Songs of Life and Hope

Cantos de vida y esperanza

Edited and translated by Will Derusha and Alberto Acereda

DUKE UNIVERSITY PRESS   Durham & London 2004

RUBÉN DARÍO

Songs of Life and Hope

Cantos de vida y esperanza

© 2004 Duke University Press   All rights reserved
Printed in the United States of America on acid-free paper ∞
Designed by Rebecca Giménez   Typeset in Quadraat by Tseng
Information Systems, Inc.   Library of Congress Cataloging-in-
Publication Data appear on the last printed page of this book.

FOR MANUEL MANTERO

Contents

Introduction

An increasing number of translations have appeared in recent years, rendering entire poetic worlds into English, often for the first time. Languages, cultures, and literary traditions have varied widely, from the somewhat familiar to the weird and wonderful. Recent English translations of Spanish and Spanish American poets such as Rosalía de Castro, Federico García Lorca, Pablo Neruda, Jorge Luis Borges, and Octavio Paz have found a receptive audience in the United States. Some of the more remarkable publications might well represent new standards for verse translation and provide encouragement for others to attempt similar works. As interest in Spanish and Spanish American poetry grows in the United States, a deeper appreciation of Rubén Darío (1867–1916) and his work is all the more urgent.

Darío — born Félix Rubén García Sarmiento in Nicaragua — became a writer of major importance to the literary history of the Spanish language, and as such he has received a lot of critical and scholarly attention. But despite his significance as one of the greatest innovators in Hispanic literature, few attempts have been made to translate his works, particularly his poetry, into English. There are practical reasons for such neglect. The very ingenuity that makes Darío so important also makes him one of the most difficult poets to translate into other languages, in part because the musicality of his rhyme and rhythm becomes extravagantly singsong when followed too tightly and sounds curiously flat when not followed closely enough. In addition, much of the original charm of his verse depends on a craftsmanship that has gone out of style in the United States and elsewhere and may sound like affectation to the contemporary ear. The scarcity of solid, representative translations since Darío's death nearly a century ago is probably the best evidence of the difficulty in expressing a real sense of his poetry in English.

A brief history best illustrates the point. In 1916, to commemorate the poet's death, Thomas Walsh and Salomón de la Selva prepared a brief anthology of eleven of Darío's poems in English for the Hispanic Society of America. A few years later, in 1922, Charles B. McMichael published a brief collection of eight poems, five of them from Prosas profanas y otros poemas (Profane prose and other poems), together with a translation of Darío's original prologue. In the following decades a handful of translations—some in verse and others in prose—appeared in anthologies and scholarly journals. In 1965, Lysander Kemp published a book-length collection of seventy-odd poems he had translated into English. Unfortunately, this volume provided no Spanish text and no annotations. The collection—long out of print—stood as the only book-length translation for over thirty years. On the eve of Darío's centennial celebration in 1967, Helen W. Patterson published a bilingual anthology that included a sampling of Darío's modernist poems among selections from twentieth-century Nicaraguan poetry. None of these translations of Darío's verses, however, enjoyed subsequent editions.

Darío's importance to Spanish and Spanish American literature, and the lack of translations and dual editions of his poetry, recently led us to prepare a bilingual anthology published in 2001 by Bucknell University Press. Our anthology addressed two pressing needs: Through our study of the original manuscripts and first editions, we endeavored first to restore the purity of Darío's text and second to reproduce in English a sense of the original poetry in all its elegance, rhythm, thematic eclecticism, and suggestiveness. Most of the texts, including the artistic credos that Darío composed for his major works, had not been previously available in English. The increasing interest in our anthology in international academic circles, especially among Anglo-American Hispanists and students, has encouraged us to carry on the task in this volume, a complete and accurate text and rigorous translation of Darío's most important—and arguably most successful—book of poetry: *Cantos de vida y esperanza. Los cisnes y otros poemas* (Songs of life and hope. The swans and other poems), first published in 1905. It is our hope that scholars will again appreciate the fidelity to the Spanish originals, while the careful rendering of the verses in English will find a ready public among teachers, students, and lovers of poetry.

Our own experience in reading Spanish poetry in English translation has generally been frustrating in terms of meaning, rhythm, and grammatical construction. In teaching Spanish poetry in translation, we have often confronted texts that baffle and discourage students and, very likely, the majority of nonspecialists. We value a text that imparts some real sense of the original poetic voice in its own time and place, rather than a sense of the translator. The atmosphere of historical or literary allusion surrounding a verse is as problematic as the acoustic dimension of what is actually written on the page. Vague or incomplete translations can mislead as much as overwritten or "enhanced" ones. Language and culture are inseparable. As recent theorists have taken pains to point out, translations carry as much ideological weight as original texts. Lawrence Venuti's vision of translation as "rewriting" takes on deeper meaning when we consider gender and similar issues, as Joyce Tolliver has shown in regard to English translations of Rosalía de Castro's poetry (see the "Translations" section of the bibliography). With all these factors in mind, we have attempted to translate Darío's poetry as meticulously as possible in order to respect his erudite tone, while also rendering much of the structural and acoustic dimensions of his language in *Cantos de vida y esperanza*. Although Darío is especially adroit at crafting intricate rhymes, we have generally preferred to forgo rhyme in favor of preserving rhythm and meaning in our translations, not only in keeping with the overall scholarly aim of this volume but also due to the vagaries of the linguistic systems involved. Anyone with a minimum of study and effort can sound out the original Spanish text and appreciate the wealth of rhyme. Not so the rhythm, depending as it does on complex rules regarding acoustic syllables, and even less so the meaning. Of course, readers familiar with Darío in the original Spanish may have their own ideas about the meaning of a favorite verse or phrase and wish we had arrived at the same conclusion. This is to be expected. We hope that such readers will be able to recognize that our version is at least as legitimate as their own. Furthermore, our translation encompasses not a verse or a phrase, but an entire book, and it aims at a unity of voice—to be more precise, a vision—that we have found in this unique and wonderful work. We wish to stress from the start that our translation is not an attempt to rewrite Darío's book but rather to suggest in English as best we can what and how Darío wrote in Spanish.

Alongside the literary translation, we reproduce the most reliable and authoritative Spanish text of *Cantos de vida y esperanza* available anywhere. As we have demonstrated in a number of articles and book editions, all previous attempts to edit Darío's volumes of poetry have included typographical errors and misreadings of the original texts. The need for further editorial interest in Darío's works is evidenced by the fact that even today no critical edition of his complete poetry is available. In the past, textual research on Darío was inhibited by three problems. In the first place, most scholars did not have access to first editions, nor to existing manuscripts. Second, many scholars followed previous studies that contained typographical mistakes and lacked proper annotation. And third, researchers proved inconsistent

3

with their own announced practices, or simply careless in execution. No doubt the universal recognition of Darío as a key figure in modern and contemporary Spanish and Spanish American literature will spur more research into his works. In order to provide a truly authoritative text, we have carefully followed the first edition of the book, as well as the manuscripts housed at the Seminario-Archivo Rubén Darío in Madrid and at the Library of Congress in Washington, D.C. This volume, then, is not only concerned with translating Darío into English but also with presenting his 1905 Spanish text in an authoritative and scholarly edition. We hope this book will introduce an important poet to readers with varying degrees of reading knowledge in Spanish, or with none at all. At the same time we know that scholars will find our critical text indispensable in their research.

In the following pages we will present a general literary biography of Darío and a more comprehensive analysis of *Cantos de vida y esperanza* to give readers the cultural and historical context of both. For further information, readers may also find the bibliography at the back of this book useful; it lists primary works by Darío himself as well as secondary sources, representative studies of the poet and his works that we consider among the best in the field, with particular emphasis on studies of *Cantos de vida y esperanza*. In an effort to make citations less obtrusive, this introduction streamlines bibliographic information according to a few simple rules: If the bibliography cites only one work by a particular author, we include here the author's name and, where applicable, a page number. In the case of multiple works by the same author, we also include the publication date. Following the bilingual edition of the poems, readers will find a glossary and annotations section that gives concise and contextual definitions of many terms found in this introduction as well as in the translations.

RUBÉN DARÍO AND HISPANIC MODERNISM

Writers and critics have long recognized Darío as one of the most influential authors of his age, the poet who changed the course of Hispanic poetry and brought it into the mainstream of twentieth-century modernity. In 1953 the Spanish poet and Nobel prize winner Juan Ramón Jiménez wrote: "Spanish poetry of that time, as in Spanish America, starts with Rubén Darío [. . .]. He is much more substantial, more wide-ranging, richer than the rest. Therefore, he embodies the very essence, the synthesis of Spanish American Modernist poets" (229–230). We could recount similar opinions from major poets such as Leopoldo Lugones, Manuel Machado, Antonio Machado, Francisco Villaespesa, Amado Nervo, Ramón del Valle-Inclán, Federico García Lorca, Gerardo Diego, Pedro Salinas, Pablo Neruda, César Vallejo, José Hierro, and many others, all of whom underscore Darío's pivotal role in Spanish-language literature. Enrique Anderson Imbert has rightly pointed out that Darío's work divides Spanish American literary history into a "before" and an "after," as many university curricula reflect in survey courses. The Mexican essayist and poet Octavio Paz, another Nobel prize winner, states in his essay "The Siren and the Seashell" (translated 1991): "Darío was not only the richest and most wide-ranging of the modernist poets: he was also one of our great modern poets. He was the beginning" (31). Paz also suggests that the movement known as Hispanic modernism—of which Darío became the undisputed leader in both Spanish America and Spain— has yet to run its course and that everything written since Darío has been influenced in one way or another by him.

The importance of Darío in contemporary Spanish American poetry has been demonstrated by Paz in his 1974 book Los hijos del limo (Children of the mire), and the Spanish poet and critic Manuel Mantero has drawn attention to the profusion of Peninsular poets— virtually all the important ones—influenced by Darío, especially in the existential aspect. The Spanish poet and literary theorist Carlos Bousoño also maintains that contemporary poetry in the Hispanic world would be vastly different today without the existence of Darío at the starting point. Specialists in comparative literature find Darío an essential figure because of his contact with U.S. (Walt Whitman, Edgar Allan Poe), French (Charles Baudelaire, Paul Verlaine), Italian (Gabriele D'Annunzio), English (Oscar Wilde, Algernon Charles Swinburne), Luso-Brazilian (Eugenio de Castro, F. Xavier), and Spanish (the Machado brothers, J. R. Jiménez) literature. At the "Encuentro Rubén Darío" in January 1967, in Varadero, Cuba, preeminent Spanish American literary critics and poets (Nicolás Guillén, Mario Benedetti, Roberto Fernández Retamar, and many others) gathered to acknowledge Darío's contribution to literature. As the twentieth century was drawing to a close, Mauricio Ostria (1991) and Manuel Mantero and Alberto Acereda (1997) carried out similar surveys among contemporary Spanish American and Spanish Peninsular poets regarding the importance of Darío, and they arrived at the same results: writers continue to admit the influence of modernism in general and of Darío's poetry in particular.

In the Hispanic literary world at the end of the nineteenth century, Darío soon became one of the leaders of a new movement called *modernismo*, which we generally translate as modernism but which should not be confused with other movements that go by this name. Each "modernism" formed a distinct historical and cultural entity with little or no direct contact with modernist movements beyond its linguistic borders, though all share some of the same impulses: Anglo-American modernism, the *Modernismo brasileiro* of Brazil, the *Modernisme català* centered around Barcelona, and all the "modern" Western artistic, literary, religious, philosophical, and cultural movements that flourished at the turn of the century and led to the avant-garde. Hispanic modernism refers most accurately to an attitude or approach to life as much as to the art that came to dominate literature on both sides of the Atlantic at the end of the nineteenth and the beginning of the twentieth centuries. Modernist poets devoted themselves to freedom, passion, and renovation in pursuit of beauty. Along with writers such as José Martí (Cuba, 1853–1895), Julián del Casal (Cuba, 1863–1893), José Asunción Silva (Colombia, 1865–1896), Amado Nervo (Mexico, 1870–1919), Leopoldo Lugones (Argentina, 1874–1938), Julio Herrera y Reissig (Uruguay, 1875–1910), Manuel Machado (Spain, 1874–1947), Antonio Machado (Spain, 1875–1939), and Juan Ramón Jiménez (Spain, 1881–1958), Darío must be counted among the most significant authors of the age, modernist or otherwise. By force of personality and sheer talent, and by publishing and traveling almost constantly, he set his stamp on the entire modernist period. In many ways Rubén Darío and Hispanic modernism are virtually synonymous.

Before dealing with Darío's personal and literary biography, we should address some important issues regarding the concept of modernism. It would prove cumbersome to lay out the whole debate over divergent and often conflicting critical approaches — whether existential, psychological, socioeconomic, or spiritual — as to what constitutes modernism. José Olivio Jiménez has already analyzed the topic, and we refer the curious reader initially to him (1994: 42–47). The view of Hispanic modernism as a normative system based on cultural and linguistic codes of modernity may be found in studies by Ángel Rama, Evelyn Picón Garfield, Ivan A. Schulman, Cathy Login Jrade, Acereda, Gerard Aching, and the compilations by Javier Blasco, Carmen Ruiz Barrionuevo, Trinidad Barrera, and others. All these works offer insights into the multiple readings of modernism as a literary, historical, and cultural phenomenon. We must emphasize, however, that Hispanic modernism appeared as one manifestation of a much larger artistic revolution in the Western world, which produced not only the different "modernisms" discussed above, but also schools and styles associated with all the variations of Art Nouveau: the French Modern Style, the German Jugendstil, the Austrian Sezessionstil, the Italian Stile Nuovo, and even the Tiffany designs in North America. For this reason we reject the distortions of any canon (as some have proposed) that attempts to divorce Hispanic modernism completely from the so-called Generation of 1898 in Spain or from comparable movements in Catalonia and, years later, in Brazil. A look at the art and the thinking anywhere in the Western world at the turn of the century soon reveals a similar picture: an increasing urgency for change (the modernists) in the face of resistance (the entrenched arbiters of taste and decorum). Suffice it to say here that Hispanic modernism was a heterogeneous cultural and artistic way of thinking, of looking at the world and the artist's place in it, that combined characteristics of such schools or movements as English Pre-Raphaelitism; French Parnassianism, symbolism, and impressionism; Italian Decadentism; and all the varieties of expressionism. To the modernist, the ideological basis or cement of these wildly assorted elements was a philosophical irrationalism in the name of freedom. The difficulty in establishing a precise definition of Hispanic modernism stems from its own diverse (and at times conflicting) tendencies, which several of the movement's own theoreticians demonstrated in screeds and manifestos and which Bernardo Gicovate, Ned Davison, José-Carlos Mainer, and others have studied at length. (For a broader look at modernism in Western literature, especially in Anglo-American literature, we suggest consulting Vassiliki Kolocotroni or Malcolm Bradbury and James McFarlane.) Beyond delineations and definitions, scholarly interest in Hispanic literary modernism and its most prominent figure, Rubén Darío, revolves mainly around a new orientation or sensibility in the Spanish language, what has come to be called modernity. Federico de Onís, one of the first critics of Hispanic modernism, has stated: "Our mistake lies in the implication that there is a difference between 'Modernism' and 'modernity,' because Modernism is essentially, as those who named it had supposed, the search for modernity" (1967: 462). Along these lines, Ricardo Gullón, José Olivio Jiménez, and Ivan A. Schulman, to mention a few, make explicit connections between these terms and the literary expressions that gave rise to them. Jrade, an outstanding scholar of Hispanic modernism and of Darío, recently pointed out that "*Modernismo* represents Spanish America's first full-fledged intellectual response and challenge to modernity" (1998: 137). Therefore, she continues, each new work produced in contemporary Spanish American literature "reconfirms the lasting foundational nature of the *modernista* vision. Each emphasizes the need to read *Modernismo* from the perspective of modernity" (145). After many years of a monolithic view that would ground modernism (and Darío) in elements of the exotic and the beautiful, it seems clear that critics now perceive Hispanic modernism more accurately and more usefully as one of the initial phases of literary modernity.

In this sense, Darío's work stands among the most influential literary efforts in the Spanish language, which underscores the value of his masterpiece, *Cantos de vida y esperanza*, in the evolution of Hispanic poetry. This book's significance becomes more readily apparent when the writer and his work are viewed in their historical context. In the second half of the nineteenth century, Spanish-language literature was just beginning to experience reverberations from a line of bohemian, doomed, and marginalized poets from other cultural traditions, particularly the French, who truly comprise the foundation of poetic modernity. The social, historical, economic, and cultural environment confronting poets in various regions of the Hispanic world seemed a somewhat stagnant counterpoint to these stirrings from abroad. Such circumstances have been studied by Rama, Noé Jitrik, and Lily Litvak, while Schulman sees a need to reorganize the critical modernist canon based on a new reading of the texts and their interrelationship with Spanish American society. It is important to bear in mind what modernism meant within a social structure that marginalized poets as unproductive members of its materialistic economy. Contrariwise, and almost perversely, such marginalized poets came to see themselves as an artistic elite, if not an aristocracy, fending off the flood of mediocrity from lesser mortals.

The latter part of the nineteenth century witnessed a second industrial revolution and the consolidation of great colonial empires, a series of profound economic shifts with their concomitant social disruptions. The turmoil and transformations would soon converge in such events as the Spanish-American War, the Russo-Japanese War, the Boxer Rebellion in China, the Mexican Revolution, the bloody General Strike in Spain, and the Bolshevik Revolution in Russia, not to mention World War I. A new social order reflected a paradigmatic shift in the relationship between capital and work. After 1870, European capitalism spread to Spanish America and, together with other transformations peculiar to Hispanic societies, conditioned the concepts of art and poetry. It was at this point that modernist poetics and

8

Darío's lyrical production entered the picture. Poetry and public life diverged, at least outside the official academies, and the ethos guiding modernist authors had no concern for wealth or power or place in society but rather centered on the cultivation of art and beauty, the bohemian lifestyle, and rebellious individualism, even an eccentricity ultimately defined by the odd, the debased, the marginalized, the debauched. Pedro Piñero and Rogelio Reyes, as well as Anthony Zahareas and José Esteban, have published significant studies on the modernist bohemia, and artistic or lifestyle marginalization is the subject of a volume edited by Anthony Geist and José Monleón.

In a world dominated by an overt consumerism hostile to their aesthetic and spiritual pursuits, modernists embraced a movement that by its very "strangeness" often achieved an extravagance and decadence that offended polite company and official institutions alike. Given the socioeconomic climate in which it found itself, modernist poetics clearly did not win the day in the Southern Cone, in Mexico, or in the Caribbean, never mind in Central America or in Spain. Modernism embodied the crisis of poets driven to create something new in a society where poetry was little esteemed and less valued, as Baudelaire had announced half a century earlier in France. Between 1880 and 1920 — the time frame of Hispanic modernism for the purposes of this introduction — all modernist poets have one thing in common, whatever the competing or conflicting literary directions to which they subscribe: a sense of having been left out, marginalized, demoted by society at large. Paz clearly perceived the tragic despair of modernist authors when he wrote: "The modern poet does not have any place in society because he is a 'nobody' " (1972: 243).

The standard-bearer of these modernist writers was Rubén Darío. His works, along with those written by others on both sides of the Atlantic, reconceived the notion of Art around the ideals of good, beauty, and truth. Art was, then, the embodiment of a divine force that provided Darío and others with the freedom they needed and craved as human beings. At the same time, their contact with Art — their own authentication as individual human beings — depended on that very freedom to be. But within the social and economic modernization of Spain and Spanish America in the late nineteenth century, nontraditional art — especially poetry — soon became isolated if it challenged, questioned, or refused to conform to what society considered art's proper function: namely, that it should be useful or profitable or simply pleasant and reassuring. From society's point of view, some degree of utilitarianism in the face of widespread poverty and cultural backwardness was not asking very much of the modernists, who were behaving like ungrateful and unruly children and had to be treated as such: sometimes rejected, often scolded, but mostly ignored. As witnesses of industrial, technological, and socioeconomic modernization, Darío and the modernists interpreted the negative response as a demoralizing affront to truth and beauty. Modern life, they suspected, kills the soul. This sense of peering into the emptiness of the world, l'*experience du gouffre* (the experience of the abyss, as the French poets would call it), produced an anguish in their personal life as well as in their literary works. Darío and the modernists sought to alleviate their despair by somehow escaping the reality in which they felt trapped. Such escapist attempts reveal themselves in often contradictory attitudes as well as in the creation of art dealing with universal themes such as existence, spirituality and religion, eroticism, and politics. In Darío's case, poetry is a direct consequence of that despair. Whereas Romantic world-weariness had led to boredom and tedium, Hispanic modernism found a new expression and sensibility for the concept of anguish. Darío, Martí, Casal, Silva, Herrera y Reissig, Lugones, Antonio Machado—all the prominent modernists—struggled desperately with a sense of doom.

Although painfully aware of his own demoted status in the sociocultural matrix in which he lived and worked, Darío still managed to leave his mark on literature as the protagonist of a movement dedicated to poetic reform. He brought in the fresh air of renovation so badly needed to reinvigorate the genre and, in consequence, opened the door on modernity for contemporary Hispanic poetry. The prevailing view that the Spanish poet Gustavo Adolfo Bécquer (1836–1870) ushered in poetic modernity is open to serious question, without denying either the value or the originality of Bécquer's *Rimas* (Rhymes), published in 1871, a scant four years after Darío's birth. The real initiator of modernity in the Spanish language must be sought in modernism and, most evidently and logically, must be Darío. Leaving aside national or personal preferences, we can easily corroborate this claim by citing the manifold qualities of Darío's verse: no other modernist offers the range and the depth found in Darío, whether we consider his thematic complexity or his handling of a purely poetic language distinct from either the Romantic tradition or Bécquer himself.

Darío broke new ground in expressing existential tragedy in verse, as well as erotic force, the religious tension between faith and doubt, the social awakening of human fraternity and solidarity, the lament of Hispanic peoples in danger of losing their cultural identity, and submersion in the occult, the Masonic, the esoteric, and the Orphic-Pythagorean. All this, and Darío's prodigious handling of poetic language at every level—from versification and rhythm to the exact adjective and the precise syllable—confirm the role of modernism, and especially of Darío, as the advent of poetic modernity in the Spanish language. Thanks to his example, Hispanic poetry again turned its attention to the formal aspects of language in its acoustic, grammatical, and lexical dimensions, a concern all but forgotten since the death of Francisco de Quevedo in 1645. In the case of Spanish America, the dislocation of poetic language and the extraordinary rupture of linguistic conventions in a poet such as the Peruvian César Vallejo owe much to the formal concerns of modernist poetry and, most of all, to Darío. Vallejo's *Los heraldos negros* (The black heralds) from 1918, for example, derived clearly from Darío's modernist ethos and aesthetics, and the poetic vanguard would later attempt to fracture and twist poetic language beyond previously known limits, in a sense to out-Vallejo the master. If Vallejo looks to Darío, and if most twentieth-century Spanish American poetry holds Vallejo in its sights, then at least indirectly Darío appears in all the poetry that follows him. In a similar vein, the view of poetry in many representative Hispanic poets of the twentieth century—poetry as queen of the arts and of all human activity—stems from the adoration the modernist writers, and especially Darío, lavished on the poetic genre.

Over the years Darío's poetry and modernist literature in general became identified with exotic affectation and the production of artsy, as in self-consciously artificial, verses detached from vital social, historical, and cultural concerns. Although some modernists obviously fit into such a framework, it would be a mistake to distil the contributions of Hispanic modernism into a precious liqueur of lakes, marquises, and swans blended together simply for art's sake. A substantial number of critics have come to recognize that modernist literature constitutes one of the most interesting manifestations of a profound transformation of Hispanic culture at the turn of the century. The 1896 publication of Darío's *Prosas profanas y otros poemas* marked the unqualified artistic success of modernism and confirmed its author as the defender of the new aesthetics, which would see in 1905, with the publication of *Cantos de vida y esperanza*, its crowning achievement. A close reading of *Cantos* proves that the traditional interpretation of modernist poets as artists locked in their ivory towers was always superficial and should no longer be accepted.

In the United States and other English-speaking countries, Hispanic modernist writers have never enjoyed the recognition they deserve and in fact enjoy in Spanish-speaking countries, and none has been adequately translated into English. As we pointed out at the start, the most prominent figure of Hispanic modernism—Rubén Darío—still lacks a rigorous English translation of the vast majority of his works. Since his death, the volume of words devoted to him is probably greater than that given to any other writer in the history of Spanish and Spanish American literature, with the exception of Cervantes. Numerous attempts have been made to interpret and evaluate Darío's written work in relation to his life (Edelberto Torres), in social and political terms (Rama), under the broad category of his rightful place in literary history (Acereda, Anderson Imbert, José María Martínez), through his use of poetic language (Avelino Herrero Mayor), of esoteric tradition and the occult (Jrade, Sonya Ingwersen, Raymond Skyrme), and through the influences of literature and the plastic arts on his poetry (Arturo Marasso).

In 1974 Keith Ellis published a groundbreaking study entitled *Critical Approaches to Rubén Darío*, in which he presented the range of methods and perspectives employed by scholars in studying Darío's life and works. A year later, Hensley C. Woodbridge compiled his *Rubén Darío: A Selective Classified and Annotated Bibliography*, which offered, along with Arnold A. Del Greco's volume, the most current information concerning an extensive bibliography on Darío's life and works. Since then, that bibliography has continued to expand, and in just the last five years we have seen notable books published by Jrade, Martínez, and Louis Bourne, to mention three prominent examples. Darío continues to intrigue scholars with a wide variety of approaches to the poet, his times, and his work. A complete understanding would require the exploration of the man's multifaceted dimensions: biographical, artistic, existential, religious, erotic, social, and political, for starters. Thankfully, little of this is necessary for the enjoyment of reading Darío. Perhaps his real contribution was the endeavor to turn poetry into a complete experience ranging from the metaphysical and existential to the erotic, from the religious to the social, all of it expressed through a new poetic language.

Darío and his fellow modernists created an art that searched the mysterious depths of life and awareness. Behind the imagery of swans, roses, fairy godmothers, princesses, and nymphs lies an attempt to interpret the enigmas of life through symbol and myth. Acereda has recently published a critical edition of Darío's *Poemas filosóficos* (Philosophical poems), in which he addresses this issue in terms of the poetics of despair, anguish, religion, and the occult. A close reading of Darío's poetry shows its connection to the broader current of modernity and its impact on twentieth-century Hispanic literary production. Nowhere is this connection clearer than in *Cantos de vida y esperanza*.

LIFE AND POETRY

Rubén Darío was born in Metapa (today Ciudad Darío), a small town in Nicaragua, on January 18, 1867. His parents wrangled over everything and soon separated. In 1869 his mother, Rosa Sarmiento, took the infant to neighboring Honduras, where they suffered extreme poverty; as a consequence, relatives had to take over his care. In 1872 Darío moved in with his adoptive parents, great-uncle Colonel Félix Ramírez and great-aunt Bernarda Sarmiento de Ramírez, who enrolled the boy in a nursery school in León, Nicaragua. He soon entered public school, where he learned to write verse with his teacher Felipe Ibarra. In 1877, a wealthy uncle sponsored his studies at a private academy but soon stopped payment owing to a quarrel between Darío and his cousin, forcing the ten-year-old to drop out of school. Between 1878 and 1880, Darío studied Greek and Latin classics with the Jesuits.

Even as a young teenager, Darío wrote and published a few poems. In León in 1881, he came into contact with the Polish intellectual and Freemason José Leonard y Bertholet, who would greatly influence the young poet's education and introduce him to Freemasonry and the occult. He later traveled to El Salvador, where he met the writer and intellectual Francisco Gavidia, who encouraged his taste for Victor Hugo and the French Parnassians. Given young Darío's fame, the Nicaraguan government decided in 1882 to defray the cost of his education. However, he never received the promised aid. In August of that same year, he broke off his engagement to Rosario Murillo, the woman who would stalk him all his life. In 1883 he gave a number of public readings of poetry and became involved once more with Rosario. A year later, at age seventeen, he was in Managua working as a clerk in the office of Nicaraguan president Adán Cárdenas. Some of his literary reviews began appearing in the local press.

In 1885 Darío was working at the National Library in Managua, reading Spanish classics in Manuel de Rivadeneyra's collection *Biblioteca de Autores Españoles* (Library of Spanish authors). He prepared his first book, *Epístolas y poemas. Primeras notas* (Epistles and poems. First notes) for publication, which he would reedit in 1888. This is a book of adolescence, at times mawkish and overly rhetorical in comparison to later books, the work of a poet just starting out. In 1886, Darío became manager of the daily El Imparcial of Nicaragua. Disillusioned with Rosario Murillo because of her relationship with a local politician, he embarked for Chile. He went first to Valparaíso and then to Santiago, where he contributed creative pieces and theater reviews to the daily La Epoca. In Santiago he met Pedro Balmaceda Toro, son of the president of Chile, and in 1887, he was named customs inspector in Valparaíso, a post he accepted for economic reasons. By this time, poetry had become a serious activity in Darío's life, and he continued to produce youthful works, correct in technique and generally praised. In the same year he took part in the "Certamen Varela," a poetry competition organized and financed by the Chilean politician Federico Varela. Darío won a prize for his Canto épico a las glorias de Chile (Epic song to the glories of Chile) and received an honorable mention for the group of compositions entitled Rimas (Rhymes) in imitation of the masterpiece by G. A. Bécquer, the Spanish Romantic poet. The "epic" is a standard patriotic ode in which Darío extols the heroism of Chile and its soldiers, a rhetorical exercise well crafted but narrowly pegged to the 1879 war between Chile and Peru. The Rimas collection, for its part, clearly reveals the adoration of Bécquer then current in Spanish America. Also in 1887, a new book of poems appeared under the title Abrojos (Thistles). It consists of a series of short poems that included texts improvised from anecdotes and reflections of the poet while in Chile.

By this time, Darío was already familiar with most of the important figures in Western literature. Like Whitman, whom he greatly admired all his life, Darío sincerely respected the past while recognizing the imperative of building a more perfect future. Italian literature interested him as a consequence of reading Giacomo Leopardi (1798–1837). But the French influence was paramount in Darío's literary life, particularly the Romantic, Parnassian, and symbolist poets. Most notable among the French poets in this regard are Baudelaire (1821–1867) and Verlaine (1844–1896); he would arrange a meeting with Verlaine during his first European travels.

Darío completed his first mature work in Chile: Azul . . . (Blue . . .), a collection of verse and prose, appeared in Valparaíso in 1888, the same year his father died. The number of texts passed through several alterations from the first edition in 1888 through the third edition in 1905, which the author considered definitive. A truly personal poetic voice emerged in this book, whose publication brought about a revolution in the poetry and prose written in Spanish and must be considered one of the turning points in literary history. Thematically, Azul . . . sings of eroticism intertwined with natural love and the pagan motif, as well as of absolute and impossible love. Poems from the section "El año lírico" (The lyrical year) pumped new energy and daring into the poetry then being written in Spanish. "Primaveral" (Spring), for instance, is a clear invitation to enjoy the season, combined with a mythological eroticism flowing sensuously in a refrain that runs from beginning to end. "Estival" (Summer), the second poem from the section, relates a tragic tale about two tigers in heat interrupted by a callous Prince of Wales, who kills one of them while out hunting. The solitary tiger's final dream of revenge lends the work a tragic tone, making it one of the best poems in the book. From the section "Sonetos" (Sonnets) we should cite "Venus," where the poet speaks to the planet as goddess of love and symbol of beauty. Her silence becomes a new source of pain, leaving him to suffer the pangs of unattainable love. Another section, "Medallones" (Medallions), contains poems addressed to real people who interested Darío by expressing either heroism or the ideal of the poet as a kind of prophet or messiah of art; such is the case in the sonnet addressed to Walt Whitman.

Stylistically, Azul . . . went beyond the use of traditional stanza forms in a deliberate search for a revolution in poetic structure, utilizing sonnet lines of twelve, fourteen, and even sixteen syllables, rather than the traditional eleven. The use of alliteration, run-on lines, epithets, metaphors, and a rich association of conceits and wordplay all point to a masterful exploration of poetry's musical possibilities. The book's prose pieces, transcending the traditional division of genres, reveal the same care and stylistic concerns. These short stories are not simply a literary game or the flaunting of Darío's considerable talent, but also become a personal metaphor of the modernist in the world. The story "El pájaro azul" (The blue bird) tells of an upper-class father who punishes his poet son with poverty. The same theme—the pain of pursuing beauty in a materialistic society—reappears in "El rey burgués" (The bourgeois king), which recounts the death of a poet in the house of a wealthy man who dismisses art as worthless and the artist as an unproductive member of society. To earn his keep, the poet is reduced to cranking the handle of a music box, producing in effect the same mechanical noise over and over; when winter sets in, he dies of exposure and starvation. Darío presents here an allegorical view of art debased and enslaved by rank materialism. Later, in *Historia de mis libros* (History of my books), Darío would write that his story was meant to symbolize "the eternal protest of the artist against someone who is all business, of the dreamer against boorish wealth." Darío uses the conflict between art and life in other stories from *Azul* . . . , perhaps the most famous being "La muerte de la emperatriz de la China" (The death of the empress of China), in which a spoiled young woman rises up against an exotic porcelain figurine and exacts a shattering revenge, never really understanding her own decorative role in life.

This book immediately brought Darío transatlantic recognition, mainly thanks to the Spanish novelist Juan Valera (1824–1905), who publicly championed the text and its twenty-one-year-old author. In 1889, Darío left Valparaíso for Nicaragua and then El Salvador, whose president appointed him manager of the daily *La Unión*, a newspaper devoted to the idea of a new Central American union. By 1890, he was the manager and owner of the daily *El Correo de la Tarde*, and in June of that year he married Rafaela Contreras Cañas. When his benefactor, the Salvadoran president, was assassinated the day after the wedding, Darío had to leave for Guatemala. The following year he traveled to Costa Rica, where his first son, Rubén Darío Contreras, was born. In 1892 he accepted a position as Secretary of the Nicaraguan Delegation that would attend festivities in Spain marking the fourth centennial of the discovery of America. In July he stopped in Cuba, where he met the modernist poet Casal in Havana. In August he arrived in Spain at La Coruña and went on to Madrid.

In November he returned to South America with stops in Havana and Cartagena de Indias (Colombia). Tragically, in January 1893, his wife, Rafaela Contreras, died. The poet was distraught, and only two months later was tricked into marrying his old flame Rosario Murillo in Managua. As soon as he sobered up, Darío began arranging his escape. After finagling an appointment as Consul General of Colombia in Buenos Aires, he left for New York in May. There he met the Cuban writer José Martí, another pioneer of modernism. Even granted the roundabout shipping lanes at the end of the nineteenth century, it would appear that Darío was in no hurry to reach Argentina. Darío left for France in July and met various poets and artists, among them his revered Verlaine. By August he was in Buenos Aires, writing for the Argentinean daily *La Nación*. In 1894, he edited the *Revista de América* (Journal of America) with Bolivian author Ricardo Jaimes Freyre (1868–1933). Darío took part in the Athenaeum of Buenos

Aires and frequented the bohemian nightlife of the cosmopolitan capital, drinking to the point of self-abuse. In 1895, his mother died in El Salvador. He lost his diplomatic post in Buenos Aires but continued to live off journalism.

In 1896, Darío was named secretary to the postal director of Buenos Aires. In December of that year, he published the first edition of *Prosas profanas y otros poemas* (Profane prose and other poems), a book that would be expanded for a second edition published in Paris in 1901. Most poems from the first edition were written in Buenos Aires between 1893 and 1896, and nearly all the poems added in 1901 were written after 1896. If *Azul . . .* reveals Darío's true poetic voice for the first time, *Prosas profanas* represents his poetic eruption, one that continued practically unabated until the end of his life. The prose introduction "Palabras liminares" (Liminary words) comprises the first of only three prologues that Darío wrote in the whole corpus of his poetic works. In these few pages he disavowed any intention of writing a manifesto but did raise important issues about the aristocracy of thought and the mediocrity of majority opinion. He also laid out his loathing of the historical moment in which he had to live, his penchant for the past, his love of the aesthetic and the erotic, the question of metrical rhythm, his Hispanic affiliation, and his admiration for French poetry. He declared his reluctance to serve as anyone's model, much less to imitate anyone else, all in the name of total artistic freedom, of every artist's need to create. He wrote:

Yo no tengo literatura "mía" — como ha manifestado una magistral autoridad — para marcar el rumbo de los demás: mi literatura es mía en mí; — quien siga servilmente mis huellas perderá su tesoro personal, y paje o esclavo, no podrá ocultar sello o librea. Wagner a Augusta Holmes, su discípula, dijo un día: "lo primero, no imitar a nadie, y sobre todo, a mí". Gran decir.

[I have no literature that is "mine" — as one knowledgeable authority has put it — in order to blaze a trail for the rest; my literature is *mine* in me; whoever obsequiously follows in my footsteps will lose his personal treasure and, page or slave, will be unable to hide the hallmark or livery. Wagner said one day to Augusta Holmes, his disciple: "First of all, imitate no one, and least of all me." A worthy saying.]

To a certain extent the prologue reveals Darío's objective for the book: nothing less than establishing a new sensibility in Hispanic poetry. Thematically, *Prosas profanas* is a multifaceted work with poems about love, mythological figures, courtiers, paganism, Christianity, freedom, destiny, and even poetry itself. Time and again he underscores the aristocracy of the poet, seen here as a courageous and at times solitary hero. The swan symbolizes the originality and spirit of the poet, frequently in an inward search for himself, but also the eternal question mark of life. The erotic theme is equally fundamental in this book, and Darío explores it in various ways, for example through the adoration of femininity and by using woman as a representation of the human soul and its longing for fulfillment. He uses color to characterize love and death, revels in overt sexuality, and champions the fusion of love and art. The past, a theme announced in the prologue, finds its embodiment in the medieval history of Spain and in eighteenth-century France as both an aspiration and an eternal presence. Pagan and Christian elements frequently alternate, whether in a mythological setting or through the contrast and reconciliation of flesh and spirit, Pan and Christ.

Some of Darío's best-known compositions are found in this book. "Era un aire suave . . ." (It was a gentle air . . .) is a splendidly erotic song in praise of woman and of the eternal power of femininity, embodied in the figure of the Marquise Eulalia. She flirts with and teases her two suitors, who represent the power of church and state, but finally slips away for an amorous rendezvous with her own page, who also happens to be a poet. Eulalia is not a brittle aristocrat, but the incarnation of Venus, manifesting the natural world order that grants the female dominion over the male. When Eulalia laughingly shreds a flower in her beautiful hands as easily and as nonchalantly as she might rend a lover's heart, the reader may well ponder to what extent Darío is celebrating such seductive power. The "Sonatina" is another poem with layers of complexity intertwined in its hypnotic rhythm. Through the portrayal of a spoiled girl's petulance and boredom as she wastes away unfulfilled in her palace, Darío creates a symbolic figure for the human soul forever dissatisfied within its material trappings, however luxurious, and forever waiting for a transcendent love that might set it free. The promised knight on the white charger, of course, fails to make his appearance. Critics have at times considered the poem little more than a decorative and superficial text driven by its musical rhythm, but Darío never strays far from a modern tragic vision of human existence as despair.

Also in *Prosas profanas*, the "Coloquio de los centauros" (Colloquy of the centaurs) is one of the great accomplishments in the Spanish language, not only for its depth of meaning but also for its perfectly precise form of expression. Penetrating timeworn myths in search of ultimate meaning, this dialogue between centaurs mines the Orphic-Pythagorean vein of universal balance and achieves an extraordinary harmonizing of the animal, the human, and the divine across millennia, the reconciliation of life, death, and love. Darío firmly believed in intercommunication within nature, imagined everything as penetrated by soul, and likened divine beauty to the beauty of a woman, thus revealing a connection to Eastern mysticism and the Cabala of the Spanish Jews. In this poem he points to the union of all nature, the universal soul of all things:

> ¡Himnos! Las cosas tienen un ser vital: las cosas
> tienen raros aspectos, miradas misteriosas;
> toda forma es un gesto, una cifra, un enigma;
> en cada átomo existe un incógnito estigma;
> cada hoja de cada árbol canta un propio cantar
> y hay una alma en cada una de las gotas del mar . . .

> [Hymns! Things have a vital being: things
> have rare aspects, mysterious gazes;
> each form is a gesture, a cipher, an enigma;
> incognito in each atom exists a stigma;
> every leaf sings its own song on every tree
> and there is a soul in each and every drop of the sea . . .]

The heartfelt "Responso" (Prayer for the dead), dedicated to Verlaine on his death, is no mournful dirge, but a kind of pagan celebration, a glimpse of the hereafter on the outer edge of Christian consciousness, with hints of reincarnation. At the end of the poem, the carnal and the spiritual are reconciled in the figure of Verlaine himself, while the final triumph of the satyr unites pagan and Christian elements. Verlaine thus receives the divine pardon Darío would later seek for himself.

Stylistically, *Prosas profanas* contains many innovations. It establishes, for example, the use of free verse, thereby pioneering a verse form that would later become prevalent in twentieth-century Hispanic poetry. In a further search for musicality, Darío turns to the hendecasyllable *serventesio* stanza, as well as to fourteen-syllable *alejandrinos*. Moreover, he experiments with compositions in *romance* form using twelve- and fourteen-syllable verses, as well as sonnets with verses of six, eight, eleven, and fourteen syllables, eleven- and twelve-syllable quatrains, serventesios in the Galician *gaita* form, mono-rhyme in tercets, and a wondrous variety of stanzas skillfully combining with age-old Castilian meters.

A close reading of both editions of *Prosas profanas* helps clarify what lies behind modernist imagery, much of which has passed into the realm of cliché and parody. Traditional interpretations of Darío's work seem increasingly outmoded and out of touch, seldom if ever looking at the figurative language of modernism in the context of modernity itself and the poetics of despair. Although the visual arts of the period have enjoyed reevaluation and serious critical study, in addition to a resurgence in popularity, many literary scholars lag behind. In the undergraduate classroom, *Prosas profanas* is generally given short shrift, cited as perhaps the best example of modernism's penchant for style over substance. The exuberant overabundance of good taste that characterizes the painting, sculpture, furniture, clothing, graphic design, and architecture of the modernist period obviously carries over to the written page. It is symptomatic of the age. A growing number of scholars realize that the aesthetic and existential concerns of modernist poetry cannot be reduced to a formula of mere decoration and escapism. *Prosas profanas* is a genuine masterpiece that might have stood—justifiably—as the crowning achievement of any poet's career, had he not gone on to create an even more profound work: *Cantos de vida y esperanza*.

In the same year as *Prosas profanas* Darío published *Los raros* (The uncommon ones), a book in prose later expanded in a second edition in 1905. His word portraits show us the rare or unique qualities he admired in the artists and writers who interested him. His own aesthetic program becomes clearer as he presents these exceptional people to us. To support himself, he continued to write for Buenos Aires newspapers. Rosario Murillo, Darío's wife in name only, kept up her relentless pursuit even as he evaded her. In 1898 he left for Spain as correspondent of the Argentinean daily *La Nación*, intending to cover the war between Spain and the United States. He arrived too late. In 1899, the war now over, he reached Madrid and there met Francisca Sánchez, his companion from that moment on. In December they moved to Paris, where Darío would report on the World's Fair. His first daughter, Carmen, was born there in 1900, but she died the following year. In September the little family traveled to Italy: Genoa, Turin, Pisa, Venice, Leghorn, Rome, and Naples.

Darío spent 1901 traveling in Europe. The articles written about Spain for *La Nación* appeared as the volume *España contemporánea* (Contemporary Spain), in which Darío saluted the talents of new Spanish authors—such as the playwright and future Nobel laureate Jacinto Benavente (1866–1954), the Machado brothers, the poet and philosopher Miguel de Unamuno (1864–1936), and the novelist Pío Baroja (1872–1956)—and looked at various aspects of Spanish daily life at the turn of the century. In 1902, always desperate for funds, he published another prose work, *La caravana pasa* (The caravan passes), a compilation of his articles on Europe. He corresponded with Juan Ramón Jiménez and finally met Antonio Machado in Paris. In March of the following year he was named Nicaraguan consul in Paris, a position he retained until 1907. His son Rubén Darío Sánchez—the "Phocas" in his poem dedicated to the child—was born in 1903 and died scarcely a year later. In 1904, Darío was able to improve his economic situation somewhat by contributing to several Spanish periodicals, including *Blanco y Negro*, thanks to the intervention of Jiménez. He also traveled to Gibraltar, Morocco, and Andalusia, trips that would serve as the raw material of his book *Tierras solares* (Lands under the sun). He toured Europe (Germany, Austria, and Hungary) and spent the summer in Asturias working on a number of compositions.

In the final years of the nineteenth century and the first years of the twentieth, Darío reached his artistic maturity, and he now poured all his knowledge and craft into creating some of his finest poems. The actual gestation of individual works was usually hurried, with little care given to sorting and preserving manuscripts. It was Jiménez, then barely twenty-four, who took charge of the poems that would become the book *Cantos de vida y esperanza. Los cisnes y otros poemas.* This book stands unquestionably with the poetic landmarks written in the Spanish language. Published by the Tipografía de la Revista de Archivos, Bibliotecas, y Museos in Madrid, it brings together compositions written in different places between 1892 and 1905, preceded by a brief but enlightening "Prefacio" (Preface). As we will show in the next section of this introduction, the poems exhibit a fascinating thematic variety and a dazzling mastery of form that would never be equaled in his lifetime.

In 1906, Darío traveled again through Europe (Great Britain, Belgium, and several other countries), then left for Brazil in June as Secretary of the Nicaraguan Delegation. He attended the Pan-American Conference in Rio de Janeiro and later went to Buenos Aires before returning to Paris. In October, his second son, Rubén Darío Sánchez—"Güicho"—was born. In November, the family traveled to the Spanish island of Majorca, where he continued to write. That year he published a book of essays entitled *Opiniones* (Opinions), in which he asserted the need for artistic originality. This was an important book because Darío expressed in it his ideas on art and modernity. In an article entitled "Nuevos poetas de España" (New poets of Spain), he writes:

> Se acabaron el estancamiento, la sujeción a la ley de lo antiguo académico, la vitola, el patrón que antaño uniformaba la expresión literaria. Concluyó el hacer versos de determinada manera, a lo Fray Luis de León, a lo Zorrilla, a lo Campoamor, o a lo Núñez de Arce, o a lo Bécquer.

> [The stagnation, the subjection to outmoded academic decrees, the same rule for everyone, the yardstick that standardized literary expression in the old days, all that is over. Writing verses in a predetermined way—whether like Fray Luis de León, like Zorrilla, like Campoamor, like Núñez de Arce, or like Bécquer—has come to an end.]

Darío's words do not imply a rejection of tradition or of any of the poets specifically named. As evidence it is enough to read his praises elsewhere of the Spanish poets Ramón de Campoamor (1817–1901) and Gaspar Núñez de Arce (1834–1903). Rather, he wants to leave no doubt that the modernists belong to a new sensibility with allegiance to none of the canonical precursors.

In 1907 Rosario Murillo pursued Darío to Europe. He then returned to Nicaragua for the first time in fifteen years and attempted, unsuccessfully, to arrange a divorce, a difficult process in the conservative Catholic culture of the Nicaraguan church, court system, and legislature. Frustrated in his bid for freedom, Darío returned to Europe. By the age of forty, then, he had reached the pinnacle of his fame as a literary figure both in Spanish America and Spain, yet remained generally unhappy and usually impoverished. In December 1907, he was named Nicaraguan minister to Spain. By this time, he had compiled enough poems, old and new, to publish *El canto errante* (The roving song) in Madrid. The title poem focuses on a symbolic figure called "the poet," who moves through a world that is not overly concerned with art and poetry. Darío passed through many periods of economic hardship that forced him to write and publish in an effort to obtain some relief. Such is the case for this volume, published at least in part with the hope of generating sorely needed funds. He had scraped together enough poems for a book by combining compositions written between 1905 and 1907 with many others published earlier in

Spain and Spanish America, as well as unpublished poems he had not considered publishable until then. The fact that this book combined older poems with more recent ones does not negate the book's overall poetic value. On the contrary, it contains a number of compositions written when Darío stood at the peak of his poetic powers.

El canto errante begins with a prologue, the "Dilucidaciones" (Elucidations), an assortment of notes and sketches published earlier in the Madrid press. In a sense, this prologue meant to serve as an act of self-defense against attacks by Darío's critics, especially in Spain. The prose here is excellent, and some observations still retain the freshness of the times. Darío, for instance, writes:

> He meditado ante el problema de la existencia y he procurado ir hacia la más alta idealidad. He expresado lo expresable de mi alma [. . .]. He cantado, en mis diferentes modos, el espectáculo multiforme de la Naturaleza y el inmenso misterio. [. . .] La poesía existirá mientras exista el problema de la vida y de la muerte. El don de arte es un don superior que permite entrar en lo desconocido de antes y en lo ignorado de después, en el ambiente del ensueño o de la meditación.

> [I have meditated on the problem of existence and have sought to reach the highest ideals. I have expressed what is expressible in my soul. . . . I have sung, in my various ways, the multiform spectacle of Nature and its immense mystery. . . . Poetry will exist as long as the problem of life and death exists. The gift of art is a superior gift that gains entrance to what was unknown before and unsuspected thereafter, in the atmosphere of fantasy or meditation.]

The book contains poems such as "Metempsícosis" (Metempsychosis), written in 1893, that reveal Darío's fascination with reincarnation; in this case, the reincarnated soul of a Roman soldier tells of his migratory history in the arms of Cleopatra. Other poems such as "Sum . . ." and "Eheu" arise from a concern for the existential human condition, a concern that drives Darío to create his deeply tragic poetry. This kind of composition, evident at every stage of his poetry, has proven to be his least-studied facet by literary scholars: a lifelong interest in esoteric doctrines, quite at odds with the usual stereotype of Darío as a synthetic poet of princesses and swans. Topical verse appears in this book as well, with poems of friendship such as one dedicated to the Spanish modernist Ramón del Valle-Inclán (1866–1936). Even in such poems, his creative talent shines through the conventions. The tone is thoughtful rather than prosaic, the language carefully controlled and often ironically tragic. The book continues the exploration of eroticism in a search for escape from the immense despair of life and death. In "Balada en honor de las musas de carne y hueso" (Ballad in honor of the muses of flesh and blood), dedicated to the Spanish author Gregorio Martínez Sierra (1881–1947), Darío confesses:

Nada mejor para cantar la vida,
y aun para dar sonrisas a la muerte,
que la áurea copa en donde Venus vierte
la esencia azul de su viña encendida.
Por respirar los perfumes de Armida
y por sorber el vino de su beso,
vino de ardor, de beso, de embeleso,
fuérase al cielo en la bestia de Orlando,
ivoz de oro y miel para decir cantando:
la mejor musa es la de carne y hueso!

[Nothing better for singing of life,
and even for smiling at death,
than the golden cup where Venus pours
the blue essence of her flaming wine.
For breathing the perfumes of Armida
and for sipping the wine of her kiss,
wine of an ardor, of a kiss, of a bewitchment,
one should take to the sky on Orlando's beast,
voice of gold and honey for speaking in song:
the best muse is made of flesh and blood!]

The Armida mentioned here, a seductive pagan woman, represents the eternal female archetype whose enchantments always fascinated Darío. Ever conscious of such power, he writes:

Líricos cantan y meditan sabios
por esos pechos y por esos labios:
¡La mejor musa es la de carne y hueso!

[Sages meditate and the lyrical sing
for those breasts and those lips:
The best muse is made of flesh and blood!]

At the end of the poem, not only is the woman desired as a means of escape from life's woes, but also as the source of artistic inspiration, as the poet tells his friend: "Gregorio: nada al cantor determina / como el gentil estímulo del beso." [Gregorio: nothing gives the singer more resolve / than the gentle incentive of a kiss].

The poem "Salutación al Águila" (Salutation to the eagle), dedicated to the United States, seems a contradictory text when compared to the earlier "A Roosevelt" (To Roosevelt) from *Cantos de vida y esperanza*. It is a matter of perspective. When focusing on the plight of the Hispanic peoples in a modern civilization dominated by non-Hispanic economies and cultures, as he does in the poem to Theodore Roosevelt in 1905, Darío expressed a heartfelt sense of outrage and despair; when admiring the power and energy of a relatively new nation of the Americas, as a sophisticated man of letters he could view the situation more objectively. At the time Darío published his poetic greeting to the Eagle, he considered himself a citizen of the whole world. Although he could be a passionate spokesman for Hispanic interests, and denounced the perceived imperialism of the United States in Central America, Darío was no ideologue. By far he was more of a poet than a political thinker, and his sense of *hispanidad*—an idealized cultural bond that, some argued, united Spain and its former colonies in the face of an outside threat, political or otherwise—emanated more from his heart than from his intellect.

The claim that it is impossible to find any level of political commitment in Darío's work is plainly wrong. In fact, from an early age he was surrounded by politics, and like everyone else in Latin America at the time, he watched his personal fortunes—such as they were—rise and fall on the political tides. Yet it must be admitted that social and political problems were not among the concerns closest to his heart, as unfashionable as such an attitude seemed to far more militant Latin American writers in the latter half of the twentieth century.

In 1907 Darío also published *Parisiana*, a book of journalistic articles and opinion pieces from Paris. In April 1908, he presented his diplomatic credentials as Nicaraguan minister to Spain to King Alfonso XIII of Spain. However, his economic hardship worsened when the Nicaraguan government, as often proved the case throughout his lifetime, failed to provide funds to back up the appointment. In 1909, Darío traveled to Italy and to Paris, remaining the most visible defender of a group of men and women who believed in art as a human expression of the divine. Yet modernism was already growing old, outstripped by revolutions in psychology (Freud) and physics (Einstein), as well as by social and political turmoil around the world. The increasing prominence of Freud in particular fostered new ways of thinking about and making art—such as surrealism—and became one of the foundations of the avant-garde. Within a decade, the groundbreaking innovations of modernism would begin to look quaint or even stale.

In 1910 José Madriz, the new president of Nicaragua, appointed Darío delegate to the festivities in honor of the Centennial of Mexican Independence, but the insurrection of Porfirio Díaz frustrated the trip. After returning to Europe, Darío published a new book of verse, *Poema del otoño y otros poemas* (The autumn poem and other poems), in Madrid. All but the final poem, which dates from 1892, were written after 1907. Most revolve around love, the cycle of life, and Hispanic identity, others composed for special occasions or to memorialize friendships. The outstanding work that opens the collection, the "Poema del otoño" (The autumn poem), is one of his most life-affirming meditations, even as it acknowledges the basic tragedy of human life. As with verses by the ancient Greek poet Anacreon or the twelfth-century Persian poet Omar Khayyam, this poem is an exhortation to live, an invitation to the sensual world, and—perhaps most of all—a vision of love as the means of approaching death with a glad heart: "¡Vamos al reino de la Muerte / por el camino del Amor!" [Let us go to the realm of Death / by way of Love!]. The poem is a satisfying turn on the carpe diem theme, proposing total, universal enjoyment, but one compounded with an awareness of death, that irremediable human destiny.

Also in 1910, he wrote the poem Canto a la Argentina (Song to Argentina) for the daily *La Nación* on the occasion of the centennial of the Argentinean Republic's independence. The next year, he barely scraped through a period of deep economic hardship by contributing pieces to the same newspaper. He went on, in 1911 and 1912 respectively, to publish two books of essays: *Letras* (Literature) and *Todo al vuelo* (Just in passing). In both books Darío defended his role as initiator of a new literary age in the Spanish language and attempted to reconstruct his literary career. Feeling the bite of real economic distress, Darío accepted the offer of the brothers Alfredo and Armando Guido and became manager of the magazines *Mundial* and *Elegancias*. In 1912, he began a promotional campaign for the magazines and traveled widely. From April to November he visited Barcelona, Madrid, Lisbon, Rio de Janeiro, São Paulo, Montevideo, and Buenos Aires. Falling ill, he returned to France. He continued to write articles for *La Nación* of Buenos Aires, some of which were collected posthumously in 1973, under the title *El mundo de los sueños* (The world of dreams). In

1913 he traveled to Barcelona, returned to Paris, and in October left for Valldemosa, on the Spanish island of Majorca, as guest of friends Juan Sureda and his wife. While there, Darío vacillated between a deep religious faith bordering on mysticism and bouts with alcohol. In December he returned to Barcelona, where he resided until April 1914. Alcohol abuse had finally caught up with him, sapping his energy and his health.

The last book of poetry Darío published in his lifetime, *Canto a la Argentina y otros poemas* (Song to Argentina and other poems), appeared in Madrid in 1914. The section "Otros poemas" includes compositions with the usual variety of themes: amorous, philosophical, religious, and topical. The long poem "La cartuja" (The charterhouse), written on the island of Majorca, swings relentlessly between the spirit and the flesh, veering between images of sanctity and salvation on the one hand, and dissipation and damnation on the other, between self-abnegation (what Darío would like to be) and indulgence (what, in fact, he is). His personal struggle with Christian dualism is clear. Another significant composition is the final poem, the "Gesta del coso" (Exploit in the bullring), dated 1890, which consists of the dramatic dialogue between an ox and a bull just before the latter goes out to fight and die in the ring. Darío underscores the anguish of death, the inevitable and tragic destiny common to all beings, and yet suggests there is something far worse: to waste a lifetime by not living fully, authentically, an idea that situates the poet at the threshold of twentieth-century existentialism.

In the same year he began to compile his complete poetic works for a Madrid publisher, starting with a personal anthology, a project Alberto Acereda has recently reedited under the title *Y una sed de ilusiones infinita* (And an infinite thirst for dreams). In October, following the outbreak of the First World War, he left Europe for the last time—along with his companion, Francisca Sánchez, and their eight-year-old son, Güicho—and sailed to New York on a pacifist voyage. He soon fell ill with pneumonia. In early 1915, the Hispanic Society of America invited him to read his poetry at Columbia University. For health reasons he was advised not to travel, but continued to tour in hopes of earning money. In May 1915, he arrived in Guatemala, invited by that country's president to write poems in his honor, and found himself unable to leave. In this last year of his life, he also compiled poems published separately in various periodicals at different stages of his career. Although the overall effect is uneven, several of these uncollected poems are significant to any assessment of the remarkable range and depth of Darío's poetry. Poems such as "Aúm" (Om), "Reencarnaciones" (Reincarnations), "La tortuga de oro . . ." (The golden tortoise . . .), and "En las constelaciones" (In the constellations) expand on the rich philosophical and metaphysical concerns we have previously mentioned. The theme of Hispanic identity shows up in poems like "Español" (Spanish), while other uncollected poems, not surprisingly, center on love, literature, classical mythology, social and political situations at the turn of the century, and religion. In these scattered efforts, the poetic mastery of their author emerges with varying degrees of success.

In late 1915, his health deteriorating, Darío was brought back to Managua by his legal wife, Rosario Murillo, and spent Christmas with her and her brother. Early in January 1916, Darío became seriously ill and was taken to the city of León. Suffering from irreversible cirrhosis, he was operated on twice without success. After receiving last rites, he died on the night of February 6, 1916, and was buried in the cathedral a week later before a packed house, following a theatrical ceremony—complete with orchestra—out of a scene worthy of the imagination of the greatest modernist himself.

Over the years Darío had tried his hand at different forms of autobiography. He wrote a history of his books in several articles published in La Nación in 1909, a semiautobiographical novel—begun in 1913 and left incomplete at his death—entitled El oro de Mallorca (The gold of Majorca), and the anecdotal memoirs La vida de Rubén Darío escrita por él mismo (The life of Rubén Darío written by Darío himself), published in 1915. These three autobiographical exercises interest readers of today chiefly for the light such details may shed on Darío's literary works and the creative genius behind them, but they are full of names of now-forgotten figures, political and artistic. An inveterate name dropper, he takes great pains in establishing his relationships with the rich and once famous but tells very little about his own personal tragedies, his lifelong struggle with alcoholism and womanizing, the grinding poverty to which he was constantly reduced, or even reliable information about what he read, what he thought, and how he wrote. Reading a good selection of his poetry gives readers a much better sense of who Rubén Darío was than the autobiographical tidbits he has left us.

Even a cursory look at his life, such as we have laid out here, suggests he suffered profoundly: the death of his young wife, Rafaela Contreras; the sham of a marriage to Rosario Murillo and her relentless pursuit of him across two decades and two continents; the death of several babies; the constant economic privation; the effects of alcohol abuse on himself and others; the unending crisis of conscience between his religious passion and his libertine lifestyle; and, at the end, the agony of a fatal disease. Much of his misery seems self-inflicted, and apparently regret often crushed out his moments of joy, as suggested by the pendulum swings of mood in a number of poems. Darío wanted to carve out a grand and noble life, and he hated himself for frittering away his precious time in the pursuit of meaningless amusement or, conversely, in brooding over it; he blamed himself for the precarious state of his health, for his weakness of character, for his sordid sex life, for his obsession with Rubén Darío. The disillusioned years he spent in restless and often pointless travels, in bohemian indulgence, in religious, psychological, and interpersonal conflicts, undoubtedly left their mark on his poetry. He exemplifies the contradictory roles many modernists assumed and discarded in the course of their lives. Champion of the poor and oppressed while in Chile, his sympathies suddenly wilted at the sight of something terrifying in the faces of workers at an anarchist meeting. Or was it the recognition that he needed to connect with the rich, the powerful, the political elite in order to survive in an uncaring world? In Paris he played the bohemian and decadent, arrogantly arty, smug in the sense of his own intellectual and spiritual superiority when not wallowing in the dens and dives of the Parisian underground; in Majorca he began by imitating the austere fervor of Carthusian monks and ended by indulging in a drunken binge. His inconsistent life seems to manifest a core of emptiness not even the creation of great poetry could fill, an inescapable despair constantly reinforced by his world and his place in it. From our point of view, of course, this vision became the hallmark of twentieth-century poetry in Spanish, and so what we term his tragic despair transcends his life and speaks to us directly.

This view of Darío's life and work calls for some final thoughts before we turn to *Cantos de vida y esperanza*. First, it is necessary to understand his poetry as a testimony of his time, grounded in and configured by the poetics of modernity. Second, his aesthetic, existential, and spiritual concerns, as expressed in his poetry, constitute at once an enduring work of art in its own right and a great leap forward within Spanish and Spanish American literary history. Third, due to Darío's importance in that literary history, his work marks the starting point of modern poetry—the way we think of poetry today—in terms of theme and the search for formal freedom. Fourth, we should understand Darío not as a particularly Nicaraguan poet, though he undeniably was, and not as a Latin American poet, nor even a Hispanic poet, though he was one of the greatest writers in the Spanish language. As a modernist writer, Darío claimed the world as his home and, unrealistic as the notion may be, consciously attempted to transcend his cultural origins. His cosmopolitan life and international experiences opened his eyes to the multifarious aesthetic and creative possibilities of modernity, and he sought to prevent or at least forestall the disappearance of art in a world where artists and poets no longer had a specific role. Anguish, despair, the yearning for transcendence: these are probably the most contemporary threads for us when we examine his poetic tapestry at the beginning of the twenty-first century. This is precisely why it is vital to read his work as an anguished poetics of despair and to see transcendence where others in the past have read escapism.

As we have seen, Rubén Darío's poetry reflects the turmoil of his life. His emotions, his sense of the way things are, and his vision of the way things should be shine through his verse with a peculiar harmony of thought and expression, especially in those collections Darío himself envisioned in book form. *Cantos de vida y esperanza* brings together pieces written in many different places between 1892 and 1905 and is divided into four parts or sections: the brief preface called "Prefacio," the fourteen poems of the section "Cantos de vida y esperanza" (Songs of life and hope), the four poems of "Los cisnes" (The swans), and the forty-one compositions of "Otros poemas" (Other poems). The entire volume is a masterful tour de force whose poems exhibit prodigious care as much on the acoustic and formal levels as on the grammatical and lexical.

The thematic variety of the book is impressive, even for Darío. The modernist view of poetry and its priestly practitioners appears with greatest force in "Torres de Dios! . . ." (Towers of God! . . .), which presents poets as heavenly lightning rods in the midst of a stormy, inhospitable world. Darío saw turn-of-the-century social and economic structures as a brutalizing snarl of hypocrisy and greed that would inexorably strangle all forms of art, everything beautiful, pure, and noble in human nature. The purpose of poets and artists, who stood among the most intellectually and spiritually evolved members of the human race, was to make a last stand against the violent forces that would—how clearly we can see it from our vantage point!—envelop the twentieth century. This interpretation of the mutual hostility between poet and materialistic society helps clarify what Darío means in the preface, when he writes: "Yo no soy un poeta para muchedumbres. Pero sé que indefectiblemente tengo que ir a ellas" [I am not a poet for the masses. But I know that inevitably I must go to them]. He weaves similar concerns about poetry and the poet in the composition—one of his most famous—that opens the book, "Yo soy aquel . . ." ("I am the one . . ."), a revealing portrait of his inner life that seeks to reconcile opposites and attain harmony within him and the universe.

Another important theme in *Cantos de vida y esperanza* revolves around Hispanic identity, in particular the dread of cultural annihilation under the advancing march of U.S. expansion. Darío undoubtedly gave voice to the profound misgivings of many Hispanics on both sides of the ocean following the so-called banana wars of the nineteenth century and the Spanish-American War of 1898. The theme took on new urgency in the face of policies under the Roosevelt Corollary to the Monroe Doctrine, which served to legitimize U.S. intervention in Central America. This was the time when the Panama Canal became a reality, in large part because a U.S. president had decided it would. Several poems of the book address this issue, for example, "A Roosevelt" (To Roosevelt), "Al Rey Óscar" (To King Oscar), and "Salutación del optimista" (The Optimist's Salutation). They generally equate life with Hispanic culture and death with the non-Hispanic world contemptuous of that culture. Darío placed his faith in the historical greatness of Spain and its former American colonies and in the enduring validity of the values that had created such historical greatness. He hoped for a rebirth of Hispanic vitality and preeminence in the world. And yet he also expressed fear. The first poem from the section "Los cisnes" (The swans) anguishes over the imminent destruction of Hispanic culture at the hand of Anglo-Saxon—read, U.S.—expansionism. In the name of all poets, Darío addresses an enigmatic swan, here a complex symbol of the poet's craft, intuition, and aspirations, as well as an oracular, almost divine presence that glimpses the future of individuals and races. As hope and disenchantment swirl around recent historical events, the poet grieves for a people dispossessed of land and soul:

Brumas septentrionales nos llenan de tristezas,
se mueren nuestras rosas, se agotan nuestras palmas,

casi no hay ilusiones para nuestras cabezas,
y somos los mendigos de nuestras pobres almas.

[Septentrional mists fill us with sorrows,
our roses die off, our palm trees dwindle away,
there is scarcely a dream for our heads,
and we are beggars for our own poor souls.]

Like many Hispanics at the turn of the century, Darío had become painfully aware of the weakness and political corruption of the Spanish-speaking world: the declining importance of Spain and the empty triumphalism of Latin America. At the same time, the United States was emerging as one of the great powers, not only of the hemisphere, but of the world. To his credit, Darío foresaw the dominant role of the United States on the world stage. He did not foresee, however, that in the next century the Spanish-speaking population of the United States would begin overtaking that of Spain itself. In any event, his opinion of the United States was a complex affair, as previously noted. He always admired the vigor, character, and perseverance of Anglo-Saxon culture, as several articles in his 1901 book *Peregrinaciones* (Pilgrimages), make clear. More important, toward the end of his life, he chose to exclude some of his political poems—such as the magnificent composition "To Roosevelt"—from a personal anthology of his works, which suggests his opinion about the U.S. president had changed considerably since the days of *Cantos de vida y esperanza*. Even in his most critical poems, however, we can detect a certain ambivalence in his attitude toward the United States. It was the home, after all, of Walt Whitman, who had revolutionized English prosody as profoundly as Darío meant to do for Spanish. In fact, such familiar (for us) ambiguity is one of the most easily identifiable elements of Rubén Darío's modernity, as would be the case for many poets after him.

Some of the most touching verses in the book emerge from the poet's disappointment and despair. To understand Darío, it is vital to understand his existential concerns, either as life-affirming optimism or as crushing hopelessness in the face of death, with the ensuing anguish over the relevance of any religious faith. The section "Otros poemas" (Other poems) contains two nocturnes that distil the anxiety that tinges almost all of Darío's poetry into palpable despair. The pain he expresses here is undeniably existential anguish, long before that term was coined. He was nearly forty years old as he completed this book and was fully aware of the inescapable and irretrievable passage of time. The same anguish would mold the final years of his life, viewed as a nightmare from which only death—personified in Spanish with the singular feminine pronoun—will awaken us:

la conciencia espantable de nuestro humano cieno
y el horror de sentirse pasajero, el horror

de ir a tientas, en intermitentes espantos,
hacia lo inevitable desconocido y la
pesadilla brutal de este dormir de llantos
de la cual no hay más que Ella que nos despertará!

[the appalling awareness of our own human slime,
and the horror of feeling short lived, the horror

of groping along, in intermittent dread,
toward the inevitable unknown and the
brutal nightmare of this weeping sleep
from which there is only She to awaken us!]

Or he conveyed this anguish by depicting life as a poison we inflict on our children, as in the poem "A Phocás el campesino" (To Phocas the peasant), written to the poet's son Rubén Darío Sánchez, who died within months of his birth. Here the disillusionment with life reaches such depths that the poet begs his son to forgive him his part in the infant's conception and birth "a este mundo terrible en duelos y en espantos" [to this world terrible with grief and dread]. Personal tragedies, such as the death of a wife and two children, along with increasingly destructive periods of alcoholism and depression, all of this aggravated by a hypersensitive temperament, moved Darío to write "Lo fatal" (What gets you), the poem that concludes the book so impressively. It is one of the high points of poetry written in Spanish, and perhaps the best of all Darío's works. Dedicated to the Chilean pianist René Pérez, a frequent companion in philosophical discussions, "Lo fatal" extracts an extraordinary modernity from nineteenth-century irrational philosophy. Sorrow and anxiety, Darío tells us, are the curses of sentient life: innocence is indeed bliss where knowledge is the source of pain. We become unwitting victims of our own nature, punished in a sense for being the most self-aware of all creatures. In only thirteen lines, Darío is able to sum up the existential problem of life and death, of awareness and despair, unique to the human condition. Far better to be a tree that will never suffer or a stone that will never feel, because human consciousness consists of the fear of what might happen and the pain of what actually does:

Dichoso el árbol que es apenas sensitivo,
y más la piedra dura porque ésa ya no siente,
pues no hay dolor más grande que el dolor de ser vivo,
ni mayor pesadumbre que la vida consciente.

[How fortunate the tree that can scarcely feel,
and more so the hard stone because it no longer cares,
since no greater pain exists than the pain of living,
nor deeper sorrow than a life self-aware.]

As the existentialists will do later in the century, Darío insists on the identity of consciousness and existence, of the human being and time: we appear out of nowhere like a brilliant flash and then vanish as mysteriously. There is more here than a foretaste of existentialism. The "temor de haber sido" [fear of having been] may well point to the awareness of a lifetime ebbing away into the past tense, but may just as readily hint at notions of reincarnation. His was a time of occultism, spiritualism, theosophy, and other esoteric doctrines, all of which interested Darío from an early age. The "futuro terror" [a terror soon at hand] may refer to the blank nothingness of death or to something even worse: perhaps the fires of hell or the migration of the soul into the horrors of a reincarnation meant to atone for the sins of this life. Nothing is certain, not the past, the present, or the future. Especially not the future. Neither his occult studies nor his Catholic faith could spare him an unbearable vertigo as he peered over the brink of the abyss. Later in *Historia de mis libros* (History of my books), Darío would write about this poem: "En 'Lo fatal', contra mi arraigada religiosidad, y a pesar mío, se levanta como una sombra temerosa un fantasma de desolación y de duda." [In 'What Gets You,' against my deep-rooted religiosity, and despite myself, a phantom of desolation and doubt rises up like a frightened shadow.] Darío intensifies the poem by twisting rules of syntax, piling up conjunctions, and snapping a prepositional phrase in two with a violent run-on line:

Y el espanto seguro de estar mañana muerto,
y sufrir por la vida y por la sombra y por

lo que no conocemos y apenas sospechamos,
y la carne que tienta con sus frescos racimos,
y la tumba que aguarda con sus fúnebres ramos

[And the dread certainty of being tomorrow dead,
and suffering because of life and shadow and

what we don't know and barely conceive,
and the flesh that tempts, fresh-picked and plump,
and the tomb that awaits with its funeral wreaths

The poem concludes in shorter and shorter lines, shifting down from the established pattern of fourteen-syllable alejandrinos, first to a verse of nine syllables, and finally to a verse of seven, or half an alejandrino, which then peters out with an ellipsis; the poem literally deflates before our eyes: "y no saber a dónde vamos / ni de dónde venimos . . . !" [and not knowing where we run / or even where we have come from . . . !]. Faced with all the questions about the origin, destiny, and meaning of human beings in the world, the poet knows only that we are all doomed to die.

Another important theme in *Cantos de vida y esperanza*, the struggle for faith in such a world, may present itself in either a Christian or pagan context, and sometimes as Christian-pagan dualism. Life's existential enigmas led Darío, as they have led many others, through periods variously described as desert, abyss, or wasteland, either way a sense of emptiness in which nothing seems to have real meaning or purpose. Such despair may explain his frequent forays into the occult and the oneiric and at the same time his reluctance, perhaps inability, to let go of Catholic teachings. He seems determined to try every door in his unending search for a way out of suffering and death. Like many writers since Romanticism, sometimes in his works he believes in God and sometimes he does not. In life he prayed to Christ every morning, kept up his devotions to the Virgin Mary, and received last rites from the bishop of León before dying with an ivory crucifix clutched tightly in his hands. Drinking and whoring through European capitals, he did not present a picture of piety; hallucinating through days and nights of delirium, he might as readily entertain a visit from Christ as from Lucifer. But he rarely glimpses divinity in the modern world, however intense his need to find it. In other spiritual traditions, in the mythological world, in his own reading of Pythagorean mysticism, he might interpret the elemental forces of nature as divine, if somewhat indifferent, but overall Darío's expression of such sentiments strikes the reader as more conventional than genuine. He was born into a Christian world and spent his life there, and so he generally interprets the sense of God's absence as a sign of his own guilt.

His anguish increases with age, culminating in a poem like "La cartuja," discussed above, in which he blames himself for God's inability to love him; but his spiritual ambivalence—his wide-open spiritual search—is already apparent in *Cantos de vida y esperanza*. When not suffused with vague tones of theosophy and other esoteric doctrines, a particular work may present an orthodox, even pious poetic voice for whom despair would be a sin, as the church teaches. Consider the wonderfully optimistic title of the book itself: *Songs of Life and Hope*. In "Spes"—the Latin word for hope—Darío seeks refuge and salvation in a merciful Jesus. "Los tres Reyes Magos" (The three Wise Men) is another example of Christian affirmation that demands absolute faith in a good and loving Savior.

The erotic theme also pervades the book, as becomes apparent in "Carne, celeste carne de la mujer! . . ." (Flesh, a woman's heavenly flesh! . . .), one of Darío's most celebrated poems. In *Historia de mis libros* he himself categorized it as "un himno al encanto misterioso femenino" [a hymn to the mysterious enchantment of the female]. The first two lines refer to the flesh, not of a particular woman but of all women. A woman's body is the heavenly stuff where men find the absolute, the ultimate union of body and spirit: flesh, clay, sacramental bread, or even better, ambrosia, the food of the gods, which, consumed with nectar, grants immortality. The poem places woman at the center of things, a divine presence that makes existence bearable:

La vida se soporta
tan doliente y tan corta,
solamente por eso:
roce, mordisco o beso
en ese pan divino
para el cual nuestra sangre es nuestro vino!

[Life is bearable,
so painful and so short,
only because of this:
a stroke, a nibble, or a kiss
upon this bread divine
for which our blood is our wine!]

The symbolism of *divine bread, blood, wine,* and the previously mentioned *ambrosia* and *nectar,* present once again the union of elements from pagan and Christian traditions, now in the context of sexual love, which from Darío's perspective is a means of salvation. Women, in their sexual aspect, acquire transcendent value and become the key to cosmic harmony:

En ella está la lira,
en ella está la rosa,
en ella está la ciencia armoniosa,
en ella se respira
el perfume vital de toda cosa

[In it (woman's heavenly flesh) is the lyre,
in it is the rose,
in it is harmonious science,
in it we breathe
the vital perfume of each and every thing]

In the second stanza Darío combines biblical and mythological allusions to reveal his view of the erotic feminine as a doorway to the mystery of existence. Women, through their superior relationship to the divine, sanctify the male elements of procreation:

Gloria, ioh, Potente a quien las sombras temen!
Que las más blancas tórtolas te inmolen!
Pues por ti la floresta está en el polen
y el pensamiento en el sagrado semen!

[Glory, O Mighty One whom the shadows fear!
May the whitest turtledoves immolate you!
Since through you the forest is in the pollen
and thought in the sacred semen!]

Not only is woman the unending source of life, the "útero eterno" [eternal uterus]; she overpowers hell itself and may even usher man into eternal life: "Porque en ti existe / el placer de vivir, hasta la muerte — / y ante la eternidad de lo probable . . . !" [Because in you / the pleasure of living exists, until death — / and considering the eternity of the probable . . . !]. Eroticism colors Darío's view of the world from first to last, especially his view of women, whom he contemplates from a number of angles: sometimes as a passive, revered, and semidivine refuge from the horrors of existence, and sometimes as a blinding, predatory, and destructive force. Death in Darío is almost invariably female, and only in part because of Spanish grammar. Glimpses of erotic despair stem from an ambivalence he himself could not resolve, perhaps due to his experience with the three most important women in his love life: his first wife, Rafael Contreras, who died so young; Francisca Sánchez, his uneducated common-law wife who supported him unconditionally; and Rosario Murillo, his second wife, who pursued him to the end. In other words, woman as the source of good and evil, as mothering saint and uncomplaining lover, or as irresistible siren and enigmatic sphinx.

The celestial female flesh he craved all his life, however, not only failed to assuage his anguish, but even brought him more torment: legal, religious, and physical. And yet flesh never lost its allure. The sonnet that begins "Por un momento . . ." [For a moment . . .] links human sexual needs to contact with the divine, represented here by the myth of Zeus and Leda. The following poem flows naturally from the same myth, from the glory of Leda ravished at the fountainhead of the erotic harmony of the universe, to the sadness of returning to this mundane existence with the memory of having touched the divine. Eroticism is an integral part of Darío's sense of cosmic harmony: "Ante el celeste, supremo acto, / dioses y bestias hicieron pacto" [In the presence of the heavenly, supreme act, / gods and beasts made a pact]. Similarly, the poem "Propósito primaveral" (Springtime purpose) celebrates the arrival of spring and its erotic symbolism as a mystical rite.

These are some guideposts to the text and context of *Cantos de vida y esperanza*. Although obviously not Darío's only book, it is likely his most important one. Here he embraces the central themes of modernity and leaves his mark on Hispanic literature of the twentieth century. Despite the shadow of swans, mythological beings, and the occasional aristocrat flitting across the modernist surface of some beautifully crafted verse, here we find one of the ground springs of poetry in our time. Here is one of the first intellects to come to grips with the conflict between artistic modernity and socioeconomic modernity, to understand that his age stood on the brink of irremediable change, to attempt to salvage the best of the past from the shipwreck of the present, and to retool poetry to survive in an unforeseeable future. Coupled with his verbal and metrical innovations, Darío's thematic concerns make *Cantos de vida y esperanza* the most influential poetic work of its time.

CRITERIA FOR REPRODUCTION AND TRANSLATION

With Rubén Darío's name so often on the lips of those familiar with the poetry of the Spanish-speaking world, it is strange that he and his works are not better known to readers in the English-speaking world. At the beginning of this introduction we emphasized this discrepancy. We also stressed the difficulty of translating a poet whose verse represents one of the high points of lyrical poetry ever written in Spanish. For the present edition and translation of *Cantos de vida y esperanza*, we have carefully borne in mind the traditional philological principles of editing and translating texts as well as some newer ideas suggested by recent advances in criticism, cultural studies, linguistics, and translation studies. We hope to offer a translation faithful to the original and a text corresponding to the intentions of the poet who first wrote and published it.

To this end we reproduce the first edition of *Cantos de vida y esperanza. Los cisnes y otros poemas* as published in 1905, under the care of Juan Ramón Jiménez. Five hundred copies of the book were originally published in Madrid nearly a century ago; the surviving copies are now scattered all over the world. The copy we have used for this edition bears a dedication and signature by the poet himself, which reads: "Al Profesor L.S. Rowe simpáticamente, Rubén Darío. En el mar, junio, 30, 1906" [To Professor L. S. Rowe, cordially, Rubén Darío. At sea, June 30, 1906]. In 1907, Darío published the second edition of the book with F. Granada y Compañía, in Barcelona. Identical to the first edition in type, margins, number of pages, and overall dimensions, it is still considered, thanks to the high quality of printing and paper, one of the jewels of Catalan publishing from that period, a product of the presses at the *Anuario de la Exportación*, on the Paseo de San Juan in Barcelona. As to specific deviations between editions, mainly of accent marks and other minor details, Ernesto Mejía Sánchez has given a full account (1977: lxvi–lxvii). For a history of the book's preparation and the relationship between Juan Ramón Jiménez and Rubén Darío, the correspondence between the poets is of special interest and may be found in the book by Jiménez himself, *Mi Rubén Darío*, as well as in a recent article by J. M. Martínez (1995).

On the question of handwritten manuscripts of poems found in *Cantos de vida y esperanza*, readers may refer to articles by Sánchez Romeralo, as well as to his edition of the Jiménez book just mentioned. Jiménez saved a number of manuscripts used for the first edition and eventually donated them to the Library of Congress in Washington, D.C., which still holds twenty-one of them. The location of another five is known, but we have few clues to suggest the whereabouts of the rest. Whenever possible, we have carried out a comparative study of manuscripts conserved in Spain, Spanish America, and the United States, giving special attention to those kept at the Seminario-

39

Archivo Rubén Darío (Madrid), in the Library of Congress (Washington, D.C.), and in the collections of the Houghton Library at Harvard University (Cambridge, MA).

In reproducing the original text, we have respected the punctuation marks used by Darío, and any alterations are in response to obvious errata. We also respected the use of spaces, indentations, Roman numerals, and other typographical peculiarities. One thing we have changed is the rather old-fashioned use of an initial capital letter for each verse, which Darío employed in some but not all of his books; we have followed the customary use of small and capital letters, with contemporary readers in mind. Similarly, in the case of the Spanish text, modernization of spelling rules has obliged us to make changes for the sake of consistency: *armonía* for *harmonía*, *hexámetro* for *exámetro*, *fue* for *fué*, and so forth. However, certain words already antiquated in Darío's time, as well as words from other languages, have been retained for their aesthetic value. In the usage of interrogative and exclamation points we respect the original choice of the poet, who at times leaves off the initial punctuation (the ¿ and the ¡) to differentiate himself from Spanish poets and to show his spirit of independence. Only by consulting the first edition of the work, the available manuscripts, and those poems published separately in journals and newspapers can serious textual problems be overcome and poems presented faithful to the original, free of typographical errata.

The fact that even Darío's most virulent detractors in his time and in ours have failed to refute his importance to the evolution of Hispanic poetry confirms the desirability of editing and translating the entire text of *Cantos de vida y esperanza*, the essence and pinnacle of Darío's art, for as wide an audience as possible. We believe the present attempt is an important first step toward the translation of all Darío's books of poetry, so woefully lacking in English. Such an ambitious project would allow scholars from all over the English-speaking world to appreciate more than ever the profundities of this poetry: its existential, religious, erotic, and social contours, and its relevance to Western literature as a whole. Darío's impact on modern Hispanic poetry bespeaks the need of faithful and rigorous translations for those who know little or no Spanish, which in turn may stimulate further critical and academic attention to the poet and his works.

As suggested at the beginning of our introduction, English versions of individual poems have been available almost from the beginning, however wildly divergent in quality and fidelity. Anthologies of Spanish and Spanish American poetry may likewise include a handful of Darío's poems in translation, though the principles behind the selection often mystify: for instance, the major poem "Yo persigo una forma . . ." (I pursue a form . . .) appears along with the minor and unrepresentative piece "El gallo" (The rooster) in a Penguin anthology; or, as in the case of Blackwell's collection, a compilation may lack a single poem from the canon for which Darío is justly famous on both sides of the Atlantic. Perhaps an individual poem's translatability determines whether it is selected for an anthology. The dearth of important poems rigorously or even accurately translated into English obliges many Hispanists and literary scholars to give their own version of one of Darío's verses or stanzas in support of an argument, with no regard for consistency from one article, chapter, or even page, to the next. Poets have also discovered Darío in their search for fresh inspiration, and not a few of them have attempted to render a specific poem in English.

Anglo-American readers have had to settle for scattered translations over the years, and any real scrutiny of those texts reveals a widespread misreading of the original Spanish, lapses in versification, and even cases of translators imposing an extraneous interpretation on the original. The failures in rendering a Darío poem into English are often due to a clash of meaning and poetics, especially poetic form, the devices of rhythm and rhyme. Among Latin American and Spanish poets, he is justly famous for the musicality—the acoustic dimension—of his verse. We will attempt a brief illustration of some aspects that are particularly problematic when translating Darío. Whereas regular English versification has come to depend on the number of metric feet, a repeated unit of stress rhythms (traditionally the iambic, trochaic, anapestic, dactylic, and amphibrachic foot), Spanish verse is measured by the number of syllables. For the purpose of measuring a verse, these syllables are acoustic rather than simply lexical, involving such processes as synizesis, elision, caesural pause, etc. The two systems—metric and syllabic—rarely coincide. Thus, for instance, the prevalent Spanish hendecasyllable may well show an iambic "tendency" but cannot in fact be a true instance of iambic pentameter due to an extra syllable. The difference is even more pronounced with a rhythm based on three-syllable feet (anapestic, dactylic, and amphibrachic): not only is an eleven-syllable verse not divisible into units of three syllables, but the Spanish hendecasyllable must follow a precise system of accentuation that precludes adherence to all but the anapestic tendency, which must fail after the second foot.

Given the vastly different morphological-syntactic systems of English and Spanish, the translator can rarely follow Darío's rhythmic patterns while retaining the sense and register of what Darío is literally saying. The best a translator can usually do is follow Darío by analogy: in other words, to use a rhythmic flow of words in English to suggest to the reader Darío's rhythmic emphasis in a certain line or stanza. An example of this occurs in the present volume in the case of the celebrated poem "Salutación del optimista" (The Optimist's Salutation). The original verse maintains a jubilant dactylic rhythm: "Ínclitas razas ubérrimas, sangre de Hispania fecunda . . ." Another three-syllable rhythm better suits the English translation, and so we have replaced the original dactyls with a decidedly amphibrachic lilt: "Distinguished, fructiferous races, blood of prolific Hispania . . ." More often than not, unfortunately, it proves impossible to follow Darío's rhythm so closely, and the translator must settle for some sort of regularity of accentuation akin to tumbling verse in order to suggest that the original is composed of regular verses.[1]

Darío's use of rhyme was extraordinary even in his time. For a sense of his rhyme schemes, and how end rhyme, interior rhyme, and alliteration seem to crackle in chain reactions all over the page, the reader may think of the Edgar Allan Poe of "Annabel Lee" and "The Raven," though Darío seems to have a more delicate touch, despite the similarities of acoustic bravura. On occasion he employs assonant rhyme, but he much prefers consonance. There are intrinsic differences here as well between the languages. Spanish verses generally end with so-called feminine rhyme, or rhymes of two syllables, stress falling on the next to last syllable: whether the consonant -oro in the words tesoro and lloro, or the assonant á-a in the words casa and mala. Darío was a master of rhyme, including rima rica, the difficult or unusual rhyme. He has somewhat toned down the almost tongue-tying intensity of some effects in Prosas profanas, which trans-

1. A particularly apt correspondence occurs in the case of "Lo fatal" (What gets you), discussed at length above. The original is composed mainly in alejandrinos, fourteen-syllable lines that divide into hemistiches with a caesural pause between them. Tumbling verse, developed from Anglo-Saxon poetry, also divides into half-lines, though with a structural rather than an acoustic pause. Each half-line includes two stresses, with the two half-lines bound together by alliteration between at least one of the stressed syllables from each half. So when Darío writes the alejandrino: "Dichoso el árbol que es || apenas sensativo," we use tumbling verse to give the reader some sense of that rhythm: How fortunate the tree || that can scarcely feel," alliteration connecting the consonant f in fortunate and feel and the near-rhyme of the long vowel sound in tree and feel.

lation can scarcely hint at, or the triple rhymes (*esdrújula*, in Spanish), such as: "Oh quién fuera hipsipila que dejó la *crisálida*! / (La princesa está triste. La princesa está *pálida*)" [Oh to be a hypsipyle that sheds its cocoon! / (The princess is sad. The princess is pale.)]. Yet in *Cantos* Darío continues to weave words in highly musical combinations. In "Augurios" (Omens) an assonant *esdrújula* verse works smoothly, if not unobtrusively, in the rhyme scheme: "irás en giras fantásticas" [you will go on fantastic flights]. The strikingly alliterative verses from the "Marcha triunfal" (Triumphal march) make us hear "los claros clarines" [the clear bugles] in the "cortejo de los paladines" [procession of the paladins]. Or consider the interior assonant rhyme (*á-a*) in a verse from "Aleluya!" (Halleluyah!): "Rosas *rosadas* y b*lancas*, r*amas* verdes" [Roses rosy and white, green branches]. The three sonnets comprising "Trébol" (Clover) cleverly interweave the names of writers, painters, and characters into musical effects. All this mastery of the acoustic dimension makes any translation difficult. The prevalence of the monosyllable in English often produces an emphatic or masculine rhyme of one syllable at the end of the verse, as in *dig* and *big* or *stop* and *shop*. Masculine rhyme, of course, exists in Spanish as well: whether the consonant *-ón* in the words *pasión* and *corazón*, or the assonant *á* in the words *universidad* and *volverán*. Like all good poets before him, Darío uses masculine rhyme on occasion, especially to vary the more subtle rhythm based on a series of feminine rhymes. But literary history suggests that a constant string of verses ending with such a jolt, so common in English, quickly tires the ear in Spanish and is almost universally avoided, except for effect. Attempts to adhere closely to Darío's rhyme schemes generally produce in English an unpleasantly precious or singsong effect, at least in our experience. Often the translation works best with softer assonant rhymes or even near rhymes that give readers a sense of the rhyming in the original without distorting the intended effect.

And here we arrive at the true question confronting every translator: given the impossibility of transferring a multifaceted work—alive and well—from one language to another, what is the essence to be conveyed? Darío's genius never resided in one aspect or another, but in the whole. His best poems, whether the first or hundredth time we read them, suggest a sense of having been inevitable. And inevitably his, for there is no mistaking that unique voice: what he says and the way he says it. Having admitted the formal limitations of translating poetry, we decided to follow as closely as possible—and, we admit, subjectively—the voice we hear when reading Darío. That voice is what so many translations so often lack. We will mention here some recourses employed in this book in an effort to approach that voice.

The pursuit of Darío's analogous voice in English involves some rather drastic hyperbaton (distorting the natural order of words in a sentence) at times: he loves to twist and turn his syntax from verse to verse, and only sometimes for the sake of a rhyme or for emphasis, regardless of what others less experienced with his poetry might think. The next generation of avant-garde writers would take this tendency and push it to the limits of comprehensibility. English grammar simply does not have the same elasticity as Spanish, but the translator should stretch it as far as possible when reflecting the original without completely obscuring the meaning (which, by the way, Darío himself occasionally does, leading to a number of possible interpretations and the ensuing scholarly arguments).

The register of Darío's diction is an important element that many translators either overlook or choose to ignore. His selection of words is precise, leaving nothing to chance, and at times rather refined, if not highbrow, as in the line from "Salutación del optimista" quoted above, and the translator must match him as closely as possible if readers are to get any sense of the original language. For instance, in the opening line of a "Nocturno" (Nocturne), the poet writes: "Los que auscultasteis el corazón de la noche," deliberately using the rare and rather technical verb *auscultar*. It so happens that a form of the same Latinate verb exists in English as well, and so an accurate translation would render the line: "Those of you who auscultated the heart of the night," bowing to Darío's word choice. In contrast, Lysander Kemp translates it in the following way: "You that have heard the heartbeat of the night," employing the most common and generic verb in English to describe the auditory sense; he then attempts to hint at *auscultate* by changing *heart* to *heartbeat*, altering the text on two levels (87). This is tantamount to correcting the poet. It is not a question of which is the most "poetic" phrase. We have not attempted an interpretation of Darío or our personal variation on a theme by Darío. After all, it is his poetry we want readers to be thinking about, not ours. Those who would prefer a more self-conscious translation that used Darío's text as a general guide to the translator's own poetic gifts, real or imagined, might not agree with us; but we have seen too many cases of inexplicably arbitrary changes in translations that falsify the original on every level. Needless to say, the sin of translators carries over to those critics who depend on such translations. Our aim is always to reproduce an accurate sense of what Darío is doing in Spanish on the facing page.

Certainly a questionable trend common to several translators and many scholars and critics is the attempt to reproduce the "meaning" of a certain poem while reducing its poetic structure to bald prose; this is the unfortunate case of recent critical studies on Darío and other modernists, which, regardless of careful documentation and research, lack a clear and consistent sense of the poetry involved. Jrade, for instance, states in the preface to her book: "I have laid out the translations of poems in paragraph form to indicate that, in trying to remain as faithful as possible to the sense of the original, I have not attempted to reproduce the poetic structure" (1998). Rosemary LoDato also admits the difficulty of translating Darío: "Unless otherwise noted, all translations are my own. I am responsible for all errors and inelegance in my translations" (10). We believe it is necessary to reproduce the atmosphere of Darío's language as faithfully as possible. It is important to see how he manages verses and stanzas. A faithful translation must also include the use of odd, artificially "poetic" words: *lymph* for a limpid stream, for example, when Darío does the same in Spanish with the equally artificial *linfa*. Given contemporary tastes, there is a general tendency to water down Darío in translation. Yet by first depriving him of his acoustic elegance through the simple act of translation and then dumbing down his expressiveness for the sake of imagined readers who do not have access to a dictionary, translators all too often produce empty verses that fail even to hint at the richness and complexity of the original. In the same vein, translators have routinely gutted the allusions—mythological, esoteric, exotic, historical—so essential to Hispanic modernist aesthetics. The motive is understandable enough: Darío's reading of myth, to give but one example, is often obscure even for Hispanic readers well acquainted with the classical world of gods, goddesses, heroes, and monsters that is part of their cultural patrimony; for an average reader from the United States, the classical world generally resonates far less than in Latin cultures and may even seem rather silly. A rigorous translation, however, should reproduce as accurately as possible the allusive world of Darío's poetry, and might then include—as ours does—a glossary of terms, names, and events with which readers may not be familiar.

What has been said regarding Rubén Darío can be extended to all Spanish and Spanish American modernist poets, from Martí to Lugones. More English translations of Hispanic poetry will encourage readers to come to know the excellent literature produced by these writers. For the cause of textual accuracy and poetry in translation, then, may the present dual edition of Darío's *Cantos de vida y esperanza* serve as a first step toward a pressing reevaluation of Darío, toward future critical editions of his poetry, in a renewed interest in translating his and Hispanic modernist poetry into English, and toward an ever-widening circle of readers who come to know and enjoy one of the great voices in literature. We believe the poems in *Cantos de vida y esperanza* have already gone beyond the barriers of time and literary trends. We would like to thank Duke University Press—J. Reynolds Smith, Sharon Parks Torian, Leigh Anne Couch, Justin Faerber, Sonya Manes, and Christine Jensen in particular—for their interest in our critical text and translation, and for the time they have devoted to them. Finally, we want to express our gratitude to the Spanish poet Manuel Mantero, whose love of poetry and of Rubén Darío continues to be an example for both of us.

Songs of Life and Hope

The Swans and Other Poems

For

Nicaragua

For the Argentine Republic

R. D.

Cantos de vida y esperanza

Los cisnes y otros poemas

A

Nicaragua

A la República Argentina

R. D.

Prefacio

Podría repetir aquí más de un concepto de las palabras liminares de Prosas profanas. Mi respeto por la aristocracia del pensamiento, por la nobleza del Arte, siempre es el mismo. Mi antiguo aborrecimiento a la mediocridad, a la mulatez intelectual, a la chatura estética, apenas si se aminora hoy con una razonada indiferencia.

El movimiento de libertad que me tocó iniciar en América, se propagó hasta España y tanto aquí como allá el triunfo está logrado. Aunque respecto a técnica tuviese demasiado que decir en el país en donde la expresión poética está anquilosada a punto de que la momificación del ritmo ha llegado a ser un artículo de fe, no haré sino una corta advertencia. En todos los países cultos de Europa se ha usado del hexámetro absolutamente clásico sin que la mayoría letrada y sobre todo la minoría leída se asustasen de semejante manera de cantar. En Italia ha mucho tiempo, sin citar antiguos, que Carducci ha autorizado los hexámetros; en inglés, no me atrevería casi a indicar, por respeto a la cultura de mis lectores, que la *Evangelina* de Longfellow está en los mismos versos en que Horacio dijo sus mejores pensares. En cuanto al verso libre moderno . . . ¿no es verdaderamente singular que en esta tierra de Quevedos y de Góngoras los únicos innovadores del instrumento lírico, los únicos libertadores del ritmo, hayan sido los poetas del *Madrid Cómico* y los libretistas del género chico?

Hago esta advertencia porque la forma es lo que primeramente toca a las muchedumbres. Yo no soy un poeta para muchedumbres. Pero sé que indefectiblemente tengo que ir a ellas.

Cuando dije que mi poesía era "mía, en mí" sostuve la primera condición de mi existir, sin pretensión ninguna de causar sectarismo en mente o voluntad ajena, y en un intenso amor a lo absoluto de la belleza.

Al seguir la vida que Dios me ha concedido tener, he buscado expresarme lo más noble y altamente en mi comprensión; voy diciendo mi verso con una modestia tan orgullosa que solamente las espigas comprenden, y cultivo, entre otras flores, una rosa rosada, concreción de alba, capullo de porvenir, entre el bullicio de la literatura.

Si en estos cantos hay política, es porque aparece universal. Y si encontráis versos a un presidente, es porque son un clamor continen-

Preface

I could repeat here more than one concept from the liminary words of *Prosas profanas*. My respect for the aristocracy of thought, for the nobility of Art, remains the same. My earlier abhorrence of mediocrity, of intellectual mongrelizing, of aesthetic shallowness, has scarcely subsided today into reasoned indifference.

The freedom movement that fell upon me to initiate in America has spread to Spain, and as much here as there, its triumph is assured. Although I could say perhaps too much about technique in a land where poetic expression is outdated to the point that mummification of rhythm has become an article of faith, I will give but one word of caution. In all civilized countries of Europe they have used the utterly classical hexameter without scaring off the educated majority and, more important, the reading minority from similar ways of singing. For a while now, Carducci (not to mention earlier poets) has made the hexameter acceptable in Italy; out of respect for the culture of my readers, I hardly dare to point out that, in English, Longfellow's *Evangeline* is composed in the same verses in which Horace spoke his best thoughts. As for modern free verse . . . Is it not truly odd that in this land of Quevedos and Góngoras the only innovators of the lyrical instrument, the only liberators of rhythm, have been the poets of the *Madrid Cómico* and the librettists of the popular stage?

I give this word of caution because form is what primarily touches the masses. I am not a poet for the masses. But I know that inevitably I must go to them.

When I said that my poetry was "mine, in me," I upheld the first condition of my existence, with no pretense at all of inciting sectarianism in the thoughts or actions of others, and in an intense love for the absolute nature of beauty.

In leading the life God has granted me, I have sought to express myself to the loftiest and most noble extent I know how; I start uttering my verse with such proud modesty only the ears of wheat can understand, and I cultivate, among other flowers, a rosy rose, concretion of a dawn, the bud of what is to come, amid the commotion of literature.

If in these songs there is politics, it is because politics appears universally. And if you find verses to a president, it is because they are a

tal. Mañana podremos ser yanquis (y es lo más probable); de todas maneras mi protesta queda, escrita sobre las alas de los inmaculados cisnes, tan ilustres como Júpiter.

R. D.

continental clamor. Tomorrow we may well become Yankees (and this is most likely); my protest stands anyhow, written upon the wings of immaculate swans, as illustrious as Jupiter.

R. D.

Songs of Life and Hope

For J. Enrique Rodó

Cantos de vida y esperanza

A J. Enrique Rodó

I.

Yo soy aquel que ayer no más decía
el verso azul y la canción profana,
en cuya noche un ruiseñor había
que era alondra de luz por la mañana.

El dueño fui de mi jardín de sueño,
lleno de rosas y de cisnes vagos;
el dueño de las tórtolas, el dueño
de góndolas y liras en los lagos;

y muy siglo diez y ocho y muy antiguo
y muy moderno; audaz, cosmopolita;
con Hugo fuerte y con Verlaine ambiguo,
y una sed de ilusiones infinita.

Yo supe de dolor desde mi infancia,
mi juventud . . . ¿fue juventud la mía?
sus rosas aún me dejan su fragancia, —
una fragancia de melancolía . . .

Potro sin freno se lanzó mi instinto,
mi juventud montó potro sin freno;
iba embriagada y con puñal al cinto;
si no cayó, fue porque Dios es bueno.

En mi jardín se vio una estatua bella;
se juzgó mármol y era carne viva;
un alma joven habitaba en ella,
sentimental, sensible, sensitiva.

Y tímida ante el mundo, de manera
que encerrada en silencio no salía,
sino cuando en la dulce primavera
era la hora de la melodía . . .

I.

I am the one who just yesterday spoke
the blue verse and the profane song,
in whose night there was a nightingale
that was a skylark of light in the morning.

I was the master of my dream garden
full of roses and vague swans;
the master of turtledoves, the master
of gondolas and lyres on the lakes;

and very eighteenth-century and very ancient
and very modern; audacious, cosmopolitan;
with straightforward Hugo and ambiguous Verlaine,
and an infinite thirst for dreams.

I've learned about pain from childhood,
my youth . . . Was mine a youth?
Its roses still leave me its fragrance,
a fragrance of melancholy . . .

An unbridled colt, my instinct took off,
my youth rode an unbridled colt;
it went about intoxicated and with a dagger in its belt;
if it didn't fall off, that was because God is good.

In my garden was a beautiful statue;
it was thought to be marble, and was living flesh;
a young soul inhabited it,
sentimental, sensitive, susceptible.

And shy before the world, so
that, locked in silence, it wouldn't come out,
except in the sweet spring
when it was the time of melody . . .

Hora de ocaso y de discreto beso;
hora crepuscular y de retiro;
hora de madrigal y de embeleso,
de "te adoro," de "ay" y de suspiro.

Y entonces era en la dulzaina un juego
de misteriosas gamas cristalinas,
un renovar de notas del Pan griego
y un desgranar de músicas latinas,

con aire tal y con ardor tan vivo,
que a la estatua nacían de repente
en el muslo viril patas de chivo
y dos cuernos de sátiro en la frente.

Como la Galatea gongorina
me encantó la marquesa verleniana,
y así juntaba a la pasión divina
una sensual hiperestesia humana;

todo ansia, todo ardor, sensación pura
y vigor natural; y sin falsía,
y sin comedia y sin literatura . . . :
si hay un alma sincera, ésa es la mía.

La torre de marfil tentó mi anhelo;
quise encerrarme dentro de mí mismo,
y tuve hambre de espacio y sed de cielo
desde las sombras de mi propio abismo.

Como la esponja que la sal satura
en el jugo del mar, fue el dulce y tierno
corazón mío, henchido de amargura
por el mundo, la carne y el infierno.

Mas, por gracia de Dios, en mi conciencia
el Bien supo elegir la mejor parte;
y si hubo áspera hiel en mi existencia,
melificó toda acritud el Arte.

Time of sunset and a discreet kiss;
time of twilight and seclusion;
time of madrigal and enchantment,
of "I adore you," of "ah," and of a sigh.

And then on the pipes it was an array
of mysterious crystalline scales,
a renewing of notes from the Greek Pan,
and a threshing of Latin music,

with such an air and a fervor so alive
that on the statue suddenly goat feet
would sprout from the virile thigh
and two satyr horns from the brow.

As much as the Galatea of Góngora
I loved the Marquise of Verlaine,
and so joined to divine passion
a sensuous human hypersensitivity;

all longing, all fervor, a pure sensation
and natural vigor; and without dissimulation,
and without comedy and without literature . . .
if there is a sincere soul, it is mine.

The ivory tower tempted my desires;
I tried to lock myself within me,
and grew hungry for space and thirsty for sky
from the shadows of my own abyss.

Like a sponge saturated by salt
in the essence of the sea, was this sweet and tender
heart of mine, swollen with bitterness
by the world, the flesh, and hell.

Yet, by the grace of God, in my conscience
Goodness learned to choose the better part;
and if there was bitter gall in my existence,
everything acrid was honeyed by Art.

Mi intelecto libré de pensar bajo,
bañó el agua castalia el alma mía,
peregrinó mi corazón y trajo
de la sagrada selva la armonía.

¡Oh, la selva sagrada! ¡Oh, la profunda
emanación del corazón divino
de la sagrada selva! ¡Oh, la fecunda
fuente cuya virtud vence al destino!

Bosque ideal que lo real complica,
allí el cuerpo arde y vive y Psiquis vuela;
mientras abajo el sátiro fornica,
ebria de azul deslíe Filomela

perla de ensueño y música amorosa
en la cúpula en flor del laurel verde,
Hipsipila sutil liba en la rosa,
y la boca del fauno el pezón muerde.

Allí va el dios en celo tras la hembra,
y la caña de Pan se alza del lodo;
la eterna Vida sus semillas siembra,
y brota la armonía del gran Todo.

El alma que entra allí debe ir desnuda,
temblando de deseo y fiebre santa,
sobre cardo heridor y espina aguda:
así sueña, así vibra y así canta.

Vida, luz y verdad, tal triple llama
produce la interior llama infinita;
el Arte puro como Cristo exclama:
Ego sum lux et veritas et vita!

Y la vida es misterio; la luz ciega
y la verdad inaccesible asombra;
la adusta perfección jamás se entrega,
y el secreto Ideal duerme en la sombra.

I freed my intellect from base thinking,
the waters of Castalia bathed my soul,
my heart made a pilgrimage and brought back
harmony from the sacred wood.

Oh, the sacred wood! Oh, the profound
emanation of the divine heart
of the sacred wood! Oh, the prolific
fountain whose virtue overcomes fate!

Ideal forest which the real complicates,
there the body burns and lives and Psyche flies;
while below her the satyr fornicates,
Philomela—drunk on blue—liquefies

a pearl of fantasy and amorous music
in the flowering cupola of the green laurel,
subtle Hypsipyle sucks on the rose,
and the mouth of the faun bites her nipple.

There, after the female goes the god in heat,
and Pan's reed rises from the mud;
Life eternal sows its seeds,
and harmony springs from the great Everything.

The soul that enters there should go naked,
trembling with desire and holy fever,
over wounding nettle and prickly thorn:
so it dreams, so it quivers, and so it sings.

Life, light, and truth: such a triple flame
produces the infinite flame within;
Art pure as Christ exclaims:
Ego sum lux et veritas et vita!

And life is a mystery; light blinds
and inaccessible truth appalls;
stark perfection never concedes,
and the secret Ideal sleeps in the shadow.

Por eso ser sincero es ser potente.
De desnuda que está, brilla la estrella;
el agua dice el alma de la fuente
en la voz de cristal que fluye d'ella.

Tal fue mi intento, hacer del alma pura
mía, una estrella, una fuente sonora,
con el horror de la literatura
y loco de crepúsculo y de aurora.

Del crepúsculo azul que da la pauta
que los celestes éxtasis inspira,
bruma y tono menor—¡toda la flauta!,
y Aurora, hija del Sol—¡toda la lira!

Pasó una piedra que lanzó una honda;
pasó una flecha que aguzó un violento.
La piedra de la honda fue a la onda,
y la flecha del odio fuese al viento.

La virtud está en ser tranquilo y fuerte;
con el fuego interior todo se abrasa;
se triunfa del rencor y de la muerte,
y hacia Belén . . . la caravana pasa!

Thus, to be sincere is to be powerful.
By being naked, the star shines;
water speaks the fountain's soul
in the crystal voice that from it flows.

Such was my intent, to make of this pure soul
of mine, a star, a resonant fountain,
with a horror of literature
and crazy with dusk and with dawn.

With the blue dusk that sets the pattern,
inspiring heavenly ecstasies;
fog and a minor key: the whole flute!
And Aurora, daughter of the sun: the whole lyre!

A stone went flying from a slingshot;
an arrow, which a violent man had sharpened, flew.
The stone from the slingshot went into the wave,
and the arrow of hate went off on the wind.

Virtue lies in being tranquil and strong;
everything burns with the fire inside it;
we triumph over spite and over death,
and on to Bethlehem . . . the caravan passes!

11. Salutación del optimista

Inclitas razas ubérrimas, sangre de Hispania fecunda,
espíritus fraternos, luminosas almas, salve!
Porque llega el momento en que habrán de cantar nuevos himnos
lenguas de gloria. Un vasto rumor llena los ámbitos; mágicas
ondas de vida van renaciendo de pronto;
retrocede el olvido, retrocede engañada la muerte;
se anuncia un reino nuevo, feliz sibila sueña
y en la caja pandórica de que tantas desgracias surgieron
encontramos de súbito, talismánica, pura, riente,
cual pudiera decirla en su verso Virgilio divino,
la divina reina de luz, la celeste Esperanza!

Pálidas indolencias, desconfianzas fatales que a tumba
o a perpetuo presidio, condenasteis al noble entusiasmo,
ya veréis el salir del sol en un triunfo de liras,
mientras dos continentes, abonados de huesos gloriosos,
del Hércules antiguo la gran sombra soberbia evocando,
digan al orbe: la alta virtud resucita
que a la hispana progenie hizo dueña de siglos.

Abominad la boca que predice desgracias eternas,
abominad los ojos que ven sólo zodíacos funestos,
abominad las manos que apedrean las ruinas ilustres,
o que la tea empuñan o la daga suicida.
Siéntense sordos ímpetus en las entrañas del mundo,
la inminencia de algo fatal hoy conmueve la Tierra;
fuertes colosos caen, se desbandan bicéfalas águilas,
y algo se inicia como vasto social cataclismo
sobre la faz del orbe. ¿Quién dirá que las savias dormidas
no despierten entonces en el tronco del roble gigante
bajo el cual se exprimió la ubre de la loba romana?
¿Quién será el pusilánime que al vigor español niegue músculos
y que al alma española juzgase áptera y ciega y tullida?
No es Babilonia ni Nínive enterrada en olvido y en polvo,
ni entre momias y piedras reina que habita el sepulcro,
la nación generosa, coronada de orgullo inmarchito,

11. The Optimist's Salutation

Distinguished, fructiferous races, blood of prolific Hispania,
brotherly spirits, luminous wings: hail!
For the moment has come when new anthems will be sung
by tongues of glory. An enormous report fills all spaces; magical
waves of life begin all at once to be born again;
oblivion recedes, death recedes, deluded;
a new realm is announced, a felicitous sibyl dreams
and in the Pandoric box from which so many misfortunes emerged
we suddenly find, talismanic, pure, laughing,
as divine Virgil might have said in his verses,
the divine queen of light, celestial Hope!

Pallid indolence, fateful misgivings that to the grave
or perpetual prison condemned noble enthusiasm,
will now see the sun coming up in a triumph of lyres,
as long as two continents, enriched by glorious bones,
evoking the shadow, imposing and grand, of old Hercules,
will say to the orb: the lofty virtue revives,
which made Hispanic progeny the master of centuries.

Abominate mouths that foretell eternal misfortunes,
abominate eyes that see only ill-fated Zodiacs,
abominate hands that stone the illustrious ruins,
or that wield the firebrand or suicidal dagger.
Deafening impulses are felt in the core of the world,
the imminence of something fateful today stirs the Earth;
mighty colossuses fall, bicephalous eagles disband,
and something has begun like a vast social cataclysm
across the face of the orb. Who says that the sleeping sap
will not thus awaken in the trunk of the giant oak
under which the teat of the Roman she-wolf was milked?
Who so pusillanimous would deny muscles to Spanish vigor
and declare the Spanish soul apterous and blind and crippled?
It is neither a Babylon nor a Nineveh buried in oblivion and in dust
nor a queen that inhabits her sepulcher among mummies and stones,
that generous nation crowned with unblemished pride,

que hacia el lado del alba fija las miradas ansiosas,
ni la que tras los mares en que yace sepulta la Atlántida,
tiene su coro de vástagos, altos, robustos y fuertes.

Unanse, brillen, secúndense, tantos vigores dispersos;
formen todos un solo haz de energía ecuménica.
Sangre de Hispania fecunda, sólidas, ínclitas razas,
muestren los dones pretéritos que fueron antaño su triunfo.
Vuelva el antiguo entusiasmo, vuelva el espíritu ardiente
que regará lenguas de fuego en esa epifanía.
Juntas las testas ancianas ceñidas de líricos lauros
y las cabezas jóvenes que la alta Minerva decora,
así los manes heroicos de los primitivos abuelos,
de los egregios padres que abrieron el surco pristino,
sientan los soplos agrarios de primaverales retornos
y el rumor de espigas que inició la labor triptolémica.

Un continente y otro renovando las viejas prosapias,
en espíritu unidos, en espíritu y ansias y lengua,
ven llegar el momento en que habrán de cantar nuevos himnos.
La latina estirpe verá la gran alba futura,
en un trueno de música gloriosa, millones de labios
saludarán la espléndida luz que vendrá del Oriente,
Oriente augusto en donde todo lo cambia y renueva
la eternidad de Dios, la actividad infinita.
Y así sea Esperanza la visión permanente en nosotros,
ínclitas razas ubérrimas, sangre de Hispania fecunda!

which fixes its longing gaze on the side of the dawn,
nor the one which, beyond the seas in which Atlantis lies entombed,
has its chorus of offspring, tall, robust, and strong.

May so many scattered strengths unite, shine, support one another;
may all of them form a single bundle of ecumenical energy.
Blood of prolific Hispania, solid, distinguished races,
show the former gifts that in olden days were your triumph.
May the old enthusiasm return, may the passionate spirit return
that will rain down tongues of fire on that epiphany.
May both the ancient heads girt with lyrical laurels
and the young heads which lofty Minerva decorates,
like the heroic manes of the primitive grandfathers,
of the eminent fathers who opened the pristine furrow,
feel the agrarian breezes of springtime returnings
and hear the murmur of grain which Triptolemical labor began.

One continent and another renewing the old bloodlines,
in spirit united, in spirit and longings and language,
see the moment coming when new anthems will be sung.
The Latin race will see the great dawn of the future;
in a thunder of glorious music, millions of lips
will salute the splendid light that will come from the East,
august East in which all will be changed and renewed
by the eternity of God, the infinite activity.
And so may Hope be the enduring vision in us,
distinguished, fructiferous races, blood of prolific Hispania!

iii. Al Rey Óscar

Le Roi de Suède et de Norvège, après avoir visité
Saint-Jean-de-Luz, s'est rendu et à Hendaye et à
Fonterabie. En arrivant sur le sol espagnol, il a crié:
"Vive l'Espagne!" —Le Figaro, mars 1899.

Así, Sire, en el aire de la Francia nos llega
la paloma de plata de Suecia y de Noruega,
que trae en vez de olivo una rosa de fuego.

Un búcaro latino, un noble vaso griego
recibirá el regalo del país de la nieve.
Que a los reinos boreales el patrio viento lleve
otra rosa de sangre y de luz españolas;
pues sobre la sublime hermandad de las olas,
al brotar tu palabra, un saludo le envía
al sol de medianoche el sol del Mediodía!

Si Segismundo siente pesar, Hamlet se inquieta.
El Norte ama las palmas; y se junta el poeta
del fjord con el del carmen, porque el mismo oriflama
es de azur. Su divina cornucopia derrama
sobre el polo y el trópico, la Paz; y el orbe gira
en un ritmo uniforme por una propia lira:
el amor. Allá surge Sigurd que al Cid se aúna.
Cerca de Dulcinea brilla el rayo de luna,
y la musa de Bécquer del ensueño es esclava
bajo un celeste palio de luz escandinava.

Sire de ojos azules, gracias: por los laureles
de cien bravos vestidos de honor; por los claveles
de la tierra andaluza y la Alhambra del moro;
por la sangre solar de una raza de oro;
por la armadura antigua y el yelmo de la gesta;
por las lanzas que fueron una vasta floresta
de gloria y que pasaron Pirineos y Andes;
por Lepanto y Otumba; por el Perú, por Flandes;

III. To King Oscar

Following a visit to St. Jean-de-Luz, the King of Sweden
and Norway traveled on to Hendaye and Fuenterrabía.
Upon touching Spanish soil, he shouted: "Long live
Spain!" — Le Figaro, March 1899.

Thus, Sire, in the air from France the silver dove
of Sweden and of Norway comes to us,
bringing instead of an olive branch a rose of fire.

An earthen Latin vessel, a noble Greek vase
will receive the gift from the land of snow.
May the native wind carry to the boreal kingdoms
another rose of Spanish blood and light;
since over the sublime brotherhood of the waves,
as your word springs forth, a greeting is sent
to the midnight sun from the Noonday sun!

If Segismundo feels regret, Hamlet grows apprehensive.
The North loves palm trees; and now the poet of the fjord
joins the poet of the walled garden, because the same oriflamme
is azure. Its divine cornucopia spills,
over pole and tropic, Peace; and the orb turns
in a rhythm consistent with its own lyre:
love. There Siegfried appears, uniting with the Cid.
Near Dulcinea shines the moonbeam,
and Bécquer's muse of reverie is a slave
beneath a celestial pallium of Scandinavian light.

Blue-eyed Sire, thank you: for the laurels
from a hundred brave men dressed in honor; for the carnations
from Andalusian earth and the Alhambra of the Moor;
for the sunlit blood of a golden race;
for an ancient armor and the helmet of heroic deeds;
for the lances that were once a vast grove
of glory passing through Pyrenees and Andes;
for Lepanto and Otumba, for Peru, for Flanders;

por Isabel que cree, por Cristóbal que sueña
y Velázquez que pinta y Cortés que domeña;
por el país sagrado en que Herakles afianza
sus macizas columnas de fuerza y esperanza,
mientras Pan trae el ritmo con la egregia siringa
que no hay trueno que apague ni tempestad que extinga;
por el león simbólico y la Cruz, gracias, Sire.

Mientras el mundo aliente, mientras la esfera gire,
mientras la onda cordial alimente un ensueño,
mientras haya una viva pasión, un noble empeño,
un buscado imposible, una imposible hazaña,
una América oculta que hallar, vivirá España!

Y pues tras la tormenta vienes de peregrino
real, a la morada que entristeció el destino,
la morada que viste luto sus puertas abra
al purpúreo y ardiente vibrar de tu palabra;
y que sonría, oh rey Oscar por un instante;
y tiemble en la flor áurea el más puro brillante
para quien sobre brillos de corona y de nombre,
con labios de monarca lanza un grito de hombre!

for Isabella who believes, for Christopher who dreams
and Velázquez who paints and Cortés who subjugates;
for the sacred land in which Herakles set
his massive pillars of strength and hope,
while Pan brings the rhythm of his illustrious syrinx
which no thunder can cut off nor tempest extinguish;
for the symbolic lion and the Cross, thank you, Sire.

As long as the world draws breath, as long as the sphere turns,
as long as the cordial wave nourishes a daydream,
as long as there is a lively passion, a noble endeavor,
a sought-after impossibility, an impossible feat,
a hidden America to find, Spain will live on!

And since after the storm you come, as a royal
pilgrim, to the abode which destiny saddened,
may the abode dressed in mourning open its gates
to the purple and ardent vibrating of your word;
and may it smile, O King Oscar, for an instant,
and may the purest jewel tremble in the golden flower
for the one who, above the gleam of crown and of name,
with a monarch's lips raises a man's shout!

IV. Los tres Reyes Magos

—Yo soy Gaspar. Aquí traigo el incienso.
Vengo a decir: La vida es pura y bella.
Existe Dios. El amor es inmenso.
Todo lo sé por la divina Estrella!

—Yo soy Melchor. Mi mirra aroma todo.
Existe Dios. El es la luz del día.
La blanca flor tiene sus pies en lodo
y en el placer hay la melancolía!

—Soy Baltasar. Traigo el oro. Aseguro
que existe Dios. El es el grande y fuerte.
Todo lo sé por el lucero puro
que brilla en la diadema de la Muerte.

—Gaspar, Melchor y Baltasar, callaos.
Triunfa el amor y a su fiesta os convida.
Cristo resurge, hace la luz del caos
y tiene la corona de la Vida!

iv. The Three Wise Men

"I am Gaspar. I have brought frankincense.
I come to say: Life is pure and beautiful.
God exists. Love is immense.
I know everything because of the divine Star!"

"I am Melchior. My myrrh perfumes everything.
God exists. He is the light of day.
The white flower has its feet in mud
and in pleasure there is melancholy!"

"I am Balthasar. I bring gold. I attest
that God exists. He is the great and strong one.
I know everything because of the pure brilliant star
that shines in the diadem of Death."

"Gaspar, Melchior, and Balthasar: shut up.
Love triumphs and bids you to its feast.
Christ reappears, makes light from chaos,
and holds the crown of Life!"

v. Cyrano en España

He aquí que Cyrano de Bergerac traspasa
de un salto el Pirineo. Cyrano está en su casa.
¿No es en España, acaso, la sangre vino y fuego?
Al gran gascón saluda y abraza el gran manchego.
¿No se hacen en España los más bellos castillos?
Roxanas encarnaron con rosas los Murillos,
y la hoja toledana que aquí Quevedo empuña
conócenla los bravos cadetes de Gascuña.
Cyrano hizo su viaje a la luna; mas, antes,
ya el divino lunático de don Miguel Cervantes
pasaba entre las dulces estrellas de su sueño
jinete en el sublime pegaso Clavileño.
Y Cyrano ha leído la maravilla escrita
y al pronunciar el nombre del Quijote, se quita
Bergerac el sombrero: Cyrano Balazote
siente que es lengua suya la lengua del Quijote.
Y la nariz heroica del gascón se diría
que husmea los dorados vinos de Andalucía.
Y la espada francesa, por él desenvainada,
brilla bien en la tierra de la capa y la espada.
¡Bienvenido, Cyrano de Bergerac! Castilla
te da su idioma, y tu alma como tu espada brilla
al sol que allá en sus tiempos no se ocultó en España.
Tu nariz y penacho no están en tierra extraña,
pues vienes a la tierra de la Caballería.
Eres el noble huésped de Calderón. María
Roxana te demuestra que lucha la fragancia
de las rosas de España con las rosas de Francia,
y sus supremas gracias, y sus sonrisas únicas
y sus miradas, astros que visten negras túnicas,
y la lira que vibra en su lengua sonora
te dan una Roxana de España, encantadora.
¡Oh poeta! ¡Oh celeste poeta de la facha
grotesca! Bravo y noble y sin miedo y sin tacha,
príncipe de locuras, de sueños y de rimas:
tu penacho es hermano de las más altas cimas,

v. Cyrano in Spain

Here is Cyrano de Bergerac, crossing
the Pyrenees in a single bound. Cyrano is at home.
Is not blood, perhaps, wine and fire in Spain?
The great Man of La Mancha greets and embraces the great Gascon.
Are not the most beautiful castles built in Spain?
Roxannes embodied with roses the Murillos
and the Toledo blade which Quevedo wields here
is familiar to the manly cadets of Gascony.
Cyrano took a trip to the moon; yet, even before,
the divine lunatic of master Miguel Cervantes
was passing between the sweet stars of his dream,
as a rider upon the sublime Pegasus Clavileño.
And Cyrano has read the written wonder,
and when uttering the name of Quixote, off comes
Bergerac's hat: Cyrano Balazote
perceives as his own tongue the tongue of Quixote.
And the Gascon's heroic nose, one might say,
is sniffing out the golden wines of Andalusia.
And the French sword, unsheathed by him,
shines bright in the land of the swashbuckler.
Welcome, Cyrano de Bergerac! Castile
gives you its language, and your soul, like your sword, shines
under the sun that in your day was never overcast in Spain.
Your nose and plume are in no strange land,
since you come to the land of Chivalry.
You are the noble guest of Calderón. Marie
Roxanne proves to you that the fragrance
of the roses of Spain contends with the roses of France,
and their supreme charms, and their unique smiles,
and their gazes—stars dressed in black tunics—
and the lyre that quivers on their resonant tongue
give you a Roxanne of Spain, enchanting.
O poet! O celestial poet of the grotesque
mien! Manly and noble and fearless and flawless,
prince of lunacies, of dreams and of rhymes:
your plume is brother to the summits most sublime,

del nido de tu pecho una alondra se lanza,
un hada es tu madrina, y es la Desesperanza;
y en medio de la selva del duelo y del olvido
las nueve musas vendan tu corazón herido.
¿Allá en la luna hallaste algún mágico prado
donde vaga el espíritu de Pierrot desolado?
¿Viste el palacio blanco de los locos del Arte?
¿Fue acaso la gran sombra de Píndaro a encontrarte?
¿Contemplaste la mancha roja que entre las rocas
albas forma el castillo de las Vírgenes locas?
¿Y en un jardín fantástico de misteriosas flores
no oíste al melodioso Rey de los ruiseñores?
No juzgues mi curiosa demanda inoportuna,
pues todas esas cosas existen en la luna.
¡Bienvenido, Cyrano de Bergerac! Cyrano
de Bergerac, cadete y amante, y castellano
que trae los recuerdos que Durandal abona
al país en que aún brillan las luces de Tizona.
El Arte es el glorioso vencedor. Es el Arte
el que vence el espacio y el tiempo; su estandarte,
pueblos, es del espíritu el azul oriflama.
¿Qué elegido no corre si su trompeta llama?
Y a través de los siglos se contestan, oíd:
la Canción de Rolando y la Gesta del Cid.
Cyrano va marchando, poeta y caballero,
al redoblar sonoro del grave Romancero.
Su penacho soberbio tiene nuestra aureola.
Son sus espuelas finas de fábrica española.
Y cuando en su balada Rostand teje el envío,
creeríase a Quevedo rimando un desafío.
¡Bienvenido, Cyrano de Bergerac! No seca
el tiempo el lauro; el viejo corral de la Pacheca
recibe al generoso embajador del fuerte
Molière. En copa gala Tirso su vino vierte.
Nosotros exprimimos las uvas de Champaña
para beber por Francia y en un cristal de España.

from the nest of your bosom a lark takes to the air,
a fairy is your godmother, and she is Despair;
and in the midst of the wood of pain and disregard
the nine muses bind up your wounded heart.
Did you find some magical meadow up there on the moon
where the spirit of dejected Pierrot wanders?
Did you see the white palace of the madmen of Art?
By chance were you met by the great shade of Pindar?
Did you contemplate the red stain that among the Alban
rocks is formed by the castle of the mad Virgins?
And in a fantastic garden of mysterious flowers
didn't you hear the melodious Nightingale King?
Don't judge my curious request as inopportune,
since all these things exist on the moon.
Welcome, Cyrano de Bergerac! Cyrano
de Bergerac, cadet and lover, and Castilian
who brings the memories which Durandal esteems
to the country where the flash of Tizona still gleams.
Art is the glorious victor. It is Art
that defeats space and time; its standard,
people of the world, is the blue oriflamme of the spirit.
Who among the chosen does not run if its trumpet calls?
And across the centuries they answer each other, listen:
the Song of Roland and the Epic of the Cid.
Cyrano falls into step, poet and knight,
to the resounding drumbeat of the solemn *Romancero*.
His lofty plume wears our halo.
His sharp spurs are Spanish made.
And when Rostand weaves the envoi into his ballad,
he must see himself challenging Quevedo with a rhyme.
Welcome, Cyrano de Bergerac! Time
doesn't wilt the laurel; the old *Corral de la Pacheca*
receives the generous ambassador of the forceful
Molière. Into a Gallic goblet Tirso pours his wine.
We press out the grapes of Champagne
to drink to France and in a wineglass of Spain.

vi. Salutación a Leonardo

Maestro, Pomona levanta su cesto. Tu estirpe
saluda la Aurora. Tu aurora! Que estirpe
de la indiferencia la mancha; que gaste
la dura cadena de siglos; que aplaste
al sapo la piedra de su honda.

Sonrisa más dulce no sabe Gioconda.
El verso su ala y el ritmo su onda
hermanan en una
dulzura de luna
que suave resbala
(el ritmo de la onda y el verso del ala
del mágico Cisne, sobre la laguna)
sobre la laguna.

Y así, soberano maestro
del estro,
las vagas figuras
del sueño, se encarnan en líneas tan puras
que el sueño
recibe la sangre del mundo mortal,
y Psiquis consigue su empeño
de ser advertida a través del terrestre cristal.

(Los bufones
que hacen sonreír a Monna Lisa,
saben canciones
que ha tiempo en los bosques de Grecia decía la risa
de la brisa.)

Pasa su Eminencia.
Como flor o pecado es su traje
rojo;
como flor o pecado, o conciencia
de sutil monseñor que a su paje
mira con vago recelo o enojo.

VI. A Salutation to Leonardo

Maestro, Pomona raises her basket. Your lineage
greets the dawn. Your dawn! May it extirpate
the stain of indifference; may it wear down
the hard chain of centuries; may the stone
from its sling crush the toad.

A sweeter smile Gioconda doesn't know.
The verse its wing, and the rhythm its wave
unite harmoniously in the same
sweetness of moon
that glides smooth
(the rhythm of the wave and the verse of the wing
of the magical Swan, upon the lagoon)
upon the lagoon.

And so, sovereign maestro
of conception,
the vague figures
of a dream are embodied in lines so pure
that the dream
receives the blood of the mortal world,
and Psyche achieves her desire
of being perceived through the earthly pane.

(*The jesters*
who make Mona Lisa smile
know songs
that long ago in the forests of Greece told the laughter
of the breeze.)

His Eminence goes by.
Like a flower or sin, his attire
is red;
like a flower or sin, or awareness
of a crafty monsignor who looks at his page
with vague suspicion or ire.

Nápoles deja a la abeja de oro
hacer su miel
en su fiesta de azul; y el sonoro
bandolín y el laurel
nos anuncian Florencia.
Maestro, si allá en Roma
quema el sol de Segor y Sodoma
la amarga ciencia
de purpúreas banderas, tu gesto
las palmas nos da redimidas,
bajo los arcos
de tu genio: San Marcos
y Partenón de luces y líneas y vidas.

(*Tus bufones*
que hacen la risa
de Monna Lisa
saben tan antiguas canciones . . .)

Los leones de Asuero
junto al trono para recibirte,
mientras sonríe el divino Monarca.
Pero
hallarás la sirte,
la sirte para tu barca,
si partís en la lírica barca
con tu Gioconda . . .
La onda
y el viento
saben la tempestad para tu cargamento.

Maestro!
Pero tú en cabalgar y domar fuiste diestro;
pasiones e ilusiones:
a unas con el freno, a otras con el cabestro
las domaste, cebras o leones.
Y en la selva del Sol, prisionera
tuviste la fiera
de la luz: y esa loca fue casta
cuando dijiste: "Basta".

Naples lets the golden bee
make its honey
in its blue festival; and the ringing
mandolin and the laurel
announce Florence to us.
Maestro, if there in Rome
the sun of Segor and Sodom burns up
the bitter science
of purple flags, your gesture
redeems our palms,
under the arches
of your genius: a San Marco
and Parthenon of lights and lines and lives.

(*Your jesters*
who bring about the laughter
of Mona Lisa
know your ancient songs . . .)

The lions of Ahasuerus
alongside the throne to receive you,
while the divine Monarch smiles.
But
you will run onto the shoals,
the shoals for your ship
if you depart in the lyrical ship
with your Gioconda . . .
The wave
and the wind
know the tempest for your cargo.

Maestro!
But you were skillful in riding and breaking in
passions and illusive hopes:
some with the bridle, others with the reins
you broke them in, zebras or lions.
And in the jungle of the Sun, you captured
the wild beast
of light; and that mad thing became chaste
when you said: "Enough."

79

Seis meses maceraste tu Ester en tus aromas.
De tus techos reales volaron las palomas.

Por tu cetro y tu gracia sensitiva,
por tu copa de oro en que sueñan las rosas,
en mi ciudad, que es tu cautiva,
tengo un jardín de mármol y de piedras preciosas
que custodia una esfinge viva.

Six months you steeped your Ester in your aromas.
From your royal rooftops the doves flew.

By your scepter and your sensitive grace,
by your golden cup in which roses dream,
in my city, which is your captive,
I have a garden of marble and of precious stones
over which a living sphinx keeps watch.

VII. Pegaso

Cuando iba yo a montar ese caballo rudo
y tembloroso, dije: "La vida es pura y bella".
Entre sus cejas vivas vi brillar una estrella.
El cielo estaba azul y yo estaba desnudo.

Sobre mi frente Apolo hizo brillar su escudo
y de Belerofonte logré seguir la huella.
Toda cima es ilustre si Pegaso la sella,
y yo, fuerte, he subido donde Pegaso pudo.

Yo soy el caballero de la humana energía,
yo soy el que presenta su cabeza triunfante
coronada con el laurel del Rey del día;

domador del corcel de cascos de diamante,
voy en un gran volar, con la aurora por guía,
adelante en el vasto azur, siempre adelante!

VII. Pegasus

As I went to ride that rugged
and trembling horse, I said: "Life is pure and beautiful."
Between its vivid brows I saw a star shining.
The sky was blue and I was naked.

Apollo caused his shield to shine upon my brow,
and I succeeded in following Bellerophon's trail.
Every summit is illustrious if Pegasus stamps it,
and I, strong, have climbed where Pegasus could.

I am the knight of human energy,
I am the one who presents his triumphant head
crowned with the laurel of the King of the Day;

tamer of the steed with hoofs of diamond,
I fly in a great rush, with the dawn as a guide,
onward in the vast azure, always onward!

VIII. A Roosevelt

Es con voz de la Biblia, o verso de Walt Whitman,
que habría que llegar hasta ti, Cazador!
Primitivo y moderno, sencillo y complicado,
con un algo de Washington y cuatro de Nemrod!
Eres los Estados Unidos,
eres el futuro invasor
de la América ingenua que tiene sangre indígena,
que aún reza a Jesucristo y aún habla en español.

Eres soberbio y fuerte ejemplar de tu raza;
eres culto, eres hábil; te opones a Tolstoy.
Y domando caballos, o asesinando tigres,
eres un Alejandro-Nabucodonosor.
(Eres un Profesor de Energía
como dicen los locos de hoy.)

Crees que la vida es incendio,
que el progreso es erupción;
que en donde pones la bala
el porvenir pones.
                              No.

Los Estados Unidos son potentes y grandes.
Cuando ellos se estremecen hay un hondo temblor
que pasa por las vértebras enormes de los Andes.
Si clamáis se oye como el rugir del león.
Ya Hugo a Grant lo dijo: Las estrellas son vuestras.
(Apenas brilla, alzándose, el argentino sol
y la estrella chilena se levanta . . .) Sois ricos.
Juntáis al culto de Hércules el culto de Mammón;
y alumbrando el camino de la fácil conquista,
la Libertad levanta su antorcha en Nueva-York.

Mas la América nuestra, que tenía poetas
desde los viejos tiempos de Netzahualcoyotl,
que ha guardado las huellas de los pies del gran Baco,

84

VIII. To Roosevelt

It would take a voice from the Bible or a verse from Walt Whitman
to get through to you, Hunter!
Primitive and modern, simple and complicated,
one part Washington and four parts Nimrod!
You're the United States,
you're the future invader
of the guileless America of indigenous blood
that still prays to Jesus Christ and still speaks in Spanish.

You're a strong and splendid specimen of your kind;
you're cultured, you're skillful; you're the opposite of Tolstoy.
And breaking horses or slaying tigers,
you're an Alexander-Nebuchadnezzar.
(You're a Professor of Energy,
as the madmen of today put it.)

You think that life is a conflagration,
that progress is an eruption,
that where you put your bullet
you set the future.
                    No.

The United States is powerful and big.
When it shudders, a deep earthquake
runs down the enormous backbone of the Andes.
If you cry out, it's heard like the roaring of a lion.
Once Hugo said to Grant: "The stars are yours."
(The Argentine sun, now dawning, has hardly begun to shine,
and the Chilean star is rising . . .) You're rich.
You combine the worship of Hercules with the worship of Mammon;
and lighting the way for easy conquest,
Liberty raises her torch in New York.

Yet this America of ours, which has had poets
since the olden days of Netzahualcoyotl,
which preserves the footprints of great Bacchus,

que el alfabeto pánico en un tiempo aprendió;
que consultó los astros, que conoció la Atlántida
cuyo nombre nos llega resonando en Platón,
que desde los remotos momentos de su vida
vive de luz, de fuego, de perfume, de amor,
la América del grande Moctezuma, del Inca,
la América fragante de Cristóbal Colón,
la América católica, la América española,
la América en que dijo el noble Guatemoc:
"Yo no estoy en un lecho de rosas"; esa América
que tiembla de huracanes y que vive de amor;
hombres de ojos sajones y alma bárbara, vive.
Y sueña. Y ama, y vibra; y es la hija del Sol.

Tened cuidado. Vive la América española!
Hay mil cachorros sueltos del León Español.
Se necesitaría, Roosevelt, ser por Dios mismo,
el Riflero terrible y el fuerte Cazador,
para poder tenernos en vuestras férreas garras.

Y, pues contáis con todo, falta una cosa: Dios!

which once learned the Panic alphabet;
which consulted the stars, which knew the Atlantis
whose name comes down to us loud and clear in Plato,
which from the first moments of life, so long ago,
has lived on light, on fire, on perfume, on love,
the America of the great Montezuma, of the Inca,
the fragrant America of Christopher Columbus,
Catholic America, Spanish America,
the America where the noble Cuauhtemoc said:
"This is no bed of roses"; that America
which shakes with hurricanes and lives on love—
men with Saxon eyes and barbarous souls, it lives.
And dreams. And loves, and quivers, and is the daughter of the Sun.

Beware. Spanish America lives!
There are a thousand cubs set loose from the Spanish Lion.
One would need to be, Roosevelt, by the grace of God,
a terrifying Sharpshooter and a mighty Hunter
to hold us in your iron claws.

And, even accounting for the rest, you lack one thing: God!

IX.

Torres de Dios! Poetas!
Pararrayos celestes,
que resistís las duras tempestades,
como crestas escuetas,
como picos agrestes,
rompeolas de las eternidades!

La mágica Esperanza anuncia un día
en que sobre la roca de armonía
expirará la pérfida sirena.
Esperad, esperemos todavía!

Esperad todavía.
El bestial elemento se solaza
en el odio a la sacra poesía
y se arroja baldón de raza a raza.

La insurrección de abajo
tiende a los Excelentes.
El caníbal codicia su tasajo
con roja encía y afilados dientes.

Torres, poned al pabellón sonrisa.
Poned ante ese mal y ese recelo,
una soberbia insinuación de brisa
y una tranquilidad de mar y cielo . . .

IX.

Towers of God! Poets!
Heavenly lightning rods
withstanding severe tempests,
like unadorned crests,
like rustic peaks,
breakwaters of eternities!

Magical Hope announces the day
when on the rock of harmony
the perfidious siren will pass away.
You must have hope, let's still hope!

Keep hoping.
The bestial element takes comfort
in its hatred for sacred poetry,
hurling brickbats of every sort.

The insurrection from beneath
spreads to the upper class and elite.
The cannibal covets his piece of meat
with red gums and sharpened teeth.

Towers, place a smile on the pavilion.
In the face of that evil and that unease
place the lofty suggestion of a breeze
and the tranquillity of sky and sea. . .

x. Canto de esperanza

Un gran vuelo de cuervos mancha el azul celeste.
Un soplo milenario trae amagos de peste.
Se asesinan los hombres en el extremo Este.

¿Ha nacido el apocalíptico Anticristo?
Se han sabido presagios y prodigios se han visto
y parece inminente el retorno del Cristo.

La tierra está preñada de dolor tan profundo
que el soñador, imperial meditabundo,
sufre con las angustias del corazón del mundo.

Verdugos de ideales afligieron la tierra,
en un pozo de sombra la humanidad se encierra
con los rudos molosos del odio y de la guerra.

¡Oh, Señor Jesucristo! por qué tardas, qué esperas
para tender tu mano de luz sobre las fieras
y hacer brillar al sol tus divinas banderas!

Surge de pronto y vierte la esencia de la vida
sobre tanta alma loca, triste o empedernida
que amante de tinieblas tu dulce aurora olvida.

Ven, Señor, para hacer la gloria de ti mismo.
Ven con temblor de estrellas y horror de cataclismo,
ven a traer amor y paz sobre el abismo.

Y tu caballo blanco, que miró el visionario,
pase. Y suene el divino clarín extraordinario.
Mi corazón será brasa de tu incensario.

x. Song of Hope

A great flight of crows sullies the celestial blue.
A millennial gust of wind smacks of pestilence.
Men are killing each other in the Far East.

Has the apocalyptic Antichrist been born?
Omens have been discovered and prodigies seen,
and the return of Christ seems imminent.

The earth is pregnant with a pain so profound
that the dreamer, preoccupied sovereign,
suffers with the heartaches of the world.

Executioners of ideals afflicted the earth,
in a shadowy pit humanity is confined
with the brutish Molossians of hate and of war.

O Lord Jesus Christ! Why do you delay, why do you wait
to stretch your hand of light upon the savage beasts
and to let your divine banners shine in the sun!

Appear at once and pour the essence of life
over such a sad, insane, or flinty soul
that—a lover of gloom—forgets your sweet dawn.

Come, Lord, to glorify yourself.
Come with a starry quake and a cataclysmic horror,
come and bring love and peace across the abyss.

And may your white horse, which the visionary saw,
pass. And may the extraordinary divine trumpet blow.
My heart will be a burning coal in your censer.

XI.

Mientras tenéis, oh negros corazones,
conciliábulos de odio y de miseria,
el órgano de Amor riega sus sones.
Cantan: oíd: "La vida es dulce y seria".

Para ti, pensador meditabundo,
pálido de sentirte tan divino,
es más hostil la parte agria del mundo.
Pero tu carne es pan, tu sangre es vino.

Dejad pasar la noche de la cena
—ioh Shakespeare pobre, y oh Cervantes manco!—
y la pasión del vulgo que condena.
Un gran Apocalipsis horas futuras llena.
Ya surgirá vuestro Pegaso blanco!

XI.

While you hold, O black hearts,
conciliabules of hatred and misery,
the organ of Love pours out its tones.
They sing: listen: "Life is sweet and serious."

For you, brooding thinker,
pale from feeling so divine,
the bitter side of the world is more hostile.
But your flesh is bread, your blood is wine.

Let the night of the supper pass
—O poor Shakespeare, and O maimed Cervantes!—
and the passion of the condemning masses.
A great Apocalypse fills future times.
Your white Pegasus will now appear!

XII. Helios

Oh ruido divino,
oh ruido sonoro!
Lanzó la alondra matinal el trino
y sobre ese preludio cristalino,
los caballos de oro
de que el Hiperionida
lleva la rienda asida,
al trotar forman música armoniosa,
un argentino trueno,
y en el azul sereno
con sus cascos de fuego dejan huellas de rosa.
Adelante, oh cochero
celeste, sobre Osa
y Pelión, sobre Titania viva.
Atrás se queda el trémulo matutino lucero,
y el universo el verso de su música activa.

Pasa, oh dominador, oh conductor del carro
de la mágica ciencia! Pasa, pasa, oh bizarro
manejador de la fatal cuadriga
que al pisar sobre el viento
despierta el instrumento
sacro! Tiemblan las cumbres
de los montes más altos,
que en sus rítmicos saltos
tocó Pegaso. Giran muchedumbres
de águilas bajo el vuelo
de tu poder fecundo,
y si hay algo que iguale la alegría del cielo,
es el gozo que enciende las entrañas del mundo.

Helios! tu triunfo es ése,
pese a las sombras, pese
a la noche, y al miedo y a la lívida Envidia.
Tú pasas, y la sombra, y el daño, y la desidia,

XII. Helios

O divine noise,
O sonorous noise!
The morning lark has launched its trill,
and over that crystalline prelude,
the golden horses —
whose rein the Hyperionid
takes up tightly —
make harmonious music as they trot along,
a silvery thunder,
and upon the serene blue
they leave rosy tracks with their fiery hoofs.
Onward, O celestial
coachman, over Ossa
and Pelion, over the living Titania.
The tremulous morning star remains behind,
and the universe activates the verse of its music.

Roll on, O master, O driver of the car
of magic science! Roll on, roll on, O dashing
handler of the fatal chariot
that in treading the wind
awakens the sacred
instrument! The summits tremble
on the highest mountains,
which in his rhythmic bounds
Pegasus touched. Throngs
of eagles circle under the flight
of your prolific power,
and if there is something that equals the pleasure of the sky,
it is the joy that ignites the bowels of the world.

Helios! This is your triumph,
despite the shadows, despite
the night, and fear, and livid Envy.
You pass by, and shadow, and damage, and lassitude,

y la negra pereza, hermana de la muerte,
y el alacrán del odio que su ponzoña vierte,
y Satán todo, emperador de las tinieblas,
se hunden, caen. Y haces el alba rosa, y pueblas
de amor y de virtud las humanas conciencias,
riegas todas las artes, brindas todas las ciencias;
los castillos de duelo de la maldad derrumbas,
abres todos los nidos, cierras todas las tumbas,
y sobre los vapores del tenebroso Abismo,
pintas la Aurora, el Oriflama de Dios mismo.

Helios! Portaestandarte
de Dios, padre del Arte,
la paz es imposible, mas el amor eterno.
Danos siempre el anhelo de la vida,
y una chispa sagrada de tu antorcha encendida
con que esquivar podamos la entrada del Infierno.

Que sientan las naciones
el volar de tu carro, que hallen los corazones
humanos en el brillo de tu carro, esperanza;
que del alma-Quijote y el cuerpo-Sancho Panza
vuele una psique cierta a la verdad del sueño;
que hallen las ansias grandes de este vivir pequeño
una realización invisible y suprema;
Helios! que no nos mate tu llama que nos quema!
Gloria hacia ti del corazón de las manzanas,
de los cálices blancos de los lirios,
y del amor que manas
hecho de dulces fuegos y divinos martirios,
y del volcán inmenso
y del hueso minúsculo,
y del ritmo que pienso,
y del ritmo que vibra en el corpúsculo,
y del Oriente intenso
y de la melodía del crepúsculo.

Oh ruido divino!
Pasa sobre la cruz del palacio que duerme,
y sobre el alma inerme

and black sloth, sister of death,
and the scorpion of hatred spewing its poison,
and Satan himself, emperor of darkness,
go under, fall. And you make the daybreak rose, and populate
with love and with virtue human consciences,
water all the arts, supply all the sciences;
overturn evil's castles of pain,
open all the nests, close all the tombs,
and upon the vapors of the gloomy Abyss,
you paint the Dawn, the Oriflamme of God Himself.

Helios! Standard-bearer
of God, father of Art,
peace is impossible, yet love eternal.
Give us always the longing for life,
and a sacred spark from your blazing torch
with which we may steer clear of the entrance to Hell.

May the nations feel
the flight of your car, may human hearts find,
in the brightness of your car, hope;
from the soul-Quixote and the body–Sancho Panza
may an unerring psyche fly to the truth of dreams;
may the broad concerns of this narrow living find
an invisible and supreme realization.
Helios! May your flame that burns us, not kill us!
Glory to you from the heart of apples,
from the white calyxes of lilies,
and from the love you pour out,
made of sweet fires and divine torments,
and from the immense volcano,
and from the minuscule bone,
and from the rhythm that I think,
and from the rhythm that vibrates in the corpuscle,
and from the intense Orient
and from the melody of dusk.

O divine noise!
Pass over the cross of the sleeping palace,
and over the helpless soul

de quien no sabe nada. No turbes el Destino,
oh ruido sonoro!
El hombre, la nación, el continente, el mundo,
aguardan la virtud de tu carro fecundo,
cochero azul que riges los caballos de oro!

of one who knows nothing. Do not upset fate,
O sonorous noise!
Man, nation, continent, world
await the virtue of your prolific car,
blue coachman steering the golden horses!

XIII. Spes

Jesús, incomparable perdonador de injurias,
óyeme; Sembrador de trigo, dame el tierno
Pan de tus hostias; dame, contra el sañudo infierno
una gracia lustral de iras y lujurias.

Dime que este espantoso horror de la agonía
que me obsede, es no más de mi culpa nefanda,
que al morir hallaré la luz de un nuevo día
y que entonces oiré mi "Levántate y anda!"

XIII. Spes

Jesus, incomparable forgiver of trespasses,
hear me; Sower of wheat, give me the tender
Bread of your hosts; give me, in the face of furious hell,
a lustral grace from rages and lusts.

Tell me this appalling horror of agony
obsessing me, comes only from my heinous guilt,
that upon dying I will find the light of a new day
and then will hear my "Rise up and walk!"

xiv. Marcha triunfal

Ya viene el cortejo!
Ya viene el cortejo! Ya se oyen los claros clarines.
La espada se anuncia con vivo reflejo;
ya viene, oro y hierro, el cortejo de los paladines!

Ya pasa debajo los arcos ornados de blancas Minervas y Martes,
los arcos triunfales en donde las Famas erigen sus largas
    trompetas,
la gloria solemne de los estandartes
llevados por manos robustas de heroicos atletas.
Se escucha el ruido que forman las armas de los caballeros,
los frenos que mascan los fuertes caballos de guerra,
los cascos que hieren la tierra,
y los timbaleros
que el paso acompasan con ritmos marciales.
Tal pasan los fieros guerreros
debajo los arcos triunfales!

Los claros clarines de pronto levantan sus sones,
su canto sonoro,
su cálido coro,
que envuelve en un trueno de oro
la augusta soberbia de los pabellones.
El dice la lucha, la herida venganza,
las ásperas crines,
los rudos penachos, la pica, la lanza,
la sangre que riega de heroicos carmines
la tierra;
los negros mastines
que azuza la muerte, que rige la guerra.

Los áureos sonidos
anuncian el advenimiento
triunfal de la Gloria;
dejando el picacho que guarda sus nidos,

XIV. Triumphal March

The procession is coming!
The procession is coming! The clear bugles are now heard.
The sword is announced by a vivid reflection;
it is coming, gold and iron: the procession of the paladins.

It is passing beneath the arches embellished with white Minervas
    and Marses,
the triumphal arches where the Fames raise their long trumpets,
the solemn glory of the banners
carried in brawny hands of heroic athletes.
You listen to the sound that the horsemen's weapons make,
the bridles the mighty warhorses chew on,
the hooves that wound the earth
and the kettle drummers
keeping in step with martial rhythms.
So the fierce warriors pass
beneath the triumphal arches!

The clear bugles suddenly raise their voices,
their raucous song,
their ardent chorus,
enveloping in golden thunder
the august magnificence of the pavilions.
It tells of the fight, the wounded revenge,
the coarse manes,
the rough crests, the pike, the lance,
the blood that with heroic crimsons waters
the earth;
the black mastiffs
loosed for attack by death, who rules war.

The golden sounds
announce the triumphal
coming of Glory;
leaving the peak that guards their nests,

tendiendo sus alas enormes al viento,
los cóndores llegan. Llegó la victoria!

Ya pasa el cortejo.
Señala el abuelo los héroes al niño: —
ved cómo la barba del viejo
los bucles de oro circunda de armiño. —
Las bellas mujeres aprestan coronas de flores,
y bajo los pórticos vense sus rostros de rosa;
y la más hermosa
sonríe al más fiero de los vencedores.
¡Honor al que trae cautiva la extraña bandera;
honor al herido y honor a los fieles
soldados que muerte encontraron por mano extranjera:
Clarines! Laureles!

Las nobles espadas de tiempos gloriosos,
desde sus panoplias saludan las nuevas coronas y lauros: —
las viejas espadas de los granaderos más fuertes que osos,
hermanos de aquellos lanceros que fueron centauros. —
Las trompas guerreras resuenan;
de voces los aires se llenan . . .
— A aquellas antiguas espadas,
a aquellos ilustres aceros,
que encarnan las glorias pasadas; —
Y al sol que hoy alumbra las nuevas victorias ganadas,
y al héroe que guía su grupo de jóvenes fieros;
al que ama la insignia del suelo materno,
al que ha desafiado, ceñido el acero y el arma en la mano,
los soles del rojo verano,
las nieves y vientos del gélido invierno,
la noche, la escarcha
y el odio y la muerte, por ser por la patria inmortal,
saludan con voces de bronce las trompas de guerra que tocan la
    marcha triunfal! . . .

stretching their enormous wings on the wind,
the condors arrive. Victory has arrived!

The procession is passing.
A grandfather points out the heroes to the child:
see how the beard of the old man
surrounds the golden ringlets with ermine.
Beautiful women prepare wreaths of flowers,
and beneath the porticos their rosy faces are visible;
and the loveliest one
smiles at the fiercest of the victors.
Honor to him who brings the strange flag captive;
honor to the wounded and honor to the faithful
soldiers who met with death at foreign hands!
Bugles! Laurels!

The noble swords of glorious times,
from their panoplies, salute the new wreaths and laurels:
the old swords of the grenadiers stronger than bears,
brothers of those lancers who were centaurs.
The warlike horns resound;
the breezes fill up with voices . . .
(Those ancient swords,
those illustrious steel blades,
that embody past glories.)
And the sun that today lights up the new victories won,
and the hero who guides his company of fierce youth;
the one who loves the insignia of his maternal soil,
the one who has defied, girt with steel and with weapon in hand,
the suns of red summer,
the snows and winds of freezing winter,
the night, the frost
and hatred and death, for the sake of his immortal homeland:
him the horns of war salute with bronze voices, playing the
    triumphal march! . . .

The Swans

For Juan R. Jiménez

Los cisnes

A Juan R. Jiménez

I.

Qué signo haces, oh Cisne, con tu encorvado cuello
al paso de los tristes y errantes soñadores?
Por qué tan silencioso de ser blanco y ser bello,
tiránico a las aguas e impasible a las flores?

Yo te saludo ahora como en versos latinos
te saludara antaño Publio Ovidio Nasón.
Los mismos ruiseñores cantan los mismos trinos,
y en diferentes lenguas es la misma canción.

A vosotros mi lengua no debe ser extraña.
A Garcilaso visteis, acaso, alguna vez . . .
Soy un hijo de América, soy un nieto de España . . .
Quevedo pudo hablaros en verso en Aranjuez . . .

Cisnes, los abanicos de vuestras alas frescas
den a las frentes pálidas sus caricias más puras
y alejen vuestras blancas figuras pintorescas
de nuestras mentes tristes las ideas obscuras.

Brumas septentrionales nos llenan de tristezas,
se mueren nuestras rosas, se agotan nuestras palmas,
casi no hay ilusiones para nuestras cabezas,
y somos los mendigos de nuestras pobres almas.

Nos predican la guerra con águilas feroces,
gerifaltes de antaño revienen a los puños,
mas no brillan las glorias de las antiguas hoces,
ni hay Rodrigos, ni Jaimes, ni hay Alfonsos ni Nuños.

Faltos de los alientos que dan las grandes cosas,
qué haremos los poetas sino buscar tus lagos?
A falta de laureles son muy dulces las rosas,
y a falta de victorias busquemos los halagos.

I.

What sign do you give, O Swan, with your curving neck
when the sad and wandering dreamers pass?
Why so silent from being white and being beautiful,
tyrannical to the waters and impassive to the flowers?

I greet you now as in Latin verses
Publius Ovid Naso greeted you long ago.
The same nightingales sing the same trills,
and in different languages it's the same song.

To you my language should not be foreign.
Perhaps you saw Garcilaso, once . . .
I'm a son of America, I'm a grandson of Spain . . .
Quevedo spoke to you in verse in Aranjuez . . .

Swans, may the fans of your cool wings
give their purest caresses to pale brows
and may your white picturesque figures
drive dark ideas from our sad minds.

Septentrional mists fill us with sorrows,
our roses die off, our palm trees dwindle away,
there is scarcely a dream for our heads,
and we are beggars for our own poor souls.

They preach war to us with ferocious eagles,
gyrfalcons of bygone days return to the fists,
yet the glories of the old sickles do not shine,
there are no Rodrigos nor Jaimes, no Alfonsos nor Nuños.

At a loss for the vital spirit which great things give,
what will we poets do, but seek out your lakes?
For lack of laurels, roses are very sweet,
and for lack of victories, let's seek out adulation.

La América española como la España entera
fija está en el Oriente de su fatal destino;
yo interrogo a la Esfinge que el porvenir espera
con la interrogación de tu cuello divino.

¿Seremos entregados a los bárbaros fieros?
Tantos millones de hombres hablaremos inglés?
Ya no hay nobles hidalgos ni bravos caballeros?
Callaremos ahora para llorar después?

He lanzado mi grito, Cisnes, entre vosotros
que habéis sido los fieles en la desilusión,
mientras siento una fuga de americanos potros
y el estertor postrero de un caduco león . . .

. . . Y un cisne negro dijo: —«La noche anuncia el día».
Y uno blanco: —"La aurora es inmortal! la aurora
es inmortal!" Oh tierras de sol y de armonía,
aún guarda la Esperanza la caja de Pandora!

Spanish America, like Spain as a whole,
stands fixed in the East of its fatal destiny;
I question the Sphinx that awaits the future
with the question mark of your divine neck.

Will we be handed over to the wild barbarians?
So many millions of men, will we speak English?
Are there no worthy nobles nor manly knights anymore?
Will we be silent now only to weep later?

I have raised my cry, Swans, among you
who have been true believers despite disappointment,
while I hear a stampede of American colts
and the death rattle of a senile lion . . .

. . . And a black swan said: "Night foretells the day."
And a white one: "The dawn is immortal! The dawn
is immortal!" O lands of sun and of harmony,
Pandora's box still contains Hope!

11. En la muerte de Rafael Núñez

Que sais-je?

El pensador llegó a la barca negra;
y le vieron hundirse
en las brumas del lago del Misterio,
los ojos de los Cisnes.

Su manto de poeta
reconocieron, los ilustres lises
y el laurel y la espina entremezclados
sobre la frente triste.

A lo lejos alzábanse los muros
de la ciudad teológica, en que vive
la sempiterna Paz. La negra barca
llegó a la ansiada costa, y el sublime
espíritu gozó la suma gracia;
y ¡oh Montaigne! Núñez vio la cruz erguirse,
y halló al pie de la sacra Vencedora
el helado cadáver de la Esfinge.

11. On the Death of Rafael Núñez

Que sais-je?

The thinker arrived at the black ship;
and when he sank
into the mists of the lake of Mystery
the eyes of the Swans saw it.

His poet's mantle
was recognized by the illustrious lilies
and the intermingled laurel and thorn
upon his sad brow.

Far away the walls
of the theological city arose, in which lives
sempiternal Peace. The black ship
came to the longed-for coast, and the sublime
spirit enjoyed the highest grace;
and—O Montaigne!—Núñez saw the cross erected,
and found at the foot of that sacred Vanquisher
the icy cadaver of the Sphinx.

III.

Por un momento, oh Cisne, juntaré mis anhelos
a los de tus dos alas que abrazaron a Leda,
y a mi maduro ensueño, aún vestido de seda,
dirás, por los Dioscuros, la gloria de los cielos.

Es el otoño. Ruedan de la flauta consuelos.
Por un instante, oh Cisne, en la obscura alameda
sorberé entre dos labios lo que el Pudor me veda,
y dejaré mordidos Escrúpulos y Celos.

Cisne, tendré tus alas blancas por un instante,
y el corazón de rosa que hay en tu dulce pecho
palpitará en el mío con su sangre constante.

Amor será dichoso, pues estará vibrante
el júbilo que pone al gran Pan en acecho
mientras su ritmo esconde la fuente de diamante.

III.

For one moment, O Swan, I will join my longings
to those of your two wings, which embraced Leda;
and to my middle-aged fantasy, still dressed in silk,
you will tell, for the Dioscuri, the glory of the skies.

It is autumn. Consolation rolls from the flute.
For an instant, O Swan, in the dark poplar grove
I will sip between two lips what Modesty forbids me,
and will leave Scruples and Jealousy bitten off.

Swan, I will have your white wings for an instant,
and the rose heart that is there in your sweet breast
will throb in mine with its steady blood.

Love will be blissful, since the vibrant jubilation
entices the great Pan to pounce
while his rhythm conceals the diamond fountain.

IV.

Antes de todo, gloria a ti, Leda!
Tu dulce vientre cubrió de seda
el Dios. Miel y oro sobre la brisa!
Sonaban alternativamente
flauta y cristales, Pan y la fuente.
Tierra era canto, Cielo sonrisa!

Ante el celeste, supremo acto,
dioses y bestias hicieron pacto.
Se dio a la alondra la luz del día,
se dio a los búhos sabiduría
y melodía al ruiseñor.
A los leones fue la victoria,
para las águilas toda la gloria
y a las palomas todo el amor.

Pero vosotros sois los divinos
príncipes. Vagos como las naves,
inmaculados como los linos,
maravillosos como las aves!

En vuestros picos tenéis las prendas
que manifiestan corales puros.
Con vuestros pechos abrís las sendas
que arriba indican los Dioscuros.

Las dignidades de vuestros actos,
eternizadas en lo infinito,
hacen que sean ritmos exactos,
voces de ensueños, luces de mito.

De orgullo olímpico sois el resumen,
oh, blancas urnas de la armonía!
Ebúrneas joyas que anima un numen
con su celeste melancolía.

IV.

First of all, glory to you, Leda!
Your sweet womb was covered in silk
by the God. Honey and gold on the breeze!
Alternately
flute and crystals sounded, Pan and the fountain.
Earth was a song, Heaven a smile!

In the presence of the heavenly, supreme act,
gods and beasts made a pact.
The lark was given the daylight,
the owls were given insight,
and the nightingale, melodies.
To the lions went victory,
for the eagles all the glory,
and to the doves all the love.

But you all are the divine
princes. Drifting like ships,
immaculate as flax,
wondrous as birds.

In your bills you have the qualities
which pure corals manifest.
With your breasts you open the pathways
which the Dioscuri indicate up above.

The dignity of your acts,
everlasting in infinity,
make these be exact rhythms:
voices of reverie, lights of myth.

You are the condensation of Olympic pride,
O white urns of harmony!
Eburnean jewels which a numen animates
with its celestial melancholy.

Melancolía de haber amado
junto a la fuente de la arboleda,
el luminoso cuello estirado
entre los blancos muslos de Leda!

Melancholy of having loved
with the fountain of the grove nearby,
the luminous neck outstretched
between Leda's white thighs!

Other Poems

For Doctor Adolfo Altamirano

Otros poemas

Al doctor Adolfo Altamirano

I. Retratos

1

Don Gil, Don Juan, Don Lope, Don Carlos, Don Rodrigo,
¿cúya es esta cabeza soberbia? ¿esa faz fuerte?
¿esos ojos de jaspe? ¿esa barba de trigo?
Este fue un caballero que persiguió a la Muerte.

Cien veces hizo cosas tan sonoras y grandes
que de águilas poblaron el campo de su escudo;
y ante su rudo tercio de América o de Flandes
quedó el asombro ciego, quedó el espanto mudo.

La coraza revela fina labor; la espada
tiene la cruz que erige sobre su tumba el miedo;
y bajo el puño firme que da su luz dorada,
se afianza el rayo sólido del yunque de Toledo.

Tiene labios de Borgia, sangrientos labios, dignos
de exquisitas calumnias, de rezar oraciones
y de decir blasfemias: rojos labios malignos
florecidos de anécdotas en cien Decamerones.

Y con todo, este hidalgo de un tiempo indefinido,
fue el abad solitario de un ignoto convento,
y dedicó en la muerte sus hechos: "¡AL OLVIDO!"
y el grito de su vida luciferina: "¡AL VIENTO!"

2

En la forma cordial de la boca, la fresa
solemniza su púrpura; y en el sutil dibujo
del óvalo del rostro de la blanca abadesa
la pura frente es ángel y el ojo negro es brujo.

Al marfil monacal de esa faz misteriosa
brota una dulce luz de un resplandor interno,

1. Portraits

1

Don Gil, Don Juan, Don Lope, Don Carlos, Don Rodrigo,
whose superb head is this? That strong visage?
Those eyes of jasper? That beard of wheat?
This was a knight who pursued Death.

A hundred times he did things so resounding and grand
that eagles inhabited the field on his shield,
and before his rough regiment from America or from Flanders
fright went blind, dread went mute.

The cuirass reveals fine workmanship; the sword
has the cross that raises fear over his tomb;
and the firm fist giving off its golden light
holds in its grasp the solid ray from the Toledo anvil.

He has the lips of a Borgia, bloodthirsty lips, worthy
of exquisite calumnies, of saying prayers,
and of speaking blasphemies: red malignant lips
flowery with anecdotes in a hundred Decamerons.

And nevertheless, this nobleman from an indefinite time
was the solitary abbot of an unknown convent,
and in death dedicated his feats: "To OBLIVION!"
and the cry of his Luciferian life: "To THE WINDS!"

2

In her heart-shaped mouth, the strawberry
solemnizes her purple; and in the subtle drawing
of the oval of the face of the white abbess
the pure brow is an angel and the eye of black is a sorcerer.

On the monastic ivory of that mysterious visage
a sweet light of inner radiance blooms,

que enciende en las mejillas una celeste rosa
en que su pincelada fatal puso el Infierno.

¡Oh, Sor María! ¡Oh, Sor María! ¡Oh, Sor María!
La mágica mirada y el continente regio,
¿no hicieron en un alma pecaminosa un día,
brotar el encendido clavel del sacrilegio?

Y parece que el hondo mirar cosas dijera,
especiosas y ungidas de miel y de veneno.
(Sor María murió condenada a la hoguera:
dos abejas volaron de las rosas del seno.)

that ignites in the cheeks a celestial rose
on which Hell placed its fatal brushstroke.

O Sister Maria! O Sister Maria! O Sister Maria!
The magical gaze and the royal bearing,
did they not cause one day in a sinful soul
the blazing carnation of sacrilege to grow?

And it seems that the deep gaze might tell of things
specious and anointed with honey and with poison.
(Sister Maria died condemned to the flames:
two honeybees flew from the roses of her breast.)

11. Por el influjo de la primavera

Sobre el jarrón de cristal
hay flores nuevas. Anoche
hubo una lluvia de besos.
Despertó un fauno bicorne
tras un alma sensitiva.
Dieron su olor muchas flores.
En la pasional siringa
brotaron las siete voces
que en siete carrizos puso
Pan.

Antiguos ritos paganos
se renovaron. La estrella
de Venus brilló más límpida
y diamantina. Las fresas
del bosque dieron su sangre.
El nido estuvo de fiesta.
Un ensueño florentino
se enfloró de primavera,
de modo que en carne viva
renacieron ansias muertas.
Imaginaos un roble
que diera una rosa fresca;
un buen egipán latino
con una bacante griega
y parisiense. Una música
magnífica. Una suprema
inspiración primitiva,
llena de cosas modernas.
Un vasto orgullo viril
que aroma el *odor di femina*;
un trono de roca en donde
descansa un lirio.

Divina Estación! Divina
Estación! Sonríe el alba

11. Because of the Influence of Spring

Above the crystal vase
there are new flowers. Last night
there was a shower of kisses.
It awoke a bicorn faun
in pursuit of a sensitive soul.
Many flowers gave their scent.
From the passional syrinx
bloomed the seven voices
that were placed in seven reeds
by Pan.

Ancient pagan rites
were renewed. The star
of Venus shone more limpid
and adamantine. The strawberries
of the wood gave their blood.
The nest was festooned.
A Florentine daydream
enflowered with spring,
so that in living flesh
dead longings were reborn.
Imagine an oak
that produced a fresh rose;
a good Latin aegipan
with a bacchante both Greek
and Parisian. A magnificent
music. A supreme
primitive inspiration,
full of modern things.
A vast virile pride
perfuming the *odor di femina*;
a rock throne on which
a lily rests.

Divine Season! Divine
Season! Daybreak smiles

más dulcemente. La cola
del pavo real exalta
su prestigio. El sol aumenta
su íntima influencia; y el arpa
de los nervios vibra sola.
Oh, Primavera sagrada!
Oh, gozo del don sagrado
de la vida! Oh, bella palma
sobre nuestras frentes! Cuello
del cisne! Paloma blanca!
Rosa roja! Palio azul!
Y todo por ti, oh, alma!
Y por ti, cuerpo, y por ti,
idea, que los enlazas.
Y por Ti, lo que buscamos
y no encontraremos nunca,
jamás!

more sweetly. The tail
of the peacock exalts
its prestige. The sun heightens
its intimate influence; and the harp
of the nerves quivers alone.
O sacred Springtime!
O delight of the sacred gift
of life! O lovely palm
upon our brows! Neck
of the swan! White dove!
Red rose! Blue pallium!
And all because of you, O my soul!
And because of you, body, and because of you,
idea, which binds them together.
And because of You, what we seek
and will never find,
not ever!

III. La dulzura del ángelus . . .

La dulzura del ángelus matinal y divino
que diluyen ingenuas campanas provinciales,
en un aire inocente a fuerza de rosales,
de plegaria, de ensueño de virgen y de trino

de ruiseñor, opuesto todo al rudo destino
que no cree en Dios . . . El áureo ovillo vespertino
que la tarde devana tras opacos cristales
por tejer la inconsútil tela de nuestros males

todos hechos de carne y aromados de vino . . .
Y esta atroz amargura de no gustar de nada,
de no saber a dónde dirigir nuestra prora

mientras el pobre esquife en la noche cerrada
va en las hostiles olas huérfano de la aurora . . .
(Oh, suaves campanas entre la madrugada!)

III. The Sweetness of the Angelus . . .

The sweetness of the Angelus, divine in the morning,
which naive provincial bells dissolve
in a breeze made innocent by the power of rosebushes,
prayer, virginal fantasies, and the warble

of a nightingale, all opposed to rude destiny
that doesn't believe in God . . . The golden vesper ball
which the evening spins behind opaque panes,
by weaving the seamless cloth of our evils

all made of flesh and scented with wine . . .
And this ghastly bitterness from enjoying nothing,
from not knowing in which direction to steer our prow

while the poor skiff in the gloomy night
sails into hostile waves, an orphan of the dawn . . .
(O gentle bells in the early morning!)

IV. Tarde del trópico

Es la tarde gris y triste.
Viste el mar de terciopelo
y el cielo profundo viste
de duelo.

Del abismo se levanta
la queja amarga y sonora.
La onda, cuando el viento canta,
llora.

Los violines de la bruma
saludan al sol que muere.
salmodia la blanca espuma:
Miserere.

La armonía el cielo inunda,
y la brisa va a llevar
la canción triste y profunda
del mar.

Del clarín del horizonte
brota sinfonía rara,
como si la voz del monte
vibrara.

Cual si fuese lo invisible . . .
cual si fuese el rudo son
que diese al viento un terrible
león.

iv. Evening in the Tropics

The evening is gray and sad.
The sea is dressed in velvet
and the deep sky is dressed
in mourning.

From the abyss arises
the bitter and reverberating complaint.
The wave, when the wind sings,
weeps.

The violins of the mist
greet the dying sun.
The white foam drones a psalm:
Miserere.

Harmony floods the sky,
and the breeze will carry
the sad and profound song
of the sea.

From the horn of the horizon
a rare symphony emerges,
as if the voice of the mountain
were vibrating.

As though it were the invisible . . .
as though it were the rough sound
given to the wind by a terrible
lion.

v. Nocturno

Quiero expresar mi angustia en versos que abolida
dirán mi juventud de rosas y de ensueños,
y la desfloración amarga de mi vida
por un vasto dolor y cuidados pequeños.

Y el viaje a un vago Oriente por entrevistos barcos,
y el grano de oraciones que floreció en blasfemia,
y los azoramientos del cisne entre los charcos
y el falso azul nocturno de inquerida bohemia.

Lejano clavicordio que en silencio y olvido
no diste nunca al sueño la sublime sonata,
huérfano esquife, árbol insigne, obscuro nido
que suavizó la noche de dulzura de plata . . .

Esperanza olorosa a hierbas frescas, trino
del ruiseñor primaveral y matinal,
azucena tronchada por un fatal destino,
rebusca de la dicha, persecución del mal . . .

El ánfora funesta del divino veneno
que ha de hacer por la vida la tortura interior,
la conciencia espantable de nuestro humano cieno
y el horror de sentirse pasajero, el horror

de ir a tientas, en intermitentes espantos,
hacia lo inevitable desconocido y la
pesadilla brutal de este dormir de llantos
de la cual no hay más que Ella que nos despertará!

v. Nocturne

I want to express my anguish in verses that tell
of my abolished youth of roses and daydreams,
and the bitter deflowering of my life
by a vast ache and petty cares.

And the voyage to a vague Orient on half-seen ships,
and the kernel of prayers that flowered into blasphemy,
and the swan's consternation between the ponds,
and the false midnight blue of a detested bohemia.

Faraway harpsichord, in silence and oblivion
you never gave the sublime sonata to the dream,
orphan skiff, renowned tree, dark nest
that softened the night with silver sweetness . . .

Hope redolent with fresh new grass, a trill
from the springtime sunrise nightingale,
a white lily cut down by a fatal destiny,
a search for happiness, a pursuit of evil . . .

The fateful amphora of the divine venom
that will bring about self-torture throughout life,
the appalling awareness of our own human slime,
and the horror of feeling short lived, the horror

of groping along, in intermittent dread,
toward the inevitable unknown and the
brutal nightmare of this weeping sleep
from which there is only She[1] to awaken us!

---

1. In Spanish the noun *death* (*la muerte*) is feminine in gender and thus
requires the feminine pronoun. The conspicuous use Darío makes
of it in this poem clearly suggests his intent to personify death, and so
we have opted to do the same by translating the pronoun literally.

VI. Canción de otoño en primavera

A Martínez Sierra

Juventud, divino tesoro,
ya te vas para no volver!
Cuando quiero llorar, no lloro . . .
y a veces lloro sin querer . . .

Plural ha sido la celeste
historia de mi corazón.
Era una dulce niña, en este
mundo de duelo y aflicción.

Miraba como el alba pura;
sonreía como una flor.
Era su cabellera obscura
hecha de noche y de dolor.

Yo era tímido como un niño.
Ella, naturalmente, fue,
para mi amor hecho de armiño,
Herodías y Salomé . . .

Juventud, divino tesoro,
ya te vas para no volver . . . !
Cuando quiero llorar, no lloro,
y a veces lloro sin querer . . .

La otra fue más sensitiva,
y más consoladora y más
halagadora y expresiva,
cual no pensé encontrar jamás.

Pues a su continua ternura
una pasión violenta unía.
En un peplo de gasa pura
una bacante se envolvía . . .

VI. Song of Autumn in Springtime

For Martínez Sierra

Youth, divine treasure,
you've already gone, never to return!
When I want to cry, I don't cry . . .
and sometimes I cry without wanting to . . .

Plural has been the heavenly
history of my heart.
She was a sweet child in this
world of pain and affliction.

She gazed like the pure dawn;
she smiled like a flower.
Her dark hair was
made of night and of pain.

I was timid as a child.
She, naturally, was,
for my love made of ermine,
Herodias and Salome . . .

Youth, divine treasure,
you've already gone, never to return . . . !
When I want to cry, I don't cry,
and sometimes I cry without wanting to . . .

The other was more sensitive,
and more consoling and more
ingratiating and expressive,
such as I never hoped to find.

Since her constant tenderness
was combined with a violent passion.
In a peplum of pure gossamer
a bacchante was wrapped up . . .

En sus brazos tomó mi ensueño
y lo arrulló como a un bebé . . .
y le mató, triste y pequeño,
falto de luz, falto de fe . . .

Juventud, divino tesoro,
te fuiste para no volver!
Cuando quiero llorar, no lloro,
y a veces lloro sin querer . . .

Otra juzgó que era mi boca
el estuche de su pasión;
y que me roería, loca,
con sus dientes el corazón,

poniendo en un amor de exceso
la mira de su voluntad,
mientras eran abrazo y beso
síntesis de la eternidad;

y de nuestra carne ligera
imaginar siempre un Edén,
sin pensar que la Primavera
y la carne acaban también . . .

Juventud, divino tesoro,
ya te vas para no volver!
Cuando quiero llorar, no lloro,
y a veces lloro sin querer!

Y las demás! en tantos climas,
en tantas tierras, siempre son,
si no pretextos de mis rimas,
fantasmas de mi corazón.

En vano busqué a la princesa
que estaba triste de esperar.
La vida es dura. Amarga y pesa.
Ya no hay princesa que cantar!

In her arms she took my fantasy
and lulled it like a baby . . .
and she killed it, sad and small,
deprived of light, deprived of faith . . .

Youth, divine treasure,
you've already gone, never to return!
When I want to cry, I don't cry,
and sometimes I cry without wanting to . . .

Another decided that my mouth
was for her passion a sheath;
and that she would madly gnaw
on my heart with her teeth,

setting her determined sights
on an excessive love,
while hug and kiss were
the synthesis of eternity;

and to imagine our weak flesh
always as an Eden,
not thinking that Springtime
and flesh also come to an end . . .

Youth, divine treasure,
you've already gone, never to return!
When I want to cry, I don't cry,
and sometimes I cry without wanting to!

And all the rest! In so many climes,
in so many lands, they forever are,
if not pretexts for my rhymes,
then phantoms of my heart.

In vain I sought the princess
who had grown sad from waiting.
Life is hard. It embitters and weighs us down.
There's no longer a princess to sing to!

Mas a pesar del tiempo terco,
mi sed de amor no tiene fin;
con el cabello gris, me acerco
a los rosales del jardín . . .

Juventud, divino tesoro,
ya te vas para no volver . . .
cuando quiero llorar, no lloro,
y a veces lloro sin querer . . .

Mas es mía el Alba de oro!

Yet regardless of stubborn time,
my thirst for love has no end;
with gray hair I approach
the rosebushes of the garden . . .

Youth, divine treasure,
you've already gone, never to return . . .
When I want to cry, I don't cry,
and sometimes I cry without wanting to . .

Yet the golden Dawn is mine!

VII. Trébol

1

De don Luis de Góngora y Argote
a don Diego de Silva Velázquez

Mientras el brillo de tu gloria augura
ser en la eternidad sol sin poniente,
fénix de viva luz, fénix ardiente,
diamante parangón de la pintura,

de España está sobre la veste obscura
tu nombre, como joya reluciente;
rompe la Envidia el fatigado diente,
y el Olvido lamenta su amargura.

Yo en equívoco altar, tú en sacro fuego,
miro a través de mi penumbra el día
en que al calor de tu amistad, Don Diego,

jugando de la luz con la armonía,
con la alma luz, de tu pincel el juego
el alma duplicó de la faz mía.

2

De don Diego de Silva Velázquez
a don Luis de Góngora y Argote

Alma de oro, fina voz de oro,
al venir hacia mí ¿por qué suspiras?
Ya empieza el noble coro de las liras
a preludiar el himno a tu decoro;

ya al misterioso son del noble coro
calma el Centauro sus grotescas iras,

VII. Clover

1

From Master Luis de Góngora y Argote
to Master Diego de Silva Velázquez

While the brilliance of your glory augurs
to be in eternity a sun that never sets,
a phoenix of vivid light, a blazing phoenix,
a diamond paragon of painting,

upon the dark garb of Spain
your name rests like a gleaming jewel;
Envy breaks its worn-out tooth,
and Oblivion laments its bitterness.

I on an equivocal altar, you on the sacred fire,
I look through my penumbra at the day
when in the warmth of your friendship, Master Diego,

playing with the harmony of light,
with the life-giving light, the play of your brush
duplicated the soul of my countenance.

2

From Master Diego de Silva Velázquez
to Master Luis de Góngora y Argote

Golden soul, fine golden voice,
on approaching me, why do you sigh?
Already the noble chorus of lyres begins
the prelude of the anthem to your decorum;

already, at the mysterious sound of the noble chorus,
the Centaur calms his grotesque rages,

y con nueva pasión que les inspiras,
tornan a amarse Angélica y Medoro.

A Teócrito y Poussin la Fama dote
con la corona de laurel supremo;
que en donde da Cervantes el Quijote

y yo las telas con mis luces gemo,
para Don Luis de Góngora y Argote
traerá una nueva palma Polifemo.

3

En tanto "pace estrellas" el Pegaso divino,
y vela tu hipogrifo, Velázquez, la Fortuna,
en los celestes parques al Cisne gongorino
deshoja sus sutiles margaritas la Luna.

Tu castillo, Velázquez, se eleva en el camino
del Arte como torre que de águilas es cuna,
y tu castillo, Góngora, se alza al azul cual una
jaula de ruiseñores labrada en oro fino.

Gloriosa la península que abriga tal colonia.
¡Aquí bronce corintio y allá mármol de Jonia!
Las rosas a Velázquez, y a Góngora claveles.

De ruiseñores y águilas se pueblen las encinas,
y mientras pasa Angélica sonriendo a las Meninas,
salen las nueve musas de un bosque de laureles.

and with new passion that you inspire in them,
once again Angelica and Medoro are in love.

Upon Theocritus and Poussin may Fame bestow
the crown of supreme laurel;
that where Cervantes gives the Quixote

and I gem the canvases with my sparkling light,
for Master Luis de Góngora y Argote
Polyphemus will bring a new palm.

3

While the divine Pegasus "grazes on stars,"
and Fortune, Velázquez, watches over your hippogriff,
the Moon plucks its subtle daisies
from the Gongorine Swan in the heavenly parks.

Your castle, Velázquez, rises on the road
of Art like a tower where eagles are born,
and your castle, Góngora, ascends to the blue like a
cage of nightingales wrought in fine gold.

Glorious the peninsula that shelters such a colony.
Here Corinthian bronze, and there marble of Ionia!
The roses for Velázquez, and for Góngora carnations.

Nightingales and eagles populate the oaks,
and while Angelica passes smiling at the Meninas,
the nine muses emerge from a laurel wood.

VIII. "Cháritas"

A Vicente de Paul, nuestro Rey Cristo
con dulce lengua dice:
—Hijo mío, tus labios
dignos son de imprimirse
en la herida que el ciego
en mi costado abrió. Tu amor sublime
tiene sublime premio: asciende y goza
del alto galardón que conseguiste.

El alma de Vicente llega al coro
de los alados Angeles que al triste
mortal custodian: eran más brillantes
que los celestes astros. Cristo: Sigue,—
dijo al amado espíritu del Santo.—

Ve entonces la región en donde existen
los augustos Arcángeles, zodíaco
de diamantina nieve, indestructibles
ejércitos de luz y mensajeras
castas palomas o águilas insignes.

Luego la majestad esplendorosa
del coro de los Príncipes,
que las divinas órdenes realizan
y en el humano espíritu presiden;
el coro de las altas potestades
que al torrente infernal levantan diques;
el coro de las místicas Virtudes,
las huellas de los mártires
y las intactas manos de las vírgenes;
el coro prestigioso
de las Dominaciones que dirigen
nuestras almas al bien, y el coro excelso
de los Tronos insignes,
que del Eterno el solio,
cariátides de luz indefinible,

VIII. "Charitas"

To Vincent de Paul, Christ our King
in sweet tones says:
"My son, your lips
are worthy of being imprinted
in the wound which the blind
opened in my side. Your love sublime
has a sublime reward: ascend and rejoice
in the high prize you have attained."

Vincent's soul comes to the choir
of winged Angels that over the sad
mortal keep watch: they were more brilliant
than the heavenly bodies. Christ: "Go on,"
he said to the beloved spirit of the Saint.

He sees then the region where
the august Archangels exist, a zodiac
of adamantine snow, indestructible
hosts of light and chaste
carrier pigeons or distinguished eagles.

Then the resplendent majesty
of the choir of Princes
that carry out the divine orders
and preside over the human spirit;
the choir of lofty Powers
that dam the infernal torrent;
the choir of mystical Virtues,
the footprints of the martyrs
and the intact hands of the virgins;
the prestigious choir
of Dominions that direct
our souls towards good, and the towering choir
of remarkable Thrones,
that support the royal dais of the Eternal,
caryatids of indefinable light,

sostienen por los siglos de los siglos;
y el coro de Querubes que compite
con la antorcha del sol.
                Por fin, la gloria
de teológico fuego en que se erigen
las llamas vivas de inmortal esencia.

Cristo al Santo bendice
y así penetra el Serafín de Francia
al coro de los ígneos Serafines.

throughout centuries of centuries;
and the choir of Cherubim that rival
the torch of the sun.
                          At last, the glory
of theological fire in which rise up
the living flames of immortal essence.

Christ blesses the Saint,
and so the Seraph of France gains entry
to the choir of the igneous Seraphim.

IX.

Oh, terremoto mental!
Yo sentí un día en mi cráneo
como el caer subitáneo
de una Babel de cristal.

De Pascal miré el abismo,
y vi lo que pudo ver
cuando sintió Baudelaire
"el ala del idiotismo".

Hay, no obstante, que ser fuerte;
pasar todo precipicio
y ser vencedor del Vicio,
de la Locura y la Muerte.

IX.

Oh, a mental earthquake!
I felt it one day in my skull
like the unexpected falling
of a Babel of crystal.

I looked into the abyss of Pascal,
and saw what he could see
when Baudelaire felt
"the wing of idiocy."

We must, nevertheless, be strong;
pass by each precipice
and be a victor over Vice,
over Madness and Death.

X.

El verso sutil que pasa o se posa
sobre la mujer o sobre la rosa,
beso puede ser, o ser mariposa.

En la fresca flor el verso sutil;
el triunfo de Amor en el mes de abril:
Amor, verso y flor, la niña gentil.

Amor y dolor. Halagos y enojos.
Herodías ríe en los labios rojos.
Dos verdugos hay que están en los ojos.

Oh, saber amar es saber sufrir,
amar y sufrir, sufrir y sentir,
y el hacha besar que nos ha de herir . . .

Rosa de dolor, gracia femenina;
inocencia y luz, corola divina!
Y aroma fatal y cruel espina . . .

Líbranos Señor de abril y la flor,
y del cielo azul, y del ruiseñor,
de dolor y amor líbranos Señor.

X.

The subtle verse that passes or pauses
upon the woman or upon the rose,
may be kiss or may be butterfly.

In the fresh flower, the subtle verse;
the triumph of Love in the month of April:
Love, verse, and flower, the gentle girl.

Love and pain. Pleasantries and spats.
Herodias laughs with her red lips.
Two executioners are there in her eyes.

Oh, to know how to love is to know how to suffer,
to love and suffer, to suffer and feel,
and to kiss the ax that will wound us . . .

Rose of pain, feminine grace;
innocence and light, divine corolla!
And a fatal aroma and cruel thorn . . .

God save us from April and the flower,
and from the blue sky, and from the nightingale,
from pain and love, save us, Lord.

XI. Filosofía

Saluda al sol, araña, no seas rencorosa.
Da tus gracias a Dios, oh, sapo, pues que eres.
El peludo cangrejo tiene espinas de rosa
y los moluscos reminiscencias de mujeres.
Sabed ser lo que sois, enigmas siendo formas;
dejad la responsabilidad a las Normas,
que a su vez la enviarán al Todopoderoso . . .
(Toca, grillo, a la luz de la luna, y dance el oso.)

xi. Philosophy

Greet the sun, spider, don't be spiteful.
Give thanks to God, O toad, for you exist.
The hairy crab has the thorns of a rose
and the mollusks reminiscences of women.
Know how to be what you are, enigmas existing as forms;
leave the responsibility to the Norms,
which in turn will hand it on to the Almighty . . .
(Play, cricket, by the light of the moon; and may the bear dance.)

XII. Leda

El cisne en la sombra parece de nieve;
su pico es de ámbar, del alba al trasluz;
el suave crepúsculo que pasa tan breve,
las cándidas alas sonrosa de luz.

Y luego, en las ondas del lago azulado,
después que la aurora perdió su arrebol,
las alas tendidas y el cuello enarcado,
el cisne es de plata, bañado de sol.

Tal es, cuando esponja las plumas de seda,
olímpico pájaro herido de amor,
y viola en las linfas sonoras a Leda,
buscando su pico los labios en flor.

Suspira la bella desnuda y vencida,
y en tanto que al aire sus quejas se van,
del fondo verdoso de fronda tupida
chispean turbados los ojos de Pan.

xii. Leda

The swan in the shadow seems made of snow;
its bill is made of amber, against the light of dawn;
the soft twilight that passes so briefly
blushes the snow-white wings with light.

And later, in the ripples of the lake turned blue,
after the aurora has lost its red glow,
its wings outstretched and its neck arched over,
the swan is made of silver, bathed in sun.

So it is, when it plumps its silken plumes,
an Olympic bird wounded by love,
and it ravishes Leda in the sonorous lymphs,
its bill searching for the flowering lips.

The beauty sighs, naked and vanquished,
and while her complaints waft away in the air,
from the verdant background of a profusion of fronds
glitter the kindled eyes of Pan.

XIII.

Divina Psiquis, dulce Mariposa invisible
que desde los abismos has venido a ser todo
lo que en mi ser nervioso y en mi cuerpo sensible
forma la chispa sacra de la estatua de lodo!

Te asomas por mis ojos a la luz de la tierra
y prisionera vives en mí de extraño dueño:
te reducen a esclava mis sentidos en guerra
y apenas vagas libre por el jardín del sueño.

Sabia de la Lujuria que sabe antiguas ciencias,
te sacudes a veces entre imposibles muros,
y más allá de todas las vulgares conciencias
exploras los recodos más terribles y obscuros.

Y encuentras sombra y duelo. Que sombra y duelo encuentres
bajo la viña en donde nace el vino del Diablo.
Te posas en los senos, te posas en los vientres
que hicieron a Juan loco e hicieron cuerdo a Pablo.

A Juan virgen y a Pablo militar y violento,
a Juan que nunca supo del supremo contacto;
a Pablo el tempestuoso que halló a Cristo en el viento,
y a Juan ante quien Hugo se queda estupefacto.

Entre la catedral y las ruinas paganas
vuelas, ¡oh, Psiquis, oh, alma mía!
—Como decía
aquel celeste Edgardo,
que entró en el paraíso entre un son de campanas
y un perfume de nardo, —
entre la catedral
y las paganas ruinas
repartes tus dos alas de cristal,
tus dos alas divinas.
Y de la flor

XIII.

Divine Psyche, sweet invisible Butterfly,
you who from the depths have come to be everything
that in my nervous being and in my sensitive body
forms the sacred spark in a statue of mud!

You peek out from my eyes at the light of the earth
and live in me as prisoner of a strange master:
my warring senses reduce you to a slave
and you scarcely wander free in the garden of dreams.

Wise with the Lust that knows ancient sciences,
at times you shake between impossible walls,
and beyond all the vulgar consciences
you explore the most dark and terrible twists and turns.

And you find shadow and pain. May you find shadow and pain
below the vineyard where the Devil's wine is born.
You alight on the breasts, you alight on the wombs
that drove John crazy and drove Paul sane.

That made John a virgin and Paul a violent soldier,
John who never knew of the supreme contact;
the tempestuous Paul who found Christ in the wind,
and John before whom Hugo becomes stupefied.

"Between the cathedral and the pagan ruins
you fly, O Psyche, O my soul!"
said
that heavenly Edgar,
who entered paradise accompanied by the sound of bells
and the perfume of spikenard:
between the cathedral
and the pagan ruins
you divide your two crystal wings,
your two divine wings.
And from the flower

que el ruiseñor
canta en su griego antiguo, de la rosa,
vuelas, ¡oh, Mariposa!
a posarte en un clavo de Nuestro Señor!

of which the nightingale
sings in his ancient Greek, from the rose
you fly, O Butterfly!
to alight on a nail of Our Lord!

XIV. El soneto de trece versos

De una juvenil inocencia
qué conservar sino el sutil
perfume, esencia de su Abril,
la más maravillosa esencia!

Por lamentar a mi conciencia
quedó de un sonoro marfil
un cuento que fue de las Mil
y Una Noche de mi existencia . . .

Scherezada se entredurmió . . .
el Visir quedó meditando . . .
Dinarzada el día olvidó . . .

Mas el pájaro azul volvió . . .
Pero . . .
      No obstante . . .
              Siempre . . .
                    Cuando . . .

XIV. The Thirteen-Verse Sonnet

Of a youthful innocence
what to preserve but the subtle
perfume, essence of its April,
the most marvelous essence!

To lament for my conscience
there remained, of a resonant ivory,
a story that came from the *Thousand
and One Nights* of my existence . . .

Scheherazade fell half-sleep . . .
The Vizier stood meditating . . .
Dunyazad forgot the day . . .

Yet the blue bird returned . . .
But . . .
      Nevertheless . . .
            Always . . .
                  When . . .

XV.

Oh, miseria de toda lucha por lo finito!
Es como el ala de la mariposa
nuestro brazo que deja el pensamiento escrito.
Nuestra infancia vale la rosa,
el relámpago nuestro mirar,
y el ritmo que en el pecho
nuestro corazón mueve,
es un ritmo de onda de mar,
o un caer de copo de nieve,
o el del cantar
del ruiseñor,
que dura lo que dura el perfumar
de su hermana la flor.
Oh, miseria de toda lucha por lo finito!
El alma que se advierte sencilla y mira clara-
mente la gracia pura de la luz cara a cara,
como el botón de rosa, como la coccinela,
esa alma es la que al fondo del infinito vuela.
El alma que ha olvidado la admiración, que sufre
en la melancolía agria, olorosa a azufre,
de envidiar malamente y duramente, anida
en un nido de topos. Es manca. Está tullida.
Oh, miseria de toda lucha por lo finito!

XV.

O misery of every struggle for the finite!
Our arm that leaves the thought written down
is like a butterfly wing.
Our childhood is worth the rose,
the lightning our beholding,
and the rhythm in the breast
that moves our heart,
is a rhythm of sea waves,
or the falling of snowflakes,
or that of the singing
of the nightingale,
which lasts as long as the perfuming
of its sister the flower lasts.
O misery of every struggle for the finite!
The soul that keeps itself simple and looks clear-
ly at the pure grace of light, face to face,
like the rosebud, like the coccinella,
that is the soul which flies to the depths of the infinite.
The soul that has forgotten the wonder, that suffers
in bitter melancholy, scented with sulfur,
by envying badly and severely, nestles
in a nest of moles. It is maimed. It is crippled.
O misery of every struggle for the finite!

XVI. A Phocás el campesino

Phocás el campesino, hijo mío, que tienes,
en apenas escasos meses de vida tantos
dolores en tus ojos que esperan tanto llantos
por el fatal pensar que revelan tus sienes . . .

Tarda en venir a este dolor a donde vienes,
a este mundo terrible en duelos y en espantos;
duerme bajo los Angeles, sueña bajo los Santos,
que ya tendrás la Vida para que te envenenes . . .

Sueña, hijo mío, todavía, y cuando crezcas,
perdóname el fatal don de darte la vida
que yo hubiera querido de azul y rosas frescas;

pues tú eres la crisálida de mi alma entristecida,
y te he de ver en medio del triunfo que merezcas
renovando el fulgor de mi psique abolida.

XVI. To Phocas the Peasant

Phocas the peasant, my son, who holds,
in the few meager months of his life, so much
pain in his eyes that await such a weeping
to judge by the fatal thoughts which his temples reveal . . .

Take your time coming to this pain you're headed for,
to this world terrible with grief and dread;
sleep beneath the Angels, dream beneath the Saints:
you'll have that Life to poison you soon enough . . .

Dream on, my son, and when you grow up,
forgive me for the fatal gift of having given you a life
I had wanted to be all fresh roses and blue;

since you are the chrysalis of my saddened soul,
and I must see you at the heart of the triumph you deserve
renewing the splendor of my abolished psyche.

XVII.

Carne, celeste carne de la mujer! Arcilla,
dijo Hugo—ambrosía más bien ¡oh maravilla!
La vida se soporta,
tan doliente y tan corta,
solamente por eso:
roce, mordisco o beso
en ese pan divino
para el cual nuestra sangre es nuestro vino!
En ella está la lira,
en ella está la rosa,
en ella está la ciencia armoniosa,
en ella se respira
el perfume vital de toda cosa.

Eva y Cipris concentran el misterio
del corazón del mundo.
Cuando el áureo Pegaso
en la victoria matinal se lanza
con el mágico ritmo de su paso
hacia la vida y hacia la esperanza,
si alza la crin y las narices hincha
y sobre las montañas pone el casco sonoro
y hacia la mar relincha,
y el espacio se llena
de un gran temblor de oro,
es que ha visto desnuda a Anadiomena.

Gloria, ¡oh, Potente a quien las sombras temen!
Que las más blancas tórtolas te inmolen!
Pues por ti la floresta está en el polen
y el pensamiento en el sagrado semen!

Gloria, ¡oh, Sublime que eres la existencia,
por quien siempre hay futuros en el útero eterno!
Tu boca sabe al fruto del árbol de la Ciencia
y al torcer tus cabellos apagaste el infierno!

XVII.

Flesh, a woman's heavenly flesh. Clay,
said Hugo—rather, ambrosia. O miracle!
Life is bearable,
so painful and so short,
only because of this:
a stroke, a nibble, or a kiss
upon this bread divine
for which our blood is our wine!
In it is the lyre,
in it is the rose,
in it is harmonious science,
in it we breathe
the vital perfume of each and every thing.

Eve and Cyprian concentrate the mystery
of the heart of the world.
When golden Pegasus
races off in morning victory
with the magical rhythm of his pace
toward life and toward hope,
if his mane stands up and his nostrils flare,
and he sets his echoing hoof upon the mountains
and snorts toward the sea,
and space is filled
with a great golden shaking,
it's because he has seen Anadyomene naked.

Glory, O Mighty One whom the shadows fear!
May the whitest turtledoves immolate you!
Since through you the forest is in the pollen
and thought in the sacred semen!

Glory, O Sublime One who is existence,
through whom there are always futures in the eternal uterus!
Your mouth tastes of the fruit of the Tree of Knowledge,
and when wringing out your hair you extinguished hell!

Inútil es el grito de la legión cobarde
del interés, inútil el progreso
yankee, si te desdeña.
Si el progreso es de fuego, por ti arde,
toda lucha del hombre va a tu beso,
por ti se combate o se sueña!

Pues en ti existe Primavera para el triste,
labor gozosa para el fuerte,
néctar, Anfora, dulzura amable.
Porque en ti existe
el placer de vivir, hasta la muerte—
y ante la eternidad de lo probable . . . !

Useless is the cry of the cowardly legion
of interest, useless Yankee
progress, if it disdains you.
If progress is made of fire, it burns because of you,
every struggle of man aims for your kiss,
because of you there is combat or there is dreaming!

For in you does Springtime exist for the sad,
joyful labor for the strong,
nectar, Amphora, agreeable sweetness.
Because in you
the pleasure of living exists, until death—
and considering the eternity of the probable . . . !

XVIII. Un soneto a Cervantes

A Ricardo Calvo

Horas de pesadumbre y de tristeza
paso en mi soledad. Pero Cervantes
es buen amigo. Endulza mis instantes
ásperos, y reposa mi cabeza.

El es la vida y la naturaleza,
regala un yelmo de oros y diamantes
a mis sueños errantes.
Es para mí: suspira, ríe y reza.

Cristiano y amoroso y caballero
parla como un arroyo cristalino.
Así le admiro y quiero,

viendo cómo el destino
hace que regocije al mundo entero
la tristeza inmortal de ser divino!

XVIII. A Sonnet for Cervantes

For Ricardo Calvo

Hours of heaviness of heart and of sadness
I spend in my solitude. But Cervantes
is a good friend. He sweetens my bitter
moments, and gives my head repose.

He is life and nature,
he presents a helmet of gold and diamonds
to my wandering dreams.
He is the one for me: he sighs, he laughs, he prays.

Christian and amorous and chivalrous,
he babbles like a crystalline brook.
For that I admire and love him,

seeing how destiny
makes the entire world delight
in the immortal sadness of being divine!

XIX. Madrigal exaltado

A Mademoiselle Villagrán

Dies irae, dies illa!
Solvet seclum in favilla
cuando quema esa pupila!

La tierra se vuelve loca,
el cielo a la tierra invoca
cuando sonríe esa boca.

Tiemblan los lirios tempranos
y los árboles lozanos
al contacto de esas manos.

El bosque se encuentra estrecho
al egipán en acecho
cuando respira ese pecho.

Sobre los senderos, es
como una fiesta, después
que se han sentido esos pies.

Y el Sol, sultán de orgullosas
rosas, dice a sus hermosas
cuando en primavera están:
Rosas, rosas, dadme rosas
para Adela Villagrán!

XIX. Exalted Madrigal

For Mademoiselle Villagrán

Dies irae, dies illa!
Solvet saeclum in favilla
when that pupil sears!

The earth runs wild,
the earth is invoked by the sky
when that mouth smiles.

The early lilies tremble
and the luxuriant trees
in contact with those hands.

The woods seem narrow
to the lurking aegipan
when that breast breathes.

Along the paths, it is
like a festival, once
they have felt those feet.

And the Sun, sultan of proud
roses, his beauties
in springtime will command:
"Roses, roses, give me roses
for Adela Villagrán!"

xx. Marina

Mar armonioso,
mar maravilloso,
tu salada fragancia,
tus colores y músicas sonoras
me dan la sensación divina de mi infancia
en que suaves las horas
venían en un paso de danza reposada
a dejarme un ensueño o regalo de hada.

Mar armonioso,
mar maravilloso
de arcadas de diamante que se rompen en vuelos
rítmicos que denuncian algún ímpetu oculto,
espejo de mis vagas ciudades de los cielos,
blanco y azul tumulto
de donde brota un canto
inextinguible,
mar paternal, mar santo,
mi alma siente la influencia de tu alma invisible.

Velas de los Colones
y velas de los Vascos,
hostigadas por odios de ciclones
ante la hostilidad de los peñascos;
o galeras de oro,
velas purpúreas de bajeles
que saludaron el mugir del toro
celeste, con Europa sobre el lomo
que salpicaba la revuelta espuma.
Magnífico y sonoro
se oye en las aguas como
un tropel de tropeles,
tropel de los tropeles de tritones!

xx. Seascape

Harmonious sea,
wonderful sea,
your salty fragrance,
your colors and resounding musics
give me the divine sensation of my childhood
when smoothly the hours
would come in a stately dance-step
to leave me a daydream or gift from a fairy.

Harmonious sea,
wonderful sea
of diamond arcades breaking in rhythmic
flights that disclose some hidden impulse,
mirror of my wandering cities in the skies,
white and blue tumult
from which emerges a song
inextinguishable,
paternal sea, holy sea,
my soul feels the influence of your invisible soul.

Sails of the Columbuses
and sails of the Vascos,
flogged by the hatred of cyclones
into the hostility of crags;
or golden galleys,
purple sails of vessels
that greeted the bellow of the bull
of the sky, with Europa on his back,
splashing the churning foam.
Magnificent and sonorous
it is heard in the waters like
a throng of throngs,
throng of the throngs of tritons!

Brazos salen de la onda, suenan vagas canciones,
brillan piedras preciosas,
mientras en las revueltas extensiones
Venus y el Sol hacen nacer mil rosas.

Arms emerge from the wave, vague songs resound,
precious stones sparkle,
while in the churning expanses
Venus and the Sun give birth to a thousand roses.

XXI. Cleopompo y Heliodemo

A Vargas Vila

Cleopompo y Heliodemo, cuya filosofía
es idéntica, gustan dialogar bajo el verde
palio del platanar. Allí Cleopompo muerde
la manzana epicúrea y Heliodemo fía

al aire su confianza en la eterna armonía.
Mal haya quien las Parcas inhumano recuerde:
si una sonora perla de la clepsidra pierde,
no volverá a ofrecerla la mano que la envía.

Una vaca aparece, crepuscular. Es hora
en que el grillo en su lira hace halagos a Flora,
y en el azul florece un diamante supremo:

y en la pupila enorme de la bestia apacible
miran como que rueda en un ritmo visible
la música del mundo, Cleopompo y Heliodemo.

XXI. Cleopompus and Heliodemos

For Vargas Vila

Cleopompus and Heliodemos, whose philosophy
is identical, like to confer under the green
pallium of the plane tree. There Cleopompus bites
the Epicurean apple and Heliodemos entrusts

to the breeze his confidence in eternal harmony.
Woe unto him who, inhumane, tempts the Fates:
once he loses a reverberating pearl from the clepsydra,
the hand that sent it will never offer it again.

A twilight cow appears. It's the hour
when the cricket makes sweet talk to Flora on his lyre,
and in the blue a supreme diamond flowers:

and in the enormous pupil of the placid beast,
Cleopompus and Heliodemos watch the music of the world
rolling in a visible rhythm.

XXII. Ay, triste del que un día . . .

Ay, triste del que un día en su esfinge interior
pone los ojos e interroga. Está perdido.
Ay del que pide eurekas al placer o al dolor.
Dos dioses hay, y son: Ignorancia y Olvido.

Lo que el árbol desea decir y dice al viento,
y lo que el animal manifiesta en su instinto,
cristalizamos en palabra y pensamiento.
Nada más que maneras expresan lo distinto.

XXII. Pity the sad soul who one day . . .

Pity the sad soul who one day on his inner sphinx
sets his gaze and interrogates it. He is lost.
That poor soul who asks for eurekas from pleasure or from pain.
Two gods exist, and they are: Ignorance and Oblivion.

What the tree desires to tell and tells the wind,
and what the animal manifests in its instinct,
we crystallize in word and thought.
Nothing more than ways and means express the distinction.

XXIII.

En el país de las Alegorías
Salomé siempre danza,
ante el tiarado Herodes,
eternamente,
y la cabeza de Juan el Bautista,
ante quien tiemblan los leones,
cae al hachazo. Sangre llueve.
Pues la rosa sexual
al entreabrirse
conmueve todo lo que existe,
con su efluvio carnal
y con su enigma espiritual.

XXIII.

In the land of Allegories
Salome always dances,
before the tiara'd Herod,
eternally,
and the head of John the Baptist,
before whom lions tremble,
falls with a chop of the ax. Blood rains.
So the sexual rose,
as it opens part way,
stirs the emotions of everything that exists,
with its carnal effluvium
and with its spiritual enigma.

XXIV. Augurios

A E. *Díaz Romero*

Hoy pasó un águila
sobre mi cabeza,
lleva en sus alas
la tormenta,
lleva en sus garras
el rayo que deslumbra y aterra.
Oh, águila!
Dame la fortaleza
de sentirme en el lodo humano
con alas y fuerzas
para resistir los embates
de las tempestades perversas,
y de arriba las cóleras
y de abajo las roedoras miserias.

Pasó un búho
sobre mi frente.
Yo pensé en Minerva
y en la noche solemne.
Oh, búho!
Dame tu silencio perenne,
y tus ojos profundos en la noche
y tu tranquilidad ante la muerte.
Dame tu nocturno imperio
y tu sabiduría celeste,
y tu cabeza cual la de Jano
que siendo una, mira a Oriente y Occidente.

Pasó una paloma
que casi rozó con sus alas mis labios.
Oh, paloma!
Dame tu profundo encanto
de saber arrullar, y tu lascivia
en campo tornasol, y en campo

XXIV. Omens

For E. Díaz Romero

Today an eagle passed
over my head,
it bears on its wings
the storm,
it bears in its talons
the thunderbolt that dazzles and terrifies.
O eagle!
Give me the fortitude
to feel in this human mire
that I have wings and strength
to resist the ravages
of perverse tempests,
and the wrath from above,
and the gnawing miseries from below.

An owl passed
over my brow.
I thought of Minerva
and of the solemn night.
O owl!
Give me your perennial silence,
and your profound eyes in the night
and your tranquillity in the presence of death.
Give me your nocturnal empire
and your heavenly wisdom,
and your Janus-like head,
which, being one, yet faces Orient and Occident.

A dove passed
almost rubbing my lips with its wings.
O dove!
Give me your profound charm
for knowing how to coo, and your lechery
in a field of sunflowers; and in a field

de luz tu prodigioso
ardor en el divino acto.
(Y dame la justicia en la naturaleza,
pues, en este caso,
tú serás la perversa
y el chivo será el casto.)

Pasó un gerifalte. Oh, gerifalte!
Dame tus uñas largas
y tus ágiles alas cortadoras de viento
y tus ágiles patas
y tus uñas que bien se hunden
en las carnes de la caza.
Por mi cetrería
irás en giras fantásticas,
y me traerás piezas famosas
y raras,
palpitantes ideas,
sangrientas almas.

Pasa el ruiseñor.
Ah, divino doctor!
No me des nada. Tengo tu veneno,
tu puesta de sol
y tu noche de luna y tu lira,
y tu lírico amor.
(Sin embargo, en secreto,
tu amigo soy,
pues más de una vez me has brindado
en la copa de mi dolor,
con el elixir de la luna
celestes gotas de Dios . . .)

Pasa un murciélago.
Pasa una mosca. Un moscardón.
Una abeja en el crepúsculo.
No pasa nada.
La muerte llegó.

of light your prodigious
ardor in the divine act.
(And give me justice in nature,
since, in this case,
you must be the wicked temptress
and the young goat chaste.)

A gyrfalcon passed. O gyrfalcon!
Give me your long claws
and your agile wind-slicing wings,
and your agile feet,
and your claws that sink deep
into the flesh of your prey.
For my falconing
you will go on fantastic flights,
and will bring me pieces famous
and rare,
throbbing ideas,
bloody souls.

The nightingale passes.
Ah, divine doctor!
Don't give me a thing. I have your venom,
your sunset
and your night of moon and your lyre,
and your lyrical love.
(Nevertheless, in secret,
I am your friend,
since more than once you have offered me,
in the cup of my pain,
celestial drops of God
with the elixir of the moon . . .)

A bat passes.
A fly passes. A botfly.
A bee in the twilight.
Nothing passes.
Death has come.

xxv. Melancolía

A Domingo Bolívar

Hermano, tú que tienes la luz, dime la mía.
Soy como un ciego. Voy sin rumbo y ando a tientas.
Voy bajo tempestades y tormentas
ciego de ensueño y loco de armonía.

Ese es mi mal. Soñar. La poesía
es la camisa férrea de mil puntas cruentas
que llevo sobre el alma. Las espinas sangrientas
dejan caer las gotas de mi melancolía.

Y así voy, ciego y loco, por este mundo amargo;
a veces me parece que el camino es muy largo,
y a veces que es muy corto . . .

Y en este titubeo de aliento y agonía,
cargo lleno de penas lo que apenas soporto.
No oyes caer las gotas de mi melancolía?

xxv. Melancholy

For Domingo Bolívar

Brother, you who have the light, tell me mine.
I am like a blind man. I go without direction and fumble along.
I go under tempests and storms,
blind with fantasy and crazy with harmony.

That is my malady. Dreaming. Poetry
is the iron jacket with a thousand bloody points
I wear upon my soul. The bloodstained thorns
spill the drops of my melancholy.

And so I go, blind and crazy, through this bitter world;
at times it seems to me that the path is very long,
and at times that it's very short . . .

And in this back-and-forth between eagerness and agony,
I am full of woes I can hardly bear.
Don't you hear the drops of my melancholy falling?

XXVI. Aleluya!

A Manuel Machado

Rosas rosadas y blancas, ramas verdes,
corolas frescas y frescos
ramos, Alegría!

Nidos en los tibios árboles,
huevos en los tibios nidos,
dulzura, Alegría!

El beso de esa muchacha
rubia, y el de esa morena
y el de esa negra, Alegría!

Y el vientre de esa pequeña
de quince años, y sus brazos
armoniosos, Alegría!

Y el aliento de la selva virgen
y el de las vírgenes hembras,
y las dulces rimas de la Aurora,
Alegría, Alegría, Alegría!

xxvi. Hallelujah!

For Manuel Machado

Roses rosy and white, green branches,
fresh corollas and fresh
bouquets: Joy!

Nests in the warm trees,
eggs in the warm nests,
sweetness: Joy!

The kiss of that girl
with blond hair, and of that dark one,
and of that black one: Joy!

And the belly of that little one
fifteen years old, and her harmonious
arms: Joy!

And the breath of the virgin forest,
and of the female virgins,
and the sweet rhymes of the Dawn:
Joy, Joy, Joy!

XXVII. De otoño

Yo sé que hay quienes dicen: ¿Por qué no canta ahora
con aquella locura armoniosa de antaño?
Esos no ven la obra profunda de la hora,
la labor del minuto y el prodigio del año.

Yo, pobre árbol, produje, al amor de la brisa,
cuando empecé a crecer, un vago y dulce son.
Pasó ya el tiempo de la juvenil sonrisa:
dejad al huracán mover mi corazón!

XXVII. In Autumn

I know that there are those who say, "Why doesn't he sing now
with that harmonious madness of days gone by?"
They don't see the profound work of an hour,
the labor of a minute, and the miracle of a year.

I, a poor tree, produced, out of love for the breeze,
a vague and sweet sound when I began to grow.
The time for youthful smiles has long since departed:
Let the hurricane move my heart!

XXVIII. A Goya

Poderoso visionario,
raro ingenio temerario,
por ti enciendo mi incensario.

Por ti, cuya gran paleta,
caprichosa, brusca, inquieta,
debe amar todo poeta;

por tus lóbregas visiones,
tus blancas irradiaciones,
tus negros y bermellones;

por tus colores dantescos,
. por tus majos pintorescos,
y las glorias de tus frescos.

Porque entra en tu gran tesoro
el diestro que mata al toro,
la niña de rizos de oro,

y con el bravo torero,
el infante, el caballero,
la mantilla y el pandero.

Tu loca mano dibuja
la silueta de la bruja
que en la sombra se arrebuja,

y aprende una abracadabra
del diablo patas de cabra
que hace una mueca macabra.

Musa soberbia y confusa,
ángel, espectro, medusa.
Tal aparece tu musa.

XXVIII. To Goya

Powerful visionary,
rare foolhardy genius,
for you I light my censer.

For you, whose grand palette,
unpredictable, blunt, restless,
every poet should love;

for your gloomy visions,
your white irradiations,
your blacks and vermilions;

for your colors, Dantesque;
for your lower-class dandies, picturesque;
and the glories of your frescos.

Because they enter your great treasury:
the man who skillfully kills the bull,
the girl with golden ringlets,

and with the brave matador,
the young prince, the knight,
the mantilla, and the tambourine.

Your crazed hand draws
the silhouette of the witch
who wraps herself in shadow,

and learns an abracadabra
from the goat-footed devil
making a macabre face.

A muse haughty and confused,
angel, specter, medusa.
So appears your muse.

Tu pincel asombra, hechiza;
ya en sus claros electriza,
ya en sus sombras sinfoniza;

con las manolas amables,
los reyes, los miserables,
o los cristos lamentables.

En tu claroscuro brilla
la luz muerta y amarilla
de la horrenda pesadilla,

o hace encender tu pincel
los rojos labios de miel
o la sangre del clavel.

Tienen ojos asesinos
en sus semblantes divinos
tus ángeles femeninos.

Tu caprichosa alegría
mezclaba la luz del día
con la noche oscura y fría:

así es de ver y admirar
tu misteriosa y sin par
pintura crepuscular.

De lo que da testimonio:
por tus frescos, San Antonio;
por tus brujas, el demonio.

Your brush bewitches, surprises;
sometimes in its bright colors it electrifies,
sometimes in its shadows it symphonizes;

with the pleasant cabriolets,
the kings, the wretches,
or the lamentable christs.

In your chiaroscuro shimmers
the dead and yellow light
of the horrendous nightmare,

or your brush lights up
the honey's red lips
or the carnation's blood.

They have murderous eyes
in their divine countenances,
your female angels.

Your unpredictable joy
would mix the light of day
with the cold dark night:

this is what, seen and admired,
your mysterious and unparalleled
twilight painting is like.

To which these bear witness:
to your frescos, St. Anthony;
to your witches, the devil.

XXIX. Caracol

A Antonio Machado

En la playa he encontrado un caracol de oro
macizo y recamado de las perlas más finas;
Europa le ha tocado con sus manos divinas
cuando cruzó las ondas sobre el celeste toro.

He llevado a mis labios el caracol sonoro
y he suscitado el eco de las dianas marinas,
le acerqué a mis oídos y las azules minas
me han contado en voz baja su secreto tesoro.

Así la sal me llega de los vientos amargos
que en sus hinchadas velas sintió la nave Argos
cuando amaron los astros el sueño de Jasón;

y oigo un rumor de olas y un incógnito acento
y un profundo oleaje y un misterioso viento . . .
(El caracol la forma tiene de un corazón.)

xxix. Seashell

For Antonio Machado

On the beach I have found a golden seashell
solid and embroidered with the finest pearls;
Europa touched it with her divine hands
when crossing the waves on the heavenly bull.

I have brought to my lips the resounding seashell
and have stirred the echo of nautical reveilles,
I have brought it to my ear and the blue mines
have softly recounted to me their secret treasure.

So the salt comes to me from the pungent winds
which the vessel *Argo* felt in its swollen sails
when the heavenly bodies loved Jason's dream;

and I hear a murmur of waves and an accent unknown
and a bottomless sea swell and a mysterious wind . . .
(The seashell has the shape of a heart.)

xxx. Amo, amas

Amar, amar, amar, amar siempre, con todo
el ser y con la tierra y con el cielo,
con lo claro del sol y lo obscuro del lodo:
amar por toda ciencia y amar por todo anhelo.

Y cuando la montaña de la vida
nos sea dura y larga y alta y llena de abismos,
amar la inmensidad que es de amor encendida
y arder en la fusión de nuestros pechos mismos!

xxx. I Love, You Love

To love, to love, to love, to love forever, with all
one's being and with the earth and with the sky,
with the bright colors of the sun and the dark colors of the mud:
To love by all science and to love by all yearning.

And when the mountain of life
is hard for us and long and high and full of chasms,
to love the immensity that is lit up with love
and to burn in the fusion of our very own breasts!

XXXI. Soneto autumnal al Marqués de Bradomín

Marqués, (como el Divino lo eres) te saludo.
Es el otoño y vengo de un Versalles doliente.
Había mucho frío y erraba vulgar gente.
El chorro de agua de Verlaine estaba mudo.

Me quedé pensativo ante un mármol desnudo,
cuando vi una paloma que pasó de repente,
y por caso de cerebración inconsciente
pensé en ti. Toda exégesis en este caso eludo.

Versalles otoñal; una paloma; un lindo
mármol; un vulgo errante, municipal y espeso;
anteriores lecturas de tus sutiles prosas;

la reciente impresión de tus triunfos . . . prescindo
de más detalles para explicarte por eso
como, autumnal, te envío este ramo de rosas.

XXXI. Autumnal Sonnet to the Marquis of Bradomín

Marquis (like the Divine that you are), I greet you.
It is autumn, and I come from a doleful Versailles.
It was very cold and ordinary people wandered around.
Verlaine's fountain of water was mute.

Lost in thought before a naked marble,
I saw a dove that suddenly passed,
and by some unconscious cerebration
I thought of you. I avoid all exegesis in this matter.

Versailles in the autumn; a dove; a pretty
marble; the common crowd wandering around, municipal and coarse;
earlier readings of your subtle works in prose;

the recent publication of your triumphs . . . I dispense
with more details for explaining to you
how, autumnal, I send you this bouquet of roses.

XXXII. Nocturno

A Mariano de Cavia

Los que auscultasteis el corazón de la noche,
los que por el insomnio tenaz habéis oído
el cerrar de una puerta, el resonar de un coche
lejano, un eco vago, un ligero ruido . . .

En los instantes del silencio misterioso,
cuando surgen de su prisión los olvidados,
en la hora de los muertos, en la hora del reposo,
sabréis leer estos versos de amargor impregnados . . . !

Como en un vaso vierto en ellos mis dolores
de lejanos recuerdos y desgracias funestas,
y las tristes nostalgias de mi alma, ebria de flores,
y el duelo de mi corazón, triste de fiestas.

Y el pesar de no ser lo que yo hubiera sido,
la pérdida del reino que estaba para mí,
el pensar que un instante pude no haber nacido,
y el sueño que es mi vida desde que yo nací!

Todo esto viene en medio del silencio profundo
en que la noche envuelve la terrena ilusión,
y siento como un eco del corazón del mundo
que penetra y conmueve mi propio corazón.

XXXII. Nocturne

For Mariano de Cavia

Those of you who auscultated the heart of the night,
who with tenacious insomnia have heard
the closing of a door, the rumble of a car
in the distance, a vague echo, a low sound . . .

In moments of mysterious silence,
when the forgotten emerge from their prison,
at the hour of the dead, at the hour of repose,
you'll know how to read these verses steeped in bitterness . . . !

As into a glass, I pour into them my sorrows
from distant memories and fateful misfortunes,
and the sad reminiscences of my soul, drunk on flowers,
and the pain in my heart, sad with festivals.

And the regret of not being what I might have been,
the loss of the realm that was to be mine,
the thinking that I could in an instant not have been born,
and the dream that has been my life ever since I was born!

All this comes in the middle of the profound silence
in which the night wraps up earthly hope,
and I feel like an echo from the heart of the world
that penetrates and deeply moves my own heart.

XXXIII. Urna votiva

A Lamberti

Sobre el caro despojo esta urna cincelo:
un amable frescor de inmortal siempreviva
que decore la greca de la urna votiva
en la copa que guarda el rocío del cielo;

una alondra fugaz sorprendida en su vuelo
cuando fuese a cantar en la rama de oliva,
una estatua de Diana en la selva nativa
que la Musa Armonía envolviera en su velo.

Tal si fuese escultor con amor cincelara
en el mármol divino que me brinda Carrara,
coronando la obra una lira, una cruz;

y sería mi sueño, al nacer de la aurora,
contemplar en la faz de una niña que llora,
una lágrima llena de su amor y de luz.

XXXIII. Votive Urn

For Lamberti

I chisel this urn over costly spoils:
a sweet coolness of immortal everlasting flower
that will decorate the fret of the votive urn
in the cup that stores the dew of the sky;

a fleeting lark, surprised in its flight
on the way to sing on the olive branch,
a statue of Diana in the native forest
which Harmony the Muse enveloped in her veil.

Like a sculptor I would chisel with love
on the divine marble Carrara provides me—
a lyre, a cross crowning the work—;

and my dream would be, as it is born from the dawn,
to contemplate upon the face of a weeping girl
a tear filled with love and with light.

XXXIV. Programa matinal

Claras horas de la mañana
en que mil clarines de oro
dicen la divina diana!
Salve al celeste Sol sonoro!

En la angustia de la ignorancia
de lo porvenir, saludemos
la barca llena de fragancia
que tiene de marfil los remos.

Epicúreos o soñadores
amemos la gloriosa Vida,
siempre coronados de flores
y siempre la antorcha encendida!

Exprimamos de los racimos
de nuestra vida transitoria
los placeres por que vivimos
y los champañas de la gloria.

Devanemos de Amor los hilos,
hagamos, porque es bello, el bien,
y después durmamos tranquilos
y por siempre jamás. Amén.

xxxiv. Morning Plan

Clear hours of the morning
in which a thousand golden bugles
sound the divine reveille!
Hail to the celestial resounding Sun!

In the anguish of our ignorance
of what is to come, let us salute
the fragrance-laden ship
that has ivory oars.

Epicureans or dreamers,
always crowned with flowers
and always with the torch ablaze,
let us love glorious Life!

Let us press from the clusters
of our transitory life
the pleasures for which we live
and the champagnes of glory.

Let us spool Love's threads,
let us do it, because good is lovely,
and afterward let us sleep peacefully
and forever more. Amen.

xxxv. Ibis

Cuidadoso estoy siempre ante el Ibis de Ovidio,
enigma humano tan ponzoñoso y suave
que casi no pretende su condición de ave
cuando se ha conquistado sus terrores de ofidio.

xxxv. Ibis

I am wary always before Ovid's Ibis,
a human enigma so poisonous and smooth
that it almost repudiates its condition of being avian
once it has overcome its terror of being ophidian.

XXXVI. Thánatos

En medio del camino de la Vida . . .
dijo Dante. Su verso se convierte:
En medio del camino de la Muerte.

Y no hay que aborrecer a la ignorada
emperatriz y reina de la Nada.
Por ella nuestra tela está tejida,
y ella en la copa de los sueños vierte
un contrario nepente: ella no olvida!

XXXVI. Thanatos

Halfway down the road of Life . . .
said Dante. His verse changes to:
Halfway down the road of Death.

And do not abhor the unknown
empress and queen of Nothingness.
Because of her our fabric is woven,
and she pours into the cup of dreams
a contrary nepenthe: she does not forget!

XXXVII. Ofrenda

Bandera que aprisiona
el aliento de Abril,
           corona
tu torre de marfil.

Cual princesa encantada,
eres mimada por
           un hada
de rosado color.

Las rosas que tú pises
tu boca han de envidiar;
           los lises
tu pureza estelar.

Carrera de Atalanta
lleva tu dicha en flor;
           y canta
tu nombre un ruiseñor.

Y si meditabunda
sientes pena fugaz,
           inunda
luz celeste tu faz.

Ronsard, lira de Galia,
te daría un rondel,
           Italia
te brindara el pincel,

para que la corona
tuvieses, celestial
           Madona,
en un lienzo inmortal.

XXXVII. Offering

A flag that is imprisoned
by the breath of April,
                crowns
your ivory tower.

Like an enchanted princess,
you are pampered by
                a fairy
of rosy color.

The roses you tread
will envy your mouth;
                the lilies
your stellar purity.

Atalanta's race
bears your flowering bliss;
                and a nightingale
sings your name.

And if while brooding
you feel a fleeting pain,
                a celestial light
floods your features.

Ronsard, the lyre of Gaul,
would give you a rondel,
                Italy
would offer you a paintbrush,

so that you might wear
the crown, celestial
                Madonna,
on an immortal canvas.

Ten al laurel cariño,
hoy, cuando aspiro a que
vaya a ornar tu corpiño
mi rimado bouquet.

Kindly accept the laurel,
today, when I aspire to
embellish your bodice
with my rhymed bouquet.

XXXVIII. Propósito primaveral

A *Vargas Vila*

A saludar me ofrezco y a celebrar me obligo
tu triunfo, Amor, al beso de la estación que llega
mientras el blanco cisne del lago azul navega
en el mágico parque de mis triunfos testigo.

Amor, tu hoz de oro ha segado mi trigo;
por ti me halaga el suave son de la flauta griega
y por ti Venus pródiga sus manzanas me entrega
y me brinda las perlas de las mieles del higo.

En el erecto término coloco una corona
en que de rosas frescas la púrpura detona;
y en tanto canta el agua bajo el boscaje obscuro,

junto a la adolescente que en el misterio inicio
apuraré alternando con tu dulce ejercicio
las ánforas de oro del divino Epicuro.

XXXVIII. Springtime Purpose

For Vargas Vila

I willingly salute and celebrate
your triumph, Love, at the kiss of the season that arrives
while the white swan of the blue lake navigates
in the magical park, a witness to my triumphs.

Love, your golden sickle has reaped my wheat;
because of you the smooth sound of the Greek flute entices me,
and because of you prodigal Venus delivers her apples
and offers me the pearls of the honeys of the fig.

On the erect boundary post I set a crown
on which the purple of fresh roses detonates;
and while the water sings below the dark grove,

beside the adolescent girl I initiate in the mystery
I will drain, alternating with your sweet exercise,
the golden amphorae of the divine Epicurus.

XXXIX. Letanía de nuestro señor Don Quijote

A Navarro Ledesma

Rey de los hidalgos, señor de los tristes,
que de fuerza alientas y de ensueños vistes,
coronado de áureo yelmo de ilusión;
que nadie ha podido vencer todavía,
por la adarga al brazo, toda fantasía,
y la lanza en ristre, toda corazón.

Noble peregrino de los peregrinos,
que santificaste todos los caminos
con el paso augusto de tu heroicidad,
contra las certezas, contra las conciencias
y contra las leyes y contra las ciencias,
contra la mentira, contra la verdad . . .

Caballero errante de los caballeros,
barón de varones, príncipe de fieros,
par entre los pares, maestro, salud!
¡Salud, porque juzgo que hoy muy poca tienes,
entre los aplausos o entre los desdenes,
y entre las coronas y los parabienes
y las tonterías de la multitud!

¡Tú, para quien pocas fueran las victorias
antiguas y para quien clásicas glorias
serían apenas de ley y razón,
soportas elogios, memorias, discursos,
resistes certámenes, tarjetas, concursos,
y, teniendo a Orfeo, tienes a orfeón!

Escucha, divino Rolando del sueño,
a un enamorado de tu Clavileño,
y cuyo Pegaso relincha hacia ti;
escucha los versos de estas letanías,
hechas con las cosas de todos los días
y con otras que en lo misterioso vi.

XXXIX. Litany of Our Lord Don Quixote

For Navarro Ledesma

King of impoverished noblemen, lord of the sad,
you breathe in strength and you dress in daydreams,
crowned by an aureate helmet of hopes and dreams;
whom no one has yet been able to defeat,
by the shield on your arm, all fantasy,
and your lance at the ready, all heart.

Noble pilgrim of pilgrims,
who sanctified all the roads
with the august step of your heroism,
against the certainties, against the consciences,
and against the laws and against the sciences,
against the lie, against the truth . . .

Knight-errant of knights,
man among men, prince of boasters,
peer among equals, master, here's to your health!
To your health, because I judge that today you have very little,
amid applause or amid disdain,
and amid the crowns and the congratulations
and all the nonsense of the multitude!

You—for whom the victories were few
in former times and for whom they would hardly be
classic glories of law and reason—
put up with eulogies, memoirs, discourses,
withstand literary contests, cards, competitions,
and, with Orpheus, you have a choral society!

Listen, divine Roland of dream,
to someone in love with your Clavileño,
and whose Pegasus whinnies at you;
listen to the verses of these litanies,
made with some everyday things
and with other things I saw in the mysterious.

¡Ruega por nosotros, hambrientos de vida,
con el alma a tientas, con la fe perdida,
llenos de congojas y faltos de sol,
por advenedizas almas de manga ancha,
que ridiculizan el ser de la Mancha,
el ser generoso y el ser español!

¡Ruega por nosotros, que necesitamos
las mágicas rosas, los sublimes ramos
de laurel! *Pro nobis ora*, gran señor.
(Tiembla la floresta de laurel del mundo,
y antes que tu hermano vago, Segismundo,
el pálido Hamlet te ofrece una flor.)

Ruega generoso, piadoso, orgulloso;
ruega casto, puro, celeste, animoso;
por nos intercede, suplica por nos,
pues casi ya estamos sin savia, sin brote,
sin alma, sin vida, sin luz, sin Quijote,
sin pies y sin alas, sin Sancho y sin Dios.

De tantas tristezas, de dolores tantos,
de los superhombres de Nietzsche, de cantos
áfonos, recetas que firma un doctor,
de las epidemias de horribles blasfemias
de las Academias,
líbranos, señor.

De rudos malsines,
falsos paladines,
y espíritus finos y blandos y ruines,
del hampa que sacia
su canallocracia
con burlar la gloria, la vida, el honor,
del puñal con gracia,
¡líbranos, señor!

Noble peregrino de los peregrinos,
que santificaste todos los caminos
con el paso augusto de tu heroicidad,

Pray for us, who hunger for life,
with our fumbling souls, with lost faith,
full of torments and devoid of sun,
for parvenu souls with broad sleeves,
who ridicule the essence from La Mancha,
the generous essence and the Spanish essence!

Pray for us, who need
the magical roses, the sublime branches
of laurel! Pro nobis ora, great lord.
(The world's laurel grove trembles,
and before your wayward brother, Segismundo,
pale Hamlet offers you a flower.)

Pray generous, pious, proud;
pray chaste, pure, celestial, spirited;
on our behalf intercede, plead on our behalf,
since we are all but sapped out, without bud,
without soul, without life, without light, without Quixote,
without feet and without wings, without Sancho and without God.

From so many sorrows, from so many pains,
from the supermen of Nietzsche, from aphonic
songs, prescriptions signed by a doctor,
from epidemics of horrible blasphemies
from the Academies,
save us, lord.

From crude backbiters,
false paladins,
and spirits fine and bland and despicable,
from the criminal underworld that sates
its lowlife-ocracy
by flouting glory, life, honor,
from the skillful dagger,
save us, lord!

Noble pilgrim of pilgrims,
who sanctified all the roads
with the august step of your heroism,

contra las certezas, contra las conciencias
y contra las leyes y contra las ciencias,
contra la mentira, contra la verdad . . .

Ora por nosotros, señor de los tristes,
que de fuerza alientas y de ensueños vistes,
coronado de áureo yelmo de ilusión;
que nadie ha podido vencer todavía,
por la adarga al brazo, toda fantasía,
y la lanza en ristre, toda corazón!

against the certainties, against the consciences,
and against the laws and against the sciences,
against the lie, against the truth . . .

Pray for us, lord of the sad,
you breathe in strength and you dress in daydreams,
crowned by an aureate helmet of hopes and dreams;
whom no one has yet been able to defeat,
by the shield on your arm, all fantasy,
and your lance at the ready, all heart.

XL. Allá lejos

Buey que vi en mi niñez echando vaho un día
bajo el nicaragüense sol de encendidos oros,
en la hacienda fecunda, plena de la armonía
del trópico; paloma de los bosques sonoros
del viento, de las hachas, de pájaros y toros
salvajes, yo os saludo, pues sois la vida mía.

Pesado buey, tú evocas la dulce madrugada
que llamaba a la ordeña de la vaca lechera,
cuando era mi existencia toda blanca y rosada,
y tú, paloma arrulladora y montañera,
significas en mi primavera pasada
todo lo que hay en la divina Primavera.

XL. Way Far Away

Ox that I saw in my childhood giving off steam one day
beneath the Nicaraguan sun of blazing golds,
in the lush hacienda, full of the harmony
of the tropics; dove of the woods reverberating
with the wind, with the axes, with birds and wild
bulls, I greet you, since you are my life.

Massive ox, you evoke the sweet early morning
that called for the milking of the dairy cow,
when my whole existence was white and pink,
and you, cooing mountain dove,
you signify in my past springtime
all that there is in the divine Springtime.

XLI. Lo fatal

A René Pérez

Dichoso el árbol que es apenas sensitivo,
y más la piedra dura porque ésa ya no siente,
pues no hay dolor más grande que el dolor de ser vivo,
ni mayor pesadumbre que la vida consciente.

Ser, y no saber nada, y ser sin rumbo cierto,
y el temor de haber sido y un futuro terror . . .
Y el espanto seguro de estar mañana muerto,
y sufrir por la vida y por la sombra y por

lo que no conocemos y apenas sospechamos,
y la carne que tienta con sus frescos racimos,
y la tumba que aguarda con sus fúnebres ramos,
y no saber a dónde vamos,
ni de dónde venimos . . . !

XLI. What Gets You

For René Pérez

How fortunate the tree that can scarcely feel,
and more so the hard stone because it no longer cares,
since no greater pain exists than the pain of living,
nor deeper sorrow than a life self-aware.

To be, and to know nothing, to be adrift,
and the fear of having been, and a terror soon at hand . . .
And the dread certainty of being tomorrow dead,
and suffering because of life and shadow and

what we don't know and barely conceive,
and the flesh that tempts, fresh-picked and plump,
and the tomb that awaits with its funeral wreaths,
and not knowing where we run,
or even where we come from. . . !

Glossary and Annotations

The following list clarifies references and resolves certain questions that may arise in reading the poems of *Cantos de vida y esperanza*. Included are cultural, historical, literary, geographical, and mythological references to some of the many and complex allusions encountered in Rubén Darío's poetry, as well as terms used in the introduction. This glossary is, no doubt, far from complete, even for our limited purposes. Also, as Darío is quite capable of recasting a particular term to fit the needs of a particular poem, all references must be understood in light of Darío's text. Each entry here offers general information that should serve as a starting point for further investigation and interpretation. We cite no particular sources: readers may consult standard reference works if they desire more information on any subject. Readers of Spanish may also wish to consult the works by Arturo Marasso (1954) and Armando Zambrana Fonseca (1998), cited in this book's bibliography. In English, as far as we can determine, our own glossary notes are the most extensive available for the works of Rubén Darío.

Aegipan: Derived from a surname of the god Pan that alludes to his goatlike features, it generally suggests an equally goatlike satyr in Darío's poems. In some traditions it stands for an independent figure with his own legend; still other traditions identify him with the constellation Capricorn.

Ahasuerus: Persian king, also known as Xerxes, who reigned from 485 to 465 B.C. In the Bible he married the Hebrew woman Esther: "this is Ahasuerus which reigned, from India even unto Ethiopia, over an hundred and seven and twenty provinces" (Esther 1:1).

alejandrino: In Spanish, a fourteen-syllable verse divided into seven-syllable hemistiches separated by a caesura. The verse was especially popular in the Middle Ages. Darío restored its use in Spanish poetry.

Alexander the Great (356–323 B.C.): King of Macedonia who set out to conquer the known world.

Alfonso XIII: King of Spain from 1902 to 1931, whom Darío met in Madrid and about whom he wrote a *retrato y semblanza* (literary portrait).

Alhambra, the: Fortified complex of exquisite palaces built in Granada, Spain, by a Moslem dynasty during the Middle Ages.

Altamirano, Adolfo: Nicaraguan Minister of Foreign Affairs under President José Santos Zelaya, who urged Darío's nomination as Nicaraguan consul to France, a post the poet held from 1903 to 1907.

amphora: A two-handled ceramic jar used throughout the Mediterranean in ancient times to store or transport wine, olive oil, and many other commodities. The amphora tapered to a point at the base and was sometimes elegantly shaped and decorated.

Anacreon: Greek poet of wine and love, who lived from about 570 to 485 B.C.

Anadyomene: Literally "she-who-rises," a name given to the Greek goddess Aphrodite (the Roman Venus) because of her birth from sea foam. Many classical artists captured this pose, in which the goddess often has a hand near each shoulder to wring out her hair.

Andalusia: The southern region of Spain, so named for the Arabic word for the Iberian Peninsula. The Moslem world retained a significant presence here from 711 to 1492, and continued to influence popular culture for centuries. The Alhambra in Granada bears architectural testimony to the power and refinement of the region's Moslem past. Always considered somewhat exotic, Andalusia is also closely associated with flamenco music and Spanish Gypsies.

Andes: Enormous mountain chain that extends north and south along the Pacific side of South America, touching nearly every Spanish-speaking country on the continent.

Angelica and Medoro: Prototypes of carnal love in the Orlando/Roland legends, they are the subject of one of Góngora's most famous *romances* (1602).

Angelus: In the Catholic Church, a devotion in honor of the Incarnation offered morning, noon, and evening with the ringing of a bell. The title comes from the first verse in Latin: "Angelus Domini nuntiavit Mariae . . ." [The angel of the Lord announced to Mary . . .].

Anthony, St. (1195–1231): Franciscan friar credited with many miracles. In 1798, the Spanish artist Francisco de Goya painted the wonderful frescos in the Ermita de San Antonio de la Florida, a small church in Madrid, where he was later buried.

Apocalypse: From the Greek word for the biblical Book of Revelation, it generally refers to the cataclysmic end of the world.

Apollo: Greek and Roman god of light, health, penance and purification, prophecy, music, poetry, and shepherds.

Aranjuez: Spanish city south of Madrid, site of an impressive royal palace that attracts many tourists.

Argentine sun: Reference to the emblem of a gold sun on the flag of Argentina.

Argo: Mythical ship on which fifty heroes—including Leda's sons, the Dioscuri—sailed with Jason on his quest for the Golden Fleece.

Armida: A beautiful Moslem woman in the epic poem *Gerusalemme liberata* (Jerusalem delivered), published in 1581 by Torquato Tasso. She wins the heart of the Christian crusader Rinaldo.

Atalanta: Woman famed for her speed and hunting skills, she sailed with the heroes of the *Argo*. If a man proposed marriage, he would have to race her. She would pursue each unarmed suitor, and, when she caught him, kill and behead him. Finally, the goddess Venus gave one man golden apples to drop during the race; as Atalanta stopped to pick up the apples, the suitor won the right to marry her.

Atlantis: Fabled lost continent, home of an advanced civilization that sank into the ocean sometime in the distant past.

234

Aurora: The Latin name for Eos, the Greek goddess of the dawn, sister (or daughter, according to Darío in "I am the one . . .") of the sun god.

Babel: In the Old Testament, a tower meant to be tall enough to reach heaven; as the people of the whole world worked together to build it, God turned their single language into many and so put an end to the cooperative project.

Babylon: Capital of an empire of the Middle East, which reached its height under Hammurabi in the eighteenth century B.C. Site of the Hanging Gardens, one of the Seven Wonders of the Ancient World, it conquered what is now Palestine.

bacchante: A priestess of Bacchus; by extension, a woman given to indulgence.

Bacchus: Latin name for Dionysus, the Greek god of wine and fertility.

Balthasar: One of the Three Wise Men of Christian tradition, who visited the Bethlehem manger with gifts for the Christ Child. Often he represents Africa, one of the three continents then known.

Baudelaire, Charles (1821–1867): French poet, forerunner of the symbolist movement, who rejected Romanticism and embraced the decadent, the urban, and at times the satanic. His most important verse is found in *Les Fleurs du mal* (The Flowers of evil), published in 1857. Darío refers to a note written by Baudelaire in 1862, in which he describes a sense of vertigo coming over him.

Bécquer, Gustavo Adolfo (1836–1870): Influential Spanish poet, considered Romantic or post-Romantic, whose most important work was the *Rimas*, published posthumously in 1871.

Bellerophon: The only human rider to mount the winged horse Pegasus successfully. After killing the monster Chimera, he attempted to ascend to the top of Mount Olympus and dwell with the gods.

blue verse: A reference to Darío's first important book, *Azul . . .* (Blue . . .), published in 1888. See the introduction to this book.

bohemia: Unconventional pleasure-seeking, sometimes illicit lifestyle of a colony of free spirits, such as the painters, writers, musicians, and hangers-on in the Paris underground frequented by Darío at the turn of the century.

Bolívar, Domingo: Colombian painter and one of Darío's companions in Paris. The poet devoted several articles to Bolívar's works. The painter left for Washington, D.C., where he committed suicide in 1903.

Borgia: Powerful Spanish-Italian noble family as famous for its patronage of the arts during the Renaissance as for its cruelty and corruption.

Cabala: Also Kabbalah, Qabalah. Jewish mystical tradition and esoteric doctrine that began to develop in Spain around 1200 A.D.

cabriolet: A small horse-drawn coach once often used as a cab in European cities.

Calderón de la Barca, Pedro (1600–1681): One of the great playwrights of Spain's Golden Age. His most famous work is *La vida es sueño* (Life is a dream), written in a variety of poetic forms, including the sonnet.

Calvo, Ricardo (1873–1966): Premier actor of the Spanish theater and a good friend to modernist writers and artists.

calyx: The cuplike outer covering of a flower.

Campoamor, Ramón de (1817–1901): Popular Spanish poet who broke with the Romantic style of long, overwrought, tragic compositions in favor of shorter and often ironic and humorous pieces written in a more prosaic tone.

Carducci, Giosuè (1836–1913): Italian poet who turned to classical meters in reaction to the extremes of Romanticism.

Carrara: Italian site famous for its marble quarries. The stone is especially prized for its color and purity by sculptors and architects.

Castalia: The spring on Mount Parnassus, consecrated to Apollo and the Muses. Its waters conferred poetic inspiration.

Cavia, Mariano de (1855–1920): Spanish journalist and tireless participant in the literary *tertulias*—a kind of semiformal discussion group—of Madrid. In addition to the poem dedicated to Cavia in *Cantos de vida y esperanza*, Darío devoted a newspaper column to him.

centaurs: According to Greek mythology, a hybrid species—half man, half horse—born of Centaurus, son of Ixion and Nephele, and the mares of Thessaly. (In another version, they are the sons of Ixion and Nephele directly, and thus "Ixionids.") Darío makes use of them to illustrate his ideas on various philosophical themes, such as life, death, the feminine element, and the mystery or enigma of existence or to represent classical virtues such as ferocity in battle.

Cervantes Saavedra, Miguel de (1547–1616): Spanish novelist and playwright who created the character Don Quixote.

charitas: Word from Latin, meaning love in its divine or spiritual sense as opposed to physical love, and thus the origin of our word *charity*, generosity and benevolence toward those in need.

chiaroscuro: Italian word referring to a painting technique that employs the dramatic contrast of light and dark.

Chilean star: Reference to the emblem of a star on the flag of Chile.

Christopher: Reference to Christopher Columbus (1451–1506), whose voyages of exploration ushered in a new age.

chrysalis: Cocoon or formative stage of a butterfly.

Cid: Arabic for lord, title given to Rodrigo or Ruy Díaz de Vivar (1043–1099), Spanish national hero, for his valor and prowess in campaigns against the Moors.

Clavileño: Supposedly the fabulous flying horse of the wizard Merlin. In fact it proved to be only a crude wooden model Don Quixote rode blindfolded so that he might be tricked into thinking it real.

Cleopompus and Heliodemos: Although their names may enjoy some association with Greek mythology, the two are symbolic philosophers—the first apparently Epicurean and the second Pythagorean—created by Darío for this sonnet.

clepsydra: Ancient water-clock marking time by controlling the rate of dripping from one vessel into another.

Columbuses: Reference to Christopher Columbus (1451–1506), whose voyages of exploration ushered in a new age.

Coccinella: A genus of beetle, including ladybugs, used to dye scarlet.

conciliabule: A clandestine meeting, usually of an ecclesiastical nature, to devise a course or a plan most likely unacceptable to others.

Corinthian bronze: Metal famous for its beauty and durability.

Corral de la Pacheca: Former name of the Teatro Español, or National Theater, in Madrid, famous since the sixteenth century.

Cortés, Hernán (1485–1547): Leader of the Spanish conquistadors who discovered and quickly overthrew the Aztec Empire of Mexico.

Cuauhtemoc: Last emperor (1520–1525) of the Aztecs of Mexico, tortured by Cortés to reveal the whereabouts of hidden treasure and later hanged. Darío cites a phrase—"This is no bed of roses"—which Cuauhtemoc reputedly uttered while being tortured.

Cyprian: A name for Aphrodite or Venus, the goddess of love, alluding to Cyprus and her great temple there in Antiquity.

Cyrano de Bergerac: French playwright Edmond Rostand's world-famous character, protagonist of a theatrical piece of the same title, which had its Spanish debut in Madrid on January 25, 1899. Set in 1640 during a war between France and Spain, the play tells of a brave and poetic soldier with an enormous nose who helps his friend Christian woo the lovely Roxanne by composing love letters for him. The task is not difficult because Cyrano himself secretly loves her. The real Cyrano de Bergerac (1619–1655) was also a soldier and man of letters who wrote about a trip to the moon, among other places.

Decameron: Boccaccio's immensely popular collection of a hundred stories, many of them humorous and others ribald or tragic, begun soon after the Black Death struck Florence, Italy, in 1348.

Diana: The Latin name for Artemis, virgin goddess of the hunt and moonlight and protector of the young.

Díaz Romero, Eugenio: Argentine poet, and Darío's associate during his days in Buenos Aires.

"Dies irae . . ." Latin hymn used in the Roman Catholic mass for the dead, referring to Judgment Day. "Day of wrath, that day when the world turns to ash . . ." Darío uses it playfully in *Cantos de vida y esperanza*.

Dioscuri: Twin heroes Castor and Pollux, brothers of Helen of Troy and the sons of Zeus and Leda, whom the god seduced in the form of a swan. Both became Argonauts.

dodecasyllable: A twelve-syllable verse, sometimes equally divided into hemistiches like the *alejandrino*, and sometimes divided into five- and seven-syllable units, the rhythm of several traditional and popular poetic forms. As with the *alejandrino*, Darío revived its use in Spanish-language poetry.

Don Quixote: Protagonist of a comic satire of popular tales of chivalry, published in two parts by Miguel de Cervantes, in 1605 and 1615, often regarded as the greatest novel in history. An elderly landholder, driven mad by a glut of chivalric romances, believes himself a knight errant out to right the wrongs of the world. In the name of his imaginary lady, Dulcinea, and accompanied by a decrepit horse, Rocinante, and one of his tenants, Sancho Panza, in the guise of a squire, the idealistic knight battles windmills and other delusions, inflicts as much pain and pandemonium as justice, and finally returns home, renounces his quest, and dies.

Dulcinea: The beloved lady to whom Don Quixote devotes his service, she is in reality a figment of his imagination, based perhaps on a glimpse of the coarse peasant girl Aldonza Lorenzo.

Dunyazad: Sister (in some texts, slave) of Scheherazade, storyteller of *A Thousand and One Arabian Nights*.

Durandal: Name of the legendary sword of Roland, hero of a number of medieval epics. In "Cyrano in Spain" Darío contrasts Roland's sword with Tizona, the sword of the Cid.

eburnean: Made of ivory.

Edgar: Darío refers to U.S. writer Edgar Allan Poe (1808–1849), probably in the context of Poe's poem "Ulalume."

"Ego sum lux et veritas et vita." Latin for "I am light and truth and life," conflation of two sayings of Jesus Christ.

Epicurus (341–270 B.C.): One of the major philosophers of the Greek Hellenistic period, whose teachings—Epicureanism—taught that atoms constituted matter, and also rejected the soul, as well as the influence of the gods. The goal of life was to achieve pleasure in this world by limiting one's desires and eliminating fear of supernatural powers and death. Darío emphasizes the hedonistic aspect.

eurekas: Invented plural form of the Greek *eureka*, "I have found it!" Archimedes (287–212 B.C.) of Syracuse, having solved a difficult problem, jumped out of the bath and ran through the streets shouting "eureka!" It generally refers to a moment of incredible insight or epiphany.

Europa: Daughter of a Phoenician king, she was carried off to Crete by Zeus in the form of a beautiful bull.

Evangeline: Epic poem by U.S. writer Henry Wadsworth Longfellow (1807–1882) about a woman's search for her bridegroom, written in hexameter.

Fames: Winged women with trumpets in hand, from Greek and Roman mythology, who tirelessly move through the air announcing the good and bad about everything.

faun: A rural deity resembling the satyr in Roman mythology.

Flanders: The northern region of Belgium, which came under Spanish control in the sixteenth century and was thereafter the site of many battles, religious and political.

Flora: Roman goddess of the springtime and of flowers.

gaita: Musical wind instrument resembling the bagpipe. In poetry, the *gaita gallega* indicates an hendecasyllable in dactylic rhythm.

Galatea: A sea nymph in love with the shepherd Acis, she is pursued by the monstrous Cyclops Polyphemus, who crushes Acis with a rock. The Spanish poet Luis de Góngora wrote a famous Baroque poem on the theme, the *Fábula de Polifemo y Galatea* (Fable of Polyphemus and Galatea), which Darío obviously admired.

Garcilaso de la Vega (1501–1536): One of the most important lyrical poets in Spanish, he revolutionized poetry by mastering and popularizing Italian versification and poetic forms such as the sonnet.

Gascon: A native of Gascony, region in western France bordering the Pyrenees and the Atlantic Ocean.

Gaspar: One of the Three Wise Men of Christian tradition, who visited the Bethlehem manger with gifts for the Christ Child. The reputed leader of the group, he is usually considered to represent Europe, one of the three continents then known.

Gaul: Roman name for the region now known as France.

Gioconda, la: Other name for Leonardo da Vinci's most famous painting, the mysteriously smiling *Mona Lisa*.

Góngora y Argote, Luis de (1561–1627): One of the great poets of Spain's Golden Age, known for an exquisite style, at times difficult and erudite, called *gongorismo* after the poet. Velázquez, as a young man, painted a now-famous portrait of the poet.

Goya, Francisco de (1746–1828): Spanish painter who created a very personal style between the Enlightenment and Romantic periods. The macabre fantasy of his so-called Black Paintings, the execution scene of *May 3, 1808*, and *The Naked Maja* are perhaps his most famous works. He is buried in the Ermita de San Antonio de la Florida in Madrid, site of his finest frescos.

Grant, Ulysses (1822–1885): U.S. general and president from 1869 to 1877. There is no record of the conversation between Grant and Hugo, to which Darío alludes in the poem "To Roosevelt." However, Grant did visit Paris in 1877, and Hugo attacked him in a number of writings.

gyrfalcon: The most spectacular of the hunting falcons, often white. In medieval Europe, only kings could own one.

hacienda: An extensive estate, plantation, or ranch. Those who work on it generally live there as well.

Hamlet: Protagonist of William Shakespeare's (1564–1616) famous tragedy, the brooding Prince of Denmark who seeks to avenge his father's death.

Harmony: Daughter of Ares and Aphrodite (Mars and Venus). Roman mythology converted her into the personification of order.

Helios: The Sun god in Greek and Roman mythology.

hendecasyllable: One of the principal verse forms in Spanish poetry since the Renaissance, when it was popularized by Garcilaso de la Vega; a verse of eleven syllables customarily accentuated on the sixth and tenth syllables or on the fourth, eighth, and tenth syllables.

Herakles: Greek name for Hercules.

Hercules: The Roman name for Herakles, the greatest of Greek heroes, son of Zeus (Jupiter) and a mortal woman. Traditionally armed with a club—sometimes with bow and arrow—and wearing a lion skin, he is generally held to be the strongest man in mythology. He set his pillars at the limits of the known world, where the Mediterranean meets the Atlantic, in the area known today as Gibraltar in southern Spain.

Herodias: Wife of Herod and mother of Salome, with whom she schemed to behead John the Baptist. The two women symbolize seduction, vengeance, and cruelty.

hexameter: Verse composed of six metric feet, the first five of which are often dactyls and the sixth metric foot a trochee, with a caesura falling between the third and fourth metric foot; the modern hexameter is based on the characteristic rhythm of Greek and Latin narrative and didactic poetry.

hippogriff: Fabulous beast, product of a male griffin and a horse, it can fly through the air faster than lightning.

Hispania: Roman name for the Iberian Peninsula, it later came to be associated with the region known today as Spain.

Holmes, Augusta (1848–1903): French composer of Irish origin and admirer of Richard Wagner.

Horace (65–8 B.C.): Roman poet famous for satires and odes.

Hugo, Victor (1802–1885): French novelist, poet, and playwright, author of such famous works as *The Hunchback of Notre Dame* and *Les Misérables*, whom Darío greatly admired.

Hyperionid: In classical mythology, one of the children of Hyperion, who fathered the sun, the moon, and dawn: that is, the gods Helios, Selene, and Eos or Aurora.

Hypsipyle: Darío uses the name for butterfly, following a classification of the Danish entomologist Johann Christian Fabricius (*Genera Insectorum*, 1776).

Inca: One of the kings of the Quechua peoples of the Peruvian Andes, whose empire fell to the Spanish in the early sixteenth century.

Ionia: An ancient people of Greek origin and their culture centered on Asia Minor and the Aegean Islands.

Isabella: Queen Isabella I of Castile, called "la Católica" (the Catholic), who lived from 1451 to 1504. With her husband Ferdinand V of Aragon, she sponsored the first voyage of Christopher Columbus across the Atlantic.

Janus: Roman god traditionally represented with two faces on his head, one looking forward and one back.

Jason: Mythic hero and leader of the Argonauts in the quest for the Golden Fleece.

Jiménez, Juan Ramón (1881–1958): Spanish poet and winner of the Nobel Prize, who was also a friend, supporter, and editor of Rubén Darío. Under his care *Cantos de vida y esperanza. Los cisnes y otros poemas* was first published in 1905.

Jupiter: Analogous to the Greek Zeus, the chief Roman god whose special province was the sky, and who, for this reason, was in charge of the weather. In a number of myths he transforms himself—into bull, swan, golden shower—in order to seduce a mortal woman.

La Mancha: Region of Castile, including the province of Toledo, that was home to the character Don Quixote.

Lamberti, Antonino: Argentine writer and friend of Darío during the time the latter spent in Buenos Aires.

Leda: A woman seduced by Zeus (Jupiter) in the form of a swan. Two eggs were produced by this union: from one egg emerged the beautiful Helen (later of Troy) and from the other the heroes Castor and Pollux, the Dioscuri. Leda symbolizes for Darío the erotic bond between the human and the celestial.

Le Figaro: French newspaper, still published today.

Leonardo da Vinci (1452–1519): Italian Renaissance painter, scientist, and inventor. His most famous painting is the *Mona Lisa*.

Lepanto: Important naval battle near Greece between a united Christian force and the Ottoman Turks. The Christian fleet won the day. Cervantes was wounded in this battle and lost the use of his arm.

Longfellow, Henry Wadsworth (1807–1882): U.S. poet who wrote the epic poem *Evangeline* in hexameter.

Luis de León, fray (1527–1591): One of the great religious poets and Renaissance scholars of Spain's Golden Age, renowned for the classical perfection of the five-verse stanza form known as the *lira*.

lymph: Poetic term for a spring of clear water.

Machado, Antonio (1875–1939): Spanish lyrical poet, author of *Soledades* (1903) and *Campos de Castilla* (1912), generally considered the greatest poet of the Generation of 1898.

Machado, Manuel (1874–1947): Spanish modernist poet and one of Darío's companions in the bohemian lifestyle in Paris; the older brother of Antonio, also a poet and friend of Darío.

Madrid Cómico: Spanish literary magazine famous for parodies, satire, and humor about cultural life in Spain in the early twentieth century.

madrigal: A song for several unaccompanied voices that was popular from the fifteenth to the seventeenth centuries; also a short lyrical poem.

Mammon: The Phoenician god of wealth and greed; also the pursuit of material riches condemned by Jesus Christ in the Bible: "Ye cannot serve God and mammon."

Manes: To the Romans, divine spirits of the dead.

Man of La Mancha: The character Don Quixote.

Marquis of Bradomín: Aristocratic and decadent narrator of the four novelistic *Sonatas* written by Ramón del Valle-Inclán (1866–1936). In the sonnet Darío identifies the author Valle-Inclán with the character Bradomín, who is described in the *Sonatas* as "ugly, Catholic, and sentimental." See Valle-Inclán.

Mars: Roman god of war identified with the Greek Ares.

Martínez Sierra, Gregorio (1881–1947): Spanish playwright and friend of Darío.

Melchior: One of the Three Wise Men of Christian tradition, who visited the Bethlehem manger with gifts for the Christ Child. He is usually considered to represent Asia, one of the three continents then known.

Meninas, Las: Probably the most famous masterpiece by the Spanish painter Diego de Velázquez (1599–1660), it is an ingenious composition showing the painter at work on a canvas in his studio, along with the five-year-old Princess Margarita and two of her ladies-in-waiting (or *meninas*, in Portuguese), two court dwarfs, a giant mastiff, three onlookers, and—in a mirror—the portrait of King Felipe IV and Queen Mariana.

Minerva: Roman goddess identified with the Greek Athena, born from the forehead of Zeus-Jupiter in full armor and goddess of wisdom and virginity.

Miserere: Title of Psalm 51 when used in the liturgy, derived from the Latin word with which it begins: "Have mercy . . ."

modernism: In the context of *Cantos de vida y esperanza*, a Hispanic movement in art and literature at the end of the nineteenth century and beginning of the twentieth, which found its first full-blown representation in Rubén Darío. Modernism reveals two principal concerns or aspects: (1) the aesthetic, typified by the sumptuous cultivation of the word and the metaphor, renovation, artistic freedom, exoticism, classicism, cosmopolitanism, symbolism, and irrationalism; and (2) the existential, centering on the poet as hero or sacred bard, as well as on eroticism, the problem of God, anguish, and rebellion. Modernism in our context should not be confused with other movements at the turn of the century or later, such as the Modernismo Brasileiro during the 1920s in Brazil or with the modernist movement of English-language writers, who may share some concerns and impulses with the Hispanic *modernistas*, but neither origin nor acquaintance.

Molière (1622–1673): Stage name of Parisian playwright Jean-Baptiste Poquelin, who changed the face of French classical comedy and whose works include *The Miser, The Misanthrope, The School for Wives, Tartuffe*, and *Don Juan*, a rewriting of Tirso de Molina's Spanish masterpiece.

Molossians: A breed of huge dogs used in war, named after the fabled semibarbarous inhabitants of Molossia, a region north of Greece, who were descended from the hero Achilles.

Montaigne, Michel de (1533–1592): French Renaissance thinker and inventor of the essay, whose skepticism of human knowledge is suggested by the question "Que sais-je?" [What do I know?] of the epigraph to the poem "On the Death of Rafael Núñez."

Montezuma (1466–1520): Aztec emperor at the time of the Spanish arrival in Mexico, he died in the early skirmishes after being taken prisoner by Cortés and was succeeded by Cuauhtemoc. His name is also spelled Moctezuma.

Moor: A Moslem of the Iberian Peninsula following the first invasion of 711, of Arab or African descent. The Christian and Moorish kingdoms share a complex history of alliances and wars throughout the Middle Ages in what is now Spain.

Murillos: Paintings by Bartolomé Esteban Murillo (1618–1682), Spanish master of religious art, whose exquisite paintings of the Virgin are especially popular.

Muses: Nine goddesses of arts and sciences who dwell on Olympus and inspire human beings: Calliope, goddess of the epic; Clio, goddess of history; Erato, goddess of love poetry; Euterpe, goddess of lyric poetry; Melpomene, goddess of tragedy; Polyhymnia, goddess of sacred song; Terpsichore, goddess of the dance; Thalia, goddess of comedy; and Urania, goddess of astronomy. Apollo was their protector.

Navarro Ledesma, Francisco: Director of the Madrid journal *Blanco y Negro*, in which Darío published on several occasions, and who attended celebrations marking the three hundredth anniversary of the publication of *Don Quixote* in 1905.

Nebuchadnezzar: Greatest of the Babylonian kings mentioned in the Bible.

nepenthe: A drug used by the ancients to relieve pain and sorrow.

Netzahualcoyotl: Aztec warrior and poet, sovereign of Texcoco until 1472, the year of his death.

Nietzsche, Friedrich (1844–1900): German philosopher and poet, whose declaration that "God is dead" caused a sensation and who insisted that superior human beings have a right to replace the mob mentality of traditional values.

Nimrod: Called in the Bible a "mighty hunter before the Lord" and the first king of Babel. He is used as a symbol of tyranny.

Nineveh: Ancient capital of the Assyrian Empire.

Núñez, Rafael (1825–1894): President of Colombia for several terms, he appointed Darío as Colombian Consul in Buenos Aires.

Núñez de Arce, Gaspar (1834–1903): Spanish moral, philosophical, and political poet who reacted against Romantic emotionalism.

"odor di femina": Italian for "scent of a woman."

Olympic: Reference to Olympus, the abode of the gods in Greek and Roman myth.

Omar Khayyam: Persian poet of the twelfth century, author of *The Rubaiyat*.

oriflamme: Sacred banner of the French kings in the Middle Ages, of red silk split into points like a flame, on a golden lance. In earlier traditions the oriflamme is blue.

Orlando: Hero of a number of epics, including Ariosto's *Orlando furioso*, he corresponds to the French hero Roland.

Orpheus: Mythical poet and one of the Argonauts, whose lyrical power could tame wild animals and move rocks and trees. His lyre was made of tortoiseshell.

Orphic: Of or relating to Orpheus or the concept of poetry as having a sacred origin or purpose.

Oscar II (1829–1907): King of Sweden and Norway, he traveled widely through Europe and always admired the arts, especially literature, and was elected to several academies.

Ossa and Pelion: Mountains in Greece, the abode of the god Apollo.

Otumba: Site of a Spanish victory over the Aztecs and their allies in 1520, near what is today Mexico City.

pallium: Roman name for a large cloak typically worn by philosophers.

Pan: Greek god of the woods and hills, associated with satyrs and Dionysus (Bacchus), he typically has goat legs and carries the syrinx or shepherd's pipe. The Romans identified him as Faunus. He is one of the most frequently mentioned gods in Darío's poems.

Pandora: Woman created out of clay whose irresistible curiosity brought all manner of woes into the world when she opened a box she had been forbidden to open. The last thing to escape the box, and quite different from the rest, was Hope.

Pandoric: Of or relating to Pandora, particularly to the evils she unleashed on the world.

Panic: Of or relating to the god Pan.

Parthenon: Famous temple of Athena from the Golden Age of Greece, whose ruins still crown the city of Athens.

Pascal, Blaise (1623–1662): French mathematician, physicist, and theologian, author of the collection of essays entitled *Pensées*, in which he speaks of a glimpse of infinite existence beyond even the power of imagination, as if looking into an abyss.

Pegasus: The winged horse of Greek mythology, associated with Eos (Aurora), goddess of the Dawn, and the Muses.

peplum: A long garment or tunic, hanging in folds, worn by women in ancient Greece.

Pérez, René: Chilean musician and Darío's friend in Paris.

Peru: Country in South America, site of the Spanish conquest of the Incan Empire in the sixteenth century.

Philomela: In Greek myth, the sister of Procne; she was turned into a nightingale. The name frequently appears in Darío as a poetic word for nightingale.

Phocas: The name in "To Phocas the Peasant" refers to the poet's son Rubén Darío Sánchez, his first child with Francisca. The boy died when he was just two years old. The name and the expression probably come from "Phocas le jardinier" (Phocas the gardener), published in 1898, by the French poet Francis Vielé-Griffin.

Pierrot: The sad clown of French pantomime.

Pindar (518?-438? B.C.): Traditionally considered the greatest lyric poet of ancient Greece, whose surviving *Odes* are justly famous.

Polyphemus: A Cyclops—a manlike giant with one eye in the center of his forehead—who figures in the legend from which the Spanish poet Luis de Góngora drew inspiration for his brilliant but difficult masterpiece, the *Fábula de Polifemo y Galatea* (Fable of Polyphemus and Galatea).

Pomona: A Roman rural divinity of Etruscan origin, protector of gardens, flowers, and fruit. She is represented with a basket full of fruits and vegetables.

Poussin, Nicolas (1594-1665): French painter of the Baroque period who sought harmony in his depiction of nature, including a "Landscape with Polyphemus," the Cyclops in Luis de Góngora's masterpiece to which Darío refers.

Profane Prose: Darío's masterpiece of full-fledged modernist poetry, published in 1896. See the introduction.

profane song: Reference to Darío's book of poetry, *Prosas profanas* (Profane prose).

Psyche: In Greek mythology, a beautiful woman with butterfly wings who personifies the human soul and is the beloved of Eros (Cupid).

Publius Ovid Naso (43 B.C.- 17 A.D.): Roman poet more commonly called Ovid, author of *Ars Amatoria* (The Art of Love) and *Metamorphoses* (Transformations).

Pyrenees: Mountain chain separating Spain and France.

Pythagorean: Of or relating to Pythagoras, Greek philosopher, mathematician, and mystic of the sixth century B.C., whose doctrine included the transmigration of souls and the harmony of the universe based on number and mathematical principles, the music of the spheres.

"Que sais-je?" French phrase for What do I know?, underscoring the skeptical methodology of French philosopher Michel de Montaigne (1533–1592).

Quevedo y Villegas, Francisco de (1580-1645): One of the great writers of the Golden Age of Spain, justly famous for his profound use of language and conceits, as well as for biting satires.

Quixote: See Don Quixote.

Rodó, José Enrique (1872-1917): Uruguayan literary critic and philosopher, the most important essayist of Hispanic modernism, whose influential book *Ariel* (1900) called on Latin America to hold fast to its cultural traditions in the face of U.S. materialism.

Roland: French hero, one of Charlemagne's legendary knights, who in the medieval epic *La chanson de Roland* (The song of Roland) dies at Roncevaux, a pass in the Pyrenees mountains, fighting Moslem invaders.

Roman she-wolf: Romulus and Remus, twin sons of the god Mars and a Vestal Virgin, are the legendary founders of Rome. As infants they were set adrift to die on the Tiber River but washed ashore and were adopted by a she-wolf, who suckled and protected them until a shepherd family found them.

romance: Traditional Spanish ballad verse-form, consisting of eight-syllable lines; only even-numbered verses are rhymed in assonance, and therefore the poem nearly always ends on an even-numbered line.

Romancero: Compilation of Spanish *romances*, which began to be published in the sixteenth century.

rondel: A French poetic form consisting of fourteen eight-syllable lines, only two rhymes, and two verses repeated as a refrain, all according to fixed rules.

Ronsard, Pierre de (1524–1585): French poet, enormously famous in his own time as the "Prince of Poets," whose principal themes were patriotism, love, and death.

Roosevelt, Theodore (1858–1919): U.S. president whose policies claimed the right of the United States to interfere in the affairs of all nations in the Western Hemisphere. After the Spanish-American War of 1898, in which he served with his "Rough Riders" in Cuba, Roosevelt's statements—"Walk softly and carry a big stick," for example—and his interventionist actions to make the Panama Canal a reality were considered by many Hispanics as provocative and imperialist.

Rostand, Edmond (1868–1918): French poet and dramatist best known for his play *Cyrano de Bergerac*.

Roxanne: The rich, beautiful, intelligent cousin of Cyrano de Bergerac in Rostand's play, she remains unaware of his love for her until the final scene.

Salome: See Herodias.

Sancho Panza: Portly neighbor of the man calling himself Don Quixote, he agrees to play the part of squire to the knight, and proves a hilarious, down-to-earth, but somewhat gullible sidekick, the perfect foil for his master's pomposity and idealism.

San Marco: Famously picturesque square in the city of Venice, Italy.

satyr: In Greek mythology, one of the hairy libertine spirits of the mountains and woods who have pointed ears, goat legs, and a short tail, gambol with nymphs, and carouse with Dionysus. They symbolize male lust and debauchery.

Segismundo: Protagonist of the drama *La vida es sueño* (Life is a dream) by Calderón de la Barca (1600–1681). Imprisoned as an infant by his father, a king of Poland, he is brought to the court as a young man and at first cannot distinguish between what is real and what is not.

Segor: City near the Dead Sea in present-day Israel, to which the patriarch Lot fled as Sodom and Gomorrah were destroyed, and where his wife was turned into a pillar of salt.

septentrional: Referring to the north or the northern regions. In Darío, it may refer to "northern" peoples: the U.S. or the Anglo-Saxon cultures.

seraphim: In Christian tradition they comprise one of the nine orders of angels, have six wings, and stand in the presence of God. The singular form is seraph.

serventesio: Stanza form consisting of four (usually eleven-syllable) verses that rhyme ABAB.

Scheherazade: Beautiful and resourceful storyteller of *A Thousand and One Arabian Nights*, daughter of the vizier, she marries a homicidal sultan in the habit of murdering his wives the morning after the wedding. By never finishing a story she holds the sultan spellbound night after night, until he relents and allows her to live and rule with him.

sibyl: In classical mythology, an oracle or prophetess.

Siegfried: Mythical Germanic hero of the *Nibelungenlied*, or Ring Cycle, descended from the god Odin.

Sodom: Biblical city near the Dead Sea destroyed for its depravity.

Spanish Lion: Reference to the emblem of a lion in the shield on the Spanish flag.

spes: Latin for "hope."

syrinx: Pan's pipe, consisting of seven to nine reeds, used by shepherds.

Thanatos: The god Death in Greek mythology.

Theocritus: Hellenistic Greek poet from the third-century B.C., who perfected the pastoral motif.

Tirso de Molina (1584?–1648): Playwright of Spain's Golden Age, whose most famous work is *El burlador de Sevilla* (The scoffer of Seville), the first known treatment of the Don Juan legend.

Titania: Another name for the moon.

Tizona: One of the Cid's legendary swords.

Toledo: Ancient city in central Spain, renowned for its swords.

Tolstoy, Leo (1828–1910): Russian writer, author of *War and Peace* and other novels. Darío mentions him in "To Roosevelt" for his austere and humble life.

Triptolemical: Of or relating to Triptolemus, the young prince of Eleusis. According to classical mythology, the earth goddess Demeter gave him a chariot drawn by flying dragons and the first grains of wheat, with which he sowed the entire earth.

triton: Mythical being in the shape of a man from the waist up and a dolphin below, he blows on a seashell to control the waves.

Valle-Inclán, Ramón del (1866–1936): Spanish poet, novelist, and playwright, author of *Sonata de otoño, Luces de Bohemia,* and *Divinas palabras,* among many other works. An extreme individualist, he evolved from a modernist style to what he himself labeled *esperpento,* a grotesque style of comedy drawing on elements of tragedy and deformation. Darío admired him and wrote in his honor the poem "*Soneto autumnal al Marqués de Bradomín*" (Autumnal sonnet to the Marquis of Bradomín), using the name of Valle-Inclán's most famous character.

Vargas Vila, José María (1860–1933): Colombian essayist and friend of Darío who traveled with him through Europe and wrote a biography of him.

Vascos: Reference to Vasco da Gama (1469–1524), navigator who discovered the sea route to India in 1498 and established Portugal as a world power.

Velázquez, Diego de (1599–1660): One of the greatest painters of Europe, he had no equal in his own time, with the exception of Rembrandt. As a young man he painted a mesmerizing portrait of the ailing and embittered Luis de Góngora a few years before the poet's death, which undoubtedly played a key role in the appointment of Velázquez as court painter at the age of twenty-four.

Venus: In classical mythology, the goddess of beauty and love, analogous to the Greek Aphrodite. It was she who gave Atalanta's suitor the golden apples to distract the huntress during their race. The planet Venus is known as both the morning and the evening star, the last to dim at dawn and the first to appear at dusk.

Verlaine, Paul (1844–1896): French symbolist poet, though he officially distanced himself from the movement, whose tempestuous and scandalous life tended to overshadow his literary genius in his own time. He is one of the writers—Victor Hugo being the other—whom Darío most admired.

Versailles: Palace built by King Louis XIV from 1664 to 1715. Surrounded by gardens and fountains, it is one of the most popular tourist sites in France.

Vincent de Paul, Saint (1581–1660): French founder of religious societies dedicated to helping the poor on a basis of practical love.

Whitman, Walt (1819–1892): U.S. writer, defender of democracy, self-styled poet of the people, and author of *Leaves of Grass*.

Zorrilla, José (1817–1893): Spanish poet and dramatist who took part in the Romantic movement and revived the archetype Don Juan in an extremely popular play written in verse, *Don Juan Tenorio*.

Bibliography

WORKS BY RUBÉN DARÍO

A la Unión Centroamericana. León, Nicaragua: Tipografía de J. Hernández, 1883.
Oda. Al libertador Bolívar. Del héroe americano. San Salvador: Imprenta de la
  Ilustración, 1883.
Epístolas y poemas. (Primeras notas.) Managua: Tipografía Nacional, 1885 and 1888.
Abrojos. Santiago de Chile: Imprenta Cervantes, 1887.
Emelina. Valparaíso: Imprenta y Litografía Universal, 1887. (In collaboration with
  Eduardo Poirier.)
"Canto épico a las glorias de Chile." Certamen Varela. Obras premiadas y distinguidas.
  Vol. 1:186–196. Santiago de Chile: Imprenta Cervantes, 1887.
"Otoñales (Rimas)." Certamen Varela. Obras premiadas y distinguidas. Vol. 1:52–66.
  Santiago de Chile: Imprenta Cervantes, 1887.
Azul . . . . Valparaíso: Imprenta y Litografía Excélsior, 1888. 2d ed. expanded, in
  Guatemala City: Imprenta de "La Unión," 1890. Definitive ed. in Buenos Aires:
  Biblioteca de "La Nación," 1905.
A. de Gilbert. San Salvador: Imprenta Nacional, 1889.
Prosas profanas y otros poemas. Buenos Aires: Imprenta de Pablo E. Coni e hijos, 1896.
  2d ed., expanded, Paris: Librería de la Viuda de Ch. Bouret, 1901.
Los raros. Buenos Aires: Tipografía "La Vasconia," 1896. 2d ed., expanded, in
  Barcelona: Maucci, 1905.
Castelar. Madrid: Rodríguez Serra, 1899.
España contemporánea. Paris: Garnier Hermanos, 1901.
Peregrinaciones. Paris: Librería de la Vda. de Ch. Bouret, 1901.
La caravana pasa. Paris: Garnier Hermanos, 1902.
Tierras solares. Madrid: Leonardo Williams, 1904.
Cantos de vida y esperanza. Los cisnes y otros poemas. Madrid: Tipografía de la Revista de
  Archivos, Bibliotecas y Museos, 1905. 2d ed., Barcelona: F. Granada y Cía., 1907.
Oda a Mitre (Chapbook). Paris: Imprimerie A. Eymeaud, 1906.
Opiniones. Madrid: Fernando Fe, 1906.
El canto errante. Madrid: M. Pérez Villavicencio, 1907.
Parisiana. Madrid: Fernando Fe, 1907.
El viaje a Nicaragua. Madrid: Biblioteca "Ateneo," 1909.
Alfonso XIII (Chapbook). Madrid: Biblioteca "Ateneo," 1909.
Poema del otoño y otros poemas. Madrid: Biblioteca "Ateneo," 1910.
Letras. Paris: Garnier Hermanos, 1911.
Todo al vuelo. Madrid: Renacimiento, 1912.
Canto a la Argentina y otros poemas. Madrid: Biblioteca Corona, 1914.
Muy siglo XVIII. Madrid: Biblioteca Corona, 1914.
La vida de Rubén Darío escrita por él mismo. Barcelona: Maucci, 1915.
Muy antiguo y muy moderno. Madrid: Biblioteca Corona, 1915.
Y una sed de ilusiones infinita. Madrid: Biblioteca Corona, 1916.
Cabezas. Buenos Aires: Ediciones Mínimas, 1916.

The following list presents some works we consider important and useful, as well as all the works cited in our introduction. For a more complete reference to the Darío bibliography, we recommend consulting Del Greco (1969), Harrison (1970), Jirón Terán (1967 and 1981), and Woodbridge (1975).

Abate, Sandro. "Elementos hagiográficos en la obra de Rubén Darío: Poesía y cuento." *Hispania* 79 (1996): 411–418.

———. *Modernismo, Rubén Darío y su influencia en el realismo mágico.* Bahía Blanca, Argentina: Editorial de la Universidad Nacional del Sur, 1998.

Abreu Gómez, Ermilo. *Crítica literaria (Temas americanos): Rubén Darío.* San Salvador: Ministerio de Educación, 1963.

Acereda, Alberto. "Darío moderno, Bécquer romántico: En torno a un lugar común de la modernidad poética en lengua española." *Cuadernos Americanos* 80 (2000): 175–193.

———. "De Quevedo a Darío: Resonancias líricas y actitud vital." *La Perinola: Revista de Investigación Quevediana* 5 (2001): 11–23.

———. *El Modernismo poético: Estudio crítico y antología temática.* Salamanca: Ediciones Almar, 2001.

———. "Introducción: Valor y modernidad en la poesía de Rubén Darío." In *Rubén Darío: Y una sed de ilusiones infinita.* Edited by A. Acereda. Barcelona: Lumen, 2000, 9–34.

———. "La creación poética en 'Salutación del optimista,' de Rubén Darío." *Ojáncano: Revista de Literatura Española* 9 (1994): 3–17.

———. "La expresión del alma en el modernismo: Relaciones contextuales entre la 'Sonatina' de Rubén Darío y algunos escritos de Amado Nervo." *Hispanófila* 115 (1995): 29–38.

———. "La hispanidad amenazada: Rubén Darío y la Guerra del 98." In *The Legacy of the Mexican and Spanish-American Wars: Legal, Literary, and Historical Perspectives.* Edited by G. D. Keller and C. Candelaria. Tempe, Arizona: Bilingual Press, 2000, 99–110.

———. "La modernidad existencial en la poesía de Rubén Darío." *Bulletin of Spanish Studies* 79 (2002): 149–169.

———. "La poesía erótica de Rubén Darío." In *Rubén Darío: Poesía erótica.* Ed. A. Acereda. Madrid: Ediciones Hiperión, 1997, 9–59.

———. "La poética del Modernismo: Una hermenéutica de la modernidad existencial." *Cuadernos Americanos* 85 (2001): 85–103.

———. "La trayectoria poética de Rubén Darío." In *Rubén Darío: Poesía selecta.* Edited by A. Acereda. Madrid: Visor, 1996, 7–37.

———. "La urgente necesidad de editar a Darío." In *Rubén Darío: Antología poética.* Edited by A. Acereda. Buenos Aires: Editorial Sudamericana, 1996, 9–38.

———. "Modernismo y modernidad: Deslindes de una poética dariana." *Chasqui: Revista de Literatura Latinoamericana* 30 (2001): 20–34.

———. "Música de las ideas y música del verbo: Versolibrismo dariano." In *Rubén Darío: La creación, argumento poético y expresivo.* Edited by Alberto Acereda and Manuel Mantero. *Anthropos* (1997): 81–89.

———. "Problemas críticos y configurativos del Modernismo literario hispánico." *Cuadernos del Lazarillo* 19 (2000): 22–29.

—. "Rubén Darío en la poesía española del siglo XX. (Recuperación de un poeta relegado)." *Letras Hispanas* 2 (1997): 46–60.

———. "Rubén Darío en la poesía española del siglo XX. (Recuperación de un poeta relegado)." *Letras Hispanas* 2 (1997): 46–60.

———. "Rubén Darío o el proceso creativo de *Prosas profanas.*" *Anales de Literatura Hispanoamericana* 28 (1999): 415–429.

———. *Rubén Darío, poeta trágico. (Una nueva visión.)* Barcelona: Editorial Teide, 1992.

———. "Textual Approaches to Rubén Darío: Was There a Primitive Edition of *Prosas Profanas?*" *Romance Notes* 39 (1998): 137–144.

———, ed. *Rubén Darío: Poemas filosóficos.* Madrid: Ediciones Hiperión, 2002.

Aching, Gerard. *The Politics of Spanish American "Modernismo": By Exquisite Design.* Cambridge: Cambridge UP, 1997.

Aguado Andreut, Salvador. *Por el mundo poético de Rubén Darío.* Guatemala City: Editorial Universitaria, 1966.

Alarcón Sierra, Rafael. *Entre el Modernismo y la modernidad: La poesía de Manuel Machado ("Alma" y "Caprichos").* Seville: Diputación de Sevilla, 1999.

Alemán Bolaños, Gustavo. *La juventud de Rubén Darío.* Guatemala City: Editorial Universitaria, 1958.

Álvarez, Dictino, ed. *Cartas de Rubén Darío: Epistolario inédito del poeta con sus amigos españoles.* Madrid: Taurus, 1963.

Ancona Ponce, Mario. *Rubén Darío y América: El Nuevo Mundo, como realidad política en la poesía rubeniana.* Mexico City: Parresia, 1968.

Anderson Imbert, Enrique. *La originalidad de Rubén Darío.* Buenos Aires: Centro Editor de América Latina, 1967.

Arellano, Jorge Eduardo. *Contribuciones al estudio de Rubén Darío.* Managua: Dirección General de Bibliotecas y Archivos, 1981.

———. *Rubén Darío en la Academia.* Managua: Academia Nicaragüense, 1997.

Armijo, Roberto. *Rubén Darío y su intuición del mundo.* San Salvador: Editorial Universitaria de El Salvador, 1968.

Balseiro, José Agustín. *Seis estudios sobre Rubén Darío.* Madrid: Gredos, 1967.

Barcia, Pedro Luis, ed. *Escritos dispersos de Rubén Darío recogidos de periódicos de Buenos Aires.* La Plata: Universidad de La Plata, 1968.

Barrera, Trinidad, ed. *Modernismo y modernidad en el ámbito hispánico.* Seville: Universidad Internacional de Andalucía—Asociación Española de Estudios Literarios Hispanoamericanos, 1998.

Barrientos Tecún, Dante. "Una lectura contemporánea de Rubén Darío: 'Canto de esperanza.' " In *El cisne y la paloma: Once estudios sobre Rubén Darío.* Edited by Jacques Issorel. Perpignan, France: Presses Universitaires de Perpignan, 1995, 12–18.

Bary, Leslie. "A Truck Named Rubén Darío: Modernismo as Chronotope and Cultural Resistance." *Siglo XX / 20th Century* 13 (1995): 321–328.

Battistessa, Ángel J. *Rubén Darío: Semblanza y florilegio.* Buenos Aires: Corregidor, 1988.

Bazil, Osvaldo. *Rubén Darío y sus amigos dominicanos.* Bogotá: Ediciones Espiral, 1948.

Beltrán Guerrero, Luis. *Rubén Darío y Venezuela.* Caracas: Instituto Nacional de Cultura y Bellas Artes, 1967.

Blasco, Javier, ed. "El estado de la cuestión: Modernismo y modernidad." *Ínsula* (special issue) (1987): 485–487.

Bonilla, Abelardo. *América y el pensamiento poético de Rubén Darío.* San José: Editorial Costa Rica, 1967.

Bosch, María del C. *Rubén Darío a Mallorca.* Palma de Mallorca, Spain: Comissió de les Illes Balears per a la Commemoració del Vé Centenari, 1992.

Bourne, Louis. "El sincretismo inestable de Rubén Darío: El escéptico se vuelve agnóstico." In *Rubén Darío: La creación, argumento poético y expresivo*. Edited by Alberto Acereda and Manuel Mantero. *Anthropos* (1997): 120–126.

———. *Fuerza invisible: Lo divino en la poesía de Rubén Darío*. Málaga, Spain: Analecta Malacitana, 1999.

Bousoño, Carlos. "Lo que debemos a Rubén." *ABC Literario* (July 30, 1988): iii.

Bradbury, Malcolm, and James McFarlane, eds. *Modernism: A Guide to European Literature (1890–1930)*. London: Penguin Books, 1991.

Briceño Jáuregui, Manuel. *Rubén Darío: Artífice del epíteto*. Caracas: Universidad Católica Andrés Bello, 1972.

Cabezas, Juan Antonio. *Rubén Darío: Un poeta y una vida*. Madrid: Ediciones Morata, 1944.

Cano, José Luis. "Juan Ramón Jiménez y Rubén Darío." *La Torre* 5 (1957): 119–136.

———. "Rubén y Unamuno." In *Rubén Darío: La creación, argumento poético y expresivo*. Edited by Alberto Acereda and Manuel Mantero. *Anthropos* (1997): 137.

Capdevila, Arturo. *Rubén Darío: "Un bardo rei."* Buenos Aires: Espasa-Calpe, 1946.

Cardwell, Richard A. "Darío and *el arte puro*: The Enigma of Life and the Beguilement of Art." *Bulletin of Hispanic Studies* 47 (1970): 37–51.

Cardwell, Richard A., and Bernard McGuirk, eds. *¿Qué es el Modernismo? Nueva encuesta. Nuevas lecturas*. Boulder, Colo.: Society of Spanish and Spanish American Studies, 1993.

Carilla, Emilio. *Una etapa decisiva de Rubén Darío: Rubén Darío en la Argentina*. Madrid: Gredos, 1967.

Celma, Pilar. *La pluma ante el espejo: Visión autocrítica del fin de siglo*. Salamanca: Universidad de Salamanca, 1989.

———. *Literatura y periodismo en las revistas del fin de siglo: Estudio e índices (1888–1907)*. Madrid: Júcar, 1991.

Caso Muñoz, Concepción. "Coloquio de los centauros" de Rubén Darío: Estudio y comentario. Mexico City: Universidad Nacional de México, 1965.

Coloma González, Fidel. *Introducción al estudio de 'Azul . . .'* Managua: Editorial Manolo Morales, 1988.

Concha, Jaime. "Los *Cantos de vida y esperanza* darianos como conjunto poético." *Cuadernos Americanos* 169 (1988): 3–11.

———. *Rubén Darío*. Madrid: Júcar, 1975.

Conde, Carmen. *Acompañando a Francisca Sánchez: Resumen de una vida junto a Rubén Darío*. Managua: Editorial Unión, 1964.

———. "El archivo de Rubén Darío en España." *Cuadernos del Congreso por la Libertad de la Cultura* 29 (1958): 29–34.

Contreras, Francisco. *Rubén Darío, su vida y su obra*. Santiago de Chile: Ediciones Ercilla, 1937.

Cuadra, Pablo Antonio. "Rubén Darío y la aventura literaria del mestizaje." *Cuadernos Hispanoamericanos* 398 (1983): 307–321.

Darío, Rubén. *Obras completas*. 5 vols. Madrid: Afrodisio Aguado, 1950–55.

Davison, Ned J. *El concepto de Modernismo en la crítica hispánica*. Buenos Aires: Nova, 1975.

Debicki, Andrew P., and Michael J. Doudoroff. "Estudio preliminar." In *Rubén Darío. Azul . . . ; Prosas profanas*. Madrid: Alhambra, 1985, 1–71.

Del Greco, Arnold A. *Repertorio bibliográfico del mundo de Rubén Darío*. New York: Las Américas, 1969.

Derusha, Will. " 'El gran Viejo' de Rubén Darío." In *Rubén Darío: La creación, argumento poético y expresivo.* Edited by Alberto Acereda and Manuel Mantero. *Anthropos* (1997): 141–145.

Derusha, Will, and Alberto Acereda, eds. and trans. *Selected Poems of Rubén Darío: A Bilingual Anthology.* Lewisburg: Bucknell UP, 2001.

Díaz-Plaja, Guillermo. *Rubén Darío: La vida. La obra. Notas críticas.* Barcelona: Sociedad General de Publicaciones, 1930.

Díez de Revenga, Francisco J. *Rubén Darío en la métrica española y otros ensayos.* Murcia, Spain: Departamento de Literatura Hispánica—Universidad de Murcia, 1985.

———. "Vitalismo y sensibilidad de Rubén Darío: Valoración actual." In *Rubén Darío: La creación, argumento poético y expresivo.* Edited by Alberto Acereda and Manuel Mantero. *Anthropos* (1997): 64–68.

Doll, Kristine. "Rubén Darío and the Escola Mallorquina." *Anales de la Literatura Española* 19 (1994): 33–45.

Doyle, Henry Grattan. *A Bibliography of Rubén Darío (1867–1916).* Cambridge, Mass.: Harvard UP, 1935.

Ellis, Keith. *Critical Approaches to Rubén Darío.* Toronto: University of Toronto Press, 1974.

———. "Un análisis estructural del poema 'A Roosevelt.'" *Cuadernos Hispanoamericanos* 212–213 (1967): 523–528.

Escudero, Alfonso. *Rubén Darío, el modernismo y otras páginas.* Santiago: Editorial Nascimiento, 1985.

Espina, Eduardo. "Rubén Darío: La timidez del cisne y el cuerpo ausente." *La Torre* 34 (1995): 201–220.

Fernández, Teodosio. *Rubén Darío.* Madrid: Historia 16—Quorum, 1987.

Fernández Retamar, Roberto. *Encuentro con Rubén Darío.* Havana: Casa de Las Américas, 1967

Ferreiro Villanueva, Cristina. *Claves de la obra poética de Rubén Darío.* Madrid: Ciclo Editorial, 1990.

Feustle, Joseph A. *Poesía y mística: Rubén Darío, Juan Ramón Jiménez y Octavio Paz.* Veracruz, Mexico: Universidad Veracruzana, 1978.

Fiore, Dolores A. *Rubén Darío in Search of Inspiration: Greco-Roman Mythology in His Stories and Poetry.* New York: Las Américas, 1963.

Fogelquist, Donald L. *The Literary Collaboration and the Personal Correspondence of Rubén Darío and Juan Ramón Jiménez.* Coral Gables: University of Miami Press, 1956.

Freixa, Mireia. *El Modernismo en España.* Madrid: Cátedra, 1986.

Fuertes-Manjón, Roberto. "La obra novelística de Rubén Darío y la narrativa centroamericana." In *Rubén Darío: La creación, argumento poético y expresivo.* Edited by Alberto Acereda and Manuel Mantero. *Anthropos* (1997): 114–117.

Gálvez Carlisle, Gloria. "Releyendo *Prosas profanas:* La figura exótica como alegoría del proceso creativo." *Acta Literaria* 21 (1996): 15–23.

García-Méndez, Javier. "*Azul . . .* de Darío: Textualización del culto a la belleza." *Cahiers du Monde Hispanique et Luso-Brésilien* 64 (1995): 91–100.

García Morales, Alfonso, ed. *Rubén Darío: Estudios en el centenario de 'Los raros' y 'Prosas profanas.'* Seville: Universidad de Sevilla, 1998.

Garciasol, Ramón de. *Lección de Rubén Darío.* Madrid: Taurus, 1960.

———. *Rubén Darío en sus versos.* Madrid: Ediciones Cultura Hispánica del Centro Iberoamericano de Cooperación, 1978.

Garfield, Evelyn Picon, and Ivan A. Schulman, eds. *'Las entrañas del vacío': Ensayos sobre la modernidad hispanoamericana.* Mexico City: Cuadernos Americanos, 1984.

Gauggel, Karl Hermann. *El cisne modernista: Sus orígenes y supervivencia.* New York: Peter Lang, 1997.

Geist, Anthony L., and José B. Monleón, eds. *Modernism and Its Margins: Reinscribing Cultural Modernity from Spain and Latin America.* New York: Garland Publishing, 1999.

Ghiano, Juan Carlos. *Análisis de "Cantos de vida y esperanza."* Buenos Aires: Centro Editor de América Latina, 1968.

———. *Análisis de "Prosas profanas."* Buenos Aires: Centro Editor de América Latina, 1968.

———. *Rubén Darío.* Buenos Aires: Centro Editor de América Latina, 1967.

Ghiraldo, Alberto. *El archivo de Rubén Darío.* Buenos Aires: Losada, 1943.

Gicovate, Bernardo. "El modernismo y su historia." *Hispanic Review* 32 (1964): 217–226.

Giordano, Jaime. *La edad del ensueño: Sobre la imaginación poética de Rubén Darío.* Santiago de Chile: Editorial Universitaria, 1971.

Gómez Bedate, Pilar. "Las joyas de Rubén Darío." In *Rubén Darío: La creación, argumento poético y expresivo.* Edited by Alberto Acereda and Manuel Mantero. Anthropos (1997): 68–75.

González, Aníbal. *La crónica modernista hispanoamericana.* Madrid: José Porrúa Turanzas, 1983.

———. *La novela modernista.* Madrid: Gredos, 1987.

———. "Modernist Prose." In *The Cambridge History of Latin American Literature: The Twentieth Century.* Edited by Roberto González Echevarría and Enrique Pupo Walker. Vol. 2. Cambridge: Cambridge UP, 1996, 69–113.

González-Gerth, M., and G. D. Schade, eds. *Rubén Darío Centennial Studies.* Austin: University of Texas, 1970.

Grass, Roland, and William R. Risley, eds. *Waiting for Pegasus: Studies on the Presence of Symbolism and Decadence in Hispanic Letters.* Macomb: Western Illinois UP, 1979.

Green Huie, Jorge. *El lenguaje poético de Rubén Darío.* Managua: Universidad Americana, 1999.

Gullón, Ricardo. *Direcciones del Modernismo.* Madrid: Alianza, 1990.

———. *El Modernismo visto por los modernistas.* Barcelona: Guadarrama, 1980.

———. "Pitagorismo y modernismo." *Mundo Nuevo* 7 (1967): 22–32.

———. "Relaciones entre Rubén Darío y Juan Ramón Jiménez." *Papeles de Son Armadans* 31 (1963): 233–248.

———. "Rubén Darío y el erotismo." *Papeles de Son Armadans* 136 (1967): 143–158.

Gutiérrez Girardot, Rafael. *Modernismo.* Barcelona: Montesinos, 1983.

Gutiérrez, José Ismael. "Crítica y modernidad en las revistas literarias: La *Revista de América* de Rubén Darío y Ricardo Jaimes Freyre." *La Torre* 3 (1997): 15–38.

Harrison, Helene Westbrook. *An Analytical Index of the Complete Poetical Works of Rubén Darío.* Washington, D.C.: Microcard Editions, 1970.

Henríquez Ureña, Max. *Breve historia del Modernismo.* Mexico City: Fondo de Cultura Económica, 1954.

Hernández de López, Ana María. *El "Mundial Magazine" de Rubén Darío.* Madrid: Beramar, 1989.

Herrero, Javier. "Fin de siglo y modernismo: La Virgen y la Hetaíra." *Revista Iberoamericana* 110–111 (1980): 29–50.

Herrero Mayor, Avelino. *El castellano de Rubén Darío: Idioma y estilo.* Buenos Aires: Ministerio de Cultura y Educación, 1972.

Hierro, José. "La huella de Rubén en los poetas de la posguerra española." *Cuadernos Hispanoamericanos* 212–213 (1967): 347–367.

Hurtado Chamorro, Alejandro. *La mitología griega en Rubén Darío*. Ávila, Spain: La Muralla, 1967.

Ibáñez, Roberto, ed. *Páginas desconocidas de Rubén Darío*. Montevideo: Biblioteca de Marcha, 1970.

Ingwersen, Sonya A. *Light and Longing: Silva and Darío. Modernism and Religious Heterodoxy*. New York: Peter Lang, 1986.

Irving, Evelyn Uhrhan de. "Francisca Sánchez and the Seminario-Archivo Rubén Darío." *Hispania* 41 (1958): 35–38.

Issorel, Jacques, ed. *El cisne y la paloma: Once estudios sobre Rubén Darío*. Perpignan, France: Presses Universitaires de Perpignan, 1995.

Jensen, Theodore W. "Modernista Pythagorean Literature: The Symbolist Inspiration." In *Waiting for Pegasus: Studies on the Presence of Symbolism and Decadence in Hispanic Letters*. Edited by R. Grass and W. Risley. Macomb: Western Illinois UP, 1979, 169–179.

———. "Rubén Darío's Final Profession of Pythagorean Faith." *Latin American Literary Review* 20 (1982): 7–19.

Jiménez, José Olivio, ed. *Antología crítica de la poesía modernista hispanoamericana*. Madrid: Hiperión, 1994.

———. "Armonía verbal, melodía ideal: Un libro, *Prosas profanas*." In *Prosas profanas*. By Rubén Darío. Edited by J. O. Jiménez. Madrid: Alianza, 1992, 7–25.

———. "Martí, Darío y la intuición modernista de la armonía universal." *Círculo: Revista de Cultura* 18 (1989): 105–121.

Jiménez, Juan Ramón. *El Modernismo: Notas de un curso (1953)*. Edited by R. Gullón and E. Fernández Méndez. Mexico City: Aguilar, 1962.

———. *Mi Rubén Darío (1900–1956)*. Edited by Antonio Sánchez Romeralo. Moguer, Spain: Ediciones de la Fundación, 1991.

Jirón Terán, José. "Bibliografía activa de Rubén Darío (1883–1980)." *Cuadernos de Bibliografía Nicaragüense* 2 (1981): 1–40.

———. *Bibliografía general de Rubén Darío (Julio 1883–Enero 1967)*. Managua: Universidad Nacional Autónoma de Nicaragua, 1967.

———, ed. *Quince prólogos de Rubén Darío*. Managua: Instituto Nicaragüense de Cultura, 1997.

Jitrik, Noé. *Las contradicciones del Modernismo*. Mexico City: El Colegio de México, 1978.

Jozef, Bella. "Modernismo y vanguardia (Del Modernismo a la modernidad)." In *Nuevos asedios al Modernismo*. Edited by I. A. Schulman. Madrid: Taurus, 1987, 62–75.

Jrade, Cathy Login. *Modernismo, Modernity, and the Development of Spanish American Literature*. Austin: University of Texas Press, 1998.

———. "Modernist Poetry." In *The Cambridge History of Latin American Literature: The Twentieth Century*. Edited by Roberto González Echevarría and Enrique Pupo Walker. Vol. 2. Cambridge: Cambridge UP, 1996, 7–68.

———. *Rubén Darío and the Romantic Search for Unity: The Modernist Recourse to Esoteric Tradition*. Austin: University of Texas Press, 1983.

———. "Socio-political Concerns in the Poetry of Rubén Darío." *Latin American Literary Review* 18 (1990): 36–49.

Kemp, Lysander, trans. *Selected Poems of Rubén Darío*. Austin: University of Texas Press, 1965.

Kirkpatrick, Gwen. *The Dissonant Legacy of "Modernismo": Lugones, Herrera y Reissig and the Voices of Modern Spanish American Poetry*. Berkeley: University of California Press, 1989.

Kolocotroni, Vassiliki, et al., eds. *Modernism: An Anthology of Sources and Documents.* Chicago: University of Chicago Press, 1998.

Larrea, Juan. *Intensidad del canto errante.* Córdoba, Argentina: Facultad de Filosofía y Humanidades—Universidad Nacional de Córdoba, 1972.

―――. *Rubén Darío y la nueva cultura americana.* Valencia: Pre-Textos, 1987.

Litvak, Lily, ed. *El Modernismo.* Madrid: Taurus, 1975.

―――. *Erotismo fin de siglo.* Barcelona: Antoni Bosch, 1979.

―――. *España 1900: Modernismo, anarquismo y fin de siglo.* Barcelona: Anthropos, 1990.

Llopesa, Ricardo, ed. *Rubén Darío en Nueva York.* Valencia: Instituto de Estudios Modernistas, 1997.

―――. *Rubén Darío: Poesías inéditas.* Madrid: Visor, 1988.

Llopesa, Ricardo, et al., eds. *Rubén Darío: Poesías desconocidas completas.* Altea, Spain: Aitana, 1994.

Lloreda, Waldo César. "Cuadro cronológico comentado de Rubén Darío en Chile." *Texto Crítico* 1 (1995): 121–168.

LoDato, Rosemary M. *Beyond the Glitter: The Language of Gems in Modernista Writers: Rubén Darío, Ramón del Valle-Inclán, and José Asunción Silva.* Lewisburg: Bucknell UP, 1999.

López-Calvo, Ignacio. "Las muertes de Rubén Darío en la poesía española." *La Torre* 37 (1996): 1–7.

López Estrada, Francisco. *Rubén Darío y la Edad Media: Una perspectiva poco conocida sobre la vida y obra del escritor.* Barcelona: Planeta, 1971.

López-Morillas, Juan. "El *Azul* de Rubén Darío: ¿Galicismo mental o lingüístico?" *Revista Hispánica Moderna* 10 (1944): 9–14.

Lorenz, Erika. *Rubén Darío: "Bajo el divino imperio de la música." Estudio sobre la significación de un principio estético.* Translated by Fidel Coloma González. Managua: Ediciones Academia Nicaragüense de la Lengua, 1960.

Loveluck, Juan. "Rubén Darío y sus primeros críticos (1888–1900)." *Revista Iberoamericana* 64 (1967): 209–235.

Lozano, Carlos. *La influencia de Rubén Darío en España.* León: Universidad Nacional Autónoma de Nicaragua, 1978.

―――. *Rubén Darío y el modernismo en España (1888–1920): Ensayo de bibliografía comentada.* New York: Las Américas, 1968.

Mainer, José-Carlos, ed. *Modernismo y 98: Historia y crítica de la literatura española.* Vol. 6. Barcelona: Crítica, 1980.

―――, ed. *Modernismo y 98. Primer suplemento: Historia y crítica de la literatura española.* Barcelona: Crítica, 1994.

Maiorana, María Teresa. *Rubén Darío et le mythe du centaure.* Tolosa: L'Amitié Guérinienne, 1957.

Mantero, Manuel. "¿Era masón Rubén Darío?" *Heterodoxia* 6 (1989): 167–172.

―――. *Poetas españoles de posguerra.* Madrid: Espasa-Calpe, 1986.

―――. "Rubén Darío: El talante existencial." In *La poesía del Yo al Nosotros.* By M. Mantero. Madrid: Guadarrama, 1971, 95–117.

Mantero, Manuel, and Alberto Acereda. "Rubén Darío: Encuesta a los poetas españoles." In *Rubén Darío: La creación, argumento poético y expresivo.* Edited by A. Acereda and M. Mantero. *Anthropos* (1997): 146–158.

Mapes, Erwin K. *L'influence française dans l'oeuvre de Rubén Darío.* Paris: Libraire Ancienne Honoré Champion, 1925.

Marasso, Arturo. *Rubén Darío y su creación poética.* Buenos Aires: Kapelusz, 1954.

Marini-Palmieri, Enrique. *El Modernismo literario hispanoamericano: Caracteres esotéricos en las obras de Darío y Lugones*. Buenos Aires: Fernando García Cambeiro, 1989.

Mario, Luis. "A los cien años de Azul . . ." *Círculo: Revista de Cultura* 18 (1989): 123–127.

Martínez, José María. "An Updated Bibliography of Azul . . . and Cantos de vida y esperanza." *Bulletin of Bibliography* 52 (1995): 203–209.

———. "Introducción." In *Rubén Darío: Azul . . . Cantos de vida y esperanza*. Edited by J. M. Martínez. Madrid: Cátedra, 1995, 11–98.

———. "Juan Ramón Jiménez y Rubén Darío: Naturaleza e intimidad en *Arias tristes*." *Revista de Literatura* 113 (1995): 171–180.

———. *Los espacios poéticos de Rubén Darío*. New York: Peter Lang, 1995.

———. "Nuevas luces para las fuentes de Azul . . ." *Hispanic Review* 64 (1997): 199–215.

———. "Para leer Cantos de vida y esperanza." *Hispanic Poetry Review* 1 (1999): 21–50.

———. *Rubén Darío: Addenda*. Palencia: Ediciones Cálamo, 2000.

———. "Una carta inédita de Rubén Darío a Algernon Charles Swinburne." *Bulletin of Hispanic Studies* 74 (1997): 279–292.

Martos, José Manuel. "Góngora, Velázquez y Rubén Darío: El diálogo imposible de 'Trébol.'" *Hispanic Review* 66 (1998): 171–180.

McGuinness, Patrick, ed. *Symbolism, Decadence, and the Fin de Siècle*. Exeter, England: University of Exeter Press, 2000.

McMichael, Charles B., trans. *Rubén Darío: Prosas Profanas and Other Poems*. New York: Nicholas L. Brown, 1922.

Mejía Sánchez, Ernesto. *Cuestiones rubendarianas*. Madrid: Revista de Occidente, 1970.

———, ed. *Rubén Darío: Poesía*. Caracas: Biblioteca Ayacucho, 1977.

Méndez Plancarte, Alfonso, and Antonio Oliver Belmás, eds. *Rubén Darío: Poesías completas*. Madrid: Aguilar, 1968.

Molloy, Sylvia. "Ser y decir en Darío: El poema liminar de *Cantos de vida y esperanza*." *Texto Crítico* 14 (1988): 30–42.

Morales, Ángel Luis. *La angustia metafísica en la poesía de Rubén Darío*. Río Piedras, Puerto Rico: Biblioteca de Extramuros—Universidad de Puerto Rico, 1967.

Morgado, Benjamín. *Rubén Darío: Ayer, hoy y siempre*. Santiago de Chile: Secretaría de Relaciones Culturales, 1988.

Nanfito, Jackeline. "Espacio y tiempo en 'Era un aire suave' de Rubén Darío." *Revista de Estudios Hispánicos* 22 (1995): 217–226.

Oliver Belmás, Antonio. *Este otro Rubén Darío*. Barcelona: Aedos, 1960.

———. *Última vez con Rubén Darío: Literatura hispanoamericana y española*. Madrid: Ediciones de Cultura Hispánica del Centro Iberoamericano de Cooperación, 1978.

Onís, Federico de. "Bibliografía de Rubén Darío." *La Torre* 55–56 (1967): 461–495.

———. *España en América*. Río Piedras, Puerto Rico: Ediciones de la Universidad de Puerto Rico, 1955.

Orringer, Nelson R., ed. *Hispanic Modernisms: Bulletin of Spanish Studies* (special issue) 79 (2002).

Ostria González, Mauricio. "Valoración de Rubén Darío: El juicio de los poetas." *Atenea* 463–464 (1991): 97–103.

Patterson, Helen Wohl, trans. *Rubén Darío y Nicaragua: A Bilingual Anthology of Poetry*. Washington, D.C.: American Literary Accents, 1966.

Paz, Octavio. *El arco y la lira*. Mexico City: Fondo de Cultura Económica, 1972.

———. "El caracol y la sirena." In *Cuadrivio: Darío, López Velarde, Pessoa, Cernuda*. By Octavio Paz. Mexico City: J. Mortiz, 1965, 9–65.

———. *Los hijos del limo: Del romanticismo a la vanguardia*. Barcelona: Seix Barral, 1974.

257

———. *The Siren and the Seashell, and Other Essays on Poets and Poetry.* Trans. Lysander Kemp. Austin: University of Texas Press, 1991.

Pearsall, Priscilla. *An Art Alienated from Itself: Studies in Spanish American Modernism.* University of Mississippi: Romance Monographs, 1984.

Pedemonte, Hugo Emilio. "Rubén Darío: Calendario bio-bibliográfico (1867–1916)." *Hora de Poesía* 59–60 (1988): 25–31.

Pedraza Jiménez, Felipe B., ed. *Manual de literatura hispanoamericana: Modernismo.* Pamplona, Spain: Cénlit, 1998.

Peñas-Bermejo, Francisco J. "El carácter existencial de la poesía de Rubén Darío y su presencia en la lírica española del siglo XX." *Alba de América* 20–21 (1993): 311–332.

Pérez, Alberto Julián. "El cliché modernista." *Crítica Hispánica* 17 (1995): 268–275.

———. "El estilo modernista." *Hispanófila* 111 (1994): 35–45.

———. "El modernismo dariano y la intertextualidad." In *Literatura como intertextualidad: IX Simposio Internacional de Literatura.* Edited by J. A. Arancibia et al. Buenos Aires: Instituto Literario y Cultural Hispánico, 1993, 94–101.

———. "La enciclopedia poética de Rubén Darío." *Revista Iberoamericana* 146–147 (1989): 329–338.

———. *La poética de Rubén Darío: Crisis post-romántica y modelos literarios modernistas.* Madrid: Orígenes, 1992.

Phillips, Allen W. "Rubén Darío y sus juicios sobre el modernismo." *Revista Iberoamericana* 47 (1959): 41–46.

———. *Temas del Modernismo hispánico y otros estudios.* Madrid: Gredos, 1974.

———, ed. *Rubén Darío: Antología poética.* Madrid: Clásicos Taurus, 1994.

Piedra, Antonio, ed. "Rubén Darío: Poesía." *Revista Ilustrada de Información Poética* 34–35 (monograph issued by the Spanish Ministry of Culture) (1991).

Piñero, Pedro M., and Rogelio Reyes, eds. *Bohemia y literatura: De Bécquer al Modernismo.* Seville: Universidad de Sevilla, 1993.

Pino, José M. del. *"Fin de siglo" and Modernity.* Anales de la Literatura Española Contemporánea (special issue) 23 (1998).

Porrata, Francisco, and Jorge A. Santana, eds. *Antología comentada del Modernismo.* Sacramento: California State UP, 1974.

Predmore, Michael P. "A Stylistic Analysis of 'Lo Fatal.' " *Hispanic Review* 39 (1971): 443–449.

Quintián, Andrés R. *Cultura y literatura españolas en Rubén Darío.* Madrid: Gredos, 1973.

Rama, Ángel. "Introducción." In *Rubén Darío: Poesía.* Edited by E. Mejía Sánchez. Caracas: Biblioteca Ayacucho 1977, ix–lii.

———. *Las máscaras democráticas del Modernismo.* Montevideo: Arca, 1975.

———. *Rubén Darío y el modernismo: Circunstancia socioeconómica de un arte americano.* Caracas: Universidad Central de Venezuela, 1970.

Ramoneda, Arturo, ed. *Rubén Darío esencial.* Madrid: Taurus, 1991.

Resina, Joan Ramon. *Un sueño de piedra: Ensayos sobre la literatura del Modernismo europeo.* Barcelona: Anthropos, 1990.

Rivera Rodas, Óscar. "La 'crisis referencial' y la modernidad hispanoamericana." *Hispania* 83 (2000): 779–790.

Rodó, José Enrique. *Hombres de América: Montalvo, Bolívar, Rubén Darío.* Barcelona: Cervantes, 1931.

Rodríguez Demorizi, Emilio. *Rubén Darío y Ecuador.* Quito: Casa de la Cultura Ecuatoriana, 1968.

———. *Rubén Darío y sus amigos dominicanos.* Bogotá: Ediciones Espiral, 1948.

Rodríguez Ramón, Andrés. *Desde el otro azul.* Santa Barbara: Schauer Printing Studio, 1959.

——. *Permanencia de Rubén Darío.* Charlotte, N.C.: Heritage Printers, 1967.

Rojas, Margarita. *El último baluarte del imperio.* San José: Editorial Costa Rica, 1995.

Rovira, José Carlos. "Espacios simbólicos y urbanos en Darío: Desde 'La sagrada selva' a 'La gran cosmópolis.' " In *Rubén Darío: La creación, argumento poético y expresivo.* Edited by Alberto Acereda and Manuel Mantero. *Anthropos* (1997): 76–80.

Ruiz Barrionuevo, Carmen, and César Real Ramos, eds. *La modernidad literaria en España e Hispanoamérica.* Salamanca: Universidad de Salamanca, 1995.

Saavedra Molina, Julio. "Los hexámetros castellanos y en particular los de Rubén Darío." *Anales de la Universidad de Chile* 18 (1935): 5–90.

——. "Una antología poética de Rubén Darío planeada por él mismo." *Anales de la Universidad de Chile* 53–54 (1944): 31–38.

Sabugo Abril, Amancio. "Cien años de *Prosas profanas.*" *Cuadernos Hispanoamericanos* 555 (1996): 73–84.

Sáinz de Medrano, Luis. "Otro notable reencuentro con Darío." *Cuadernos Americanos* 258 (1985): 185–191.

——. "Rubén Darío: Un periodista ante la modernidad." *Revista de Filología Románica* 14 (1997): 407–421.

——. "Un episodio de la Autobiografía de Rubén Darío: La conmemoración del IV Centenario del descubrimiento de América." *Anales de Literatura Hispanoamericana* 4 (1975): 395–401.

Salgado, María A. "El alma de la 'Sonatina.' " *Anales de Literatura Hispanoamericana* 4 (1975): 405–411.

——. "Félix Rubén García Sarmiento, Rubén Darío y otros entes de ficción." *Revista Iberoamericana* 146–147 (1989): 339–362.

——. " 'Mi esposa es de mi tierra, mi querida, de París': El hispanismo ingénito de Rubén Darío." In *Rubén Darío: La creación, argumento poético y expresivo.* Edited by Alberto Acereda and Manuel Mantero. *Anthropos* (1997): 51–58.

Salinas, Pedro. *La poesía de Rubén Darío: Ensayo sobre el tema y los temas del poeta.* Buenos Aires: Losada, 1948. 2d ed. 1957.

Salvador Jofre, Álvaro. *Rubén Darío y la moral estética.* Granada, Spain: Universidad de Granada, 1986.

Sánchez-Castañer, Francisco. *Estudios sobre Rubén Darío.* Madrid: Cátedra Rubén Darío — Universidad Complutense, 1976.

——. *La Andalucía de Rubén Darío.* Madrid: Cátedra Rubén Darío — Universidad Complutense, 1981.

Sánchez Romeralo, Antonio. "Los autógrafos de *Cantos de vida y esperanza:* Papel de Juan Ramón Jiménez en la edición del libro y en la conservación de sus autógrafos." *Revista Hispánica Moderna* 41 (1988): 45–60.

——. "Los *Cantos de vida y esperanza:* Historia del libro y sus autógrafos." In *Rubén Darío: La creación, argumento poético y expresivo.* Edited by Alberto Acereda and Manuel Mantero. *Anthropos* (1997): 93–100.

Scholz, László. *Ensayos sobre la modernidad literaria hispanoamericana.* Murcia, Spain: Universidad de Murcia, 2001.

Schulman, Ivan A. "El modernismo de Rubén Darío: La otra dimensión." In *Rubén Darío:. La creación, argumento poético y expresivo.* Edited by Alberto Acereda and Manuel Mantero. *Anthropos* (1997): 40–51.

——. "Génesis del azul modernista." *Revista Iberoamericana* 25 (1960): 251–271.

——. "Registros alternativos en la obra de Rubén Darío." In *Recreaciones: Ensayos sobre la obra de Rubén Darío.* Edited by I. Schulman. Hanover, N.H.: Ediciones del Norte, 1992, 29–46.

———. *Rubén Darío: La tradición cultural y el proceso de modernización.* Hanover, N.H.: Ediciones del Norte, 1990.

———, ed. *Nuevos asedios al Modernismo.* Madrid: Taurus, 1987.

———, ed. *Recreaciones: Ensayos sobre la obra de Rubén Darío.* Hanover, N.H.: Ediciones del Norte, 1992.

Schulman, Ivan A., and Evelyn P. Garfield. *"Las entrañas del vacío": Ensayos sobre la modernidad hispanoamericana.* Mexico City: Cuadernos Americanos, 1984.

———, eds. *Poesía modernista hispanoamericana y española: Antología.* Madrid: Taurus, 1986.

Schulman, Ivan A., and Manuel Pedro González. *Martí, Darío y el modernismo.* Madrid: Gredos, 1969.

Seluja, Antonio. *Rubén Darío en el Uruguay.* Montevideo: Arca, 1998.

Serrano Alonso, Javier, et al., eds. *Literatura modernista y tiempo del 98.* Santiago de Compostela, Spain: Universidad de Santiago de Compostela, 2001.

Sequeira, Diego Manuel. *Rubén Darío criollo o raíz y médula de su creación poética.* Buenos Aires: Guillermo Kraft Ltda., 1945.

———. *Rubén Darío en El Salvador: Segunda estada o atalaya de su revolución poética.* León, Nicaragua: Editorial Hospicio, 1964.

Silva Castro, Raúl. *Génesis del "Azul . . ." de Rubén Darío.* Managua: Ediciones de la Academia Nicaragüense de la Lengua, 1958.

———. *Rubén Darío a los veinte años.* Madrid: Gredos, 1956.

———. *Rubén Darío y Chile.* Santiago de Chile: La Tracción, 1930.

———. *Rubén Darío y su creación poética.* Santiago de Chile: Prensas de la Universidad de Chile, 1935.

Skyrme, Raymond. *Rubén Darío and the Pythagorean Tradition.* Gainesville: University of Florida Press, 1975.

Solares Larrave, Francisco J. "A Harmony of Whims: Towards a Discourse of Identity in Darío's 'Palabras Liminares.' " *Hispanic Review* 66 (1998): 447–465.

———. "El discurso de respuesta en la obra primigenia de Rubén Darío (1888–1898)." PhD Diss., University of Illinois, 1997.

Solares Larrave, Francisco J., and Frances Jaeger, eds. *Rubén Darío y "El Correo de la Tarde."* Valencia: Instituto de Estudios Modernistas, 1996.

Southworth, Susan L. "Sounding the Great *Vacío*: The Abyss in the Poetry of Rubén Darío and Amado Nervo." *Neophilologus* 85 (2001): 397–409.

Torre, Guillermo de. *Vigencia de Rubén Darío y otras páginas.* Madrid: Guadarrama, 1969.

Torres, Edelberto. *La dramática vida de Rubén Darío.* San José: Educa, 1996.

Torres Bodet, Jaime. *Rubén Darío: Abismo y cima.* Mexico City: Fondo de Cultura Económica, 1966.

Torres Pou, Joan. "Un escritor centroamericano ante el 98: Rubén Darío cronista de fin de siglo." *Bulletin of Hispanic Studies* 76 (1999): 261–266.

Torres-Rioseco, Arturo. *Casticismo y americanismo en la obra de Rubén Darío.* Cambridge: Harvard UP, 1931.

Trueblood, Alan S. "El 'Responso a Verlaine' y la elegía pastoril tradicional." In *Actas del Tercer Congreso Internacional de Hispanistas.* Mexico City: El Colegio de México, 1970, 861–870.

———. "Rubén Darío: The Sea and the Jungle." *Comparative Literature Studies* 4 (1967): 425–456.

Tünnermann Bernheim, Carlos. *Estudios darianos*. Managua: Fondo de Promoción Cultural, 1997.

Uceda, Julia. "El rostro interior: La imagen femenina en Rubén Darío." In *Rubén Darío: La creación, argumento poético y expresivo*. Edited by Alberto Acereda and Manuel Mantero. Anthropos (1997): 105–111.

Urbina, Nicasio, ed. *Miradas críticas sobre Rubén Darío*. Managua: Centro de Investigación sobre la Realidad Americana, 2002.

Valle-Castillo, Julio. "Cronología." In *Rubén Darío: Poesía*. Edited by E. Mejía Sánchez. Caracas: Biblioteca Ayacucho, 1977, 487–553.

Vargas Vila, José María. *Rubén Darío*. Barcelona: Ramón Sopena, 1935.

Villacastín, Rosario M. *Catálogo-archivo Rubén Darío*. Madrid: Editorial de la Universidad Complutense, 1987.

Walsh, Thomas, and Salomón de la Selva, trans. *Eleven Poems of Rubén Darío*. New York: Putnam's, 1916.

Watland, Charles D. *La formación literaria de Rubén Darío*. Managua: Publicaciones del Centenario de Rubén Darío, 1966.

———. *Poet-errant: A Biography of Rubén Darío*. New York: Philosophical Library, 1965.

Weinberg de Magis, Liliana. "Poesía pura: Rubén Darío y el campo de las letras." In *Rubén Darío: La creación, argumento poético y expresivo*. Edited by Alberto Acereda and Manuel Mantero. Anthropos (1997): 59–63.

Whitesell, David R. *Rubén Darío en Harvard: Libros y Manuscritos de la Biblioteca Personal del Poeta*. Managua: Fundación Internacional Rubén Darío, 1999.

Woodbridge, Hensley C. *Rubén Darío: A Selective Classified and Annotated Bibliography*. Metuchen, N.J.: Scarecrow Press, 1975.

Ycaza Tigerino, Julio. *Los Nocturnos de Rubén Darío*. Managua: Academia Nicaragüense de la Lengua, 1954.

———. *Los Nocturnos de Rubén Darío y otros ensayos*. Madrid: Ediciones de Cultura Hispánica, 1964.

Yurkievich, Saúl. *La movediza modernidad*. Madrid: Taurus, 1996.

Zahareas Anthony N., and José Esteban, eds. *Los proletarios del arte: Introducción a la bohemia*. Madrid: Celeste Ediciones, 1998.

Zambrana Fonseca, Armando. *Para leer a Darío: Glosario básico*. Managua: Francisco Arellano Oviedo, 1998.

Zapata-Whelan, Carol M. " 'With Faces Turn'd Sideways': Walt Whitman and Rubén Darío." PhD Diss., University of California–Los Angeles, 1994.

Zavala, Iris M. *Colonialism and Culture: Hispanic Modernisms and the Social Imaginary*. Bloomington: Indiana UP, 1992.

———. *Rubén Darío bajo el signo del cisne*. Río Piedras: Editorial de la Universidad de Puerto Rico, 1989.

———, ed. *Rubén Darío: El modernismo y otros ensayos*. Madrid: Alianza Editorial, 1989.

Zepeda-Henríquez, Eduardo. *Estudio de la poética de Rubén Darío*. Managua: Comisión Nacional del Centenario, 1967.

Zuleta, Ignacio M. "Introducción biográfica y crítica." In *Rubén Darío: Prosas profanas y otros poemas*. Edited by I. Zuleta. Madrid: Clásicos Castalia, 1983, 9–54.

———. *La polémica modernista: El modernismo de mar a mar (1898–1907)*. Bogotá: Publicaciones del Instituto Caro y Cuervo 82, 1988.

———. " 'Las ánforas de Epicuro' y la difusión del modernismo." In *Simposio sobre Villaespesa y el Modernismo: Comunicaciones*. Almería, Spain: Comisión del Centenario del Poeta Villaespesa, 1977, 9–54.

Bassnett, Susan, and André Lefevre. *Constructing Cultures: Essays on Literary Translations.* Bristol: Multilingual Matters, 1998.

García Yebra, Valentín. *Teoría y práctica de la traducción.* 2 vols. Madrid: Gredos, 1989.

Gentzler, Edwin. *Contemporary Translation Theories.* Buffalo, N.Y.: Multilingual Matters, 2001.

Hulet, Claude L. *Latin American Poetry in English Translation: A Bibliography.* Washington, D.C.: Pan American Unions, 1965.

Landers, Clifford E. *Literary Translation: A Practical Guide.* Buffalo, N.Y.: Multilingual Matters, 2001.

Lefevre, André. *Translating Literature: Practice and Theory in a Comparative Literature Context.* New York: Modern Language Association of America, 1992.

López Morales, Humberto. *Estructura interna, estructura externa y traducción.* Río Piedras, Puerto Rico: Publicaciones de la Facultad de Humanidades, 1974.

Sonntag Blay, Iliana L. *Twentieth-Century Poetry from Spanish America: An Index to Spanish Language and Bilingual Anthologies.* Lanham: Scarecrow Press, 1998.

Tappscott, Stephen, ed. and trans. *Twentieth-Century Latin American Poetry: A Bilingual Anthology.* Austin: University of Texas Press, 1996.

Tolliver, Joyce. "Rosalía between Two Shores: Gender, Rewriting, and Translation." *Hispania* 85 (2002): 33–43.

Venuti, Lawrence. *The Scandals of Translation: Towards an Ethics of Difference.* New York: Routledge, 1998.

Library of Congress Cataloging-in-Publication Data
Darío Rubén
Songs of life and hope / Cantos de vida y esperanza / Rubén Darío; edited and translated by Will Derusha and Alberto Acereda.
p. cm.
ISBN 0-8223-3282-5 (cloth : alk. paper)
ISBN 0-8223-3271-X (pbk. : alk. paper)
I. Title: Cantos de vida y esperanza.   II. Derusha, Will.
III. Acereda, Alberto.   IV. Title.
PQ7519.D3C2713 2004
861'.5—dc22
2003017793

W9-AWE-724

A WORSHIP MINISTRY DEVOTIONAL

Times of Refreshing

TOM KRAEUTER

WITH GERRIT GUSTAFSON

KENT HENRY

BOB KAUFLIN

PATRICK KAVANAUGH

BILL RAYBORN

AND ARLEN SALTE

Emerald Books

P.O. Box 635
Lynnwood, WA 98046

Training Resources
Hillsboro, Missouri

Emerald Books are distributed through YWAM Publishing. For a full list of titles, including other great worship resources, visit our website at www.ywampublishing.com or call 1-800-922-2143.

Times of Refreshing: A Worship Ministry Devotional
Copyright © 2002 by Training Resources, Inc.
8929 Old LeMay Ferry Road
Hillsboro, MO 63050
(636) 789-4522
www.training-resources.org

10 09 08 07 06 05 04 03 02   10 9 8 7 6 5 4 3 2 1

Published by Emerald Books
P.O. Box 635
Lynnwood, Washington 98046

ISBN 1-883002-91-5

Printed in the United States of America.

To Dr. Judson Cornwall
who, in many ways, has influenced
an entire generation of worshipers.

Other books by Tom Kraeuter

Keys to Becoming an Effective Worship Leader

Developing an Effective Worship Ministry

Worship Is...What?!

*Things They Didn't Teach Me
in Worship Leading School*

*More Things They Didn't Teach Me
in Worship Leading School*

Oh, Grow Up!

Living Beyond the Ordinary

*If Standing Together Is So Great,
Why Do We Keep Falling Apart?*

Contents

Introduction

If you're a worship leader or minister of music or even if you're involved in the ministry of praise and worship, this book was created with you in mind. We, the writers, want to help hold up your arms and offer some practical, biblical insights to strengthen you.

The idea behind this book was to create a devotional book that can be used independently or with a group. Each chapter is a separate devotion. Each contains a theme Scripture passage with a story or teaching from a respected worship leader. You may choose just to read the devotion, or in a group setting, you may use it as a springboard for discussion or ministry time.

The devotions are not arranged topically. This is intentional to give variety to the readings. If you plan to use this in a group setting, rather than just picking up the book and reading the next devotion aloud, you might want to check the one coming next to make sure it's right for your group. You may even want to page through the book, marking the ones you think are most appropriate for your setting. Some of the devotions might be more applicable to certain churches and specific situations than others. The variety of writers offers a broad spectrum of experiences, and some may be more suitable to your church and where your people currently are in their spiritual lives.

Our prayer is that this book will help strengthen you as well as the overall ministry of praise and worship in your church.

Meet the Authors

GERRIT GUSTAFSON is a conference speaker, songwriter, and worship teacher who conducts seminars and conferences throughout North America and abroad. Gerrit has been actively involved in the "worship revolution" that has dramatically affected the Church over the past twenty years. He was part of Integrity Music's original creative team. Later he founded WholeHearted Worship (www.wholeheartedworship.com), which offers products to accompany worship. Many of his songs are being sung throughout the world—songs like "Only by Grace," "Lord We Welcome You," and "Mighty Is Our God." Gerrit and his wife, Himmie, have five children and live in Brentwood, Tennessee.

KENT HENRY was the worship leader on six Integrity Music albums and has produced twenty-three of his own worship recordings. These live albums are worship times that have captured the essence of true worship to the one true God. For the past seventeen years, Kent has been traveling and ministering to thousands of worshiping believers around the world. Kent, his wife, Carla, and their three children reside in St. Louis, Missouri. Two of those children, Jessica and Matthew, are currently involved in worship ministry and serve on the staff of Kent Henry Ministries (www.kenthenry.com).

BOB KAUFLIN, after twelve years with GLAD, left in 1984 to pursue pastoring in the local church. He has led worship on numerous CDs, including Integrity's *Chosen Treasure* and Word's *A Passion for His Presence*. Since 1997 he has served as director of worship development for PDI Ministries (www.pdinet.org), leading worship at various conferences, training worship leaders and teams, and contributing to PDI's

Come and Worship recordings. Bob also leads worship at Covenant Life Church in Gaithersburg, Maryland, pastored by C. J. Mahaney. Bob's column "Worship Matters" appears weekly on Crosswalk.com. He and his wife, Julie, have six children.

Dr. Patrick Kavanaugh is the author of seven books, including *Worship—A Way of Life* and *The Spiritual Lives of the Great Composers*. Patrick has composed in a wide variety of genre, from orchestral to chamber music, from opera to electronic music. He now serves full-time as the executive director of the Christian Performing Artists' Fellowship, representing over 1,000 members from fifty different denominations. He is also the artistic director of the MasterWorks Festival in New York. Patrick resides near Washington, D.C., with his wife, Barbara—a cellist—and their four children.

Tom Kraeuter (pronounced Kroyter) is one of the most prolific authors and teachers on the contemporary worship scene today. His books are available worldwide in multiple languages. Tom's biblical, practical teaching transcends all denominational lines and has made him a sought-after speaker for conferences. Nearly 20,000 people have attended his worship seminars in churches all across North America. Tom has been a part of the leadership team of Christian Outreach Church near St. Louis, Missouri, since 1984. He is the executive director of Training Resources, Inc. (www.training-resources.org). Tom and his wife, Barbara, and their three children reside in Goldman, Missouri.

Bill Rayborn served for thirteen years as full-time minister of music in various churches in Missouri, South Carolina, and Texas. Entering the Christian music industry, Bill became director of record promotion for Word, Inc. Later he was executive director for Andraé Crouch and the Disciples and then vice president of Christian Artists Corporation, where he planned the first three years of the music seminar held at Estes Park, Colorado, each summer. From there he became director of music publication for Tempo Music. Today Bill publishes a popular newsletter, *The Church Music Report* (www.tcmr.com). Bill lives with his wife, Lynann, and her daughter, Amber, in Grapevine, Texas.

ARLEN SALTE is the founder and executive director of New Creation Ministries (www.new-creation.net). In addition to hosting the largest creative ministry conference in Canada, they provide practical worship skills training and worship resources for churches. Arlen travels the world, giving concerts, leading worship, preaching, and teaching contemporary worship and music skills. Arlen is Canada's top-selling gospel artist, the worship columnist for *Strategies for Today's Leader* magazine, and author of the Break Forth contemporary worship manual. Arlen lives in Sherwood Park, Alberta, Canada, with his wife, Elsa, and their three children.

Fireworks and Finishing Well

BY TOM KRAEUTER

 *I have fought the good fight, I have finished
the race, I have kept the faith.*
2 TIMOTHY 4:7

Where I live in Missouri it is legal to shoot off fireworks around
Independence Day. We live out in the country, and generally there are
lots of folks around us who put on quite a show with their fireworks. I
remember watching one of those homegrown fireworks displays last
year. One rocket shot off from the ground and left a pretty impressive
trail of sparks as it rose into the night sky. I thought, "This one's gonna
be good!" Suddenly, the trail of sparks stopped, there was a little
"poof," and then...nothing. "Was that it?" I wondered.

We've all known or at least seen *people* like that. They start off with
great promise. Perhaps they are exceptionally gifted in a certain area.
Maybe they have an outgoing, friendly personality that automatically
causes people to like them. Perhaps they are the creative, visionary type
who is a natural leader. Whatever their situation, they begin well. Unfortunately, over time, the zeal fades, the passion withers, and their end is
nowhere close to what they had hoped for. They fizzle out like that rocket.

Certainly I am not talking about all gifted people. Many fulfill the
plans and purposes of God throughout their entire lifetime. However,
many do not.

12

Jesus came to earth with a final purpose in mind—the eternal salvation of mankind. Nothing would deter Him from accomplishing that purpose. Being pursued by a maniacal king just after He was born didn't stop Him. Neither did living in total obscurity most of His life. Jesus was not diverted from His goal when He had a direct confrontation with Satan. Neither was He hindered when the bulk of His followers abandoned Him or when the religious leaders rejected Him. He was not even deterred when He was nailed to the cross. He had a goal, and no matter what He faced, He pursued the goal and completed the task that was set before Him. At the end of His life, Jesus could say with confidence, "It is finished" (John 19:30).

Not long ago I read an article in *Worship Leader* magazine by J. Robert Clinton. The article was entitled "Four Observations on Giftedness." Two of his observations startled me. His third observation on giftedness was stated simply but emphatically: "Few leaders finish well." What he was saying is that many people start off with a bang and then fizzle out over the long haul. They don't finish well.

Clinton's final observation was even stronger. "Leaders in general and worship leaders in particular who do not finish well do not usually do so as a result of lack of giftedness." He went on to explain this final observation like this: "Leaders who fail generally do not do so because of giftedness but as a result of other inner life characteristics." He described these "inner life characteristics" as deficiencies in areas such as integrity, relational issues, lack of intimacy with God, etc.[1]

Not finishing well is not because of a lack of ability. In fact, it is often because of too much ability. I have an observation of my own that I have often stated in seminars. "It seems to me that the people who are the most gifted have the most difficulty maintaining their heart for God." My remedy for this is simple: "Guard your heart!" I usually repeat that statement for emphasis because it is so very important.

The writer of Proverbs says, "Above all else, guard your heart, for it is the wellspring of life" (Proverbs 4:23). As a writer, it seems obvious to me that when a writer says, "Above all else," what follows this statement is of supreme importance. Solomon said, "*Above all else,* guard your heart." Don't just go out and do a bunch of great things for God. Guard your heart. Why? Because otherwise you can end up like the fireworks failure—lots of promise but no lasting results.

The Lord does not want us to fizzle out. His desire is for us to complete what we began. At the end of our lives, He wants us to be able to echo Paul's words: "I have fought the good fight, I have finished the race, I have kept the faith" (2 Timothy 4:7).

Jesus finished well because He took time for His relationship with His heavenly Father. He also took time to nurture relationships with those for whom He cared. Certainly, He accomplished many wonderful things along the journey of His life, but He didn't fizzle out at the end because He had maintained the important things along the way.

What about your life? Are you guarding your heart? Above all else? Will you be a fizzling firework, or will you be able to say, "I have fought the good fight, I have finished the race, I have kept the faith" (2 Timothy 4:7)?

The Cobbler's Shoes

BY ARLEN SALTE

> *Kenaniah the head Levite was in charge of the singing; that was his responsibility because he was skillful at it.*
>
> 1 CHRONICLES 15:22

You'd think that after all these years I'd know better.

I'm on the road about 100 days a year. I know my way around airports, fast-food chains, and look-alike hotel rooms. I love what I do, but there are times when touring does get tiresome. When I feel that way, I make the big mistake.

I get home, see that I have a luxurious three weeks without having to pack my suitcase, and promptly set my guitar aside. Three weeks later I'm jostling through airports and praying that my luggage didn't go to Biloxi, Mississippi, when I'm in Phoenix, Arizona.

Do you remember that the Bible says that our sin will find us out? It finds me every time. Some people may think that the grimace on my face when I'm playing an acoustic guitar solo is there because I'm trying to give one of those 1980s stadium rock-guitar poses. Nope. I'm really, for truly, absolutely, no doubt about it, in pain. My fingertips are whining from being neglected. Every guitar player knows that you can't set your acoustic guitar aside for three weeks and still expect to have calluses on your fingertips. My sin of laziness catches up with me.

There seem to be two extreme camps in the worship opinions being taught today. One camp teaches that passion is everything and

15

excellence is just a handy accessory. The other camp teaches that precision in musical execution is to be revered above heart and soul.

It's a common saying that the pendulum of opinions seldom rests in the middle. I believe we need to set goals for our worship teams that strive for both musical improvement and spiritual development.

However, for today let's take a look at your fingertips.

In our Bible reading for today it talks about Kenaniah being assigned the responsibility of being in charge of the singing because he was skillful at it. He wasn't just given this task because he had a warm, fuzzy heart. He had worked hard at developing his skills. He probably graduated with honors from the Hebrew school of quarter tonal singing. He knew how to get the altos to sing in tune, even though their hearing had been blown out years ago by standing between the loud crashing cymbals and the ram's horn section in the orchestra.

Skill is a high calling of God. When we employ our gifts to the best of our ability, we give God praise. Martin Luther said, "The cobbler gives God the highest praise when he makes the finest pair of shoes."

This makes a lot of sense. When I give my children presents and they spend hours playing with them, I receive the joy of knowing that they see my gifts as valuable. If they are more enthralled with the color of the wrapping paper than the gifts, it shows that they don't really value my gifts.

I believe that it's similar with God. He is the Giver of all good gifts. When we spend quality time exploring and developing these gifts, we are actually worshiping God. We let God know that we are grateful. We let God know that He is the Giver of something precious. We let our Father know that His gifts are not taken for granted.

When God established priests who were dedicated to worship, they took their gifts and calling seriously. In 2 Chronicles 34:12b, it talks about "the Levites—all who were skilled in playing musical instruments..."

Did you note that? It didn't say a few were skilled. It didn't say some. It didn't even say the majority. It said *all* were skilled. They deeply valued the gift they were given by God.

So, how are your calluses? This applies to keyboard players, vocalists, drummers, sound technicians, multimedia ministers, and more.

Are you stretching to the next level in your musical skills? Are you showing your gratitude to your heavenly Father by exploring and developing the gifts you've been given? Are you like the cobbler, making the finest pair of shoes?

Wherever you are in your skill level, there are always new things to learn. Are you a keyboard player who needs to learn to play by chord? Give God praise by rising to the challenge. Are you a drummer who needs to learn to play with more solid timing? Play with a metronome, and worship the King. Are you a guitar player who needs to learn to play in E flat? Come worship the Lord with straining fingers.

God truly is the Giver of all good gifts. Let's show our gratitude in how we use them. May you still be discovering new techniques on your instrument and calling out, "Eureka" at the age of eighty-five!

Let's be great cobblers for the glory of God.

The True Foundation

BY TOM KRAEUTER

> *Because of the LORD's great love we are not consumed, for his compassions never fail. They are new every morning; great is your faithfulness.*
> LAMENTATIONS 3:22–23

My youngest son, Stephen, has a quilt with glow-in-the-dark material as part of the pattern. I'm sure you've seen glow-in-the-dark items, and you know how they work. You place the item under a light, then put it in a dark room and it glows...for a while. Eventually it stops glowing. In order to get it to glow again, you have to put it back under the light. Do you understand the application of what I'm saying for your life? We were not designed to walk out this life apart from relationship with God. Without Him we're empty.

During His earthly ministry, Jesus said it like this: "I am the true vine.... Remain in me, and I will remain in you. No branch can bear fruit by itself; it must remain in the vine. Neither can you bear fruit unless you remain in me" (John 15:1–4). It is our relationship with Him that makes us able to do anything. Jesus continues by saying, "I am the vine; you are the branches. If a man remains in me and I in him, he will bear much fruit; *apart from me you can do nothing*" (John 15:5). In order to accomplish anything at all, we must get our strength, our abilities, from Him. Apart from our relationship with Him, there is absolutely nothing of any lasting value that you or I will ever accomplish.

18

In the middle section of 2 Corinthians 12:9, God tells the apostle Paul, "My power is made perfect in weakness." A dear friend of mine, Daryl Roth, has a favorite saying based on this passage about his relationship with the Lord. Daryl says, "It's a team effort. I supply the weakness and God supplies the strength."

He's right. It is God's power living and active within us that begins and ends His work in us. "…for it is God who works in you to will and to act according to his good purpose" (Philippians 2:13).

"Let us fix our eyes on Jesus, the *author and perfecter* of our faith…" (Hebrews 12:2). It is the Lord who first reached out to begin the relationship, and it is He who will complete it. In essence, when we understand that God's love is the foundation for our relationship with Him, we've come full circle. We need to be in constant relationship with God, but the only way we can be in that relationship is through what He has done for us. It is God's grace and love that establish us in that relationship initially, and it is also His love and mercy that cause that relationship to be ongoing. It all begins and ends with His grace. "He who began a good work in you will carry it on to completion until the day of Christ Jesus" (Philippians 1:6).

It is because of the everlasting love of the Lord that our relationship with Him is a settled issue. There is no need to wonder whether God loves you ("Can I really have a relationship with Almighty God?"). Jesus' atoning work on the cross proves His love once and for all.

One of the earliest glimpses in the Bible of God's heart is right after Adam sinned. "But the LORD God called to the man, 'Where are you?' " (Genesis 3:9). This picture of the loving Father in search of His lost child is the underlying theme of all Scripture. The main message throughout the Bible is that God loves us. If we see Him as the evil taskmaster waiting to beat us when we do wrong, we have not understood His care for us. "God *is* love" (1 John 4:16).

Regardless of how long we have walked with the Lord, there is something refreshing about receiving God's love anew. One of my favorite present-day songwriters is Mark Altrogge. One of his songs, "The Love of a Holy God," says this: "I'm ruined for this world for I've tasted Your love, the love of a holy God." The fact that God is so holy and yet still loves sinful creatures like us makes His love even more wonderful. All the treasures of this world pale in comparison.

This matter of God's love and grace is the foundation on which we must build our entire lives. We must stop trying to earn God's favor and recognize the reality of what His love and grace have already done for us. "Therefore, there is now *no condemnation* for those who are in Christ Jesus" (Romans 8:1).

God is not impressed by how well you or I play or sing. The long hours you put into the worship ministry do not cause Him to love you more fervently. Regardless of all the fine achievements we will ever accomplish, there is still only one foundation: the love and grace of God in the form of the blood of Jesus shed for the forgiveness of our sins in order to make us acceptable to God. In reality, all the rest are just peripheral issues.

If all that we do in life is not built on the foundation of His love, then the structure will never be solid. We are all simply sinners saved by the immeasurable grace and sacrifice of the Lord Jesus.

"Because of the LORD's great love we are not consumed, for his compassions never fail. They are new every morning; great is your faithfulness" (Lamentations 3:22–23).

Right now, thank God for His wonderful love and mercy.

Adapted from the book *Living Beyond the Ordinary* by Tom Kraeuter (Lynnwood, Wash.: Emerald Books, 2000).

Be Careful How You Button Your Coat

BY BILL RAYBORN

In everything set them an example by doing what is good. In your teaching show integrity, seriousness and soundness of speech that cannot be condemned, so that those who oppose you may be ashamed because they have nothing bad to say about us.
TITUS 2:7–8

Many years ago I was serving as minister of music at the First Baptist Church of Aiken, South Carolina. During my tenure there, we organized a Junior Boys' Choir for ages 9–12. Taking advantage of the normal aversion to members of the female sex (we even had a male pianist), our rules said that "no women were allowed in the rehearsal room."

The boys went on camping and fishing trips together and participated in lots of other outdoor activities. The group worked hard at their music and soon gained a statewide reputation as a fine choir. They were even invited to go to the state capital, Columbia, South Carolina, to appear on statewide television. It was quite an honor.

For such an auspicious occasion we thought it would be good not only to sound great but also to look nice. Because of this, each boy was asked to purchase a new blue blazer to give the group a unified look. Through a special contest we even had exclusive patches made and sewn on their pockets. The kids really looked sharp!

Although we had been through a lot together, in the midst of all this attention, I often wondered if I was actually having any impact on these young men. Would they remember anything I said other than "be quiet"? Would they be different because of the countless hours I had spent working with them? I just wasn't sure.

Then, one Sunday morning the boys were to sing in our worship service. That morning all my wonderings snapped into perspective with one innocent comment made just before the service began.

As I watched the boys arrive at church that morning, it was hard to believe this well-groomed assembly was the same group of loud, dirty-faced boys who had been playing football in the church yard before rehearsal just four days earlier. (Although their musical prowess had deservedly received a great deal of recognition, they were, after all, still boys.)

As I made my way toward the sanctuary, I was brought up short by one of the choir parents. "Mr. Rayborn," the woman said, "may I tell you something?"

My verbal response was, "Of course." However, having been a minister of music for several years, I was steeled for a possible complaint.

"I hope you never do anything wrong," she remarked. I told her that I hoped so, too, but asked why she would say such a thing.

She explained that when they had arrived at church that morning, she told her son to button his blazer when he got out of the car. Uncharacteristically, the lad had refused. When she inquired as to why, he replied that he wanted to wait and see how Mr. Rayborn buttoned his coat. He wanted his coat buttoned the same way. "I hope you never do anything wrong," she said again and walked away.

Stunned by the impact of that comment, I couldn't help but stand just a little straighter as I walked into the worship center, checking to make sure my coat was buttoned correctly. You just never know when others are watching and listening.

Anyone involved in the church worship ministry is seen by people in the congregation as a leader. You may not want that to happen. You might dislike it when it occurs, but that won't change the fact that people see *you* as a leader. Whether you want to be or not, you are an example to someone. People will look at not only how you button your coat but also how you treat your spouse and children. They will take notice of how you drive and how you respond when you're tired or overworked. They will observe your actions when you're at a restaurant, at the mall, or in church. You will be an example for someone.

As our verse today says, we must be willing to set an example by doing what is good. No, this is not an easy task, but for those involved in any up-front ministry, it is essential.

More Than Anything

BY BOB KAUFLIN

> *Whom have I in heaven but you? And earth has nothing I desire besides you. My flesh and my heart may fail, but God is the strength of my heart and my portion forever.*
> PSALM 73:25–26

From the moment of birth, we become aware of wants. Our first wants are genuine needs. We realize Mom is no longer supplying oxygen, so we frantically flex our lungs, gasp for air, and let the world know we're not particularly happy about what just happened to us. Soon we crave nourishment, and we gladly receive whatever is provided. Shortly thereafter, however, our wants move beyond basic needs. As we grow, we increasingly desire a variety of things we don't possess or think we don't have enough of: toys, clothes, friends, free time, cars, money, pleasure, prestige, CDs, tools, hobbies. The list grows faster than we do.

It is not wrong in and of itself to want anything (as long as that thing isn't inherently sinful). The real issue is how much we want it. Any desire can begin to compete in our hearts for the place that only God should hold. Author and pastor John Piper has suggested that the essence of worshiping God is wanting God more than anything else. He goes on to say that the essence of praising Christ is *prizing* Christ. We could add that the essence of devotion to Christ is desire for Christ. This is the true heart of a worshiper.

The Bible knows nothing of a worship that relates to God out of mere duty or performance. Again, Dr. Piper helps us see the place of desire in worship. "I believe it can be shown Biblically that all our behavior should be motivated by a thirst for more and more satisfaction in God.... When our whole life is consumed with pursuing satisfaction in God, everything we do highlights the value and worth of God. Which simply means that everything becomes worship."

In other words, wanting God more than anything shows that He is more important to us than anything else. Of course, worship is about exalting, praising, and honoring God. Worship is about wholeheartedly responding to God's self-revelation. Worship is about experiencing an intimacy with God through the substitutionary sacrifice of Jesus on the cross. However, the glory these actions bring to God is directly related to how much we *want* to do them. And, of course, that depends on how much we want God Himself.

There are countless things in this life that can draw our attention away from God. Some of these include clothes, cars, careers, relationships, money, and fame, just to name a few. Too often we are more enamored with the things of this world than we are with God Himself. As worshipers, our thoughts, attention, and desires should be focused on the life to come. If we set our sights only on the joys of this life, we are mistaking the introduction for the story!

The apostle Paul was certainly well-positioned to seek a ministry that brought him fame and glory. Yet he told the Philippians, "For to me, to live is Christ and to die is gain...I am torn between the two: I desire to depart and be with Christ, which is better by far; but it is more necessary for you that I remain in the body" (Philippians 1:21–24). What motivated Paul to consider death as a desirable alternative to a fruitful ministry?

Paul was a worshiper of God, first and last. He lived for a purpose beyond himself or his own life: that moment when he would look into the eyes of his Maker and receive what was due him for the things he had done on earth (2 Corinthians 5:10). Paul's view of death was an informed view. He knew that our time on earth is only a preparation. He recognized that death is the beginning of the life that is truly life. So Paul commanded the Colossians to do what he did: "Set your minds on things above, not on earthly things. For you died, and your life is now hidden with Christ in God" (Colossians 3:2–3).

As believers in Jesus Christ, our lives, too, are hidden with Christ in God. Is that how you live? What are the greatest desires of your heart? Where are you storing up your treasures? What do you want more than anything?

True worshipers of God understand that even with all the good of this life, nothing is better than God Himself. A worshiper lives in eager anticipation of the time when he or she will bow at the very throne of God to declare the glories of the Lamb forever. There, in His presence, our words, our worship, and our passion for God will have no bounds.

May God, by His Spirit and grace, make each of us that kind of worshiper in this life.

Let's Go to the Movies

BY TOM KRAEUTER

> *For you make me glad by your deeds,*
> *O LORD; I sing for joy at the works of*
> *your hands. How great are your works,*
> *O LORD, how profound your thoughts!*
> PSALM 92:4–5

I remember the first time we took one of our children to a movie theater. Everything about the experience was fascinating for the youngster. Even before we got inside the building, just buying the tickets was an adventure. Of course, after that, giving the just-purchased tickets to the guy who rips them in half took some explaining. Walking down the softly lit corridor to the correct theater caused questions about all the other movies being shown. Choosing a seat was a big dilemma: Was the first row too close to the screen? Was the back too far away? Would somewhere in the middle be best? Which side of the aisle? Near the aisle or closer to the wall? By the way, where is the rest room?

Everything was brand-new. I had to keep reminding myself of that. Over my lifetime, I'm sure I've been to a few dozen movies. This was old stuff for me. Though perhaps I had never been to this particular theater before, I had been to many movies. My child, on the other hand, was a first-timer. Everything he saw was a brand-new experience for him. There was a wonder and amazement that I had lost in the movie-going experience.

Once we've done something once or twice it becomes old hat to us. Our usual reaction today to practically anything in life is, "Been there, done that." What would be the reaction of Wilbur and Orville Wright if they took a ride on a modern jet. Their first flight was the distance of the equivalent of the wingspan of a 747. We, on the other hand, get on a plane and open a book or magazine to keep from being bored.

Unfortunately, we can too easily have the same complacency in our worship. Over time we can become accustomed to the words, the actions, the emotions, the music and begin to tune it out.

On the other hand, in our verse for today, the psalmist said, "You make me glad by your deeds...I sing for joy at the works of your hands. How great are your works...how profound your thoughts!" These are not words of complacency. There is clearly a freshness and enthusiasm in these words.

The New Living Translation says it even more strongly: "You thrill me, LORD, with all you have done for me!" (Psalm 92:4, NLT). When was the last time you honestly *told* God that you were thrilled by all He's done for you? Beyond just telling Him about it, when was the last time you actually *were* thrilled by what the Lord has done in your life?

The book of Revelation is believed to have been written in the 90s, just sixty years after the death and resurrection of Jesus. It starts off with the Lord's messages to the seven churches. One of His major grievances is their complacency. Get the picture here. Some of these folks had parents who saw and perhaps walked with Jesus during His visible earthly ministry. Now they are being lambasted for becoming complacent.

Those of us involved in the ministry of praise and worship are not exempt from the same thing happening in our lives. It can be very easy for us to come in on Sunday morning and play our instrument or sing our part and never really connect with God. I would rather not tell you how many times I have caught myself playing guitar for a Sunday service and thinking, "Let's see, this week I've really got to finish cleaning the basement and..." Oh, you know this story.

In his book *One Thing Needful*, Dr. Gary Mathena suggests that if the greatest commandment is to love God with all our heart, soul, and mind (Matthew 22:37), then it follows that the greatest sin is not to love God with all our heart, soul, and mind. In other words, being complacent.

Personally, I find that comforting. Not that I like the idea of being complacent. I just was not exactly certain what to do about complacency. However, I know how to deal with sin. I repent. Maybe you need to do that also. Let's pray together.

"Lord, I'm sorry for being complacent. Please forgive me. Wrench the ugly sin of complacency out of my life. Instead, by Your Word and by Your Spirit, cause me to sing for joy at the works of Your hands. Cause me to be thrilled by the things You do in my life, just like the excitement of that little kid at the movie theater. Let me not be bored or complacent about You, but recognize that You are what makes everything else in life worthwhile. I love You, Lord. Teach me to love You more each day."

Imperfect Scores

BY ARLEN SALTE

> 🌿 *There is no fear in love. But perfect love drives out fear, because fear has to do with punishment. The one who fears is not made perfect in love.*
>
> 1 JOHN 4:18

It was my first recording session with an orchestra. I was twenty-one. Writing for an orchestra wasn't exactly a skill that I'd picked up playing the Rolling Stones songs in my rock band days. Mick Jagger could certainly pout and prance, but I don't think he cared too much for the oboe.

The moment of truth arrived when the orchestra showed up. They filled the studio, took their chairs, tuned their instruments, and started looking over the score I had written. They ran through the pieces. The lush sounds gave me goose bumps. I was in heaven.

Unfortunately, something was about to suddenly change my mood. These fabulous players couldn't control themselves any longer. Soon laughter came rolling through the expensive microphones. The conductor showed me that I had placed the stems on the wrong sides of many of the notes. Needless to say, this was the last time I transcribed my parts by hand for an orchestra.

Quite frankly, I was so embarrassed that day that I wanted to pack in the entire idea of music. I had shown my ignorance in front of all these awarded musicians. However, I take great courage in the following true story.

There was a man who desperately wanted to become a conductor. He put his very heart and soul into it. During soft passages, he would signal the orchestra by crouching low. During loud passages he'd leap into the air with enthusiasm. He'd even shout to the orchestra in excitement.

Despite his passion, however, he was not exactly blessed with a great memory. In concert, he once forgot that he had instructed the orchestra not to repeat a section. As instructed, the orchestra didn't repeat the section. He lost his temper and yelled at the orchestra for not repeating the section. He was horribly embarrassed!

For his very own piano concerto, he tried conducting from the piano. He thought he could do it all. At one moment in the concert, he leapt from the piano bench, knocking the candles from the piano. At another concert, he knocked over a choirboy.

His hearing started to rapidly deteriorate, which left him with even bigger challenges. Not only did he have a bad memory, a clumsy body, and a poorly controlled temperament, now he couldn't hear well. It got so bad that the orchestra started to get their cues from the first violinist rather than from the inept conductor.

After great pleas from the musicians to give up conducting, he finally gave up and went home. His name: Ludwig Van Beethoven.

While he is one of the greatest composers the world has ever known, he was an absolute failure as a conductor. However, this did not make Beethoven a failure as a person. He pushed beyond his fear of failure to take on new challenges, and the world is richer for it.

One of the most inhibiting fears we will ever face is the fear of failure. This is the fear that has stopped great moments throughout human history. This may also be a fear that has stopped you from taking new steps in your ministry. Maybe you have pulled back because you failed before. Maybe you tried to play by ear before, and it sounded as though you actually were playing with your ears. Maybe you stretched out to try a vocal solo, but that little hormonal demon of adolescence made you yodel instead. Or perhaps you wrote orchestral arrangements for an album, but you put the stems on the wrong sides of the notes.

Whatever your past failures may be, they may have limited your reach. God is asking you to take great new strides, but you fear the embarrassment of past failure so much that you remain in your comfort zone.

This is why it is so important to ground our ministries in God's unconditional love and not in legalism. We need to know that whether our efforts gain great applause or rotten tomatoes, God's view of us will never change. His love is with us no matter what side we have placed the stems of the notes. This surety gives us freedom to try new things in ministry, knowing that we will never be viewed as a failure in God's eyes.

In our Bible verse today, we see that there is no fear in love. God's love sets us free to spread our wings and to face the possibility of failure head on. Perfect love drives out fear. When we know that we are perfectly loved by the Creator and Sustainer of all life—the highest authority in the universe, the One who holds planets in their orbits— we are freed to take great steps of faith. When we know that our failure in the eyes of the "crowd" is really nothing to fear at all, then we are free to stretch and become all that God wants us to be.

Who knows how many great songs or poems or voices have gone to their graves because of a fear of failure? As a child of God, *you* have been given a new authority in ministry. God is waiting for His children to step out in the authority that comes with the gift of grace. Do you have past failures that are holding you back? In God there are always new beginnings.

Today, I challenge you to live in the reality of God's grace. Step out of your comfort zone. Spread your wings, knowing that God's perfect love for you drives out the fear of failure. Have you been challenged to learn how to sing alto? Do you need to dust off that old Hofner Beatle bass from the '60s? Take the step.

I still have those original orchestral scores in my files, but now I don't look at them with shame. I see them as another step taken in the reality of God's grace. Every day we're called on to write imperfect scores. God wants to use the ink of your life poured out for others. Let's get writing!

Are You a Puddle or a Hero?

BY TOM KRAEUTER

> So then, just as you received Christ
> Jesus as Lord, continue to live in him.
> COLOSSIANS 2:6

Not long ago I went on a field trip with my daughter's elementary school class. Aside from the tornado warnings later in the afternoon (that's another story), it was a beautiful day to enjoy the St. Louis Zoo.

My daughter's teacher had scheduled a special learning time at the zoo with one of the employees. The employee taught us about vertebrates, animals with a backbone. At one point during her talk she asked, "What good are bones?"

One of the students answered, "They hold us up." My immediate reaction was to think that this was a rather simplistic answer but that the employee probably expected it coming from a third grader.

Her response, however, surprised me. She said, "If you didn't have bones, you'd be a big puddle of yourself." We all laughed. What a picture that conjures up!

Actually, I frequently feel like I'm just a big puddle of myself. More often than I care to admit, I am keenly aware of my shortcomings. I am very mindful of the myriad of things I can't accomplish by myself. However, in the midst of recognizing that on my own I am just a big puddle of myself, I find hope in the Word of God.

Try this. Make a list of the people in the Bible who you view as heroes. Write down all those from the pages of Scripture whose lives you would like to emulate, the ones through whom God clearly accomplished wonderful deeds. When you've finished that little project, you will have a list of sinful people who struggled with many of the same passions and quirks with which you and I struggle. In spite of their deficiencies, the Spirit of God worked in and through their lives.

In his book *Twelve Steps for the Recovering Pharisee (Like Me)*, John Fischer talks of growing up with Bible characters as his heroes. They captured his childhood imagination, and he admired them greatly. Fischer said this:

> Solomon was the wisest, Samson was the strongest, Jacob was the cleverest, Gideon was the bravest, Jonah was the luckiest, Moses was the boldest, Joshua was the most courageous, and David was the greatest of them all, because he defeated the giant Goliath with nothing but a slingshot...
>
> At some point in my life I had to face the disappointing fact that Solomon was a bigamist, Samson was a womanizer, Jacob was a deceiver, Gideon was an idolater, David was an adulterer and murderer, and Jonah was running away from God even after he got to Nineveh.[2]

Those are stark contrasts, but realities nevertheless. These "heroes" were sinful human beings like you and me. They weren't perfect by any stretch of the imagination. They were, in essence, big puddles of themselves.

However, they did not let that keep them from accomplishing God's plans and purposes. They ultimately recognized their need for God's mercy. They saw that on their own, they couldn't accomplish anything.

God doesn't have a lot of perfect people in His kingdom. He's got folks like you and me. From my perspective on Scripture, the truth is that Jesus went out of His way to hang out with people who were a mess, people who were in great need of His mercy and grace.

If you're waiting for the day when you'll be more "together" before God can really use you, stop waiting. He has only ever had one absolutely pure, completely perfect vessel to work through: Jesus. All the rest of us have been marred by sin.

I am not trying to make light of sin. Sin is heinous in the sight of God. It is the thing that sent Jesus to the cross. God hates sin. However, God's grace will always be more powerful than sin. It is only because of that grace that we can do anything at all. It is not because we somehow reach a certain level of sinlessness in our lives that God will work through us. No, it is simply because of His tremendous mercy.

Our verse for today says, "So then, just as you received Christ Jesus as Lord, continue to live in him" (Colossians 2:6). How did you receive Christ Jesus as Lord? By faith, recognizing your need for forgiveness, right? So, *as* you received Him, *continue* to live in Him. In the same way you received Him—by faith, recognizing your need for forgiveness—continue to live in Him.

Realize that each day you desperately need the grace and mercy of the Lord. The only difference between remaining as a big puddle of yourself and being someone who truly accomplishes the plans and purposes of God is the unfathomable mercy of the Lord Most High. Rest in His grace. Allow Him to cause you to fully accomplish His plans and purposes for you as an individual and as part of the worship ministry.

Mother Teresa and Your Church's Worship

BY GERRIT GUSTAFSON

 Whatever you did for one of the least of these brothers of mine, you did for me.
MATTHEW 25:40

Tucked away in an alley off a dingy street in Calcutta is a very non-descript doorway. I was a bit uncertain that it was even the right place. However, that humble doorway, through which I was warmly welcomed by the Missionaries of Charity, also became an entrance for me into an understanding of worship that is branded deeply in my mind and heart.

Mother Teresa was probably not someone you would have thought of as a worship consultant to your church. However, as you retrace with me that conversation in 1988, I think you might just discover an insight that if put into practice could deepen your life of worship and increase the sense of God's pleasure in it.

After presenting her with simple gifts—a booklet I had written and two popular worship tapes—*Give Thanks,* with Don Moen, and *Glorify Thy Name,* with Kent Henry—I exuberantly described what I saw going on internationally in the area of worship. "It's a worldwide revival of joy," I reported. "God is clothing His people with garments of praise!" Surely, I thought, I would declare the good news of what God was doing and introduce these faithful servants of God to a greater and more glorious worship!

36

Her eyes were kind, but unimpressed, as she pushed back the cassettes saying that they didn't have any cassette players. They had chosen to live without such distractions.

I thought to myself, "How can you be a worshiper and not be able to keep up with all the new songs!" I was daunted but quickly regained equilibrium and tried again. "What kind of music do you like? What kind of instruments do you use? Do you like faster or slower songs?"

No instruments, I learned. Their early morning worship times were very reverent, and prayer was more prominent than singing. A chance-of-a-lifetime conversation, and I was blowing it. It was as though we were speaking different languages.

I desperately recalled the words of my friend who had invited me to India and had helped set up this meeting. He had said to me, "Ask what worship means to her." So I did.

Finally, her eyes brightened as her answer went something like this: "If you really want to bless the Lord and pour out your love on Him, He has told us how to do it." And then she quoted Jesus' words in Matthew 25: "Inasmuch as you did it to one of the least of these My brethren, you did it to Me" (NKJV). She said that when the Missionaries of Charity minister to lepers from the streets of Calcutta, they do it as an act of worship to Jesus. She challenged me with these words: "If you really want to lavish your love on God, pour out your life on the needy."

"Mother Teresa," I said, "would you pray for me that I would be a true worshiper?" She answered, "Only if you'll pray for me first that I would be one, too." We prayed for each other.

On my flight home, somewhere between Delhi and Frankfurt, I came across these words in Hebrews 13: "Through Jesus, therefore, let us continually offer to God a sacrifice of praise—the fruit of lips that confess his name. And do not forget to do good and to share with others, for with such sacrifices God is pleased" (Hebrews 13:15–16).

With such sacrifices—vocal praise *and* acts of mercy and generosity—God is pleased! I thought, "What a great title for a worship conference: 'With Such Sacrifices!' "

Just as the cross of Christ is vertical and horizontal, and just as the two great commandments—to love God and love your neighbor—reach upward as well as outward, so the true worship of God has two components: spoken praise to Him and selfless service to others. One without the other is an incomplete expression of worship.

So what would Mother Teresa have said to help the worship in our churches? Maybe her words would go like this: "You mustn't think worship happens only when you are singing. It happens also when you're serving others. Until we are vitally connected with those our Lord calls 'the least of these,' we are not yet the worshiping churches He is looking for. Until we find delight in serving the insignificant— the children, the powerless, the prisoners, the unborn—God's pleasure in our worship is incomplete."

So if you're part of the worship ministry in your church and it's all starting to feel a bit empty, maybe it's time to cancel the regular worship band or choir practice and find out where the "least of these" are so you can tell Jesus how much you really love Him.

A Team Effort

BY TOM KRAEUTER

> *The eye cannot say to the hand,*
> *"I don't need you!"*
>
> 1 CORINTHIANS 12:21a

U sually when I teach worship seminars I utilize video projection software. In this way I am able to project the outlines for the teachings and use attention-grabbing graphics to enhance those teachings. The opening slide for one of my outlines features a collage of photos of individual musicians. These range from a man in a Mexican hat playing the bongos to a tuxedo-clad saxophonist. The guy in jeans and a T-shirt bending backward playing a screaming lead on his electric guitar is next to a rather staid-looking, middle-age woman playing the piano. There are several other varied photos as well. My comment is that this conglomeration of musicians reminds me of the average church worship ministry. There are people from all different backgrounds and, oftentimes, even extremely varied musical tastes.

Over the years I have frequently used 1 Samuel 22:2 as an example of what many church worship ministries look like to me: "All those who were in distress or in debt or discontented gathered around him [David], and he became their leader." Church music ministries are usually quite the assortment of different kinds of people. Getting all these different types of folks to work together is often a major chore.

Scripture tells us, "The eye cannot say to the hand, 'I don't need you!' And the head cannot say to the feet, 'I don't need you!' On the contrary, those parts of the body that seem to be weaker are indispensable, and the parts that we think are less honorable we treat with special honor.... Now you are the body of Christ, and each one of you is a part of it" (1 Corinthians 12:21–23a, 27).

Although we may differ immensely in our backgrounds, styles, tastes, and thinking, we still need one another. We could never accomplish alone what we can accomplish together.

In his wonderful book *The Heart of the Artist*, Rory Noland, music director at Willow Creek Community Church, said this:

> One thing that we learned very quickly at Willow Creek is that ministry is best done in teams. The beauty of working in teams is that together we can accomplish greater things for God than if we were on our own. We have a saying around Willow Creek that goes like this: We come together to do what no one of us could do alone. With all of us pitching in and pulling in the same direction toward a goal, we reap huge dividends from our individual investments. If we try to do all alone what is better done as a team effort, the result will be limited...[3]

Those of us involved in church worship ministry need to understand a concept that much of corporate America appears to have grasped: synergy. A dictionary definition of synergy is "the simultaneous action of separate elements which, together, have greater total effect than the sum of their individual effects." The idea is the mathematically impossible equation where the whole is equal to more than the sum of its parts.

Have you ever seen a flock of geese flying in "V" formation? Each goose is aided by the windbreak caused by the goose in front of him. When they fly in such a manner, geese are able to fly much farther and with much less effort than if they each tried to fly on their own. This is synergy.

Some time ago, I read a fascinating illustration of synergy. On the average, one farm horse can pull six tons. So if you put two farm horses together, how much should they be able to pull? Twelve tons, right? Wrong. Two horses can pull thirty-two tons! That is synergy.

Even the Bible declares this to be true. "Five of you will chase a hundred, and a hundred of you will chase ten thousand" (Leviticus 26:8). Mathematically, if five can chase a hundred, then a hundred should be able to chase two thousand. But that is not what it says. A hundred can chase *ten thousand*. That is synergy. We must understand that God has made it inherent within His creation that if we will walk together and work together, we can accomplish far more than each of us can on our own.

Though we may not see eye to eye on everything—we are, after all, very different from one another—we still need one another to accomplish fully what God wants us to do. "The eye cannot say to the hand, 'I don't need you!'" Even with all of our differences, we need one another.

Hold the Onions

BY BILL RAYBORN

> To the weak I became weak, to win the weak. I have become all things to all men so that by all possible means I might save some. I do all this for the sake of the gospel, that I may share in its blessings.
> 1 CORINTHIANS 9:22–23

I HATE ONIONS!

I mean, if you really want to ruin the taste of something for me, just load it with onions. Garlic is nearly as bad, but nothing—absolutely nothing—tastes as bad to me as onions! Please understand, I do not like the taste. I do not like the texture. There is nothing about raw onions that has any redeeming value to me at all! I hate onions!

Now, this is not an *inherited* repulsion. I recall my mother telling how as a child she would take a salt shaker to the onion patch, pull an onion from the ground, peel back the outer layer, salt it, and eat away. UGH! To even write these words doesn't sit well with me. I don't like onions. Have I made that clear?

But you know what? I have fellowship each Sunday, as well as days in between, with fellow Christians who like onions. I can't say I understand them. I can't even say I think the way they do about this subject. However, *they like onions*. Why they like onions I cannot understand for the life of me. But I will have to admit it is possible to like onions and still be a Christian!

Sometimes, in my saner moments, I even realize that not everyone feels the same as I...nor should they! Why, McDonald's even puts onions on their hamburgers unless you tell them to hold the onions. And McDonald's seems to be doing very well, thank you.

Okay, you are probably already way ahead of me in what this has to do with church music and those of us in the choir. We know that we are not all going to agree on worship or even worship music. In every congregation there are always those who would like more praise and worship choruses or fewer praise and worship choruses. There are those who love the great old hymns of the church, and those who consider anything written before 1980 to be out of date. Some want a cookin' praise band, while others prefer the solitude of a pipe organ. Some will raise both their hands in worship, while others stand with their hands firmly entrenched in their pockets.

I have tried something with choirs across the country, and *the results are always the same*. I have asked choir members to take the music that we are rehearsing and rank it in order of most meaningful down to least meaningful. Not the prettiest or easiest to sing or most popular, but the most meaningful to *them*. No one is to look and see what his or her neighbor is doing until everyone is through. Even though I have done this many times all across the country, the result is always the same. Someone's *most* meaningful song is someone else's *least* meaningful.

I remember the first time I heard "Mercy Saw Me" by Geron Davis as it was published in the musical *Mighty Cross*. I was at a special meeting being held by Integrity Music in Mobile, Alabama, for music distributors from across the country. I had just gone through some difficult times, and to hear the words of this great tune rendered me into one big puddle right there in front of God and about two dozen of my fellow music industry compadres. As I looked around the room, I noticed that not everyone's eyes were leaking.

People at your church come from differing backgrounds. Some love classical music. Some love country. Some may think music is not that important at all. Those of us leading in music ministry must minister to them all. If you don't like a certain song being sung in the congregation or as a choir special number, just wait. That one may not be for you. As Will Rogers said about weather, "If you don't like it, just wait a few minutes."

So I think it's okay for me to hold the onions on my hamburger. It's when I decide that other people can't have onions on their burgers that I do not really minister.

If we serve our people a variety of musical dishes seasoned in a variety of ways, then we will have hungry folks coming back to be served over and over again. And if you don't like McDonald's, just wait. Sooner or later you can "Have It Your Way."

Leaky Pipes and Humility

BY TOM KRAEUTER

> *Pride goes before destruction,*
> *a haughty spirit before a fall.*
> PROVERBS 16:18

We were having company that evening. It was a friend my wife and I had not seen for more than twenty years. All three of us had gone to high school together, and we were finally reuniting after all those years. So why, you may wonder, did I choose that afternoon to try to fix a slowly leaking water pipe valve in the basement? Good question!

Keep in mind that home repairs are not my area of expertise. (Friends and family reading this are thinking, "That's a gross understatement!") However, fixing the leak seemed like such a small project, one that would take only a very short time. As my wife worked diligently in the kitchen fixing a rather involved meal, I dutifully pulled together all the necessary tools to make the repair. I turned off the water throughout the house (to keep from flooding the basement while I worked) and proceeded to begin the necessary repairs.

It took almost an hour to get enough water finally drained out of the pipes to start removing the old shutoff valve. Almost immediately after that I encountered another small setback, but I was certain I could solve the problem. Over two hours later, my wife was still waiting patiently for the water to be turned back on so she could finish the meal preparations. I assured her I was almost done. Finally, I reassembled the section of plumbing with the new shutoff valve. When all the joints had been soldered, I looked at my work and smiled. I was sure I had done a really good job. In fact, I had done such a good job that I thought I could offer my services to help others with their plumbing. "That wasn't too difficult," I thought. "I'm pretty good at this."

Then I reached up to grab the pipe as I climbed off the ladder. Two of the four solder joints were done so poorly that the entire assembly twisted in my hand. I knew I was in trouble.

What did that opening Bible passage say? "Pride goes before destruction, a haughty spirit before a fall" (Proverbs 16:18).

Have you ever been prideful, only to find out you weren't really as good as you thought? After a service, have you ever thought, "I sure nailed that solo this morning. I'm sure everyone was really impressed"? Guess what. God could have done that solo much better than you could ever do. The longer I walk with the Lord, the more I am amazed that He is willing to work through haughty, prideful people like you and me.

God spoke through the prophet Isaiah, "I am the LORD; that is my name! I will not give my glory to another or my praise to idols" (Isaiah 42:8). He will not allow us to compete with Him for the glory. He gets it all.

Several years ago my pastor, Nick Ittzes, made a statement that I have often shared at worship seminars. Even though I have read it aloud many times, every time I read it I am still pierced by the truth of the words. "Any success that comes apart from humility will, on the last day, be labeled the illegitimate child of a wicked heart." It's true. God has no use for our prideful attitudes.

James told us, "Humble yourselves before the Lord, and he will lift you up" (James 4:10). Peter said it in very similar fashion: "Humble yourselves, therefore, under God's mighty hand, that he may lift you up in due time" (1 Peter 5:6). Those are tremendous promises. We want to be lifted up. However, to get lifted we must first humble ourselves. Matt Redman reminded us in his popular song "The Heart of Worship" that it's not about us; it's all about Jesus.

In his book *Fresh Wind, Fresh Fire*, Jim Cymbala, pastor of Brooklyn Tabernacle, said this:

Our forebears back in the camp meeting days used to say that if people left a meeting talking about what a wonderful sermon the preacher gave or how beautifully the singers sang, the meeting had failed. But if people went home saying things like 'Isn't God good? He met me tonight in such a wonderful way,' it was a good meeting. There was to be no sharing the stage with the Lord.[4]

We need that kind of attitude in the Church today. Do you ever exhibit just a bit of a prideful attitude? Avoid the destruction and the fall that today's Bible verse warns of. Stay away from pride and haughtiness. Choose to be humble.

Why?

BY PATRICK KAVANAUGH

> 🍃 *God is love. Whoever lives in love lives in God, and God in him.*
> 1 JOHN 4:16b

Why does God desire our worship? When we read passages like the one about Jesus and the woman at the well, we note that the Father is seeking (that is, desires) our worship. Perhaps you, after pondering this idea, have asked the classic one-word question, "Why?"

Many scriptures make it clear that God commands us to worship Him. But why? Usually our difficulties with this question can be placed in one of two categories:

1. "Is God conceited, so that He wants to be the center of everything?"
2. "Why would an all-powerful God *need* anything from us?"

To answer these questions, look at the character of God. To begin with, "God is love" (1 John 4:16). This means that all He does toward us is done in love; that is, all His actions toward us are done for *our* good. Therefore, His desire for our worship cannot come from any motives of conceit or egotism. It must be concluded that He wants us to worship Him for *our* good. So much for the first question.

The second question is a bit trickier. Obviously, an all-powerful God cannot have needs in the same way that we have needs. As the

48

great London preacher Charles Spurgeon pointed out, "The Lord says nothing of friends and helpers: He undertakes the work alone, and feels no need of human arms to aid Him."

This is also true in regard to worship. It is clear that if no person ever worships the Lord, God has not lost anything. Indeed, God was God—without any needs whatsoever—long before He even created us.

So God does not *need* our worship. Yet He certainly *desires* our worship. He insists on it. He commands it of us. Why?

Anyone who has ever read the delightful *Autobiography of Benjamin Franklin* knows that this man had tremendous gifts of intellect and diligence. *Poor Richard's Almanac* clearly shows that Franklin was also a man of much practical wisdom. Yet I believe that he made a critical mistake concerning the subject of worship.

In his *Articles of Belief and Acts of Religion*, Franklin declared, "I cannot conceive otherwise that He, the Infinite Father, expects and requires no worship or praise from us, but that He is infinitely above it."

How did Franklin come up with such an idea? Very logically...almost. He correctly discerned that God is "infinite," indeed, infinitely above us. Franklin saw correctly that God was all-powerful, all-knowing, and utterly without need. Since God was without need, Franklin logically concluded that God did not need our praise and worship. Also correct.

The mistake was that of omission. Our brilliant patriot concluded wrongly that the only reason God might command praise from us is that He *needed* us to praise Him, which, of course, He does not. Franklin did not see that there might be another reason that God commands us to worship Him.

So what is this other reason? The answer, clearly understood, reveals one of the most profound aspects of the Christian life. The reason that God desires our worship is that *He desires a personal relationship with each of His children.*

Why is this? God desires this relationship with us, not because He needs it but because of His own nature and character. Everything we see in Scripture indicates that it is in God's essential nature to desire relationship with those He has created. Consider the Lord's words as He cries out for our fellowship: "Here I am! I stand at the door and knock. If anyone hears my voice and opens the door, I will come in and eat with him, and he with me" (Revelation 3:20).

This "desire of God" is poetically described toward the beginning of Milton's *Paradise Lost*. According to this epic masterpiece, as soon as creation was complete, God had an "unspeakable desire to see and know all these His wondrous works, but chiefly Man, His chief delight and favour, him for whom all these works so wondrously He ordained."

Why did He create us except to have relationship with us? It is because God is love—and love is essentially concerned with giving—that He created us.

Adapted from the book *Worship—A Way of Life* by Patrick Kavanaugh (Grand Rapids, Mich.: Chosen Books—a division of Baker Book House Company, 2001).

Are You a Servant?

BY TOM KRAEUTER

> *"If anyone wants to be first, he must be the very last, and the servant of all."*
> MARK 9:35

Jesus told His followers, "[T]he Son of Man did not come to be served, but to serve" (Matthew 20:28). If we understand this statement, and if we understand that Jesus always told the truth, then it appears obvious that Jesus did not sit around while others waited on Him hand and foot. Jesus clearly could not have honestly made this statement about not coming to be served if he had sat around like a potentate expecting others to jump at His every whim.

I imagine Jesus helped collect firewood for their cold evenings in the countryside. I picture Him offering to carry water. With His carpentry skills, He most likely repaired more than one door or chair in a home where He stayed.

What about you? Do you offer to help prepare the music sheets for Sunday? Do you help stack the chairs or move the music stands and other equipment? Are the menial tasks of life beneath you? Are you really a servant?

Jesus summarized the servant attitude we should have when He spoke these words: "Suppose one of you had a servant plowing or looking after the sheep. Would he say to the servant when he comes in

51

from the field, 'Come along now and sit down to eat'? Would he not rather say, 'Prepare my supper, get yourself ready and wait on me while I eat and drink; after that you may eat and drink'? Would he thank the servant because he did what he was told to do? So you also, when you have done everything you were told to do, should say, 'We are unworthy servants; we have only done our duty' " (Luke 17:7–10).

Quite some time ago I attended a large Christian conference. Toward the end of the conference there was an appreciation ceremony to honor those who had done such a marvelous job of taking care of all the details of the event. Especially honored were the husband and wife who had tirelessly spearheaded coordinating all of the volunteers necessary for the conference. Several people expressed what a tremendous job this couple had done. Finally, when it was time for them to respond, they stood. The wife said nothing and the husband said just four words: "It was our pleasure." Then they sat down. There was not even a hint of, "Look at us. Didn't we do a great job?" Their servant hearts shone through clearly.

In Matthew 25, Jesus told the parable of the talents. Toward the end of the story the master says to those who were faithful, "Well done, good and faithful servant!" (Matthew 25:21, 23). This story was meant to parallel the kingdom of God. The ending represents the great last day when we will meet the Lord face-to-face. It is my personal conviction that as long as we are part of His kingdom we will all hear those words, "Well done, good and faithful servant." Please realize that it has very little to do with us, but everything to do with God's faithfulness. However, when we hear those words, what will our reaction be? "Oh yeah, God, remember the time we were leading worship and four people gave their hearts to You while we played and sang?" At that point, who cares?!

When I look into my Savior's eyes and He tells me, "Well done, good and faithful servant," the only possible response will be to look at Him through tear-filled eyes and say, "Lord, thank You so much for the opportunity just to serve You!"

That should be our attitude here and now also. We're really no one special, just unworthy servants doing our duty.

Let's be really candid for a moment. I have ministered in churches of nearly every conceivable background and size all across North America. I have encountered churches where the worship "team" consisted of one person and other churches where the ministry included horns and a string section. I have seen hundreds, perhaps thousands, of very gifted musicians. However, I have not found nearly as many servants.

What about you? Are you comfortable and active serving others? Do you need to allow God to work in your heart an attitude that counts it a privilege to serve?

Adapted from the book *Oh, Grow Up!* by Tom Kraeuter (Lynnwood, Wash.: Emerald Books, 2001).

Carriers and Couriers of God's Presence

BY KENT HENRY

> *Whenever the spirit from God came upon Saul, David would take his harp and play. Then relief would come to Saul; he would feel better, and the evil spirit would leave him.*
> 1 SAMUEL 16:23

Through the example of David's life, we catch a glimpse of the power of a vessel who is a carrier of the presence of God. It's actually hard to believe that anyone could have this kind of effect on a king terrorized by an evil spirit. Yet, this is exactly how David was used as he played his harp and worshiped. He released a power from the Lord. And the results were astonishing.

First Samuel 16:20–23 tells the story of David, the shepherd boy, who loved to sing songs to the Lord. King Saul had sent word to Jesse, David's father, to release David to serve in his court. It was in this place that David took harp in hand and played until the king was changed. Saul was made well and refreshed because of David's ministry. The evil spirit would depart as David played.

This must have been a very potent power working through David. The power was in the music that he played, but more important, it was the Lord within him. David was clearly a useful vessel and a carrier of a power that sent an evil spirit fleeing.

In the same way, God has called you and me to be couriers of His holy presence. First Corinthians 6:19–20 proclaims, "Do you not know

54

that your body is a temple of the Holy Spirit, who is in you, whom you have received from God? You are not your own; you were bought at a price. Therefore honor God with your body."

Have you ever thought about yourself in this way, as a reservoir of God's presence? If not, it's time to readjust your focus. We are believers, whom God has called, and that makes us vessels in the truest sense of the word. In essence, we are the "postmen" of His presence, transmitting it to everyone we see and touch throughout the day.

This is one of the constant mindsets and heart attitudes that I take with me into worship services. I pray, "Father, come and meet with us. As we loose the power of your Holy Spirit in worship, let the abundance of Your presence bring healing, restoration, and refreshing to Your people. In this time, we loose the ability of Your presence to transform human hearts and minds. Do in us by Your presence what we cannot do for ourselves."

The word *carrier* is defined as "one who carries on the business of transporting; a person employed to transport goods or passengers." It was because of this very idea that the early believers were called Christians. Literally that means "little Christs." They were the "little anointed ones" transporting the same Spirit that was in Jesus. Anointed with what? Carriers of what? God's holy presence, of course.

In the study of chemistry, a carrier is a catalytic agent that causes an element or radical to be transformed from one compound to another. We can be men and women, just like those in the Bible, who carry His presence to our generation, bringing help and healing wherever we go. In essence, we are God's catalytic agents, helping others be transformed in His presence.

Let's look at this from a slightly different angle. Besides being carriers of God's presence, we are couriers. The word *courier* is defined as "a messenger, usually sent in haste with important letters or messages; one hired to accompany travelers and take care of hotel accommodations and luggage."

A few years ago I woke up on the day I was to teach at a pastors' conference in Louisiana. As the reality of where I was and what I was about to do dawned on me, my first thoughts were, "Who do I think I am? Who am I to be teaching these pastors about moving their churches forward in worship?" Immediately I sensed the Lord speaking back to me in that still, small voice: "Who *are* you? Part of My body. My vessel, an errand boy delivering a life-changing message for Me." That day my life was significantly impacted. It became clear to me that we are not simply accidents going someplace to happen. Rather, we are couriers of His presence, carriers of His message, and those called to fulfill His purposes.

Like David playing his harp and bringing relief to the tormented King Saul, so we, as carriers and couriers of God's presence, can bring true life wherever we go—especially through our music and worship. Recognize anew the power of "Christ in you, the hope of glory" (Colossians 1:27). Then as we go forth, let's remember that we are carriers and couriers of His presence!

God's Softest Whisper

BY TOM KRAEUTER

> *Paul and his companions traveled throughout the region of Phrygia and Galatia, having been kept by the Holy Spirit from preaching the word in the province of Asia. When they came to the border of Mysia, they tried to enter Bithynia, but the Spirit of Jesus would not allow them to.*
> ACTS 16:6–7

It was a cold, rainy Sunday morning as we prepared to leave for church. Our entire family was nearly ready to walk out the door when my oldest son asked if he could take my keys and start the car. I agreed, and everyone else scrambled toward the door to follow him. I was the last one out of the house, so I locked and closed the door. As I started to move toward the car, I realized that my coat was stuck in the closed door. I couldn't open the door. It was locked, and I didn't have my keys. I couldn't move toward the car because my coat was caught. Oh, and did I mention that it was raining?

At first my family couldn't figure out what I was doing. Once they realized my predicament, however, they did the only sensible thing. They laughed. And not just little snickers hidden behind hands for the sake of politeness. No, this was uproarious, sidesplitting laughter. I couldn't move, and they knew it.

The apostle Paul was once kept from going where he was planning to go also. However, it was not a stuck coat that stopped him. It was God. Our Bible verse for today tells us that the Spirit of Jesus would not allow Paul and his companions to enter Bithynia. Please realize that Paul was not being rebellious by trying to go to Bithynia. He was endeavoring to fulfill the mandate that the Lord had given him. He was, after all, the apostle to the Gentiles (Romans 11:13). He was simply trying to walk out the fullness of that to which the Lord had called him.

It seems apparent to me that God does not generally show us the whole plan ahead of time. If He did, our normal human reaction would be to take the big picture and run with it, never waiting to find out the specific steps God has in mind. When we do this we are relying more on ourselves than on God. We want to reach the goal when, often, the Lord seems more interested in the means.

If Paul had not been listening to the Lord all along the way, he easily could have gone right on into Bithynia. Had he done so, Paul would have missed the important work God had for him and his companions in Macedonia. There is a chance Paul may have even seen good things happen in Bithynia, but it would not have been God's best.

We, also, sometimes get glimpses of what the Lord is saying, and we run off, half-cocked, ready to achieve the goal. We'll overcome anything in the way to get to the end.

Perhaps we should consider the possibility that more important than arriving at the finish line is paying attention to God along the way. After all, if we get to the end and have missed His lessons along the way, have we really succeeded?

In everyday life as well as in the worship ministry, we must be seeking the Lord regularly about our next steps. We may have an overall idea or plan, but the specifics also need to be done with God's direction.

Perhaps you didn't get to play the solo you were hoping to play. However, was it possible that God was speaking to you about humility? Or when you sang the words of the second verse when you should have been singing the first verse, you were embarrassed for several days. Was the Lord perhaps dealing with you about your overactive perfectionist attitude? You see, it's very easy to get so lost in reaching a particular destination that we miss God's hand in events along the way.

I recently conducted a retreat for the worship ministry of a church. During the weekend a woman made a statement that has had a profound impact on me. She said, "I am on a quest to hear God's softest whisper." She wanted to know the Lord not just in the big events and arriving at the final destination, but in the everyday moments of life.

That should be our goal, also. Whether we're the drummer, the violist, the harmony singer, or the worship leader, we should desire to follow God. More than giving a flawless musical performance, we want to know Him, follow His directions, know His voice.

Together, let's seek the Lord's guidance in everyday life. Let's be more concerned with learning the lessons along the way than simply arriving at a final destination.

Soft Hearts on a Dangerous Mission

BY ARLEN SALTE

Therefore, since we are surrounded by such a great cloud of witnesses, let us throw off everything that hinders and the sin that so easily entangles, and let us run with perseverance the race marked out for us. Let us fix our eyes on Jesus, the author and perfecter of our faith, who for the joy set before him endured the cross, scorning its shame, and sat down at the right hand of the throne of God. Consider him who endured such opposition from sinful men, so that you will not grow weary and lose heart. In your struggle against sin, you have not yet resisted to the point of shedding your blood.
HEBREWS 12:1–4

As long as I live, I will never forget the scene. My wife and I were on the way to work during rush hour. Suddenly, a young boy dashed out into the middle of the road. A pickup truck turning left hit him head on. His little body flipped under the truck and was caught on the undercarriage until his clothes tore and he was left crumpled in a heap.

Nobody moved. Like statues, people on the street corners refused to run to the rescue of this little boy in the busy road.

Finally, my wife could restrain herself no longer. She leapt from the car into the path of rush-hour traffic and ran to this young boy's side.

While I screamed at people to call 911, my wife knelt in the danger of the street. By now the boy's face was blue. He wasn't breathing. He was dying.

My wife restored his breathing and held him until the ambulance showed up.

The boy was taken away, and we never saw him again. The fact remained, however, that my wife was covered in blood because she ran to help when everyone else stayed in the comfort of the sidewalk. There were no thank you's. No one applauded. The crowd didn't hoist my wife on their shoulders and parade her downtown to get a medal. No journalist took her name. My wife was simply left with bloodied clothes and dirty hands.

Today, maybe you feel a little like my wife, out in the danger of the street. Ministry is a dangerous business. Being involved in your church's music ministry is one of the hardest places to be. When you deal with people's music, you don't just deal with their personal tastes. You deal with the very language of their hearts.

Week after week you lay your soul bare before the congregation. In the process of exposing your soul, it's easy for your heart to get battered in the battle. Maybe you wish someone would acknowledge your gifts, place you on his shoulders, and parade you to the church office to be awarded a medal. Unfortunately, you are generally left standing alone with little applause, and the traffic has just picked up where it left off.

Along the way, we can begin to carry the staining scars of ministry. These come in many forms. Sometimes we have been taken for granted. At times we ourselves are the little boy hit by a truck called slander. Perhaps we've had face-to-face confrontations about our drum volume, our choice of music, or style of playing.

The most common result of having our heart stepped on in ministry is bitterness.

Our Bible reading today talks about throwing off everything that hinders. Bitterness is one of the greatest hindrances to an effective worship ministry. It impacts every word we say and every note we sing. We cannot proclaim both bitterness and praise at the same time and have an effective ministry.

James 3:9–12 says, "With the tongue we praise our Lord and Father, and with it we curse men, who have been made in God's likeness. Out of the same mouth come praise and cursing. My brothers, this should not be. Can both fresh water and salt water flow from the same spring? My brothers, can a fig tree bear olives, or a grapevine bear figs? Neither can a salt spring produce fresh water."

Is the sin of bitterness entangling your life and sabotaging the effectiveness of your worship ministry? Have the words of hurt that have been leveled at your gift left you shackled by the chain of resentment?

Mark 11:25 says, "And when you stand praying, if you hold anything against anyone, forgive him, so that your Father in heaven may forgive you your sins."

If you are trying to retain a soft heart in ministry while having a concrete shell against your brother or sister, you are damaging your worship ministry, the person you are bitter against, and your own heart as well.

In his book *The Art of Forgiving*, Lewis Smedes writes, "When we genuinely forgive, we set a prisoner free and then discover that the prisoner we set free was us."[5]

If you think this is still too hard, take a look at the apostle Paul's challenge today. Use Jesus as an example. Isaiah 53:3 says, "He was despised and rejected by men, a man of sorrows, and familiar with suffering. Like one from whom men hide their faces he was despised, and we esteemed him not."

Nothing we face in our dangerous ministries will ever compare to the danger of His mission. Yet, He retained a soft heart and cried out from the cross, "Father, forgive them, for they do not know what they are doing" (Luke 23:34a).

Jesus ran into the rush hour of our lives with no guarantee of our response. He came to us when all others stood by, watching our destruction. His hands ended up covered with blood. However, the blood wasn't even ours. It was His own.

It's time to throw off the hindrance of bitterness. Why not begin the process today?

Real Worship

BY TOM KRAEUTER

> *Seek justice, encourage the oppressed.*
> *Defend the cause of the fatherless, plead*
> *the case of the widow.*
>
> ISAIAH 1:17

The section of Scripture that precedes today's verse depicts God lambasting His people for going through the motions of worship but missing the real heart motivation. For several years I had taught from this portion of Scripture. However, one day I realized that I had not really paid much attention to this particular verse. "Seek justice, encourage the oppressed. Defend the cause of the fatherless, plead the case of the widow." At the end of God's tirade against His people about what was wrong with their worship He tells them to "seek justice." He says they should "encourage the oppressed." God charges them to "defend the cause of the fatherless," even to "plead the case of the widow." Did I miss a curve somewhere, or is the Lord relating worship to acts of kindness? Coincidence? Read on.

The prophet Amos says, "I hate, I despise your religious feasts; I cannot stand your assemblies. Even though you bring me burnt offerings and grain offerings, I will not accept them. Though you bring choice fellowship offerings, I will have no regard for them. Away with the noise of your songs! I will not listen to the music of your harps. But let justice roll on like a river, righteousness like a never-failing stream!" (Amos 5:21–24).

There it is again! It *appears* that the Lord is saying that unless we are performing deeds of kindness, unless there are acts of justice within our lives, our songs of praise are meaningless. God is far more interested in our lives than our words. We can come into our church buildings singing songs of praise, but if our ears are deaf to those who cry out for justice, is it really of any value? "To obey is better than sacrifice" (1 Samuel 15:22).

Several years ago, as I began to study this concept earnestly, I found more and more evidence that God really does link our worship with our acts of kindness. "Religion that God our Father accepts as pure and faultless is this: to look after orphans and widows in their distress" (James 1:27a). Amazing! It says nothing about singing or lifting hands. No reference is made to prayer or intercession. Pure religion is looking after those in need.

In the context of bearing one another's burdens, Paul prays that God would "give a spirit of unity...so that with one heart and mouth you may *glorify God*" (Romans 15:5–6). By bearing the burdens of one another we can come into a degree of unity whereby God is glorified. In this instance, glorifying God, or worship, appears to be a by-product of helping one another in times of need.

I also came across some rather fascinating verses in Psalm 68. "Sing to God, sing praise to his name, extol him who rides on the clouds— his name is the LORD—and rejoice before him. A father to the fatherless, a defender of widows, is God in his holy dwelling. God sets the lonely in families, he leads forth the prisoners with singing" (Psalm 68:4–6). Right in the middle of simply glorifying God, David begins to expound upon God's heart toward those in desperate situations, the heart of a loving heavenly Father who is far more interested in actions than in words.

Worship is more than just singing songs on Sunday morning. Ultimately, it must be even more than singing songs all through the week. Worship must be a way of living. It should encompass all that we say and do, even those little acts of kindness.

One day, during the course of my studying this connection between acts of kindness and worship, I was driving along in my car singing praises to God accompanied by a worship tape. I was on a long stretch of highway when I noticed a car on the side of the road with a flat tire.

On the opposite side of the road I noticed an older woman walking. I felt a nudge inside to turn around and go pick her up. I resisted, but immediately I remembered that this was a perfect opportunity for a real act of worship. I turned around and took her to a service station. On the way I learned that although we were each more than fifteen miles away from our respective homes, she lived only two houses away from our church. I had the opportunity to introduce myself and invite her to church.

I could have continued on driving, singing my words of worship. Instead, I chose to glorify God with my deed, a simple act of kindness to a person in need. That's the real heart of worship.

Often at worship conferences I have heard Hebrews 13:15 shared: "Through Jesus, therefore, let us continually offer to God a sacrifice of praise—the fruit of lips that confess his name." Frequently this passage is used to help people understand the necessity of giving vocal expressions of praise in every situation. This is indeed a correct understanding, but if we stop there we miss the context of the passage. The next verse says, "And do not forget to do good and share with others, for with such sacrifices God is pleased." Simply verbalizing our praise and worship to God is not enough—He wants our lives and our actions.

Will *you* accept the challenge? Beyond the Sunday morning singing, let's live lives of worship. Let us model real worship of God for all those around us. Let's not be so caught up in the intricacies of music performance that the heart of the Lord is forgotten. He cares greatly about *people*. Let's take our worship beyond the four walls of the church and offer our lives to the Lord through acts of kindness to anyone who is in need. That's real worship.

Adapted from the book *Worship Is...What?!* by Tom Kraeuter (Lynnwood, Wash.: Emerald Books, 1996).

Worship and the Visitor

BY GERRIT GUSTAFSON

> *I will praise you, O LORD, among the nations;*
> *I will sing of you among the peoples.*
> PSALM 108:3

An American church-planting pastor in Japan told me this story. Two Japanese, who had never had any previous contact with Christianity, came into a tiny Christian gathering. The worship that day, he said, was especially good. After the meeting, the two visitors eagerly approached the pastor with this question: "When you were singing those songs, we felt something. Was that God?" The pastor was able to explain how God dwells in the praises of His people and how they could know Him personally.

People are looking for spiritual reality. In previous decades a secular rationalism created antagonism toward spiritual expression. Currently, however, there is a broad reaction to that worldview and an unabashed hunger for spiritual experience. For the most part, the Church is surprisingly uncomfortable with its transcendent nature.

In his book entitled *The Contemporary Christian*, John Stott makes this observation:

> This quest for transcendence is a challenge to the quality
> of the church's public worship. Does it offer what people are

craving—the element of mystery…in biblical language "the fear of God"…in modern language "transcendence"? My answer to my own question is "Not often." The church is not always conspicuous for the profound reality of its worship…. No wonder those seeking Reality often pass us by![6]

We shouldn't assume that the visitor is incapable of apprehending spiritual phenomena. After all, each one is made in the image of God, and as Ecclesiastes 3:11 says, He has "set eternity in the hearts of men." The worship experience corresponds to that universal "itch." That explains the recent finding of the largest study of American congregational life ever undertaken—the FACT report conducted by the Hartford Institute for Religion Research: "Vibrant worship is at the heart of church growth."

Let's look at some principles of how hearty worship can help our fellowships and congregations communicate the Christian life to visitors.

PRINCIPLE #1—WORSHIP GIVES A PICTURE OF KINGDOM LIFE

A man I met at a conference told me this story. At a time in his life when he was far from God, he was hurrying through a hotel lobby and happened to catch in the corner of his eye a television broadcast of a large gathering of people worshiping. Less than a minute later, he stopped in his tracks, went back to the TV, and watched intently through his tears, knowing that God was drawing him back. God apprehended this man through a picture of worship.

Jesus said in Mark 12 that loving God totally and wholeheartedly is the greatest commandment. Christian worship should be living pictures of the society of those who have exchanged self-centered living for God-centered living. The act of corporate worship beautifully demonstrates this new lifestyle where God is the center. The visitor needs such a picture.

PRINCIPLE #2—MEAN WHAT YOU SING AND SING WHAT YOU MEAN

The biggest hindrance to visitors is not that they encounter something they don't immediately understand. It's encountering something that is not genuine. Mahatma Gandhi, after several years of studying in London, said he would have become a Christian if he had ever met one.

Whatever version of Christianity he saw, he apparently didn't see the real thing.

One study concluded that 55 percent of all communication is non-verbal. The visitor is not just listening to what you say. He is intuitively observing how connected you and your group really are with what you espouse. He's looking for emotional and intellectual honesty, depth of conviction, and heartfelt compassion. How we worship reflects these things—or their absence—more than we know.

The discipline for worship teams to learn is to mean what you sing and sing what you mean. This will affect not only what you sing but also how you sing it. Worship leaders, choose songs that are appropriate to your group's experience. There's no place for meaningless expression. Then learn the songs so well that they are literally part of you.

Also, make sure that the transitions between songs and between the segments of your meetings are natural and believable.

PRINCIPLE #3—ONE SIZE DOES NOT FIT ALL

To some, Jesus revealed mysteries; to others He veiled His message. In the same way, we need to discern the level of hunger among those who are visiting.

People who come to our meetings will be at many different levels of spiritual experience. Since the Holy Spirit knows and loves each one so deeply, being sensitive to the Holy Spirit is the best thing you can do for the visitor.

Don't get in a rut. Being sensitive to the Holy Spirit may mean on one day to stir in bigger portions of fun songs; other times, the songs may be more thoughtful. The smaller the meeting, the more flexible you can be, but this principle of sensitivity to the Holy Spirit needs to apply to all our gatherings.

Why is it so important to me that we not try to hide our worship from the visitor? It's because I was once the visitor, as you probably were too. I can still remember that meeting in Tallahassee, Florida, in 1968, when I, for the first time, saw people abandoned to God in worship. It awakened in me a deep sense of hope and destiny. Like the Queen of Sheba in 2 Chronicles 9, when she was the visitor observing Israel's worship, I was "breathless." I'll really never be the same.

Don't you think that those who visit us should be given the same privilege?

Reaching for Excellence

BY TOM KRAEUTER

> Whatever you do, work at it with all
> your heart, as working for the Lord,
> not for men....
> COLOSSIANS 3:23

Some time ago I had the opportunity to visit a fascinating exhibit at the St. Louis Zoo. In it were numerous displays of exotic animals from around the world. Unfortunately, all through the exhibit I saw blatant, as well as subtle, references to evolution. As I walked through the display, two feelings came over me. The first was pity for the learned scientists who believe that all of these things came into being simply by chance. The second was an overwhelming awe of the God of creation who made all of these creatures. His creativity is limitless. The variety in those creatures was so great that it seems to take more faith to believe that they were an accident than to believe in a God who created them.

God apparently held nothing back when He created the earth on which we live. Why, after all, did the Lord make the creatures in the ocean depths that no human would even discover until this century? Why did He make each animal unique? Why so many different kinds? Would not just a few dozen have been sufficient? It seems apparent that God chose to make creation not just a halfhearted effort but the absolute best it could be. This attitude was manifest in Jesus also. When the people witnessed His healing ministry, they responded, "He has done everything well" (Mark 7:37).

We in the Church need to grasp the concept of excellence more fully. I frequently have the opportunity to interact with those involved in worship ministries in churches. There have been more times than I care to remember when I have encountered someone doing a half-hearted job with the attitude of, "It's good enough for church." This attitude is totally opposite from God's perspective.

Proverbs 18:9 tells us, "One who is slack in his work is brother to one who destroys." From the Lord's perspective, not doing your best is akin to being a destroyer. Clearly God is interested not in a halfhearted effort but in excellence.

> In the second century, Christian apologist Justin Martyr grew up over the hill from Galilee. Interestingly, he notes that the plows made by Joseph and Jesus were still being used widely in his day. How intriguing to think of Jesus' plows...to wonder what it was that made His plows and yokes last and stand out.[7]

Wooden plows that were used regularly and lasted more than 100 years? This was not merely "acceptable" craftsmanship. The work of Joseph and Jesus was apparently outstanding. The reality is that they could have cut some corners and not done such a quality job. After all, if the plows lasted just thirty years, surely the purchaser would have been satisfied. There certainly could not be any recourse for any type of reimbursement if a regularly used plow made it through fifty years of plowing. Why expend so much effort to make plows that would last so amazingly long? As Colossians 3:23 tells us, "Whatever you do, work at it with all your heart, as working for the Lord, not for men."

Author and teacher Os Guiness, in his book *The Call*, said, "Instead of doing things because of their intrinsic importance—their value in themselves—we do things for instrumental reasons—their value for our self-expression, our fulfillment, our profit, and our publicity."[8] Unfortunately, he's right. We are too often more self-motivated than God-motivated. "What's in it for me?" is a common thought. Instead, our attitude should be, "What's the right thing to do?" and "How can I glorify the Lord in this?"

If we really want to follow the Lord, then we have no choice but to desire and pursue excellence in everything we do. The standard of excellence is simply a part of the nature of the God whom we serve. We need to strike the death blow to mediocrity within the Church. If we can grasp and implement this attitude in our lives, we will see the blessing of God poured out upon us to maintain it.

We should have the attitude of, "Regardless of what others think, regardless of what it costs me, I will pursue godly excellence, even as my Creator has pursued it." If we will pursue this attitude of excellence in all that we do, God will be honored and, in return, honor our efforts.

Work at your musical abilities. Don't rest on past accomplishments. Don't compare yourself (favorably or unfavorably) with someone else. Honor God by working to do the best you can. Reach for excellence.

Adapted from the book *Living Beyond the Ordinary* by Tom Kraeuter (Lynnwood, Wash.: Emerald Books, 2000).

Encountering God's Presence in Worship

BY BOB KAUFLIN

> Then Moses said to Him, "If Your
> Presence does not go with us, do not
> send us up from here."
> EXODUS 33:15

Exalting God is our first priority in the corporate worship of God. Our worship must be God-focused (God is clearly seen), God-centered (God is clearly the priority), and God-honoring (God is clearly exalted). We should come away from public praise with a renewed understanding of who God is and what He has done.

However, if we stop there, our congregational worship is incomplete. A unique aspect of corporate praise is God's presence. In his significant book *God's Empowering Presence*, Gordon Fee writes, "For Paul the gathered church was first of all a worshiping community; and the key to their worship was the presence of the Holy Spirit." If this is accurate, how then do we experience God's presence when He is already present everywhere? (Psalm 139:7–10).

Although God is omnipresent—equally present in all places at all times (ponder that for a while!)—He also reveals His presence to us in unique ways, especially as we gather in His name. One striking example occurs in 2 Chronicles 5:13–14, when God's people began to praise Him at the dedication of the temple. "They raised their voices in praise to the LORD and sang: 'He is good; his love endures forever.' Then the temple of the LORD was filled with a cloud, and the priests could not perform their service because of the cloud, for the glory of the LORD filled the temple of God."

God desires to come near to us as we draw near to Him (James 4:8). Hebrews 4 urges us to approach the throne of grace with confidence "so that we may receive mercy and find grace to help us in our time of need." This certainly includes (although it isn't limited to) times of corporate worship.

As we worship God, He meets with us and directly ministers to us, strengthening our faith, making us more aware of His presence, and refreshing our spirits. This is what it means to encounter God's presence.

During these times, He may also convict us of a particular area of sin in our lives or our sinful state in general. This seems to be the effect of the prophetic utterances in the public meeting Paul describes in 1 Corinthians 14:23–25. Regardless of your view of the gift of prophecy, this passage plainly shows that God seeks to encounter us as we gather to worship Him.

In corporate worship, God encounters His people today the same way He has for centuries: through His Word and His Spirit. In one instance you may be particularly moved by a passage of Scripture that is being read. At another you may suddenly be gripped by the mercy of God as you share in the bread and cup at communion. Or you may find yourself overflowing with joy at the glorious thought that "my sin, not in part, but the whole, has been nailed to the cross, and I bear it no more!"

We want to be clear: The primary goal of corporate worship must not be any particular emotional experience. (That is the very definition of man-centered rather than God-centered worship!) But let us not so overreact to perceived emotional excesses, whether real or imagined, that we fail to respond appropriately to God's Spirit working in our hearts. He desires and intends for us to encounter Him as we worship Him. As you enter a corporate meeting, are you actively desiring to encounter God?

Worship is more than a one-sided conversation. While we sing and pray, God wants to reveal some aspect of His character to us. As He does so, it is crucial that we respond to His presence.

I've been in meetings—you may have been also—in which little or no opportunity is provided for a congregation to respond to what God is evidently saying during a time of corporate worship. We move on to the next event in the program as though we had exhausted all God had for us. I don't believe this is biblical or helpful. We need to remember that God's Holy Spirit is actually in our midst, seeking to encourage, convict, and edify the members of the church. The New Testament seems to indicate that the meetings of the early church, while maintaining a sense of order, provided opportunity for people to respond to what the Spirit was saying, through either spiritual gifts or the preached Word (1 Corinthians 14:24–33; 1 Thessalonians 5:19–21; Acts 20:7). The singing itself was to be a time of "teaching and admonishing" (Colossians 3:16). How could the effects of that activity be measured without some kind of response?

A wise worship leader will be sensitive to the Spirit's leading and, under the authority of his pastor, help the congregation respond appropriately to God's emphases during a meeting. A common response in corporate worship is prayer led by the pastor or prayer for one another. A testimony of someone's conversion might give rise to songs of exaltation and celebration. Every response brings glory to God because we are acknowledging that God has revealed Himself to us.

Second Corinthians 3:17–18 says, "Now the Lord is the Spirit, and where the Spirit of the Lord is, there is freedom. And we, who with unveiled faces all reflect [or contemplate] the Lord's glory, are being transformed into his likeness with ever-increasing glory, which comes from the Lord, who is the Spirit." We are transformed as we meditate and reflect on the Lord's glory. Transformation emerges from response.

Which of these two options brings God more glory: to faithfully execute our plan for the service each week or to respond wholeheartedly when, in the midst of our plans, the Spirit of God enlightens our hearts to understand better who He really is and what He has done? I believe this is part of what Paul is referring to when he describes us as those who "worship by the Spirit of God" (Philippians 3:3).

Encountering God's presence in our times of worship is a precious gift we should not only hope for but also eagerly expect. Do you?

"Who Me—Selfish?"

BY TOM KRAEUTER

🌿 *But he answered his father, "Look! All these years I've been slaving for you and never disobeyed your orders. Yet you never gave me even a young goat so I could celebrate with my friends. But when this son of yours who has squandered your property with prostitutes comes home, you kill the fattened calf for him!"*
LUKE 15:29–30

These verses, of course, are from near the end of Jesus' parable about the lost son, commonly referred to as the prodigal son. The wayward child had just returned home, and the father told his servants to prepare for a celebration. Big brother, however, was not in a festive mood.

Can you sense the anger in the older son's voice? He wouldn't even refer to the returning son as his brother. Instead, he says to his father, "…this son of *yours.*"

If Jesus had told this parable in our day, the older brother's monologue might have sounded like this: "Dad, this just isn't right! I can't believe this is happening! I've hung around here at home for all these years doing everything you've asked me to do. I have not complained or grumbled at the chores you gave me. I never rebelled against your authority. And this…this young punk—this miserable excuse for a human being—goes off and squanders his entire inheritance on…on debauchery…and you give *him* a feast?! Tell me, Dad, what's wrong with this picture?!"

Have you ever felt like this? Oh, perhaps the situation and circumstances were radically different, but the heart attitude was the same. "I've been a Christian for practically my entire life. Why does it seem like the people who have lived horrendous lives and then had a powerful conversion experience as adults are the ones who get all the attention? What about those of us who have been faithful for years?" Or perhaps a closer-to-home scenario: "Why does the new guy get the solo part? I've been faithfully doing my musical part for a very long time in this church, and *he* gets the limelight? It's really not fair!"

In the early 1600s Thomas Coryat traveled extensively on foot and wrote of his adventures. In a magazine article novelist Anthony Weller wrote of Coryat that he "traveled not for plunder or science or God but for his own personal pleasure, and to our eyes he seems modern in this regard."[9] In other words, Weller believes that to be modern means to be totally self-centered. Actually, that's not modern at all. It's been human nature right from the very beginning. Like the older brother in the prodigal story, we have a propensity to see everything that happens through a lens that has been tainted by our own self-centeredness.

Remember the story of Martha and Mary? Martha wanted to make a really good meal because the Master was coming to her house. She wanted to bless Him. That's a good and noble aspiration. Martha started out well. Her motivation was right. Where she got into trouble was when she demanded that Mary have the same motivation. She switched from wanting to bless Jesus to meeting her need to get the meal prepared. When Mary didn't cooperate, Martha got upset.

Have you ever done something like that? There have been times that I have begun a project—large or small, it seemingly makes no difference—with good intentions. I wanted to help. However, as I undertook to complete the endeavor, I saw those who were not working on this now-beloved project of mine. "What's wrong with them," I wondered. "Can't they see I could use some help? Don't they recognize how important this is?" Just like Martha, I started out right, but my focus switched along the way. How come? Because I'm selfish. Oh, and, by the way, so are you.

Paul sums up the dilemma well in his letter to the Philippian church: "For everyone looks out for his own interests" (Philippians 2:21a). Let's face it. We're selfish. We want *our* way.

Although God clearly knows our hearts better than anyone, he showed *His* heart in the parable of the lost son. The father responds to the faithful son, "My son...you are always with me, and everything I have is yours" (Luke 15:31–32). Yes, the son was being selfish. Yes, his response was way out of line. The father, however, articulated his compassion.

If today you're feeling a bit alienated in life—if you're having a selfish pity party—listen to the words of your heavenly Father to you: "You are *always* with Me. *Everything* I have is yours." God is with us. He's given us everything we need. In light of this promise, let's be less focused on ourselves—our wishes, our desires—and be more focused on God—His plans and His purposes—as well as the needs of others.

"Lord, forgive me for being so focused on me. Help me to be more in tune with Your desires and with the needs of others. Amen."

Are You Vegetating or Worshiping?

BY PATRICK KAVANAUGH

> Be very careful, then, how you live—not as unwise but as wise, making the most of every opportunity, because the days are evil.
>
> EPHESIANS 5:15–16

Do you desire to worship God more than you do right now? I think it is safe to assume that none of us is 100 percent satisfied with our overall worship life. Improvements could be made. So how do we do that?

It is clear that each of us has exactly twenty-four hours each day. So for you to *add* any new activity (such as worshiping God) will mean, of course, that you will first have to *subtract* some other activity in which you are presently involved.

Now, don't panic! I do not mean that you have to quit your various clubs, throw out any hobbies, and kick in the television. (God may or may not be telling you to do so at times, but I am not.) We need a degree of rest, relaxation, and recreation, and there is no need to feel guilty about it. How you spend your relaxation and recreation time is your own business. Certainly, we each should check ourselves from time to time to reevaluate our priorities. However, this is not my present purpose.

No, we must learn to worship God more in our *present* lifestyle, although, as was mentioned above, we cannot add without subtracting. What then shall be subtracted to make room for worshiping the Lord?

The answer is, for lack of a better word, *vegetating*. That is, every day we waste a huge amount of time vegetating, when we could be worshiping.

What is vegetating? Let me explain by asking a number of questions:

What were you thinking about when you showered yesterday?

What were you thinking about when you were waiting in the bank line yesterday?

What were you thinking about when you shaved yesterday?

What were you thinking about when you waited for your computer to start up yesterday?

Do you know the answer to any of these questions? Most of us haven't a clue. You may answer, "I suppose I was thinking something, but it wasn't that important, and I can't remember what it was today." Perhaps. However, for most of us, the honest truth was that we weren't really thinking about anything in particular at those times. We were zoned out. We were wasting mental time. We were vegetating.

Is this such a horrible crime? Of course not. It does, however, represent a vast amount of time every day that could have been better spent worshiping the Lord. As Thoreau reminds us, "You cannot kill time without injuring eternity." Trying to spend less time vegetating is simply the price one must pay to spend more time consciously worshiping.

You see, when many of us read about someone like Brother Lawrence, the medieval monk who coined the phrase "practicing the presence of God," we make a critical mistake. We think that he was able to practice the presence of God while scrubbing dishes because he was such a wonderful, holy person. In other words, we assume that he could do this because of some special ability or talent that *he* had but we do not. This is both a mistake and a cop-out—one that we all too often use to excuse our own lack of worshiping.

The real reason Brother Lawrence was able to practice the presence of God while scrubbing dishes was that instead of zoning out, as most of us do while scrubbing dishes, he consciously worshiped, prayed, sang, and spoke praise (at least mentally) during those times of ordinary work. Instead of vegetating, he chose to worship.

How much of our time could be spent like this? How many things do we do every day that do not take any real thinking but are rather automatic? Some scientists have estimated the amount as high as 50 percent to 70 percent of our day. Most of our routine activities—unless they are directly involved with speaking, writing, or communicating with someone—fall into this category. Whatever our lifestyle, we all indulge in some amount of unnecessary vegetating every day.

Of course, few of us are guilty of wasting *large* amounts of time. However, it is in the small moments that we could improve. The great Christian teacher G. Campbell Morgan once exhorted those around him, "Let the year be given to God in its every moment! The year is made up of minutes: let these be watched as having been dedicated to God. It is in the sanctification of the small that hallowing of the large is secure."

Again, please understand that I am *not* talking about rest, relaxation, or recreation. These are beneficial and necessary, and we should consciously choose them. Vegetating is neither beneficial nor necessary. It is not even something we consciously choose to do. It is a waste: Our body is busy, but our minds are vacant, unoccupied, meaningless, a blank.

All those times we could have been worshiping the Lord.

Adapted from the book *Worship—A Way of Life* by Patrick Kavanaugh (Grand Rapids, Mich.: Chosen Books—a division of Baker Book House Company, 2001).

Are Your Fields Trimmed?

BY TOM KRAEUTER

> *What is more, I consider everything a loss*
> *compared to the surpassing greatness of*
> *knowing Christ Jesus my Lord....*
> PHILIPPIANS 3:8a

Years ago I attended a worship conference. In one workshop, the speaker began by asking those involved in the worship ministry of their local church a poignant question: "What would you do or what would your reaction be if your pastor told you that for the foreseeable future, worship at your church would be very different? There would be no extended times of worship, only three or four songs. Even those would utilize only the piano or organ, no other instruments. There would be no worship choir or harmony singers, just one person leading the songs. What would you do?"

We all pondered the question, but only briefly. He didn't give us much time to think before continuing, "That happened at my church...and it was the right thing." This man went on to explain that the pastor had recognized that the majority of those involved in their worship ministry were only there to, as he put it, "do their musical gig." They were not so much interested in worshiping God as they were in playing their instrument or singing their part.

In my experience this scenario is extreme. Most of us involved in the worship ministry started because of a desire to use the talents God has given us. We began playing or singing to honor the Lord. The idea of people involved in worship ministry who have no desire to truly worship is foreign to us. Although I have to admit that I have encountered a few people like that, they are clearly in the minority. The vast majority of people involved in worship ministry got into it because of an honest desire to worship their Creator/Redeemer. That is definitely the norm.

However, even with such a positive beginning, there often comes a time when that desire begins to wane. Over time, the monotony of things like preparation, weekly rehearsals, and working at your musical part can begin to take its toll. Originally we thought, "I can't wait until _____ night for rehearsal." Eventually, in some cases, that can be transformed into, "I don't want to go to rehearsal tonight. Maybe I'll call and say I can't make it."

Not long ago some friends of mine, Paul and Gretyl Haglin, said this in their ministry newsletter:

> A few years ago, while we were hiking together around the big pasture in front of our home, we became aware for the first time of how really far back into the woods from the edge of the field were the old fence lines. We realized that over the years we and our predecessors had allowed the woods to encroach on the fields by as much as fifty feet in some areas. This process had been gradual and over a long time because some of the trees inside the fence line were mature and rather large. A sizable area of our property that had at one time been a productive field had become woods and scrub brush and weeds and poison ivy vines.
>
> The Lord made the equation in our hearts that the same thing happens to our spiritual "fields" if we do not keep them trimmed and cultivated and productive.[10]

This is true for us as musicians also. We must recognize that worship is not simply a matter of coming to church and playing our instrument or singing our harmony part. It is a matter of relationship with the living God. We, as those leading the congregation in worship, need to be regularly trimming and cultivating our spiritual fields. If we don't, we really have nothing to give.

So what exactly does that mean? Okay, let's be specific. Are you growing in your relationship with the Lord? Are you reading and studying His Word? Are you praying regularly? When you play your instrument for church, is your heart engaged? Or is it just another musical gig?

C. S. Lewis, in his classic book *Mere Christianity*, said this:

> God made us: invented us as a man invents an engine. A car is made to run on gasoline, and it would not run properly on anything else. Now God designed the human machine to run on Himself. He Himself is the fuel our spirits were designed to burn, or the food our spirits were designed to feed on.[11]

The apostle Paul said, "What is more, I consider *everything a loss* compared to the surpassing greatness of knowing Christ Jesus my Lord" (Philippians 3:8a).

What a statement! This is Paul, the apostle. Paul, a brilliant man. Well-educated. Righteous. The Pharisees' Pharisee. Outgoing. Friendly. Well-traveled. Articulate. Still, he says that none of these things make any difference compared to knowing Christ.

Please notice in Paul's statement that he did not say, "knowing *about* Christ Jesus." The Greek word very clearly indicates not just head knowledge but relationship.

When my oldest son, David, graduated from sixth grade in a small Christian school, the parents of the class were invited to a luncheon and brief ceremony. The teacher asked each of the parents to share a section of Scripture with their child during the celebration. When my turn came I shared Philippians 3:8. I explained to David that he reminded me a lot of Paul. "You're articulate and well-educated. You've gotten straight A's in everything this year. You're friendly. You're persuasive in speech. However, the reality is that without your relationship with the Lord none of these things are of any value at all."

The same is true for each one of us. No matter how well you play your instrument or sing, without the ongoing relationship with God—if you don't keep your spiritual fields trimmed and cultivated—the rest is worthless.

Careening Down a Mountain in Unity

BY ARLEN SALTE

 Two are better than one, because they have a good return for their work: If one falls down, his friend can help him up. But pity the man who falls and has no one to help him up!...
Though one may be overpowered, two can defend themselves.
A cord of three strands is not quickly broken.
ECCLESIASTES 4:9–10, 12

They were a pretty scraggly group of people. (If the truth be told, they probably thought the same about us.) They were hitchhikers in need of a ride and a shower, but even more in need of the gospel.

We were a band on a mission. We had a tour bus, so we saw it as the ultimate mobile evangelistic tool. We were a virtual tent meeting on wheels. We picked up every hitchhiker we saw. We were going to evangelize the world, even if it took us forever to get to our next destination. The back of the bus was filled with gospel tracts. Yet, the hitchhikers didn't seem to want to read them. That is, until we lost our brakes on the way down the Canadian Rocky Mountains.

It's amazing how quickly your mind can turn from thoughts of *this* life to thoughts of the *next* life when you're careening down a mountain. This is enhanced even more when the driver is shouting out the distances printed on signs that tell you where the next runaway lane is. They say that speed kills, but it also does very well at concentrating the mind on eternity.

A few minutes earlier the hitchhikers were a diverse group of people who really didn't care to know one another or us either. As we slalomed down the twisting mountain without the benefit of skis, however, we were all like brothers. Suddenly, the fact that we were Christians didn't matter to them. And I'll tell you frankly that their body odor really didn't matter to me either during those tense minutes.

Having a passionate dedication to survival can bring amazing unity and make differences seem pretty trivial. However, having a passionate dedication to *any* common goal can have the same effect.

There are so many attitudes that can hinder unity in our praise teams. This lack of unity also impacts the effectiveness of our worship leading. I have known many worship groups that are filled with tremendously talented musicians, singers, and technicians. Yet, the church's worship never gets off the ground because their internal strife acts like a ballast on a balloon. When this happens, it's time to revisit our common vision.

We can get so bogged down with each other's imperfections that we forget our higher purpose of unity. In John 17:20–21, Jesus prays, "My prayer is not for them alone. I pray also for those who will believe in me through their message, that all of them may be one, Father, just as you are in me and I am in you. May they also be in us so that the world may believe that you have sent me."

Did you catch that? Jesus prays that we may be one *"so that the world may believe that you have sent me."* Jesus was saying that our unity is a sign of His divinity to the world.

At every service in our churches, there are people who are at different levels in their spiritual walks. Some don't know Jesus as their Savior. Some know Christ but have wandered far away. They watch us to see if Jesus truly makes a difference in our lives. They often reason that if discord is the signature of the church, then Jesus may lack the power to change their lives. If our worship team is filled with disunity, then we may be a huge stumbling block in their spiritual awakening. This should restrain our discordant thoughts with great sobriety.

Jesus spoke directly to this issue of unity in the Church when he said, "Therefore, if you are offering your gift at the altar and there remember that your brother has something against you, leave your gift there in front of the altar. First go and be reconciled to your brother; then come and offer your gift" (Matthew 5:23–24).

Often, this is quoted as a reference to the time we come together to take communion. However, it goes far beyond communion. The musical gifts that we offer in front of the altar are to be taken very seriously. Jesus challenges us to lay our gifts aside and be reconciled first. We are not even to continue with offering our gifts until we have settled matters with our fellow Christians.

It is essential that we keep our eyes on the significance of what we're here to accomplish. Whenever our praise team is torn apart with strife, it's time to set aside our musical gifts at the altar and deal with the issues that prevent us from being a singular voice of praise.

What is the blessing of doing this? As our verse for today states, *"A cord of three strands is not quickly broken."* We all will face times in our ministries when the brakes go out and we're careening down the mountain. If we keep our eyes on the ultimate goal, we can remain strong in Jesus Christ.

Prayer Mining

BY TOM KRAEUTER

> The eyes of the LORD are on the righteous
> and his ears are attentive to their cry.
> PSALM 34:15

T hose of us involved in the ministry of praise and worship in the local church often view music as the most important thing. Oh, certainly we understand that our hearts must be in the right place. That's a given. However, after that, as long as we come in and play and sing well, that's what really matters, right?

Let me offer you some further thoughts from my own life. Although I have been involved in music and worship for years, God has given me a stronger gift in teaching. It's just a natural thing for me to teach. Because of the teaching gift, I have often thought, "If people just have enough information, they'll change." Wrong!

In his book *Fresh Wind, Fresh Fire*, Jim Cymbala, pastor of Brooklyn Tabernacle, said it like this:

> Prayer is the source of the Christian life, a Christian's lifeline. Otherwise, it's like having a baby in your arms and dressing her up so cute—but she's not breathing! Never mind the frilly clothes; stabilize the child's vital signs. It does no good to talk to someone in a comatose state. That's why the great

87

emphasis on teaching in today's churches is producing such
limited results. Teaching is good only where there's life to be
channeled. If the listeners are in a spiritual coma, what we're
telling them may be fine and orthodox, but unfortunately, spir-
itual life cannot be taught.[12]

You see, information alone does not fully empower people. I need
to pray for the people whom I am teaching. Even if the full counsel of
the Word of God is preached, unless it is undergirded with prayer, it
will not have the fullest possible effect.

Likewise, you may sing or play your instrument extremely well.
You may even give an absolutely flawless musical performance.
However, if you don't pray for the people to whom you are ministering,
it will not have the same impact in their lives.

I read a lot. I often jot down quotes from books or articles for future
use in teaching. Usually I remember to note the source of the quote.
Occasionally I forget. This quote is so pertinent that although I
neglected to obtain the source information, I want to share it anyway:

Mining is hard work. Boring into solid rock is no easy
task. It requires patience and commitment, but it is essential
to the mining process. Once the boring is complete a charge
is placed in the hole, and large amounts of rock are then
blasted away. If the blast occurred on the surface it would not
have the same impact. Many Christians today are eager to par-
ticipate in lighting the fuse, but few are willing to give them-
selves to the difficult job of boring into solid rock. Anyone can
light the fuse. It takes commitment and patience to do the
hard work.

Likewise, you can play your instrument or sing, but unless you're
willing to do the hard work of prayer, the full impact of the ministry
will never be realized.

Please understand that I am not suggesting that you must spend
hours and hours praying for the people in your church (I'm not sug-
gesting that you shouldn't either!). It is not so much a matter of how
long you pray or how often you pray that is important.

Perhaps you are familiar with international evangelist Reinhard Bonnke. Hundreds of thousands of souls have come into the kingdom of God through his ministry. Bonnke credits a great measure of the success he has experienced to the people who consistently pray for him. A few years ago I heard the woman who leads the intercession team for Bonnke. Please understand that this is her job. She spends hours a day praying. However, she made one simple statement that has stuck with me ever since. She said, "It is not how long you pray or how 'powerfully' you pray—it is that you pray that counts."

Our verse for today, Psalm 34:15 says: "The eyes of the LORD are on the righteous and his ears are attentive to their cry." God is waiting for us to cry out to Him.

He wants you to pray for those people you're leading in worship. And not just a quick sixty-second prayer right before the service. Throughout the week, pray that their hearts would be open to all that God has for them—in the service and in their lives. Pray that they will come to the service prepared not just to sing but to worship God with all their heart. What would happen if everyone on your team did that? Would it make a difference the next time your church gathers corporately?

What about praying for the other team members? Pray that the peace of God will reign in their hearts, in their lives, and in their families. Pray that they will be ready to minister, not just to play their instrument and sing their part. What would happen if everyone on your team did that?

Pray for your worship leader. Pray for your pastor. Oh, you get the idea. Don't be content just to sing and play your instrument. Cry out to God. Pray!

Anybody Here Know Jesse Rayborn?

BY BILL RAYBORN

 But store up for yourselves treasures in heaven, where moth and rust do not destroy, and where thieves do not break in and steal. For where your treasure is, there your heart will be also.
MATTHEW 6:20–21

W e thought we had lost him. My dad had been admitted to the hospital with a serious gall bladder attack. The operation was successful, but later he burst his stitches. A serious infection set in, and he almost died. Fortunately for Dad—and us, his family—penicillin had just been discovered. His life was saved for several more years. God was not through with him yet.

When Dad came out from under the anesthetic, he said he had a marvelous story to tell us. It became a story that he repeated many times to unsaved people over the years, before a heart attack finally took him home to be with the Lord.

He told us that while he was anesthetized he had seen some wonderful things. First, there was the obligatory bright light reported by so many people in such experiences. Traveling toward the light he found himself before a multitude of people, all dressed in white robes.

All was quiet for a time. Then, suddenly, a great voice boomed, *"Does anyone here know Jesse Rayborn?"* Daddy said there was silence for another moment, and then the voice asked again, *"Does anyone here know Jesse Rayborn?"*

Then, the crowd began to part as a young boy stepped forward, saying, "I know Jesse Rayborn. He is the reason I am here!" He went on

90

to recount how my dad had told him about Jesus, and how he had accepted Christ while talking with my father. "I'm not the only one," said the young man. "There are several of us here."

Daddy smiled and said that once the boy was through talking, my father was clothed in a white robe and visited with others in the throng. Then, just as quickly as it had begun, the experience ended. Dad told us, "I don't know if it was real, or if it was just too many 'hypos.' What I *do* know is that it seemed real to me, and I have no reason to believe it wasn't."

That experience was years ago. To this day I'm still not sure what *I* believe about those "near death experiences." To my mind, there is no reason to believe they are *not* real. But whether the veil between earth and heaven is sometimes lifted just a bit so we can see the eternal, I don't know. I do occasionally think that if the Lord let us see too much we would be most unhappy with our mortal existence.

There is, however, one thing I do know for certain. I know that for most of his adult life Jesse Rayborn taught young people in Immanuel Baptist Church in Tulsa, Oklahoma, and led many of them to Christ. I can remember our yard being full of kids playing croquet, badminton, and a hundred other games. Whether Dad actually met one of those boys the night he almost died, I really don't know.

There is another thing I can guarantee you. One day I'll meet many of Daddy's "kids" in heaven…when I get my white robe. My dad took the time to invest in kids' lives. He will most certainly reap a great reward in heaven because of it.

Now, let me ask you, what are you investing in? I'm not talking about your bank account or stocks and bonds. Today's verse says that we should store up treasures in heaven. Dad did that through kids' lives. Where are you investing?

Has God given you abilities and gifts? Are you using those gifts and talents in God-honoring, God-pleasing ways? Are you storing up heavenly treasures, or are you getting your full reward here and now?

Beyond that, are there people you should be nurturing in areas where the Lord has gifted you? Are there people who need the knowledge and wisdom God has worked in your life? Are you investing in those people?

Maybe the greatest question to ask would be, "Who would come forward if that great voice were to ask if anybody knows you?"

God Is Here!

BY TOM KRAEUTER

> *Day and night they never stop saying: "Holy, holy, holy is the Lord God Almighty, who was, and is, and is to come."*
> REVELATION 4:8b

Several places in John's revelation we can see glimpses of heaven. One of the most profound pictures is found in the fourth chapter of the book of Revelation. It says this:

> In the center, around the throne, were four living creatures, and they were covered with eyes, in front and in back. The first living creature was like a lion, the second was like an ox, the third had a face like a man, the fourth was like a flying eagle. Each of the four living creatures had six wings and was covered with eyes all around, even under his wings. Day and night they never stop saying: "Holy, holy, holy is the Lord God Almighty, who was, and is, and is to come" (Revelation 4:6–8).

The four living creatures described here are clearly nothing we have ever seen. They are not earthlings of any type. These beings were most likely created just for heaven. Whatever their precise origin, there is no indication—not even a hint—that they have a fallen nature. Nothing even remotely suggests that they were in need of redemption.

Unlike us descendants of Adam, these creatures are holy by nature. Certainly their holiness does not approach the fullness of the holiness of God. However, being sinless creatures automatically means they are holy. These four may be aware of sin, or perhaps they have even seen sin. They have not, however, experienced it firsthand. They have not been immersed in it as we have. Because of this there is automatically a purity—a holiness—about them that we have never experienced.

All of this makes their ongoing chanting even more poignant: "Day and night they never stop saying: 'Holy, holy, holy is the Lord God Almighty, who was, and is, and is to come.' " If they, in their holy state, found God so holy that it required them to repeat over and over and over, "Holy, holy, holy..." what will we do when we look upon the holiness of God? We who are fallen by nature, we who have been steeped in sin since birth, what will our reaction be when we gaze upon the holiness of God Almighty?

Let's look at this from a different perspective. What would happen if in the middle of a worship service God came up and tapped you on the shoulder? "I'm here." I'm not talking about just sort of imagining it. In reality He *is* there. "For where two or three come together in my name, there am I with them" (Matthew 18:20).

Too often we see the people but we miss Christ. The problem is that we have lost the sense of awe. Unfortunately this is not a new phenomenon. The Israelites saw the blessing of God day after day. For forty years He supplied food for them (manna) in an obviously miraculous fashion. It was there every morning. There was no other possible explanation for this means of sustenance other than the hand of God. Yet they took it for granted. We also too often take the presence and actions of the Lord for granted. We need to cultivate a sense of awe and wonder toward God.

Dr. Donald McCullogh wrote a fascinating book entitled *The Trivialization of God*. In it McCullogh said this:

> Visit a church on Sunday morning—almost any will do— and you will likely find a congregation comfortably relating to a deity who fits nicely within precise doctrinal positions, or who lends almighty support to social crusades, or who conforms to individual spiritual experiences. But in many churches, you

will not likely find much awe or mystery. The only sweaty palms might be those of the preacher unsure whether the sermon will go over; the only shaking knees could be those of the soloist about to sing the offertory.[13]

No wonder our services are so often mundane. We have lost all sense of expectancy. We do not act as though God is really there. If He really did tap us on the shoulder, we would most likely not even notice.

Let's not settle for such a lackadaisical attitude. Instead, ask the Lord to help you recapture—or perhaps find for the first time—a sense of awe toward Him. In addition, purpose in your heart to not settle for the mundane but to recognize the wonder of God. Cultivate a sense of expectancy in your heart. Recognize anew the holiness of God that caused those already holy creatures to cry out, "Holy, holy, holy is the Lord God Almighty, who was, and is, and is to come."

Back to Kingdom Basics

BY KENT HENRY

 ...whoever wants to become great among you must be your servant.
MATTHEW 20:26b
Humble yourselves, therefore, under God's mighty hand.
1 PETER 5:6a
The fear of the LORD teaches a man wisdom.
PROVERBS 15:33a

How do we define the phrase "back to the basics"? If you and I were forced to cut out half of our daily activities, for whatever reason, which ones would remain, and why? What are the top three kingdom principles by which we are to live our lives?

These are important questions. Hopefully we would each come up with some worthwhile answers. So exactly where should our life focus be? Obviously, our focus should be on the Lord and on the characteristics of Jesus' life that were displayed in the Gospels.

In considering these things, there are three qualities that stand out in a big way for me: servanthood, humility, and reverence for God. When I'm considering getting back to kingdom basics, these three are at the top of my list.

In the Gospels we find that these great qualities continued to surface in Jesus' ministry. Through His life He modeled the idea that true greatness is based on becoming a servant to all. Through His actions He sent a very clear message: The walk of humility leads to a life of true greatness. Further, Jesus demonstrated that those people who revere, fear, and worship the living God are undergirded by the fullness of God's provision and help.

As a lifelong woodsman and a hunter, I've spent countless hours in the woods. Have you ever watched animals in their natural habitat? Birds fly to and fro, eating, nesting, and resting. There is a real simplicity about their lives. The same goes for the squirrels, rabbits, and all of God's other creatures in the woods.

My point here is that our lives need to get back to the basics, the simple yet essential things. There's a constant clutter of so many different things to do, and we are asked to do them in so many different ways. We get to the place where we forget about the most important things of life. In this case we lose sight of servanthood, humility, and reverence for God.

A friend of mine was a jet pilot in Vietnam during the war. Every day he faced some pretty tough circumstances, but he found his way through and has been in ministry now for many years. He tells a story about testing jet pilots in a flight simulator.

As a pilot is flying in the simulator, his commander causes (with a flip of a switch) one thing to go wrong with the plane. Ninety-nine percent of the pilots will correct that problem as they continue on their mission. However, the percentage begins to drop when the commander causes two or three things simultaneously to go wrong with the plane. Finally, when four or five problems occur at the same time, everybody crashes and burns. Here is the point: No one can function for long with too much commotion in his or her life.

The basics for living life are not meant to be a mystery. We are servants of the Lord, called to walk the walk of humility while living a life of worship.

These elements are not very popular things today. We live in a very self-centered society. These three basics stand out in stark contrast to today's social norms and ethics. We have drifted a long way from truly serving others with an attitude of humility. As we look around, we see so little reverence for God in the world around us.

As a nation—even more so as the Church—we are in desperate need of a fresh wind of His Spirit touching our hearts deeply. God-centered ministry releases the help and benefits of an awesome God to people both saved and unsaved.

It's time for each one of us to reassess our priorities. How do we invest our time and energy daily? We need to honestly consider our motivations. Are we operating from the heart, revering and worshiping God while serving Him and others in the true grace of humility? If we are honest, we would probably have to say that we often miss the mark. So let's pray. Let's ask God to breathe new life and understanding into these three areas. Whoever wrote the following song lyrics was absolutely right: "It's time to get back to the basics of life"—the kingdom basics.

Stretching Ourselves

BY TOM KRAEUTER

[F]an into flame the gift of God,...
2 TIMOTHY 1:6

God has given each one of us certain gifts to use for His glory. "Now to *each one* the manifestation of the Spirit is given for the common good. To one there is given through the Spirit the message of wisdom, to another the message of knowledge...to another faith...to another gifts of healing...to another miraculous powers, to another prophecy, to another distinguishing between spirits, to another speaking in different kinds of tongues, and to still another the interpretation of tongues. All these are the work of one and the same Spirit, and he gives them to *each one*, just as he determines" (1 Corinthians 12:7–11).

There is no question that we have each been given at least one gift. The friction comes when we consider nurturing the gift(s). We would much rather simply wait for the Lord to act in a sovereign manner within our lives to make the gift come forth in its fullest potential. We really do not want to work at the gifts He has given us. We just want them to happen. Unfortunately, that's not the way the Lord designed it.

In writing to Timothy, his son in the faith, Paul exhorts, "[F]an into flame the gift of God, which is in you through the laying on of my hands" (2 Timothy 1:6). Other translations say to "stir up" and "kindle afresh." Fan into flame. Stir up. Kindle afresh. These are phrases demanding action. They require a response. But was not the gift already within Timothy? Was it not a gift from the Lord? Then why did Paul tell him to do something? Because that is how God has chosen to develop people's gifts.

In the same letter where Paul wrote about all the various gifts we looked at earlier, he also says this: "Since you are eager to have spiritual gifts, *try to excel* in gifts that build up the church" (1 Corinthians 14:12). How can we seek to excel at the gifts of God unless we somehow have a part in developing them?

The Lord gives us gifts and then expects us to learn to use them to their fullest potential. Certainly He will lead us and guide us, but we have to work with the gifts to learn to "excel" at them. It is very rare, even in Scripture, for the Lord to sovereignly give a full-blown gift to someone.

In cultivating the gifts God has placed within you, do not neglect prayer. Faithful prayers have the ability to do far more than all the other work we can do. And yet prayer alone is not all that the Lord requires. We must work diligently at the gifts that He has given so that when this life is over we may hear, "Well done, good and faithful servant!" (Matthew 25:21, 23).

In practical terms, we need to use and work at the gifts He has bestowed on us as leaders of worship. Do you have musical gifts? Have you continued to cultivate them and learn more? Do you practice your instrument on a regular basis? Depending on your level of proficiency, you should perhaps consider further music courses at a local junior college or from a private instructor or even by correspondence. Perhaps music theory would be in order or further lessons on your instrument(s). If you are experienced enough and have developed your gift to a high degree of expertise, maybe you should consider giving lessons. Regardless of the subject, I almost always learn something when I have the opportunity to teach others.

Are you a would-be songwriter? Have you considered taking a music composition course? Perhaps a class on poetry or grammar would be in order. Maybe researching other song writers would be helpful. Even attempting to correspond with some of today's writers of popular worship songs might be a worthwhile endeavor.

Has God given you the ability to communicate effectively with others? Endeavoring to enhance this gift with a seminar on public speaking would be a good idea.

All of these things and more are there for the doing. Regardless of what your gifts are there is still room for improvement.

The apostle Paul, who wrote about the various gifts and then also said to stir them up, apparently wanted no part in complacency. In his letters he uses phrases like "I press toward the goal," "straining toward what is ahead," and "run in such a way as to get the prize." He's not sitting with his feet up waiting for God to expand his gifts and abilities. He's working, and working hard. He is stretching himself to be the best he can be at what he does.

God has already given us the gifts. How far we go with them is now up to us.

Adapted from the book *Keys to Becoming an Effective Worship Leader* by Tom Kraeuter (Lynnwood, Wash.: Emerald Books, 1991).

Why Do We Sing?

BY BOB KAUFLIN

> *Let the word of Christ dwell in you richly as you teach and admonish one another with all wisdom, and as you sing psalms, hymns and spiritual songs with gratitude in your hearts to God. And whatever you do, whether in word or deed, do it all in the name of the Lord Jesus, giving thanks to God the Father through him*
> COLOSSIANS 3:16–17

Whether it's a praise chorus or a hymn, an anthem or an amen, whenever God's people gather, they sing. But why? Does it really matter to God whether we sing or not? Are there other ways He wants us to praise Him when we gather? Does He even like the sound of our voices?

I believe God has given us singing as a means of developing and deepening our relationship with Him. A quick word study on variations of the word *sing* in the Bible reveals that there are over 500 favorable references to singing. Fifty of them are direct commands to sing to God, including Psalm 47:6: "Sing praises to God, sing praises; sing praises to our King, sing praises."

Obviously, God is concerned not only that we praise Him but also that we *sing* our praises to Him. As I've considered why this might be, I believe there are at least three reasons.

First, singing enables us to remember God's Word to us. Colossians 3:16 commands us, "Let the word of Christ dwell in you richly...as you sing psalms, hymns and spiritual songs." There is an apparent connection between singing and causing God's Word (or any words) to dwell in us. In fact, before people knew how to read or write, poems and music were often used for significant events such as treaties, blessings, covenant promises, and prophecies to help people remember what was taking place. Although it might be difficult for us to imagine a president singing his inaugural vows, it wouldn't have been out of place in ancient times.

If you've ever played the musical game Encore or found yourself spontaneously singing songs you knew ten, twenty, even thirty years ago, you realize that we don't easily forget what we sing. Singing helps the Word of Christ dwell in us richly by helping us remember it.

A second purpose for singing is to help us respond fully to God. In Colossians, we are not told simply to sing. We are to sing psalms, hymns, and spiritual songs with gratitude in our hearts. Whatever the threefold distinction might mean, it certainly encompasses a variety of styles as we seek to worship an infinite God.

A parallel passage in Ephesians 5:19 says as we sing we are to make music in our hearts to the Lord. God is interested in getting His Word not only into our heads but also into our hearts. Singing helps us do that. As pastor and author John Piper has commented, we sing "because there are depths and heights and intensities and kinds of emotions that will not be satisfactorily expressed by mere prosaic forms, or even poetic readings. There are realities that demand to break out of prose into poetry and some demand that poetry be stretched into song."

Singing enables us to combine intellect with emotion. Objective truth becomes linked with our response to it. Singing is meant for emotional expression. It is never to be done halfheartedly. Scripture also teaches us that singing is to be enjoyable! "Praise the LORD, for the LORD is good; sing praise to his name, for that is pleasant" (Psalm 135:3). We bring no honor to God when we squelch our emotional responses of gratefulness and joy while meditating on the mercy and kindness He has shown us. In fact, the emotion that singing is most often connected to in the Bible is joy.

The book of James has more instruction for us along these lines. "Is any one of you in trouble? He should pray. Is anyone happy? Let him sing songs of praise" (James 5:13). Not "let him speak" but "let him sing." In the words of the Billy Graham film, we have "something to sing about!"

A third reason God gave us singing is to reflect His glory in us. Singing is not simply a means to the ends of edification and emotional expression. It is an end in itself. It is an act of worship that reflects the glory of the One we worship.

Singing reflects God's glory, for He Himself sings. In fact, all three members of the Trinity sing or inspire song within us. We read in Zephaniah 3:17 that God the Father will rejoice over us with singing. In Hebrews 2:12 (quoting Psalm 22:22) Jesus is described as singing the Father's praise in the midst of the congregation. In Ephesians 5:18–19, we find that the Spirit inspires song.

Singing also glorifies God by reflecting His infinite creativity. God is the ultimate source of every creative idea in music. We must not think for a moment that God is pleased with our worship because our music is so sophisticated, so cultured, so current, or performed with excellence. God receives our simple, sincere attempts at glorifying Him as pale, distorted, but genuine reflections of His vast creativity, made acceptable through the perfect offering of His own Son.

Lastly, singing reflects God's glory because it is a foretaste of the eternal glory yet to come. The book of Revelation gives us a breath-taking picture of the singing around the throne by the heavenly creatures, the twenty-four elders, countless angels, and the redeemed. Whether these pictures represent what was taking place in the early church liturgy or were meant simply to inspire them, we're not sure. For our purposes, it makes little difference.

A logical response to hearing of the worship in heaven is to sing of God's ultimate triumph and outworking of His redemptive purposes in Christ, even before those events have been fully worked out. We sing as though the last chapter has already been written—because it has been.

Remembering God's Words, responding fully to His works, and reflecting His glory. May these three reasons inspire us all the more to sing the glory of His name and to make His praise glorious!

Like It or Not, You're an Example

BY TOM KRAEUTER

> *Join with others in following*
> *my example, brothers....*
> PHILIPPIANS 3:17

Many years ago, when I first became part of the worship team at our church, I had a stunning realization. I remember well my reaction to people looking at me, the bass player on the worship team, as an example of a worshiping Christian. Quite simply, I hated it. I had absolutely no desire to be a role model. That was not the reason I had become a part of the music ministry at our church. I simply wanted to worship the Lord with the gifts He had given me. But an example for others to follow? Me?! No way!

I soon stumbled across this passage in Paul's letter to the church at Philippi: "Join with others in following my example, brothers, and take note of those who live according to the pattern we gave you" (Philippians 3:17). "Well sure, Lord, but that is the apostle Paul talking. Certainly You do not expect people to follow *my* example," I reasoned. However, I realized that I really did not have much of a choice. People's attitudes are such that if you minister in front of the church, even if you are just the bass player, you are considered a leader.

This is even more true for the worship leader. Your leadership and example even carry over into your "off" time. Regardless of where you are or what you are doing, people observe you to see what a worshiping Christian is really like. If you are playing with your kids at a park, people want to see how you act. If you are yelling at the manager of the local department store because of some ongoing problem, people will watch to see how a worshiping Christian behaves. Wherever you find yourself, people will observe your actions. This is at least part of the reason why Scripture demands that leaders have their lives somewhat in order (1 Timothy 3:1–13, etc.). Being an example even includes the entire concept of moral integrity. I have heard it said of worship leaders, or any leader for that matter, "Others may, but you may not." As a leader, your life should be exemplary.

This whole concept can be very unnerving unless you are prepared to have others view you as an example. (It can sometimes be unnerving even if you are prepared for it.) Few people like to accept the responsibility of being a model for others to follow. However, like it or not, being an example comes with the territory. If you are a worship leader, people will watch your example whether you want them to or not. I realized that it is easier just to accept this than to fight against it. Besides, if people can't watch us to see what a worshiper is really like, whom can they watch?

David apparently understood this idea when he demonstrated his worship of God in front of all of Israel. "David, wearing a linen ephod, danced before the LORD with all his might, while he and the entire house of Israel brought up the ark of the LORD with shouts and the sound of trumpets" (2 Samuel 6:14–15).

King Solomon perceived the importance of being an example at the temple dedication. In 2 Chronicles 6:13, we learn that Solomon built a large platform and knelt down on it "before the whole assembly of Israel and spread out his hands toward heaven" and prayed. Unquestionably, the king wanted the people to see how he prayed. He was setting a pattern that the people could follow.

Paul again, in his second letter to the Thessalonians, said of himself and his companions that we "make ourselves a model for you to follow" (2 Thessalonians 3:9). Paul, probably more than anyone, understood how vital it is to have role models. Did he start out to be a role model? Probably not. Did he enjoy it? That answer is unclear. What is clear, however, is that Paul accepted the responsibility of being an example for others to follow.

People have a need to be taught, not only by your words but just as much by your actions. The "don't do as I do, do as I say" mentality must be removed from our way of thinking. We as the people involved in the ministry of praise and worship cannot just talk about worship being a way of life. We must live it. And we must live it to the extent that others can look at us and see what worshipers are really like. Refusing to accept this responsibility is not an option. Like it or not, people will learn from *your* example.

Adapted from the book *Keys to Becoming an Effective Worship Leader* by Tom Kraeuter (Lynnwood, Wash.: Emerald Books, 1991).

Waiting to Be Discovered in Your Basement

BY ARLEN SALTE

> 🍃 *"His master replied, 'Well done, good and faithful servant! You have been faithful with a few things; I will put you in charge of many things. Come and share your master's happiness.'"*
> MATTHEW 25:23

They're in basements all across the nation. It's an underground movement. They're everywhere! They're hiding in your town as well. Maybe they're your neighbors. Maybe they're sitting next to you right now. Maybe they're you!

No, I'm not talking about an alien body snatchers B-grade movie. Your neighbor's body hasn't been taken over by an extraterrestrial being. Now, stop looking at your keyboard player! He's probably just fine.

What I'm talking about is a huge percentage of musicians who are waiting for the "big break" before they're willing to put their heart, soul, mind, and strength into the task that's already set before them. Until that time, everything else is "just another gig." It's just "another day, another dollar." Maybe for church musicians it's more accurate to say, "another day, another potluck."

Today's verse is taken from the story of the talents. Two servants took what they had, gave no evidence of whining, used their talents, and saw a tremendous return on their investment. The third buried what he had been given.

I can hear him now: "Why wasn't I given five talents like my neighbor? Certainly I'm as deserving as he is. If he loses one talent, he still has four left. If I lose one talent, I have zippo. I'm hanging on to this. My neighbor gets all the breaks. Until I'm given five talents, I'm not doing anything."

As crazy as this story seems to us, I'm afraid it happens all too frequently. In fact, it happens in some way to all of us because its root is pride. None of us escapes that particular sin.

I've known many musicians who wouldn't give of themselves because they were waiting for a more "significant" opportunity. Yet, all the time, God's call was right in front of them. It may not always be glamorous, but it's always significant if it's from God.

These people are like musicians sitting in their basements, waiting to be discovered. They may sit there for weeks, months, or years making no progress.

Maybe this person is your neighbor. Or maybe it's you.

Maybe you're in the worship team that isn't used as often as the "A" list. Maybe you've been asked to lead worship for the church youth group retreat but you feel it's not a big enough event. Maybe you're playing second keyboard and you really feel you should be the worship leader.

Maybe you're tempted to say, "Until my talents are fully recognized, I'm packing my gear into the basement."

There's an old phrase that simply says, "Bloom where you are planted." This is so true. It was also true of Joseph in the Old Testament. His brothers had sold him to a passing caravan of Ishmaelites. As he walked behind the smelly, spitting camels on his way to Egypt, I wonder if he asked God, "Hey, in my dream, my brothers were supposed to bow to me. What's with this slavery gig?"

However, Joseph remained faithful as a slave. He was faithful in a little, and God granted him a serious promotion in Potiphar's house. Even in the midst of severe temptation, Joseph was faithful where he was planted. In turn, he was thrown into prison. I wonder if he sat in his stinking Egyptian prison cell and asked God, "Hey, my brothers were supposed to bow to me. According to my project management software, we're not meeting our critical path to greatness. So what's with the prison gig?"

Yet, Joseph remained faithful in prison for years, and God worked on him there. His attitude changed from pride to humility. His heart surrendered to God's timing, plan, and purpose.

In the end, Joseph was promoted to the second most powerful position in Egypt. Yet, when God's dream from years before came true, it was not so his brothers could laud Joseph. It was so that a greater good was accomplished. A remnant of God's people was spared.

Leading worship for the youth lock-in is not an Egyptian prison. Playing guitar in the back row of the worship group is certainly not walking in the desert behind a herd of camels.

I challenge you today. Bloom where you are planted. Be willing to sing to the shut-in. Be willing to give a turn at the drums to the thirteen-year-old who is showing promise. Be faithful wherever God has placed you.

The greatest thrill you get won't be when people bow to you and acknowledge your greatness. It will be when you are overcome in humble amazement that God has used you for His greater purposes.

It's time to leave the basement.

Levi's Genes

BY TOM KRAEUTER

> 🌿 *In this way you are to set the Levites apart from the other Israelites, and the Levites will be mine. After you have purified the Levites and presented them as a wave offering, they are to come to do their work at the Tent of Meeting. They are the Israelites who are to be given wholly to me....*
> NUMBERS 8:14–16a

Without question the Levites' main purpose was simply to be given unto God. They were an offering, as it were, unto Him. Anything else in their lives was of secondary importance. All that they did and said was consecrated unto God. Nothing outweighed the fact that they belonged to Him.

Obviously, we are not Levites in the literal sense, because we are not direct descendants from the tribe of Levi. However, even beyond the clear musical similarities, there seems to be a strong correlation between what God required of the Levites and what He requires of those of us involved in the ministry of praise and worship. He is not just looking for talented musicians. He wants our hearts. Our main purpose in life is simply to *be* to His glory.

Ephesians 1:12 tells us that as believers we are to "*be* for the praise of his glory." How much more is this true for worship leaders. We, as the people involved in the ministry of praise and worship, should model for others this idea of existing for God's glory. However, we too often get so busy with the things of God that we miss simply *being* for the praise of His glory. The Lord isn't nearly as interested in our abilities as He is interested in us. The very essence of our existence is not to *do* but to *be* for His glory.

The opening Scripture passage in this chapter clearly states that the Levites were "given wholly" to God. In 1 Chronicles 16:4–6, Scripture tells us that the Levites were ministering regularly before the Lord. It wasn't a once-in-a-while thing for them; this was their life.

This attitude of being given completely to the Lord needs to permeate our lives also. Some years ago my wife and I decided to build a house. At the time, I was the bass player on the worship team at the church where I now lead worship. This was obviously not a full-time or even part-time position. My full-time occupation was in sales for a company located forty miles from our church.

In choosing a location to build our house, we considered many factors. Anyone who has ever moved into a new home can relate. We considered how far it was to work, to schools, shopping, and major highways. We discussed utilities, garbage pickup, zoning restrictions, etc., etc., etc. All of these were important and needed to be considered. Ultimately, however, one factor proved to be decisive: the proximity to our church. Even though I was at church only two or three times per week, and even though I was only the bass player, God had put within me this Levitical heart attitude. I realized that my main reason for being was to be given totally to the Lord. This meant that my first priority was Him and what He had called me to. Everything else, including the daily eighty-mile round trip for work, paled in comparison.

It is important to mention that I did not do this to get something from God. My motivation was that I simply wanted to honor Him with my life, regardless of the consequences.

I share this story, not in hopes that you will think I am a great guy, but to stir all of us more toward the daily attitude of being totally given to God. All the abilities that I possess, all the talents I can claim are, in the final analysis, of very little importance to God. He wants my life. Without that, He cannot even begin to use the other things to their full potential.

Our giving ourselves unto Him must be without any conditions. Too often we say or think something like this, "God, I will be totally

Yours if You will let me be important, if You will let people esteem me." The Lord has no use for our restrictions. He requires our lives.

The bottom line is this: We must decide that if God never uses us in any "big" way that we will still be His. We are to *be* for the praise of *His* glory, regardless of circumstances or situations. No restrictions, no hidden clauses. We are His...Levites, given totally to Him.

Adapted from the book *Keys to Becoming an Effective Worship Leader* by Tom Kraeuter (Lynnwood, Wash.: Emerald Books, 1991).

Exuberant Dancer or Staff Leaner?

BY PATRICK KAVANAUGH

> We have different gifts, according
> to the grace given us.
> ROMANS 12:6a

Many of us read of King David publicly "dancing before the Lord with all his might," or perhaps we see someone in our congregation ecstatically praising God, and we say to ourselves, "That's not me." It is common for sincere Christians to feel guilt because of their lack of overt worship. Does God really want us (or command us) all to worship Him in the same way?

Of course not. Even within the Scriptures we see a wide variety of expression. The spectrum might be said to span from King David's exuberance to that of the aged Jacob, who "worshiped as he leaned on the top of his staff" (Genesis 47:31b). There are many other biblical examples that are at various places between these two extremes.

Let's face it. Though some of us are exuberant dancers, others may prefer to quietly lean on our staff. The question, then, becomes, "Is this okay?" Well, yes and no.

1. Yes. We are each unique individuals. Who made us this way? God did, so He doubtless enjoys each of our personalities, which were a gift from him. As Paul explains, "We have different gifts, according to the grace given us" (Romans 12:6a). The Lord loves people who are

shy, outgoing, analytical, or emotional. He loves introverts, extroverts, and everyone in between.

Furthermore, the Lord wants to be worshiped by those of every personality type, the exuberant dancers to the staff leaners. This is one reason why the Bible gives us so many different portraits of worship, from dancing and leaping (Psalm 149:3) to simply kneeling down before the Lord (Psalm 95:6). It is our job to find those actions that enhance our times of worship and to avoid any guilt trips about what we are doing (or not doing).

Yes, it is appropriate for you to worship God in your own "style." The important thing is *to worship*, not to worship in a certain way. Yet our personality types, or rather our fixation upon our personal preferences, can sometimes become a hindrance to worship. That is why the above question, "Is this okay?" was answered, "Yes and no."

2. No. We must never use our personalities as an excuse not to worship the Lord. If we are the kind of person who is naturally withdrawn, reclusive, or even crotchety, we still must remind ourselves that God *commands* us all to worship Him. No excuses.

If we are one who finds it difficult to praise the Lord, we may be comforted in the knowledge that He understands our difficulties. He knows that this is a challenge for us, and He is surely all the more pleased with us for our extra efforts. He knows that some of us worship more easily than others, but He also knows that *all* of us need to spend time worshiping our Creator.

Of course, for most of us, it is sometimes hard to determine where our natural personality ends and where an area of sin begins. For instance, it is not a sin to be a reserved person, but it becomes so if we are inhospitable to others in need. It is fine to be gregarious and enjoy society, yet there are many scriptures about "controlling the tongue." The Bible certainly commends a "gentle and quiet spirit," but not if we use this trait as an excuse never to witness verbally for Christ.

We need to look honestly at our natural personality and find our distinctive ways of worshiping God. But we must never use our personality types as an excuse for ingratitude or a lack of worship.

Perhaps this is why the author of Hebrews uses the rather surprising word *sacrifice* in the following passage: "Through Jesus, therefore, let us continually offer to God a sacrifice of praise—the fruit of lips that confess his name" (Hebrews 13:15). For many of us, worshiping and praising God may indeed be a great sacrifice.

Nevertheless, if it seems difficult or unnatural to praise God, discipline yourself to do so anyway. God will give you the grace needed, and the more you worship God, the easier and more natural it will become. Like any other action you do in life, from playing the piano to driving a car, the action of worship is improved with practice.

Adapted from the book *Worship—A Way of Life* by Patrick Kavanaugh (Grand Rapids, Mich.: Chosen Books—a division of Baker Book House Company, 2001).

I'm Not Okay, and Neither Are You

BY TOM KRAEUTER

> For who makes you different from anyone
> else? What do you have that you did not
> receive? And if you did receive it, why do
> you boast as though you did not?
> 1 CORINTHIANS 4:7

Years ago there was a very popular book entitled *I'm Okay, You're Okay*. It was a best-seller for quite a long time. The problem with that idea is this: I'm not okay, and neither are you. Apart from the unmerited favor of God, we would be destined for eternity in hell.

In interacting with worship ministries in various churches, I have frequently encountered people with proud, haughty, self-righteous attitudes. "I'm really good on my instrument. I deserve to be doing this." Or "I'm a better person than John (or Linda or Sue or Shawn). Of course I should be involved in the worship ministry." Though I have seldom heard those words, I have seen the attitude clearly displayed all too often.

Jesus spoke these words in Revelation 3: "You say, 'I am rich; I have acquired wealth and do not need a thing.' But you do not realize that you are wretched, pitiful, poor, blind and naked" (Revelation 3:17). These words were written not to unbelievers but to the believers at Laodicea. Jesus had just declared that they were not "cold" but "lukewarm." The problem was not that they were not saved but that they thought they were okay. They were self-righteous. They no longer needed God. In the midst of their self-assuredness, God calls them "wretched, pitiful, poor, blind and naked."

Those of us involved in the ministry of praise and worship must recognize that we are not there because we are "worthy." Not one of us, on our own merits, is worthy to stand before a holy God.

My pastor recently made a statement that struck me. He said, "The forgiveness of sins has a catch: It's only for the guilty." There is lack of understanding in the North American church that we are guilty. We are much more apt to blame-shift or use self-justification. However, it is only when we honestly confess our need for God's grace—our utter dependence on His forgiveness—that we are truly justified before Him.

Jesus told a story in Luke 18 that illustrates this point:

> Two men went up to the temple to pray, one a Pharisee and the other a tax collector. The Pharisee stood up and prayed about himself: "God, I thank you that I am not like other men—robbers, evildoers, adulterers—or even like this tax collector...." But the tax collector stood at a distance. He would not even look up to heaven, but beat his breast and said, "God, have mercy on me, a sinner." I tell you that this man, rather than the other, went home justified before God. (Luke 18:10–14)

Each one of us must realize that apart from God's grace we are completely and totally lost. On our best days, we still fall far short of God's holy standards. Romans 14:23 tells us that "everything that does not come from faith is sin." Most of us probably do something "that does not come from faith" before we even brush our teeth in the morning. However, recognizing and admitting that fact points us in the right direction. When I realize that I'm really not okay on my own, when I recognize how desperately I need God's grace and mercy, then I am ready to admit that I am completely dependent on God. Not on my own abilities or merits, but on His unmerited favor.

C. S. Lewis had a unique way of looking at this concept. In his book *Perelandra*, the second book in his fantasy space trilogy, two angels are discussing man.

> "Look on him, beloved, and love him," said the first. "He is indeed but breathing dust and a careless touch would

unmake him. And in his best thoughts are such things mingled as, if we thought them, our lights would perish. But he is in the body of [Christ] and his sins are forgiven."[14]

Even our best thoughts, our best ideas, our best actions—our best everythings—fall woefully short of God's righteous standards.

Let's be honest. Prior to our coming into the kingdom of God, how much of God's law were we guilty of breaking? Years later, if we have reached the point where there are fewer areas of sin in us, are we any less in need of His mercy and grace? No! "For whoever keeps the whole law and yet stumbles at just one point is guilty of breaking all of it" (James 2:10). We must recognize that in and of ourselves we have nothing to offer. Apart from the Lord's grace we are nothing.

"For who makes you different from anyone else? What do you have that you did not receive? And if you did receive it, why do you boast as though you did not?" (1 Corinthians 4:7). Don't be proud or haughty about your abilities or your goodness. Everything you have is a gift from God's mercy and grace.

Adapted from the book *Living Beyond the Ordinary* by Tom Kraeuter (Lynnwood, Wash.: Emerald Books, 2000).

Are You a Joy to Lead?

BY BOB KAUFLIN

> *Obey your leaders and submit to their authority. They keep watch over you as men who must give an account. Obey them so that their work will be a joy, not a burden, for that would be of no advantage to you.*
> HEBREWS 13:17

Music and worship teams, unfortunately, are legendary for their examples of infighting, bitterness, and bad attitudes. Every time I've attended a worship conference, I've gained fresh examples of struggles that leaders face in handling their teams. It shouldn't be that way, however, in the church of Jesus Christ. As those charged with leading the church in the worship of God, we should be a living demonstration of the reconciliation Jesus purchased for us on the cross.

It's probably safe to assume that your worship leader or music director doesn't have the Bible verse for today hanging on the wall in your rehearsal room. He probably doesn't open up many Bible studies with it. However, it's also safe to assume that while this verse concerns pastors and churches, its content should also characterize our participation on the music team. The writer of Hebrews gives us a clear command on how we are to interact with our leaders. Whenever they think of us, it should bring a smile to their faces. Here's the question: Does your worship leader consider you a joy to lead? If not, here are some practical ways you can pursue change.

119

First, demonstrate a passion for God's glory in your daily life. Worship begins not just when we gather corporately, but in our everyday lives. While all worship leaders love to have notes sung in tune and instruments played skillfully, their greatest concern is that we be worshipers of God. This means that we are pursuing a deepening relationship with God through regular prayer and Bible study. We take it upon ourselves to maintain a consistency in seeking God's presence and power.

We can also develop passion for God by growing in our knowledge of Him through disciplined study of doctrine and theology. For some of us, those words strike fear in our hearts. It doesn't need to be that way, however. Theology is just the study of God. Doctrine is the summation of everything the Bible has to say about a certain subject. Whether you know it or not, you're already a theologian. The question is, are you a good theologian or a bad one? Books like *Concise Theology* by J. I. Packer and *Knowledge of the Holy* by A. W. Tozer can help you know God for who He really is rather than who you *think* He is.

A second way we can bring joy to our worship leader is through practical demonstrations of gratefulness. Let him know how much you appreciate the time he invests to prepare for meetings, to make calls, to keep his heart focused on God. Communicate your appreciation by being punctual for rehearsals and meetings. Don't accept the stereotype that musicians are always running late. As Philippians 2:3 says, we want to consider others as more important than ourselves. Being warmed up and having your instrument tuned in advance are simple but effective ways of applying that scripture.

We can also take time to encourage other members of the team in specific ways. Whenever my family is together, it brings me great joy when I see my children honestly encouraging one another and looking for ways to serve. It's no different on a worship team.

Finally, we can bring joy to our leaders by seeking to lead worship with musical skill. Are you still struggling with the same musical deficiencies that afflicted you a year ago? Can you identify one way in the past six months you've sought to become a better musician? Taking lessons, reading books, listening to CDs, and attending conferences are all effective ways we can expand our musical horizons. When every person on the team is pursuing growth in his or her musical ability, it creates a climate that discourages the status quo and minimizes ungodly competition.

In groups of varying skill levels, those who are more experienced can teach the younger musicians. Possibilities for training include music theory, phrasing, riffs, vocal health, microphone usage, and repertoire. Another important area for growth, especially on larger teams, is learning to play in a way that allows room for others to be heard. If much of your music involves reading chord charts, this is a crucial area to deal with. Churches are filled with music teams where everyone plays so much that it's difficult to distinguish any one musician. A less-than-ideal solution is a sound man who simply pulls out all but a few musicians from the mix. The general rule is: The more people playing, the less each one should play. Learning to listen is one of the greatest needs for contemporary worship teams.

We've just scratched the surface here of how to be someone your worship leader loves to lead. We didn't get to things like joyful submission, serving, faithfulness, or prayer. I'm sure that with a little effort, you can come up with a list of your own. You may even want to invite your worship leader's input. That may be the most important step you can take in becoming a true joy to lead.

God Does the Lifting

BY TOM KRAEUTER

> *Humble yourselves before the Lord,*
> *and he will lift you up.*
> JAMES 4:10

The ultimate musician in twenty-first-century America is one who spends nearly his entire life studying music and usually a specific instrument. His course is fixed on one singular purpose: to make it to the top. Good is not good enough. He must be the very best, or he is a complete and utter failure. He will use and abuse people to accomplish his goals. If his talents and training are of a high enough caliber, and if he gets to know the right people, he will ultimately be rewarded with the opportunity to regularly perform before hundreds, before thousands, and even before the leaders of society.

The ultimate worshiper in approximately 1000 B.C. Israel spends his time guarding the family's sheep and making up songs about the faithful God he serves. He apparently has no aspirations toward anything more and is quite content in what he is doing. If no one ever sees or recognizes his talents, he is satisfied to worship and serve the Lord. His reward is to know God intimately and to know that God Himself will protect and provide for him. Although it was never his aim, he ultimately finds that his musical gifts, which he has diligently cultivated before the Lord, make a way for him to stand before the ruler of the nation.

Is it not amazing how different the modern philosophy of success is from David's? The difference is probably even more significant when you realize that the Bible refers to David as a man after God's own heart (1 Samuel 13:14). If David's attitude really reflects the heart of God, then what does this other attitude reflect?

In Psalm 51:17, David writes "The sacrifices of God are a broken spirit; a broken and contrite heart, O God, you will not despise." It was with great trepidation that I realized one day that these words *broken* and *contrite,* although written by a musician, characterize the hearts and lives of very few musicians today...even in the church. It seems that "making the big-time" is "where it's at." Even "making it big for God" is often-used terminology.

Ultimately, though, the Lord doesn't need our talents—He wants our hearts. All the abilities we can muster are of very little eternal consequence. God is looking for a broken and contrite heart, one that is not self-centered but focused on Him.

Long before Jesus was ever born, David understood the concept of being a humble servant and being faithful in the little things (Luke 19:17). He simply did whatever was put before him, knowing that God was the One who held the future. If promotion was to come, it would come by His hand, not by David's attempting to manipulate the circumstances. Even after Samuel anointed him as king, David refused to take matters into his own hands. Instead, he chose to allow the Lord to move sovereignly on his behalf. How contradictory to our normal ways today!

When people tell you how gifted and talented you are, how do you react? "Well, yes, God has certainly invested much of Himself in me, hasn't He?" Proverbs 27:21 tells us, "The crucible for silver and the furnace for gold, but man is tested by the praise he receives." How you react to those compliments regarding your abilities says much about your humility (or lack thereof).

Jesus told us that He did not come to be served but to serve. He taught that His followers should do as He did. In Mark 9:35, Jesus tells us, "If anyone wants to be first, he must be the very last, and the servant of all." Again, how contrary this is to our society's view of success. We do not really understand what it means to be humble. We need to pray that God will reveal how we can manifest this humble servant attitude within our lives.

In practical terms, we can humble ourselves in many ways. We can humble ourselves before the Lord by worshiping and obeying Him in all that we do and say. We can humble ourselves before our church by constantly learning and growing in the things that will enable us to do better in our position in leading others in worship. We can humble ourselves before our pastor by honoring him with our words and our actions. We can humble ourselves before our fellow worship team members by stepping out of the limelight and letting them shine. We can daily decide that in all we do and say we will, like Jesus and like David, be humble servants.

"Humble yourselves before the Lord, and He will lift you up." Ultimately His promise will become manifest in us: If we humble ourselves, He will lift us up. But remember, we do the humbling; God does the lifting.

Adapted from the book *Keys to Becoming an Effective Worship Leader* by Tom Kraeuter (Lynnwood, Wash.: Emerald Books, 1991).

Nomads

BY ARLEN SALTE

> As he was praying, the appearance of his face changed, and his clothes became as bright as a flash of lightning. Two men, Moses and Elijah, appeared in glorious splendor, talking with Jesus. They spoke about his departure, which he was about to bring to fulfillment at Jerusalem. Peter and his companions were very sleepy, but when they became fully awake, they saw his glory and the two men standing with him. As the men were leaving Jesus, Peter said to him, "Master, it is good for us to be here. Let us put up three shelters— one for you, one for Moses and one for Elijah." (He did not know what he was saying.)
>
> LUKE 9:29–33

Flash back with me twenty years. I'm on tour across North America. I'm a young man full of more faith than strategy. I've just incorporated a ministry, bought equipment, converted a bus, and headed off on the road with two other young men. We sing where we can and eat when we're able. Sometimes there isn't enough money in the offering plate to take us to the next town. Yet God always shows up in time with a few dollars. Sometimes there isn't a place to sleep, so we stretch out a sleeping bag across speakers in the back of the bus, or we sleep under the stars. One time we drive for twenty-six hours and find ourselves at 7:00 a.m. with only enough money between all of us to buy a pound of Polish sausage and a quart of chocolate milk. It's the worst breakfast I've ever had in my life.

Along the way we find churches humming with spiritual vitality and cutting-edge ministries.

- In one Midwest state a church is booming with the newest ministry models. They fill Bible schools with new students. They reach their community with powerful impact.
- On the West Coast, the renewal movement has touched a mainline church. You need to show up an hour early just to get a seat.
- In an inner city, a community is formed in a run-down church. They reach out to street people, prostitutes, and young university students looking for direction. Many lives are touched and transformed by the power of God.

All along the tour are churches that are fresh, leading edge, and high impact. Enthusiasm swells. People study their methods. Conferences are held in their churches.

Now flash forward with me today.

- The church in the Midwest? It began declining years ago. It should probably shut its doors.
- The church on the West Coast? It was sold to a realty company. The church has long since died.
- The inner-city church? It folded up fifteen years ago.

One of the sobering realities that has come with being in full-time ministry so many years has been seeing the "hot" thing come and go. The inability to change and to stay fresh is one of the greatest challenges in ministry. This is true in our worship ministries as well.

In the Bible passage for today, the disciples must have been slack-jawed, ashen-faced, and shaken to their very bones. Of course, they wanted to do what any self-respecting church would do. Here they are, confronted by one of the most magnificent divine interventions in human history, and they wanted to start a building program. At some time down the line, I imagine that Peter even would have started a fight about the color of the carpet in the booths.

It's so easy to become like the disciples at the Transfiguration. We want to build booths around our experiences. Booths that have sides and corners to them. Booths that maintain our nostalgia and quell our fear of obsolescence. Booths that have doors that allow us to control what comes in and what goes out. Booths that freeze the present like a statue in a museum, safely set aside for admiration.

The churches I encountered twenty years ago did just that. They built booths around their current methods and experiences.

It is said that the only difference between a rut and a grave is the dimensions. Has your church's worship format sunk its foundation so far into the ground that you're in danger of repeating the same mistake the other churches did? Are you personally longing for a return to the good old days, whether that's three years ago or thirty years ago? Are these the good old days that you're comfortable with and you've started to build booths?

The disciples wanted to maintain a nostalgic moment in time. Yet, Jesus had a higher goal that went far beyond His comfort zone or any sense of nostalgia. His goal was the salvation of us all.

Instead of constructing cathedrals of stone in our hearts, let's be nomads. Let's make our worship ministries more like tents that can move, flex, and change.

Are you stretching to reach people in a new way. Are you moving your tent outside your comfort zone for the sake of a higher goal? If not, I encourage you to be a nomad.

An Artist and a Minister

BY TOM KRAEUTER

 Sing to him a new song; play skillfully....
PSALM 33:3

Not long ago my wife and I visited the St. Louis Art Museum. It was an impromptu outing with my favorite person, and we thoroughly enjoyed our time together. However, I must admit that I was a bit taken aback by some of the "art" objects at the museum. One was a blank white canvas, about eight feet square, with a straight red line that was maybe eighteen inches across running from top to bottom. Nothing else. In another room there was a "sculpture" that was simply old car parts stuck together in no particular order and forming no particular shape. I could go on, but I don't want to bore you with the details.

Let me explain why I was amazed at finding these things at the art museum. You see, from the beginning of time, art has been revered because it is not something that just anyone can do. Real art takes both ability and the discipline to develop that ability. Natural inclination and plenty of hard work are both necessary ingredients.

Go buy yourself a canvas, some oil paints, and some brushes and try to make a copy of Leonardo da Vinci's *Mona Lisa.* Betcha can't! Or try picking up a violin and playing like Itzhak Perlman. It's just not going to happen. How come? Because not only are those artists gifted, but they spent years practicing and perfecting their abilities. Perlman didn't just decide one day, "Hey, I think I'll try playing the fiddle today. I wonder if I could do it." No, he expended the necessary effort to learn the instrument and still works diligently at it daily. Although apparently naturally gifted, his abilities have undergone years of honing to get them to the point of being the master violinist he is today.

Not just anyone can create true art. That's why we all are so enamored when we encounter the real thing. "Wow! That's amazing!" is our initial thought. Whether it is an exquisite sculpture, a beautifully handwoven oriental rug, or a highly trained vocalist, our reaction is, "I would love to be able to do that." However, we are keenly aware that it took that person a long time to get to be so good at it. We are impressed that someone would be so gifted and also disciplined enough to develop that gift. That is not something just the average guy on the street can do. That is true art.

So now you understand why I found some of those "art" pieces objectionable. Not that they were evil or anti-Christian. They just weren't art. If my ten-year-old son could create that piece with no lessons and no real effort, it is clearly not really art. Painting a straight line down a piece of canvas is hardly a major achievement. (I'm no painter, and I could probably have done a wavy line and given it a bit more character!) Throwing together some old parts from an automobile does not take any particular discipline. I would suggest that more likely than not, the person who would create such "art" is unwilling to pay the price of true discipline to create *real* art. Perhaps his or her attitude is, "What is the least amount of effort I can get by with and still have someone think my work is worthwhile?"

I've seen people involved in church worship ministries who appear to have a similar attitude. "It's only church. It doesn't need to be *that* good." Many church instrumentalists only ever play their instrument at the worship ministry rehearsal or for actual services. How do they ever expect to become more accomplished on their instrument?

My mom is a quilter. Quilts of various sizes adorn the walls of her home. She has made quilts for just about everyone in our entire extended family and many people outside of our family. She has been quilting for years. Recently she won an award for a wall-hanging quilt she had designed and made. A contest was held in the local quilting group. Many people entered their small quilts, but Mom's won. I think in part it's because she's been at it for a very long time, but also because she spends time working on quilts almost every day. The first quilt she made years ago probably would not have won an award. However, because she has worked at her skills for years, she is now reaping some rewards for her diligence.

What about you? Are you regularly working at your abilities. Are you endeavoring to "play skillfully" as Psalm 33 says we should?

Don't just have a "this-is-adequate" mentality. Do the best you can to honor God with your abilities.

Extravagant Worship

BY KENT HENRY

> *A woman came to him with an alabaster jar of very expensive perfume, which she poured on his head as he was reclining at the table.*
> MATTHEW 26:7

If ever I've heard a powerful example of what wholehearted worship is, this would be it. This woman's act of worship reminds us that we should open our hearts on a consistent basis in worship to God. We have been given a gift and a ministry to anoint the Lord with our worship. We can "enter in" on a daily basis. Romans 12:1 tells us that this is really just our reasonable service and offering to the Living God.

This woman in Matthew 26 who gave her expensive perfume is still known today throughout the world. For what event is she remembered? Wasting her best on the Lord Jesus. She "wasted," or poured out, her most precious possession on the main focus of her life and love.

Here's the full story.

While Jesus was in Bethany in the home of a man known as Simon the leper, a woman came to Him with an alabaster jar of very expensive perfume, which she poured on His head as He was reclining at the table.

When the disciples saw this, they were indignant. "Why this waste?" they asked. "This perfume could have been sold at a high price and the money given to the poor."

Aware of this, Jesus said to them, "Why are you bothering this woman? She has done a beautiful thing to me. The poor you will always have with you, but you will not always have me. When she poured this perfume on my body, she did it to prepare me for burial. I tell you the truth, wherever this gospel is preached throughout the world, what she has done will also be told, in memory of her" (Matthew 26:6–13).

Three very important points are made in this passage of Scripture. The first is this extraordinary account of her worship. By giving her most precious gift, this woman showed much love to the Lord Jesus while being extravagant with her own possession.

Some Bible scholars say that the bottle of expensive perfume was equal in value to three years' wages. For us today as New Testament believers, can we even begin to match this woman's act of giving her all? Further, will we learn to offer extravagant worship on a daily basis?

I'm not so much concerned with people just receiving teaching and revelation from God's Word concerning the lifestyle of worship. The more important question is, will we change our lives and become doers of the profound things we've learned about worship from the Bible?

The second point is the attitude of the on-looking disciples. They were such a bunch of know-it-alls that they almost missed one of the most powerful times of ministry that Jesus ever received. They sat and watched this act of worship as spectators who did not understand its true significance.

Many times I, too, have missed the power of God working among His people because I had become a spectator rather than a participant. This is such an important point. God wants participants, not spectators.

Even though the disciples got upset with her for her "wasteful act," Jesus was blessed and His heart was touched by her. Remember this: Nonworshipers (or spectators) will always be on a different wavelength. Until they change their heart posture, extravagant worship seems to be, at least to them, an overstatement, even a gaudy display of affections or emotions.

I find the disciples' attitude unrighteous, even shameful. Why? Because selfless worship is exactly what blesses the heart of our heavenly Father. People who worship God unashamedly serve as working models and examples for others. Extravagant worship can help other people lose their inhibitions and enter into honest, heartfelt worship.

Finally, we must look at the response and admonishment of Jesus to the disciples. He said, "She has done a beautiful thing to me." This speaks of the beauty of worship in God's sight. In this case, it was the beauty of her act and the fragrance that was left over in the room after she anointed Jesus. It was a beautiful thing!

The fragrance...the fragrance of our worship! It's an aroma that comes from the overflow of heartfelt love toward God. Many people still stand on the sidelines, never fully entering into the place of extravagant worship. Their heart is rarely let out of the box so it can be enjoyed by God and His people.

So here is our challenge: to open our hearts and pour out extravagant worship. It's time to yield up to the Lord the most precious and costly things of our lives in sweet communion with Him. This is a place of worship you'll be drawn back to time and time again.

Only Building Others Up

BY TOM KRAEUTER

> *Do not let any unwholesome talk come out of your mouths, but only what is helpful for building others up according to their needs, that it may benefit those who listen.*
> EPHESIANS 4:29

For several years now my family and I have taken a vacation/ministry trip during the summer. It is generally a two-week trip with both times of ministry and times of family fun mixed together. When we were planning our first such trip, my wife and I decided that we wanted to utilize some of the extended time together in the van for more than just reading, listening to tapes, and arguing. We made the decision that we would memorize a lengthy section of Scripture together as a family.

The section we chose for that first trip began with Ephesians 4:29: "Do not let any unwholesome talk come out of your mouths, but only what is helpful for building others up according to their needs, that it may benefit those who listen." We liked the idea of our children (at that point ages three, seven, and eleven) getting hold of the principles of that verse: no unwholesome talk, only what is helpful for building others up. Practicing those things could radically alter their interaction with one another. However, as we drove together and recited this verse (and the following verses) aloud each day, it dawned on me that these principles were not just for the kids. I needed to practice these things.

134

One day Jesus told His followers, "You have heard that it was said to the people long ago, 'Do not murder, and anyone who murders will be subject to judgment.' But I tell you that anyone who is angry with his brother will be subject to judgment. Again, anyone who says to his brother, 'Raca,' is answerable to the Sanhedrin. But anyone who says, 'You fool!' will be in danger of the fire of hell" (Matthew 5:21–22).

The word *raca* (rhak-ah´) literally means "empty head." Today, our equivalent of this word would be "airhead." Jesus is telling the people that simply calling one another names puts them in danger of judgment!

A normal form of verbal interaction in our society is put-downs—cutting remarks designed to destroy one another or, at least, to bring others down a notch or two. The truth is that we Christians should be doing the opposite. We have enough detractors in the world. We should use our words to build one another up.

Some time ago I heard a story that really makes the point clear. A junior high school teacher had been trying to instruct her class in a particularly difficult mathematical concept. They had spent much of the week on this concept. Unfortunately, it was now Friday afternoon, and they still weren't getting it. Partly out of frustration and partly out of wanting to shift gears and get away from the math, the teacher asked the students to put away their books and get out a blank sheet of paper. She then asked them to list the name of each person in the class on their paper. After they had all the names listed, she instructed them to write one encouraging thing, a single attribute, about each of their fellow students. By the time they finished, school ended for that week, and the teacher collected their papers as they left for home.

Over the weekend the teacher compiled the comments. She made a separate sheet for each student, putting all the encouraging words about each on his or her own sheet. Monday morning, when the students returned, she gave each one his or her own list of encouraging comments made by fellow students.

Several years later, one of the students from that class was killed in the Vietnam war. Because of her influence in his life, the junior high teacher was invited to the funeral and subsequently back to his parents' home afterward to be with family and close friends. While she was there, the young man's wallet was brought out by his father. In it was a well-worn piece of paper that had encouraging comments from his fellow students of years ago. It had meant so much to him that he had carried it with him through all those years.

If I stopped right there, it would be a tremendous example of the power of building others up, but that's not the end of the story. Three or four of the young man's junior high classmates were also there at the home after the funeral. One by one they each pulled out their sheets of paper. They too had been so moved by the words of their fellow students that those papers had become part of their lives.

Encouragement—this building up of one another—is so lacking in our culture that when we receive even a little we hang on to it. It is a powerful force in the lives of those who do the building up as well as of those who receive it.

What would happen if each of us honestly did "not let any unwholesome talk come out of [our] mouths, but only what is helpful for building others up according to their needs, that it may benefit those who listen"? Would it make a difference in your life? Would it make a difference in the worship ministry of your church? Of course it would.

Let's try it!

Our Greatest Battle

BY BOB KAUFLIN

> *Even while these people were worshiping the LORD, they were serving their idols.*
> 2 KINGS 17:41a

What is our greatest hindrance in worshiping God? We could come up with a number of believable answers. Laziness, pride, and distractions could start the list. We could move on to sins of lust, self-sufficiency, and apathy. All of these, however, have their root in something even more serious and pervasive: the sin of idolatry.

The passage from 2 Kings referenced above describes a situation that can potentially exist in our church services today. We can engage in what we perceive to be all the proper elements of worship—singing, giving, praying, kneeling, listening to God's Word, etc.—and be actively serving false gods in our hearts. God makes it clear in Exodus 20 that He will not tolerate any competition for the allegiance and affections of our hearts. "You shall have no other gods before me." That succinctly describes idolatry.

In the Old Testament, there is no sin God confronts more frequently than that of idolatry. In the second chapter of Jeremiah, God asks, "Has a nation ever changed its gods? (Yet they are not gods at all.) But my people have exchanged their Glory for worthless idols" (Jeremiah 2:11). These idols were not always something external. God

137

told Ezekiel in chapter 14, verse 3, that the Israelites had set up idols in their hearts and could no longer hear Him. Time after time, God's people are guilty of esteeming other people and things as more important than God Himself. At one point it's a golden calf. Another time it's the pleasures of Egypt. In the Promised Land they submit themselves to all kinds of detestable practices as they worship the gods of the Canaanites. In every case, a desire to pursue and be ruled by something other than God results in disobedience, rebellion, and unbelief.

In the New Testament, we don't hear much talk of idols. What we do find is a focus on the sinful desires of the heart. Peter tells us "As obedient children, do not conform to the evil desires you had when you lived in ignorance" (1 Peter 1:14). Romans 6:12 says, "Do not let sin reign in your mortal body so that you obey its evil desires." What do sinful desires have to do with idolatry?

At its root, idolatry is wanting something other than God to rule over us. The key words are *wanting* and *rule*. While our tendency is to think that our hearts are uninvolved spectators in life waiting to be acted upon, the reality is quite different. John Calvin spoke truly when he said our hearts are idol factories, constantly creating new objects for our attention and affections. We are always pursuing the things we think are most valuable. Those objects of our pursuit become our idols.

They also become the things that rule us and direct our actions. An idol is any person, situation, possession, thought, or emotion that we feel compelled to serve above all else. The idols we seek to worship in God's place are rarely as obvious as a golden calf or a tottering wooden image. They surprise us with their subtlety, pervasiveness, and power. We find ourselves wanting the silliest things more than we want God. Things like power, pleasure, a job, or a relationship—any one of them can usurp God's right to rule us and start to govern our lives.

Idols are often revealed by the thoughts that run through our mind when we're not purposefully thinking about something else. I've been ashamed at times of how frequently my mind dwells on the next item I'm going to buy, when I already have more "stuff" than 95 percent of the populated world. Do I really think my life will be more complete with a faster computer or a more current wardrobe? That's idolatry at work.

What kind of idols might we deal with as we participate on a worship team? Certainly the idol of man's approval is one. We might more appropriately call it the idol of man's applause. No, if we want to get to the heart of it, we are really serving the idol of man's adoration. How tragic that we can be proclaiming the glory of God while secretly desiring glory for ourselves! "What does my worship leader think of me?" "Why didn't my pastor encourage me?" "Do people appreciate my contribution?" All these questions could be evidences of an idolatrous heart.

Another area we might deal with is the idol of control. When things don't go your way, when you're asked to play a part you don't particularly prefer, or when your suggestion is ignored, how do you respond? What if the worship leader takes the meeting in a direction you don't agree with? It's at those moments we face a choice to bow down to our own wants and desires to rule or to humbly submit to an all-wise, all-loving God who carefully places us under leaders He knows will expose our sinful hearts!

A third idol we may confront is the idol of pleasure. In a culture that places a high value on immediate gratification, we're prone to think that the temperature, sound, lights, and environment must suit our personal tastes at all times. If that were true, how could anyone worship God in impoverished third-world countries? While we don't want to view ourselves as martyrs for the faith, there will be times we simply ignore discomforts because the glory of God has captivated our hearts and our minds.

"While they were worshiping the Lord, they were serving their idols." What a merciful reminder. Let's be diligent to expose all the ways we serve anything other than God, knowing that the blood of Jesus has redeemed us from an empty way of life (1 Peter 1:18). He alone is truly worthy of all our thoughts, all our affections, and all our obedience.

Worshiper or Watcher?

BY TOM KRAEUTER

> As the ark of the covenant of the LORD was entering the City of David, Michal daughter of Saul watched from a window. And when she saw King David dancing and celebrating, she despised him in her heart.
> 1 CHRONICLES 15:29

Some time ago I was walking along a country road. It was a beautiful summer afternoon, and I was praying and enjoying the day. As I walked along under some trees, I suddenly found myself entangled in a huge spiderweb. I had not even noticed it, but just that quickly it seemed as though it was everywhere. I felt it on my arms and legs, my face, even in my hair. I flailed my arms and danced around, trying to get the invisible sticky web off of me. It took a few moments, but finally I was satisfied that I was completely free of the web.

It was then I noticed a man on the next hill staring at me. What a picture I must have been from his perspective. Surely he could not see the spiderweb from his vantage point. All he saw was a guy dancing around on the road and flailing his arms. It must have been quite a sight. I still wonder what he must have thought.

Often, we can look in judgment on someone else, inwardly ridiculing their form of worship, simply because we have not gone through what they have. They may raise their hands or dance or jump up and down—all biblical forms of worship, by the way—but because these things are not part of our experience, we find fault with them.

Obviously, we must recognize that there are biblical boundaries for worship. However, within those boundaries there is a lot of freedom. You can say, "That particular form is outside of my comfort zone, my culture, my taste, and my style. I'm not ready right now to go so far out in this area." That's okay. However, we must be very careful that we don't judge someone else simply because he or she is willing to do things differently than we do them. We must not have a critical or judgmental spirit.

In the Old Testament, King David was excited that finally, the Ark of God—the place where the Lord chose to manifest Himself—was being returned to Israel where it belonged. In essence, the presence of God was coming back to His people. Because of this, David danced with joy. He wasn't showing off. He was not trying to demonstrate his talent as a dancer. No. David was genuinely enthusiastic.

When I drive into our driveway after being gone for a few days, I can often hear excited cries from inside the house: "Daddy's home!" Sometimes one or more members of my family will burst through the door and hug me before I am completely out of the car. That's what David was doing in this situation. He was excited that the Ark of God was back home. For David this was not a show. It was an honest expression of that which was in his heart.

David's wife should have affirmed her husband's heart before God. Even though she didn't like the dancing, he was worshiping. She should have looked past her dislike of the movements and seen his heart. But she didn't. Instead, "she despised him in her heart." What a shame.

Luke's Gospel records the story of Jesus eating at the home of a Pharisee named Simon. While He was eating, a "woman who had lived a sinful life" came in. She went over to Jesus and "she stood behind him at his feet weeping, she began to wet his feet with her tears. Then she wiped them with her hair, kissed them and poured perfume on them" (Luke 7:38).

The host was indignant. He could not understand why this woman would do such a thing nor why Jesus would allow it. Jesus knew Simon's heart and asked him a question: "Two men owed money to a certain moneylender. One owed him five hundred denarii, and the other fifty. Neither of them had the money to pay him back, so he canceled the debts of both. Now which of them will love him more?" (Luke 7:41–42).

Of course Simon knew the correct answer: "The one who had the bigger debt canceled." Jesus went on to explain that the one who has been forgiven much would love much, "but he who has been forgiven little loves little" (Luke 7:47b).

There would not be such an extravagant act of worship from Simon. Why not? Because he had not received forgiveness. He was self-righteous. However, this woman would gladly make a fool of herself to honor the One who had canceled her great debt. And, of course, Simon would gladly judge her.

We must be very careful to not allow our traditions—"I've never done it that way before"—to cause us to sit in judgment against our brothers or sisters in Christ. We cannot see their heart. As long as their form of worship has honest, biblical basis, allow them the freedom to worship God.

The Table, the Pulpit, and the Throne

BY GERRIT GUSTAFSON

> *To him who sits on the throne and to the Lamb be praise and honor and glory and power for ever and ever!*
> REVELATION 5:13b

In his excellent book *Worship His Majesty*, Jack Hayford asks an exceedingly provocative question: "Are we in the earthquake throes of a new Reformation?" He boldly proposes that, like Martin Luther nailing the Ninety-Five Theses to the Wittenberg door, we drive a nail in the altar, or the pulpit, or the communion table, or whatever, to announce again the preeminence of God's Word and His Spirit over our own traditions.

I, for one, am pulling for such a new Reformation. It is my conviction that the Church is, in fact, in a historic transition that is as significant as the Protestant Reformation. The resulting changes from this new Reformation will not just redecorate the house, but they will fundamentally affect the very structure of the house. To properly view this moment of history, we need to think in terms of a once-in-a-millennium event, not just a once-in-a-lifetime event. It is not just a new season; it's a new epoch.

The first Reformation brought with it a new reason for the Church to exist. To illustrate, imagine that you could go back in time seven hundred years to several pre-Reformation Christian worship services and interview one hundred people as they were entering their various places of worship.

"Excuse me, I am conducting a religious survey. Could I ask you a simple question: 'What do you expect to be the most important part of the meeting you are about to attend?'"

After some very interesting exchanges about your tennis shoes, your unusual accent, and how a tape recorder works, you will probably begin to get a very high percentage of answers indicating that the meaningful moment for most is the participation in the Eucharist, or the Lord's Supper. You have just identified the Eucharistic model of worship, where the communion table is the central piece of furniture. Check "Eucharistic" on your survey form.

Now jump ahead six hundred years from there. Ask the same question to one hundred people entering several Protestant churches. "Excuse me...etc."

Now you are going to find that there is a new explanation. The answers will run along these lines: "The main event will be when the preacher brings us a message from God's Word." Since "kerygma" refers to the proclamation of God's Word, and since we need a fancy name to identify this second model of Christian assembly, let's call it the Kerygmatic model, where the pulpit is the central fixture. Just check "Kerygmatic" on the form.

Now, if you are not too worn out from your time travels, let's drop in on Christians twenty-five years into the third millennium where we will find that the Second Reformation has already had its effect. "Excuse me,..." you begin.

This time the results reveal a new basis for gatherings of believers. They have a gleam in their eyes as they answer: "We are coming to worship God. The main event will be when we offer our sacrifices of praise to God!"

Go ahead and check "Leitourgistic" on the survey, and then let me explain what the Leitourgistic model is. (By the way, you won't find that in the dictionary yet. But very shortly we will need a such a term.)

Ministry unto the Lord will be the chief occupation of this twice-reformed Church, as it was of the early Church. "Leitourgeo" is the Greek word used to describe this activity. It's translated in Acts 13:2, for instance, as "ministered to." "While they were worshiping the Lord and fasting, the Holy Spirit said..."

As we acquire the habit of coming into God's presence to minister unto the Lord in worship, we will not be Word-less. Instead, there will be a powerful revelation of the Word of God, Himself! And in His presence, the Lord's Supper will be more meaningful than ever! The table and the pulpit will still be there, but neither will be center stage. Instead, there will be an invisible throne, and God Himself will be center stage.

Consider Paul's description in Ephesians 5 of Christ's unfolding love for His Church in light of the three phases of Church history: 1) He "gave himself up for her," 2) "cleansing her by the washing with water through the word," so that 3) a radiant Church may be presented to Him.

The Eucharistic model celebrates His sacrifice for us. The Kerygmatic model celebrates the Word of God that washes us. But the end result is that the bride may be presented to the bridegroom. In Romans 12, Paul says that the presenting of ourselves as sacrifices is worship. The first two stages focus on His ministry to us; the third centers on our ministry to Him. Can you imagine such a Church where ministry to the Lord is the priority?!

So how can we prepare for this Second Reformation? How can we minimize the trauma of this coming earthquake of change? First, get the picture firmly in your mind of the Church that ministers unto the Lord. Next, evaluate your present priorities as an individual and as a congregation and set new ones if necessary. Finally, begin to function as a fellowship of those who minister unto the Lord.

God will be pleased, and you'll be part of history in the making!

The Essential Element

BY TOM KRAEUTER

> "Love the Lord your God with all your
> heart and with all your soul and with all
> your mind and with all your strength."
> MARK 12:30

Some time ago I heard an elderly gentleman discussing how his priorities had changed over the years. As a youth he had been taught that certain things were important. Over time he had abandoned many of those values and embraced new ideals. But as he grew in years and wisdom, he found himself doing another reversal. Those things that he had left behind were once again becoming top priority. He had realized that the standards he had learned as a youngster really contained lasting value.

I have gone through much the same process in my years of leading worship. I first began leading worship mostly out of a deep, intense gratitude to the Lord. He had redeemed me! He had, as the psalmist said, "lifted me out of the slimy pit, out of the mud and mire; he set my feet on a rock and gave me a firm place to stand" (Psalm 40:2). I wanted to verbalize my appreciation. Beyond saving me, He had become my friend and constant companion. To this day I still have trouble grasping that the almighty God of all creation would desire *me*. But I had accepted the truth of His Word, and my heart was filled with unending gratitude toward God.

From the beginning of my walk with the Lord, it was obvious to me and others that He had called me to leadership. Therefore, it was only natural that my gratitude would spill over onto others, and I would end up leading others into this same expression of appreciation, or worship. Then the expression itself was more important to me than leading others in it. I just wanted to love and honor God.

As time went on, however, I began to realize that other dynamics played into the worship-leading process. My musical abilities and understanding became increasingly important. I looked at the type and style of music being used and its effect on the song service. I began to grasp how people's relationships affected their worship. Even the other musicians and their abilities came to play a more important role in my understanding of how worship "works." I began more and more to take my cues from people's reactions to the "worship" instead of from the Lord. I had almost completely abandoned the once simple, gratitude-based relationship I had with God. Concepts affecting worship leading had become my focus more than the Lord Himself. I was more in touch with the process than I was with God. I was not spending time with the Lord developing our relationship. In fact, the only real quality time I was spending with God was while I was leading.

At first I was able to fool most of the people while I went through the above scenario, due at least in part to the strong gifts that God had given me. No one really knew that I was more conscious of the techniques than I was of the Lord. Still, as time went on, my drifting from God became more obvious and had the potential for getting much worse.

I had reached bottom. I was not leading worship from a heart full of worship; I was leading by using techniques alone. The tools that God had provided to be effective in leading *worship* had become an end in themselves. The reactions of people had become more important to me than having a heart that desired to please God. I was not really leading worship. In reality, I was only toying with people's emotions, including my own.

Fortunately, I once more experienced the rescuing, redeeming power of the Lord. His unending mercies touched me where I needed them most, and I saw the falsehood of what I was doing. By His grace, I was able to recognize that the path I was on was quite a distance from the one I should have been on. The Lord graciously brought me back into that simple grateful relationship we had before. There were no lightning bolts from heaven or earthshaking revelations, just a simple understanding of His new-every-morning mercies. I could once again lead worship out of a heart that radiated true worship.

In going through this process, I learned some lasting principles. The most obvious was this: The only way to be effective long-term as a worship leader is to maintain a close relationship with the Lord.

If I am not in constant pursuit of a close relationship with the Lord, if I am not continually allowing Him to fill this empty vessel, then I will have nothing to give to others. I may have some nifty tricks that will pull me through a few services, but beyond that, I'm empty. I need to be daily renewed and refreshed by Jesus, the living water. If I forego this ongoing relationship with Him, I have really missed the fullness of His calling on my life.

Anyone aspiring to be effective in the worship ministry must have as his or her main anchor point maintaining a relationship with the object of worship, the almighty God. You would not expect to be a close friend of a person with whom you never spend time. Relationships take time, and lots of it, to develop. In the same way, it is essential to spend time with the Lord, just as you would spend time cultivating an earthly friendship. Nothing—absolutely nothing—is more important.

Adapted from the book *Keys to Becoming an Effective Worship Leader* by Tom Kraeuter (Lynnwood, Wash.: Emerald Books, 1991).

Beulah Land

BY BILL RAYBORN

> *A new command I give you: Love one another. As I have loved you, so you must love one another. By this all men will know that you are my disciples, if you love one another.*
> JOHN 13:34–35

My phone rang today. It was a church music leader saying he was having some trouble in his church. He knew I had been around the block a few times, and maybe I could help him understand why people in his church were so hard to please. It seems he had gone through two or three weeks of people saying they didn't like this and didn't like that, why *didn't* he do this, why *did* he do that. He continued his lament saying that he was trying to do the very best he could, but it just didn't seem to please anyone. Then in an incredulous tone, he said that some of these people complaining were actually *choir members* and one sang on the *praise team*!

I responded, "Can you imagine that...a critical choir member? What is this world coming to?"

He didn't seem to enjoy the humor in my comment, so I took a more serious approach. I told him of some of my own experiences and shared a few "battle scars" and war stories from my many years in the music ministry. I assured him that what he was experiencing was not unusual (though I wish it were) and that it could actually be a positive experience, though it would be hard to see that now.

I told him something my father told me many years ago. He said, "If they are shooting at you from both sides, you are probably in about the right place." That seemed to help some, and I continued by telling him that I had found that the leader who is not subject to *some* criticism is probably not doing much.

We talked about a small musical group of wonderful young people in my church in Nederland, Texas, called *The New Generation*. They were an outreach group that ministered mostly beyond the stained-glass windows. Although the group was very successful, there were those critics who did not like us singing this secular tune or singing in that location. Some didn't like our choreography, and others criticized our outfits. These were young people who were very sensitive to the Lord's leading and would sometimes say, "No one has criticized us lately. We need to pray." Kidding? Not even a little bit. Some of our most wonderful times with the Lord followed a comment such as that.

But I digress. Back to my friend on the phone. At this point I told him one of my favorite stories.

Several years ago I heard Dr. Travis Shelton teaching at the LifeWay Assembly in Ridgecrest, North Carolina. He was a professor at Southern Methodist University and directed the music in a small Dallas church. He began telling us how he would occasionally have a "request service" where the people would choose certain congregational songs. He said this gave some members, especially the older ones, a chance to sing some of the "good ol' songs" they seldom sang anymore.

Dr. Shelton said that when he would have one of these special events there was a little old lady who would *always* request "Beulah Land." (Actually "Dwelling in Beulah Land.") Dr. Shelton sort of smiled, then grimaced as he commented that he just did *not like* "Beulah Land." "It's a great dance tune," he quipped. "There is even this one little spot where it echoes 'Praise God' in kind of an old gospel quartet fashion."

Well, this particular evening, sure enough, she raised her hand and requested "Beulah Land." Shelton's choir was in the service, and they knew how he felt about "Beulah Land." So as the church started singing, the choir began to sway from side to side. Then, when they got to that "Praise God" spot, they all threw their hands in the air in mock worship.

Dr. Shelton said, "I knew we had finally put that old lady in her place!"

His voice lowered as he continued the story. "Two days later I received two unsigned postcards. One of them is framed and hangs in my office to this day. It said simply, ' "Beulah Land" is here to stay. You ain't necessarily.' "

Professor Shelton said that day *he* was the pupil, and he learned a valuable lesson from that postcard. You don't change people by making fun or being critical.

It is possible that we get so hung up on our musical preferences that we miss the opportunity to worship. Sometimes we don't show respect for others' feelings just because they see things from a different mountaintop than we do.

Next time you don't like a particular song or feel inclined to criticize something about the church or music ministry, remember Dr. Shelton and "Dwelling in Beulah Land."

Not one of us is "here to stay" very long. The way we support our ministers, the way we worship, and the spirit we show toward one another will last long beyond our short term on this earth.

When Jesus talked about loving one another, He called it a new *command*, not a new *suggestion*.

The song says, "They'll know we are Christians by our love." Let's love one another. After all, there ain't any of us that's here to stay very long!

A Little Encouragement
Goes a Long Way

BY TOM KRAEUTER

> *Therefore encourage one another and build each other up....*
> 1 THESSALONIANS 5:11

Several years ago I was teaching an all-day worship seminar. At one point I finished a section of teaching and asked for questions. I was amazed when several of those asking questions offered lightly veiled criticism aimed at those with whom they ministered. Unfortunately, it became obvious that the people being talked about were present.

As I listened and responded, I could not help feeling deep sorrow for the people making the comments as well as those at whom they were directed. There was no encouragement, only tearing down. Paul tells us to "encourage one another and build each other up" (1 Thessalonians 5:11).

Without question, one of the things sorely lacking in our society today is encouragement. Encouragement among close friends is a rare commodity. Between those who are not so close it is usually nonexistent.

Yet despite all of this, I am constantly amazed at the power of an encouraging word. A simple, "You can do it," spoken to my young son can be transforming. A brief, encouraging phone call to someone who is having trouble can make a world of difference. Telling the people around you what you appreciate about them will have a powerful, long-term effect.

One of the best things you can do to encourage people is to look for their strengths. One night at our home fellowship group the leader took half of the people into another room and gave them an "assignment." Those of us who remained behind had no idea what those in the other room had been asked to do. When they returned, each person who had been given the assignment began to speak with another person. They explained why they appreciated us as friends. They described the strengths they saw in us. They spoke of specific times when we had been of help to them. It was a *very* encouraging time. The idea, we found out later, was simply to encourage. It was powerful.

Later, as we discussed what took place with the entire group, it was interesting to note that very few of us really felt comfortable. Both the encouragers and those receiving encouragement were a bit uneasy. However, we all agreed that the benefit of encouragement is well worth the effort.

Sometimes we have difficulty encouraging others because we are not quite certain what to say. We may be afraid we will sound silly. However, we do not need to wait for big events or accomplishments to give a word of encouragement. We can even comment on the little things our friends say or do that we appreciate. In so doing, we will undoubtedly bless them as well.

In his book *You Gotta Keep Dancin'*, Tim Hansel, a former physical education instructor, shares a letter from a former student. Allow me to quote a brief portion of that letter.

I may not be burned deeply into your memory, Tim, but you are in mine. And now that you've surfaced once again in my life, I thought I'd let you know that.

I remember the first day I had you for P.E. when I was a freshman in 1966. We all had to run the 600-yard dash, and I didn't want to. I was always coming in last, no matter how hard I ran (and I always ran as hard as I could). But this one was different.

Oh, I still came in last—by about 150 yards, as I remember. But I remember you running alongside of me that last 100 yards yelling, "Good effort, Lou! Great effort! Absolutely magnificent..."

I felt like I'd won the Olympic Gold Medal for the marathon. And I became totally devoted to you because no one had ever encouraged me like you.[15]

This one little incident of encouragement had an effect for years! In the ministry of music and worship, we need to encourage one another and build one another up. We have enough detractors in the world. From one another, we need encouragement.

Seize every opportunity possible to encourage your brothers and sisters involved in the music ministry with you. Tell them how much you appreciate their efforts, their time commitment, their attitude, their gifts, their love for God, their life, their family, their friendship...oh, you get the idea. Encourage them a lot and often.

Encourage one another and build each other up.

Adapted from the book *If Standing Together Is So Great, Why Do We Keep Falling Apart?* by Tom Kraeuter (Lynnwood, Wash.: Emerald Books, 1994, 1998).

First Things First

BY PATRICK KAVANAUGH

> *Could you men not keep watch with me for one hour?*
> MATTHEW 26:40

When Jesus was asked, "What is the greatest commandment?" He answered, "Love the Lord your God with all your heart and with all your soul and with all your mind. This is the first and greatest commandment" (Matthew 22:37–38). *After* giving this supreme command, Jesus continued, "And the second is like it. Love your neighbor as yourself" (Matthew 22:39).

There is a reason that He gave them in this order. It is that the first must be *first*. It is no good trying to keep the second command until we have kept the first. It is like trying to perform the second in a series of instructions before you have performed the first task. It doesn't work. It was not meant to.

Getting us to act on this supreme commandment has been the endeavor of all the great preachers and teachers throughout the past two millennia. This was the urging of Augustine in his masterpiece *The City of God:* "Let us love Him as we ought to love Him. For this is the great reward, this is royalty and pleasure, this is enjoyment, and glory, and honor, this is light, this is the great happiness, which language or reasoning cannot set before us nor mind conceive."

"All right," you concede, "we should love God first. But how *do* we love God? How can we show Him our love, except through keeping His command to love others?"

Jesus indeed made it clear that one of the ways we can show Him our love is by loving others. "Whatever you did for one of the least of these brothers of mine, you did for me" (Matthew 25:40). His emphasis on keeping the first commandment does not mean we are to ignore the second. Nevertheless, this cannot be the only way we can show our love for God. We ought to be able to express our love to the Lord even if we were the only human left on earth. But how?

Anyone who has ever raised children knows that kids spell the word *love* "T-I-M-E." That is, if you want to show love to your children, you need to spend *time* with them. This is what they want from us; not things, or money, or lectures, etc. They want us to spend time with them. There is no better way to show them our love. If you have children, you know exactly what I mean.

For that matter, any relationship needs time. For those who are married, do you remember when you first met your spouse? You wanted to spend *all* your time with him or her! And now that the honeymoon is long since over, if a marriage is to continue and grow, it will still take time spent together. All friendships take a degree of time in getting to know each other and doing things together that will cement the relationship.

How we use our time is the ultimate stewardship. Each of us is given only so much, and we must take care to spend it carefully. For if it is wasted or stolen, we cannot get it back. Even Napoleon had to admit, "There is one kind of robber the law does not strike at, though he steals what is most precious to men: Time." The time we have is indeed precious, and how we spend it demonstrates to the world what is most important to us.

In the same way, if we want to show our love for God, it will cost us some time—time to spend with the Lord, time to get to know Him, time to prepare our hearts for His service. It takes time. It is, however, the most worthwhile investment of our time we can ever make.

During Jesus' three-year public ministry on earth, notwithstanding the wonderful teachings our Lord gave the crowds, He primarily spent His time with His disciples. Jesus tells them, "Come with me by yourselves to a quiet place and get some rest" (Mark 6:31). Some of this was spent with the entire group, but the Gospels also refer to times spent alone with specific disciples. Certainly, these times were often used for instruction, but much of the time was doubtless spent in nurturing their deep relationships. It took time.

One is reminded of the poignant words of Jesus when He found His closest disciples asleep in Gethsemane: "Could you men not keep watch with me for one hour?" (Matthew 26:40).

This spending time with God, focusing on Him and putting aside the cares of the world, gives us time to mature our relationship with Him. It is called worship. It may happen in groups (large or small), or it may be in private. Even in the largest group, what we usually call *corporate* worship is still a private experience between each worshiper and God. Worshipers simply happen to be together in the same room, outwardly doing many of the same things.

Make time with God the real priority in your life.

Adapted from the book *Worship—A Way of Life* by Patrick Kavanaugh (Grand Rapids, Mich.: Chosen Books—a division of Baker Book House Company, 2001).

Of Aram or Guitars

BY TOM KRAEUTER

> For the eyes of the LORD range throughout the earth to strengthen those whose hearts are fully committed to him.
>
> 2 CHRONICLES 16:9a

There was a lengthy period of time in the Old Testament when Judah and Israel were not only divided but also at sharp odds with each other. At one point in this conflict, Baasha, king of Israel, was tormenting Judah. Rather than resort to an army-to-army direct attack, Asa, king of Judah, decided to try forming an alliance. To make this work, he stripped the temple of the Lord as well as the royal palace of all gold and silver. All of this he sent to the king of Aram, asking him to side with Judah against Israel. It worked. Aram attacked Israel, and consequently, Israel left Judah alone.

As I read this section of Scripture, it struck me as odd that Asa resorted to taking the valuables from the temple to bribe another nation to help him. Why did he not instead simply call on the Lord? Why do something that would clearly alienate God from them? He took the temple treasures—the things devoted to the Lord Most High—and used them to gain some temporary help.

Later, God spoke to Asa through a prophet: "Because you relied on the king of Aram and not on the LORD your God, the army of the king of Aram has escaped from your hand. Were not the Cushites and

158

Libyans a mighty army with great numbers of chariots and horsemen? Yet when you relied on the LORD, he delivered them into your hand. *For the eyes of the LORD range throughout the earth to strengthen those whose hearts are fully committed to him*" (2 Chronicles 16:7–9a).

God's help would have been far better. The Lord would have been a far greater ally than any ten nations Judah could have found to side with them. In fact, this scripture says that God is looking for those He can strengthen. His desire is to assist and support those whose hearts are fully committed to Him.

Too often, those of us involved in the ministry of praise and worship have a tendency to rely on things other than God. We upgrade our sound system to give the music and words more clarity. We add instruments to be able to use songs and even musical styles that were previously unapproachable for us. We invest time and money to help the choir or praise vocalists be able to sing better. Please realize that all of these can be *very* good things. However, if our reliance in leading worship is on these things, then our focus is in the wrong place.

A number of years ago the Lord blessed me with a phenomenal guitar. It is much too lengthy a story to go into, but God sovereignly brought it about. People regularly comment on the clarity and brilliance of the tone of the instrument. It was custom-made just for me— my style of playing and particular **taste** in sound. The woods were hand selected by the builder to offer the timbre I prefer. It was specially made for the type of strings I use. The guitar was designed and built by a very dedicated Christian man who prayed over it from inception to completion. I have dedicated it to the Lord and intend that it will always be used for His glory.

Not long after I got the guitar, there was a time that I began to rely on it more than on the Lord. "With a guitar that sounds this good and has been dedicated to Him, of course people will respond in worship," I thought. As long as I had my "blessed" guitar, worship would always be great.

I soon realized my focus was all wrong. Like Asa, I was counting on something other than God. Oh, the circumstances were different, of course, but the heart was the same. Asa put his trust not in the Lord but in his hired army. My confidence **was** not in God but in my instrument. Both of our heart attitudes were putrid to the Almighty.

What the Lord wants is for us to be fully committed to *Him*. God desires for our trust, our confidence, to be placed squarely in Him. Not in our abilities. Not in our ideas. Not in all that we have or possess. We depend solely on the Lord Most High.

When we are fully committed to Him—and not to ourselves or something else—then the Lord Himself looks for ways to strengthen us. "For the eyes of the LORD range throughout the earth to strengthen those whose hearts are fully committed to Him" (2 Chronicles 16:9a).

Vikings, Moon Landings, and Buses

BY ARLEN SALTE

🌿 *Your attitude should be the same as that of Christ Jesus: Who, being in very nature God, did not consider equality with God something to be grasped, but made himself nothing, taking the very nature of a servant, being made in human likeness. And being found in appearance as a man, he humbled himself and became obedient to death—even death on a cross!*
PHILIPPIANS 2:5–8

I'm driving a gray 1965 Ford school bus. I'm young. I'm a musician. I'm on the road. I have no food. I have no money. I have a guitar and a prayer. I'm ecstatic.

It's the afternoon, and the sun is beating down. I pull up to the church where I'll hold a concert that night. No one shows up to welcome us, so my sound man and I go ahead and set up the sound equipment. Just when we're wondering what to do about dinner, we notice a note on the door of the church. It simply says, *"For supper tonight, head east out of town. The first white house on the left-hand side of the road is where you'll eat before the concert."*

We drove east out of town. After about a mile we noticed a white house on the left side of the road. We pulled up to the farmhouse, marched up to the front, knocked on the door, introduced ourselves, and walked in. We went into the kitchen and carried on a conversation for a while until we noticed that it was getting a little close to the concert start time. We hadn't been offered anything but finally decided to assert ourselves.

"I'm sorry to impose, but would it be possible to eat now? It's getting kind of late."

With more than a little discomfort, they said, *"Frankly, we have no idea who you are or why you're here."*

We'd gone to the wrong house and had let ourselves in.

We had another one of our band members experience worse. He showed up at a house late at night after a concert. It was back when long hair and ripped jeans were in vogue. He stepped into the house and visited with the elderly people who lived there. It was only after he asked where his bed was to sleep in that night that they informed him they had no idea who he was.

Now, let's fast-forward twenty-four years to today. You walk up to a house, knock on the door, step into the kitchen, and ask where your meal and bed are for the night.

In both of these cases, we were fortunate to run into hospitable people in rural areas. In most large cities today, you'd be shot or at least chased outside by a butcher knife.

What's the significance of this illustration? It's simply this: You cannot take your congregation into a new place in worship unless you are willing to go there yourself. You need to introduce them to the experience as one who is willing to go ahead of them.

For many of us, this means that we need to step outside of our comfort zones. That's not always very easy. It is, however, a critical part of leadership. If leadership remains in the comfort zone, nothing fresh is experienced.

In the Bible reading for today, we see that Jesus Christ emptied Himself. For the sake of the gospel, He even gave up His cultural preferences. He did not bring heaven's music, language, architecture, clothes, or physical appearance with Him. For the sake of the gospel, He became incarnate, spoke in simple ways of sheep and shepherd, weeds and grain. He walked among us and became us. Not only was He life, He showed us how to live life. He was the example. People followed.

People follow your example as well. When you step to the platform in worship services, many eyes are upon you. To a great extent you will determine just how far the congregation will go. Your forging ahead provides a level of safety, acceptability, and permission. You cannot be an indifferent worshiper and ask the congregation to go ahead of you in expressing themselves in worship.

When the first Viking landed on the shores of Newfoundland, he gave permission to other Vikings to jump on those ships and head for North America.

When the first step was taken on the moon on July 20, 1969, future Apollo missions were given faith and courage.

When a black woman stayed in her seat on a bus and refused to give it up to a white person, she gave bravery to millions.

You *are* Leif Eriksson. You *are* Neil Armstrong. You *are* Rosa Parks. This takes bravery and determination.

I'm often asked in more reserved churches, "How do we get people to clap and raise their hands?" While there are many tips I can give, the starting point is always the praise team. They need to lead the way. They need to give permission. They need to stretch out of their comfort zone.

Whenever we want to pull back into our comfort zone, we need to look at Jesus. His road to the cross was a long ways from His comfort zone.

What comfort zones do you need to step out of? Maybe it's time to hold some of your congregation's hands and take them to a deeper place in worship than they've ever been before.

Look around the room at your worship team. You're looking at Leif Erikssons, Neil Armstrongs, and Rosa Parkses. Now, let's head for uncharted territory. It's a great adventure!

So, Who Was Enoch, Anyway?

BY TOM KRAEUTER

> *He has showed you, O man, what is good. And what does the LORD require of you? To act justly and to love mercy and to walk humbly with your God.*
> MICAH 6:8

The eleventh chapter of Hebrews has been referred to as the "hall of faith." The star players of the Old Testament are there. Noah is mentioned. Abraham is there along with Isaac and Jacob. Moses receives a deservedly lengthy section. Included, of course, are the likes of Gideon and Samson, David and Samuel. Nearly all the Old Testament heroes of the faith are there, just the way it should be.

However, one of the first names on the list is a guy named Enoch. Please excuse my apparent disrespect, but I'm not sure that Enoch belongs on the same list with folks like David, Abraham, Noah, and Moses. After all, we know David was arguably the greatest warrior and most renowned king in the history of Israel. Abraham has become known as the father of the faithful, the beginning of our heritage. Amidst many scoffers, Noah spent years building the ark—a massive feat—in obedience to God. Moses led the people of Israel out of Egypt and through the desert for forty years. These guys did stuff that you or I would be proud to say we had done. Each one of these folks is what legends are made of. There is no doubt that they should be on the list. But Enoch? Who is he?

Consider this: His entire life story is summed up in the span of just seven short verses in Genesis 5:18–24. Scripture does not give much background on Enoch at all. We don't even know if he was a stonemason, a wood cutter, a preacher, or an unemployed homeless person. However, we do know this: He had pleased God. Hebrews 11:5 says, "He was commended as one who pleased God." So, you might ask, how did he do that? Genesis 5:24, the last verse in his life story, gives us the answer: "Enoch walked with God."

There's hope in that statement for you and me. You see, I'm uncertain about what I would do if the Lord asked me to lead His people into battle. Or build an ark. Or rule over His people. These and the other feats of the heroes of the faith seem overwhelming to me. But I can walk with God. I may not know much about parting seas, but I can walk with God. The thought of hand-to-hand combat with Philistine warriors scares me, but I can walk with God. You and I may be intimidated by the idea of doing great exploits in the name of Jesus, but we can walk with God. More than all the great accomplishments that you or I will ever achieve, walking with God is the most important.

Unfortunately, there are lots of things in life that will try to hinder us from walking with God. Things like being overly busy or undisciplined or lazy. Any (or all) of these (as well as many other things) can keep us from walking with God in the way that He desires for us to walk with Him.

I live near St. Louis, Missouri. Recently I went on a personal prayer retreat, and the retreat facility where I stayed overlooked the Mississippi River. One day as I walked along the shore of the river, I noticed several places where man-made piles of rock jutted out into the water. These were not just small accumulations of stones but large boulders forming blockades, fifty feet out into the river. At the time I wondered why they had been made.

Later, as I sat outside the small hermitage where I was staying, I noticed that just downriver from each of these collections of rocks was a place where the shoreline was considerably worn away. These stone barricades were not just someone's personal piers for walking on. The ferocious waters of the mighty Mississippi were wearing away large sections of shoreline. The never-ceasing current of that great river had pulled away rocks and soil from the edge. Left unchecked, those waters would have destroyed even more of those sections of riverbank. These blockades were obviously designed to help keep any more of the shore from eroding.

In our own lives we need blockades just like these. We need to keep our spiritual life from eroding. We need to make time in our busy schedules to spend with the Lord. We need to make sure that laziness or lack of discipline is not keeping us from the relationship He desires for us to have with Him. We need to be certain that we, like Enoch, are indeed walking with God.

What does God ask of you? In our Bible verse for today God speaks through the prophet Micah, telling the people to do good things, love His mercy, and *walk humbly with Him.*

Of Table Lamps and Flashlights

BY ARLEN SALTE

> When Moses came down from Mount Sinai
> with the two tablets of the Testimony in his
> hands, he was not aware that his face was
> radiant because he had spoken with the LORD.
> EXODUS 34:29

It was April sixteenth. I was in Nashville in a downtown hotel. A breathless announcement was given that a tornado was ripping through town. We needed to leave the meeting room immediately. We quickly took the stairs down to the relative safety of the parking garage.

The tornado did terrible damage to Nashville. Maybe you remember the front-page story.

When the damage was done, we were told to leave the downtown area immediately. There were open gas lines. Downtown Nashville looked like a windblown ghost town, full of broken glass and twisted metal.

I took the elevator up to my room and gathered my luggage. Then the power went off. I headed for the stairwell.

I entered the staircase, and the fire door slammed behind me. The emergency lights weren't working. It all went black. I'm not talking gray. I'm not talking slivers of light. I'm talking absolute darkness. I couldn't even see my hand in front of my face.

That's when the complications of my situation hit me. I'm 6' 4", over 200 pounds, carrying a guitar flight case in one hand and a suitcase big enough to hold my mother in the other. I'm on the fourth floor, I'm in a hurry, and I can't see a thing. How many steps were there? Where was the next landing? How many times could a tall person cartwheel downward while still holding on to his guitar? I had visions of all the *Roadrunner* cartoons from my childhood passing in front of me.

That's when I remembered it. I had made the pledge years ago as a Boy Scout always to be prepared. If I could live through the childhood traumas of Boy Scout camp, I could handle a pitch-black Nashville stairwell. Desperation gave birth to inventiveness, and I pushed my finger to the Indiglo button of my Timex. Guess what? In absolute dark, an Indiglo light can show you how many steps there are to the next landing. I made it all the way down—intact.

I was grateful that I had a portable light with me. The table lamp back in the hotel room wouldn't have done much good. I needed a light source with me wherever I went.

All too often, our worship is more like a table lamp than a flashlight. We walk into church, flick on the "switch," and go into "worship mode." Then, we leave the church and turn off the lights as we're walking out the door. If we always require a certain setting to engage our hearts in worship, we'll rise and fall, dependent on our circumstances.

What's more, it is impossible for an authentic heart of worship to be transmitted to the congregation if we are not living a lifestyle of worship every day and in every circumstance.

This is a challenge to all of us as worship leaders, whether we're sitting behind drums or strumming a guitar. Authenticity in public worship is birthed in the real stuff of life that happens in our private worship.

One of the most powerful books on worship is the three-hundred-year-old spiritual classic *The Practice of the Presence of God* by a humble cook named Brother Lawrence. He writes of how he had come to the state where he was in constant communion with God. He remained in this state whether he was washing pots and pans in the noise of the kitchen or on his knees in prayer. He called this the art of "practicing the presence of God in one single act that does not end."

Brother Lawrence wrote, "There is no sweeter manner of living in the world than continuous communion with God."

Oh, how the worship in our churches would be revolutionized if we would only follow the example of Brother Lawrence. Oh, how the attitude in our worship teams would be transformed if we abided in

God's presence whether we were leading the congregation, packing up the drum set, or changing a flat tire.

The light of God's presence doesn't need an extension cord. He is with us at all times. So how do we come to this realization like Brother Lawrence? It really comes down to the basics.

1. Pray without ceasing: Talk to God throughout the day. Acknowledge His presence in the mundane things and the exhilarating times.

2. Spend time in His Word. Christian worship doesn't happen in a vacuum. It is always in response to God's activity in our lives. How can we worship if we don't know why He's worthy of our praise?

3. Sing in the shower and the sanctuary. Fill your home and car with the sounds of worship. How many times a day do we need to hear the news? Do we really need to listen to so much whining on talk radio?

All of these are spiritual disciplines. That means that they require dedication. It also means that just like an investment with compound interest, they grow over time.

Right now, you're in the dark stairwell of the world. A table lamp back in the sanctuary won't do you much good. However, an Indiglo just might save your neck. Practice the presence of God so that when you come down from the mountain like Moses, your face will be a radiant light wherever you go.

Hope for the Weary

BY TOM KRAEUTER

> *But now, Lord, what do I look for?*
> *My hope is in you.*
> PSALM 39:7

No hope. This often describes the world around us. Sometimes it captures our feelings as well. We can get to the point where we are too discouraged to even trust God any longer. But Jesus is the One who bids us try again and gives us the hope to do so.

One day Jesus was teaching by the Lake of Gennesaret. Because so many people were crowding around Him, He thought it would be best to get into a boat and teach from there. He asked one of the nearby fishermen who were washing their nets to put out a little from the shore. The man, Simon, did as Jesus asked. Then Jesus sat down in the boat and taught the people from there.

"When he had finished speaking, he said to Simon, 'Put out into deep water, and let down the nets for a catch.' Simon answered, 'Master, we've worked hard all night and haven't caught anything. But because you say so, I will let down the nets' " (Luke 5:4–5).

This was apparently one of Simon's (later to be known as Peter) first encounters with Jesus. In his bold, matter-of-fact manner, Peter was probably thinking, "Jesus, You may be an excellent teacher, but fishing is my life. What do You know about fishing?"

In this instance, instead of speaking his mind, he basically said, "We're tired and discouraged. We haven't caught a thing all night. I can't see how it could possibly be any different this time. Nevertheless, because You say so, we'll try it again."

You know the rest of the story. "When they had done so, they caught such a large number of fish that their nets began to break. So they signaled their partners in the other boat to come and help them, and they came and filled both boats so full that they began to sink" (Luke 5:6–7).

Sometimes we can become so discouraged and tired that we too can lose hope. Situations and circumstances seem completely the opposite of our ideal. Everything seems to be going wrong. Occasionally, we feel so hopeless that we do not even have the desire to try again. It is at these times that if we listen carefully, we can still hear the voice of Jesus, saying, "Try it again. This time will be different."

In Psalm 39, David sounds rather discouraged. "Show me, O LORD, my life's end and the number of my days; let me know how fleeting is my life. You have made my days a mere handbreadth; the span of my years is as nothing before you. Each man's life is but a breath. Man is a mere phantom as he goes to and fro: He bustles about, but only in vain; he heaps up wealth, not knowing who will get it" (Psalm 39:4–6).

Sounds pretty grim, huh? "[D]ays a mere handbreadth...years as nothing...life but a breath...man a mere phantom...bustles about in vain...heaps up wealth, not knowing who will get it." These words sound as though David is struggling. To our normal thinking his next statement should be something like, "Oh, woe is me!" But it isn't.

David goes on to say, "But now, Lord, what do I look for? *My hope is in you*" (Psalm 39:7). His attitude is, "This life may look pretty crummy at times, but my hope and my confidence are in God." David knew where to look for hope.

Yes, clearly this devotion is about life in general. However, it is also about worship ministry. If you have been involved in the worship ministry of your church for any length of time, there have probably been some disappointments along the way. You may have seen your share of discouraging moments. Perhaps there was a time (several times?) you caused a crash-and-burn ending to a song during corporate worship. Maybe there have been times when people have not truly recognized the time and effort you and the others have devoted to worship ministry. Maybe the extra time away from family has occasionally taken its toll. Or perhaps someone was critical of you or the others.

Whatever the case, you have certainly been disappointed. There may have been times when your hope for things getting better had vanished. Perhaps you're there now.

Even in the midst of difficult times God still offers you hope. Do you have the courage to fish again? Will you call to God in time of trouble? For those who are willing, His hope is still there.

Pressing In Again...to Worship

BY KENT HENRY

> 🍃 *Come near to God and he will*
> *come near to you.*
> JAMES 4:8

A few years ago I helped organize a worship summit in Portland, Oregon. It was a small gathering of thirty or so worship leaders from the West Coast. We had come together for a couple of days of worship, prayer, and encouragement. As my friend Gerrit Gustafson was sharing with the group the elements of priesthood, he said an amazing thing: "The life definition of a true priest is 'one who draws near to the divine presence.'"

Internally I thought, "What did you say?" As the thought continued to grip my heart, my thought process went something like this: "Okay...one who draws near...(I am saying this slowly on the inside) draws near to the divine presence. Yes! That's it! I've finally heard in one simple phrase my life's passion and cry—to linger in God's presence."

James 4:6–8 tells us, "But he gives us more grace. That is why Scripture says: 'God opposes the proud but gives grace to the humble.' Submit yourselves, then, to God. Resist the devil, and he will flee from you. Come near to God and he will come near to you."

Since becoming friends with Jesus, I've found my heart consistently preoccupied with God, His person and presence, and why He

173

would choose to work through such a lowly vessel like me. You see, for quite a while I thought maybe there was something very amiss with my priorities. My heart was on fire. I was burning to worship God. I longed to consume the Word of God. I had a deep desire to continue to worship and fellowship with like-hearted believers.

As Gerrit spoke, I realized that this passion is not unique. We are built to continually be hungry for the things of God, especially in our inner man. Jesus tells us in Matthew 5:6, "Blessed are those who hunger and thirst for righteousness, for they will be filled." That's my heart's desire.

In the physical realm, each day we go through a regular cycle of being hungry and being filled. We get hungry, and we eat food to satisfy that hunger. We need to take a lesson from God's creation. Just as our physical man cannot operate for long without foods that have good nutritional value, neither can our spiritual man operate at the highest levels without His presence and His Word.

I have a deep concern that you who are reading this may have struggled with the concept of living your life in His presence. Perhaps even worse, you are burned out at even making an attempt at drawing near to the Lord. Maybe you have encountered those who have ridiculed your attempts to walk closely with God. I'm sorry that people have hurt and abused you. I'm very sorry that your heart and idealism were spurned. However, as a friend and a fellow worshiper, I invite you as the Father would to once again come deeply into His presence.

I shudder to think that mere words on a page could be so encouraging or invasive as to begin a healing deep in your heart. Unfortunately, it's all that I have at this moment—these words on this page—to say to you. Turn to the Lord. Turn and keep turning to the Lord. Even if you've become weary, even if you've become very tired of your human condition, make the choice right now to begin once again to worship.

Honestly, in twenty-seven years of worship ministry there have been times when I have hit the wall. There were times when I was not able to discern or feel His presence. I have learned to worship anyway. God's Word tells us that His strength is perfected in weakness. It is not in the ability or the power of the very gift He gave us to sing or play music. It is in our moments of weakness that His strength is perfected in us.

So it's time to press on. It's time to press in again. What is left except to press on? To continue to press in for the highest and deepest things of the heart of God. Ultimately, we are giving our lives to see everyday people touched by the power of His holy presence. Take heart; start anew and afresh to draw near to the Lord with true worship. We remain His worshipers until every tribe, every tongue, every dialect, and every nation has an opportunity to worship at His holy mountain.

The Right Tools for
the Right Situation

BY TOM KRAEUTER

 Praise the LORD.... Praise him with the sounding of the trumpet...with the harp and lyre...with tambourine...with the strings and flute...with the clash of cymbals...with resounding cymbals.
PSALM 150:1a, 3–5

My father was an extremely talented person. He had the ability to do auto repair work, woodworking, electrical work, plumbing, etc., and all with a very high degree of professionalism. Having done all of these kinds of things for years, he had accumulated quite a collection of tools. He had more *toolboxes* full than I have tools. (Unfortunately, I did not inherit much of his ability to work with his hands. I did, however, learn a lot from him.) It always amazed me that regardless of the task, he had just the right tool to do the job. Regardless of the task ahead of him, he would reach into a toolbox—often a small drawer in a seldom-used box tucked away in the corner—and pull out just the right implement to do the job. He very seldom used a tool to accomplish something for which it was not intended. He always seemed to use the *right* tool for the job.

As the people involved in the ministry of praise and worship, we need to understand this concept in our music. We need to learn to use just the right tool—instrument—for just the right purpose. Too frequently we use all the instruments all the time. Just as my dad would never have used a screwdriver when a wrench was needed, or a pocketknife when a lathe was necessary, so we should use the right instruments at the right times.

Some time ago I had the opportunity to attend a production featuring a major symphony orchestra. Throughout the evening nearly the entire gamut of human emotion was portrayed using only musical instruments. The audience was transported from a calm peace to a point of severe tension. We experienced deep sorrow, tremendous joy, excitement, and much more. Each emotion was depicted by the use of appropriate instrumentation. It was interesting to note that this would have been impossible to do if all of the instruments had played continuously throughout the entire concert. Instead, the various instruments helped to create the proper setting and feel for what the music attempted to convey.

We in the church need to learn this concept. We need to be more sensitive with our use of music. Do not just plow through during your praise and worship time. Instead, strive to be sensitive to how you might enhance the worship experience through the use of your musical instruments. A good friend of mine drives home the point: "Most church praise and worship music is put through a 'blander.' It all comes out sounding the same!" If it all sounds at least somewhat similar, we are not adequately expressing the various themes and moods of our songs. We must use more variety in what we do.

To that end, we need to learn to use each of the instruments we have available as tools. Just as my father used certain tools at certain times, it is necessary for us to choose carefully which instruments will most effectively portray what we are trying to say with our worship. If we are in a slow, intimate time of communing with the Lord, a blaring electric guitar solo or loud cymbal crashes would probably be out of order. On the other hand, during a boisterous time of jubilant celebration these things might be very appropriate. Obviously these are extreme cases, but we need to learn even subtle nuances of musical enhancement of our worship. Use *all* of the instruments you have available to their fullest potential, but do not overuse them.

Psalm 150 depicts using quite the variety of instruments. I get the impression that the ones listed were just a sampling of what was available. They probably had enough instruments to add lots of variety to their music.

As a side note, some music folks at smaller churches have told me this is impossible for them. They have said, "All we have is a slightly out of tune piano and a guitarist who plays only every other week."

"That's okay," I respond. "On some songs use just the piano. On others use just the guitar. Other times you can use both. Still other times you can sing a capella. You may have a limited number of instruments, but you can still use variety in ways that will enhance the songs."

The bottom line is this: We need to learn to be sensitive and creative with our music in order to enhance what God wants to do. If we simply blanderize our music, we will miss at least part of the purpose of the Lord for us and our ministries. Like my father using just the right tools for the right situation, we need to learn to use just the right instrument(s) to enhance what we are doing musically.

Adapted from the book *Keys to Becoming an Effective Worship Leader* by Tom Kraeuter (Lynnwood, Wash.: Emerald Books, 1991).

Losing Your Good Reputation

BY BOB KAUFLIN

> *Fear of man will prove to be a snare, but whoever trusts in the LORD is kept safe.*
> PROVERBS 29:25

Few of us appear more "spiritual" than when we gather with the Church to praise God in song. Voices raised, faces bright, hands uplifted (or maybe holding a hymnal)—surely, worship is taking place, right?

Worship is definitely taking place. The question is, "Who is being worshiped?" It can be dangerous to assume that if we're leading other Christians in praising God, then we must be praising God, too. As you're probably aware, self-focused and ungodly thoughts can pass through our minds even as we sing worshipful words. Is it possible to worship God on the outside while worshiping myself on the inside? Sadly, yes.

Jesus confronted this type of hypocrisy among the religious leaders of his day. "Everything they do is done for men to see" (Matthew 23:5). What a sobering indictment. While others esteemed the piety of their clothing, prayers, and teachings, Jesus detected their true motives. He pointed out how they loved the most important seats in the synagogues and enjoyed having others call them "Rabbi." What was the issue? "They loved praise from men more than praise from God" (John 12:43). It wasn't that they desired a good reputation. It was that they wanted it too much. Fear of man became a snare for them.

179

We shouldn't be too quick to comfort ourselves that we're not first-century Pharisees strutting about in flowing robes. The spirit of the Pharisees is alive and well in our generation. Let's take a moment to look at some of the ways it's revealed.

Ask yourself a few questions. What am I most conscious of as I'm standing in front of my closet on Sunday morning picking out the clothes I'll wear? Have you ever thought, "Oh, I can't wear that old thing. It's so out of fashion." Or perhaps, "This new outfit is going to make people sit up and take notice!" Or maybe, "I just don't have anything to wear!" Of course, wanting to look your best is not evil in itself. It's when we are more concerned with how we appear to others than how we appear before God that our true heart has been exposed. Whose opinion matters most to you? That's the real question.

Here's another example. When we arrive at the corporate gathering, what fills our minds? Do we eagerly look forward to expressing wholehearted devotion to the King of the universe? Or do our minds drift to checking out what everyone's wearing, taking mental note of who doesn't greet us, or struggling with the attention that someone else is receiving?

Worship teams and leaders face a unique challenge in this area. While seeking to draw attention to God during worship, we can be tempted to draw attention to ourselves. (A pop culture that tends to worship trendy musicians only complicates the issue.) In reaction, some churches limit the role of the worship team, perhaps by placing the band off to the side or restricting the role of the leader. I believe such efforts ultimately fail to address the real issue: the sinful human heart.

Leadership always brings the temptation of self-glorification, although most of us are smart enough to avoid blatant expressions of arrogance. "Wasn't I great this morning?" isn't something we typically ask, even though we might be thinking it! Here are some more questions that will help reveal what's going on in our hearts, even when we're unaware of it.

1. Am I insecure about how others might perceive me, and does this sometimes lead to a fear of stepping out into a new area of involvement in the worship ministry? If I'm asked to do something I'm not completely confident in, I have a choice. Either I can seize this fresh opportunity to trust God to use me in my

weakness, or I can keep quiet so that no one will see me make a mistake. Stepping out requires humility. Keeping quiet might be an evidence of pride.

2. Am I distracted by, threatened by, or resentful of the gifts God has given others? Am I able to sincerely encourage those who are more gifted than I am? Current members of the worship team should be the first to detect and encourage other gifted musicians. This will be difficult to do if we constantly compare ourselves to others, favorably or unfavorably. Sometimes we try to avoid exposing our true thoughts by belittling our contributions or talents. Actually, this can lead others to "balance" our assessment through encouragement and flattery. We may even secretly hope that will be the result. Speaking negatively of our own gifts makes it more difficult for others to give us an honest evaluation.

3. Am I bitter or depressed about not being chosen or used more? This is more likely to happen when singers and players are on a rotating schedule or when a special event is approaching. God gives out gifts of varying degrees; we're foolish to think otherwise.

4. In remembering a meeting where I was particularly effective, do I tend to reflect on how God used me as opposed to all the other people God might have used? Do I bring up the meeting in conversation, hoping someone will point out the great contribution I made?

If your toes are feeling stepped on right now, you're not alone. A preacher I know likes to say, "If it still hurts, it ain't dead yet." What "ain't dead yet" is our desire to receive more glory than God. Or maybe just to share a little bit with Him. Fortunately, God won't let that happen. He loves us too much to let us live in that deception.

When questions like these hurt, we must be ruthless in dealing with the sin that has been revealed in our heart. One of the most effective ways I've found is to confess proud thoughts to others on the worship team. It may be frightening at first, but God has promised to give grace to the humble. And what sweet fruit humility bears!

Let's be thankful we have a Savior who cleanses even our "holy" acts, as well as a Deliverer who can turn our hearts to desire His glory above our own.

Fresh Batteries

BY TOM KRAEUTER

"Apart from me you can do nothing."
JOHN 15:5

It is clear from both Scripture and experience that God gives specific gifts to certain people. Some folks have an inborn ability to communicate. Others possess a seemingly natural aptitude for understanding mechanical reasoning. Still others may have an innate penchant for music or administration or leadership or hospitality or any number of other possibilities. The Lord graces people with unique gifts.

Once we recognize that God has indeed blessed us with certain gifts, there can come a problem. We can have the idea that we are now fully responsible for the function of that gift. The reasoning seems rational: If someone gives me a gift for my birthday, then I now own that gift. It is 100 percent my responsibility to maintain and use that gift. Although there is a dimension of truth in this way of thinking, it is not the entire truth.

A more accurate understanding of God's gifts would be a battery-powered item. The batteries are a very special kind and can be obtained only from the one who gave you the gift. You can use that gift on your own for a while. Eventually, though, the batteries will wear down. At that point, there is only one source for new batteries. Of course, you may able to nurse that gift along on its original batteries. You might even be able to find some novel use for it that doesn't use the batteries. However, to use the gift fully for its originally intended purpose, you're going to need some fresh batteries. And there is only one source for those batteries.

I am convinced that the Lord has given me some pretty amazing gifts. I have been consistently overwhelmed by the ways the seminars I have taught and the books I have written have impacted people. To say that the responses I have received have been way beyond what I could have imagined would be an understatement. However, if I took all the gifts I have and even added to them all the gifts of all of my friends, they still would not make me able to bear fruit on my own. It makes no difference the talents and abilities you or I possess. We still have a desperate need for the Lord of Life within our lives and ministries. Apart from Him we can do nothing.

When the Israelites were coming into the Promised Land, God gave them a warning. In essence He said, "Don't think you have won this land because of your goodness or on your own strength. I gave it to you." We too must be on guard lest we think we have done something on our own.

This is especially true for those of us involved in the ministry of music. Music is a very powerful medium. We can easily become intoxicated by it and the effect that it has. When we see people swayed by "our" ministry, it is easy to think that we are really something special. When we continually receive words of affirmation about the times of worship, we can begin to feel that it is because of our own abilities. It is especially at these times that we must stop and remind ourselves that apart from Jesus we can do nothing.

In 1 Corinthians 4:7 it says: "For who makes you different from anyone else? What do you have that you did not receive? And if you did receive it, why do you boast as though you did not?" We must always recognize that everything we possess is simply a gift from Him. All of our abilities are not really ours at all. They are His.

The reality is that left to ourselves there are actually many things we can do. If we have strong personalities, we can influence people personally. We may be able to sway their emotions with our artistic abilities. We can even convince people on an intellectual basis. However, only God can touch their heart and make long-term changes.

Clearly the Lord works in us and through us, but it is still His work. This idea can be likened to when we learned to ride a bike. Mom or Dad was running next to us, pushing the bike and holding us up. We really didn't do anything, but Mom or Dad encouraged us, "You're doing great!"

Do you remember the centurion who came to Jesus and wanted Jesus to heal his servant? Scripture says that Jesus marveled at his faith. Where did he get that faith? It was from God. Yet Jesus encouraged Him for having it. In reality, there is nothing of any value that you or I have that we did not receive from God.

In Psalm 16, David made this statement, "I said to the LORD, 'You are my Lord; apart from you I have no good thing'" (Psalm 16:2). David realized that all his talents and gifts were of little value without God. Do *you* recognize this in *your* life? Are you completely dependent on Him? Ask God for some fresh batteries today to truly empower you to do the things He has called you to do.

The Creative Variety of the Worshiping Church

BY PATRICK KAVANAUGH

> *Therefore let us stop passing judgment on one another.*
> ROMANS 14:13a

L et us consider a number of different church worship services. But before setting out, let us first establish an important proposition: No two churches are alike. Not only are the worship services of various denominations different from one another. Each church within a given denomination is different from all the rest.

Anyone who has ever moved from one town to another already knows this. While "shopping" for a new church, a part of you is constantly comparing the churches you visit to the one you just left in your old town. There never seems to be a church that is quite like the one you left. There never will be. They are all different.

This was even true in the early Church. A reading of Paul's letters gives us a variety of church styles, from Philippians to Galatians, from Corinthians to Colossians. They each had different strengths and weaknesses. The contrast is even greater among the seven churches from the book of Revelation (see Revelation 2–3).

Did you ever stop to think about the congregations in these various New Testament churches? How different they must have been, and how different their worship services might have been! Suppose one of the Ephesians traveled on business to Corinth and decided to go to the Christian church in town.

185

Doubtless he would have been delighted to find other believers who were worshiping together. But as we are all prone to comparing, as he left the service there might have been other thoughts going through his Ephesian head.

"That worship service certainly was longer than the ones we have in Ephesus. Too long! And why did they sing those strange, boring songs? I really didn't enjoy those. And another thing, I wish they didn't use those modern Greek instruments."

I am not trying to seem irreverent. The early saints were people just like you and me. They, too, had their preferences concerning worship, and when these were not encountered, they doubtless had just as much difficulty being patient and tolerant as we do. Because, as I have pointed out, every church is different.

Why are churches so different from one another? Don't we read the same Bible and pray to the same God? Certainly. Our differences arise from another factor. Churches are made up of *people*. Every person is unique, and therefore each church will also be unique.

This seems to be fine with God, who, after all, is *very* creative. He inspired four different Gospels, each of which tells the same life-changing story, but each with its own distinct characteristics. He clearly accepts all types of people into His kingdom—intelligent people, not very intelligent people, exciting people, boring people, nice people, and, well, a number of grouchy people. I'm sure you have met some of these people.

Knowing this to be true, it shouldn't bother us so much that there is such a variety of churches and denominations. To meet the needs of the different people, there will have to be wild churches, dignified churches, churches that are very loud, and churches that are rather quiet. After all, each church is made up of people—and some of these people are loud, while others are quiet.

God's kingdom is surely large enough for a very diverse group of Christian churches. Consider His creativity at giving gifts and talents throughout His people: "There are different kinds of gifts, but the same Spirit. There are different kinds of service, but the same Lord. There are different kinds of working, but the same God works all of them in all men" (1 Corinthians 12:4–6).

Certainly there are sincere doctrinal differences between various denominations. However, for every obscure point one can find to argue about, there are probably a hundred essential points on which we can all safely agree. As elucidated so well in C. S. Lewis's great work *Mere Christianity*, it is far better to concentrate on our commonalities than our controversies. The differences between any two denominations within Christianity are minuscule compared with the difference between Christianity and anything else.

Of course, one church may begin with a song, while another church begins with a prayer. Perhaps another begins with a word of exhortation, while still another begins with a Bible reading. These are differences not in content but simply of order. Some of the clergy dress in beautiful vestments, while others wear suits. I have seen church services in which the leaders wore old blue jeans. In the same way, some churches are beautiful edifices in marble and stained glass, while others are very plain and utilitarian. However, the same God can be worshiped in both "high" churches and "low" churches. The differences in worship styles among all these churches do not seem to bother our Lord. Perhaps they shouldn't bother us either.

Doubtless the most obvious difference that is heard about so frequently concerns worship music. Some churches sing older hymns, while others sing contemporary songs. Some use organ, some synthesizer. Some add orchestral instruments; others add the drums and electric guitars. And yes, the music of some churches is quiet, while for others LOUD music is definitely preferred.

These differences in style may not sit well with Christians who have been taught that their church or denomination is "right" and all the others are wrong. Maybe the Ephesians thought that about the Galatians and Philippians. But Paul did not think so, and I suggest that our Lord does not either.

The biblical injunction given throughout the fourteenth chapter of Romans clearly forbids us to censure another Christian church on such debatable matters as worship styles: "Therefore let us stop passing judgment on one another" (Romans 14:13a). One is reminded of a maxim of Augustine: "In essential matters, unity; in debatable matters, liberty; in all things, charity."

Adapted from the book *Worship—A Way of Life* by Patrick Kavanaugh (Grand Rapids, Mich.: Chosen Books—a division of Baker Book House Company, 2001).

God Looks at the Heart

BY TOM KRAEUTER

*Man looks at the outward appearance,
but the LORD looks at the heart.*
1 SAMUEL 16:7b

One of my favorite stories in the Bible is found in 2 Chronicles 30. Hezekiah was the king of Judah. The nation was about to celebrate the Passover for the first time in many years. The law clearly stated that the people must purify themselves in order to eat the Passover. Although a large number of the people who came had not purified themselves, they ate the Passover anyway, contrary to what was written. However, Hezekiah prayed for them, saying, " 'May the LORD, who is good, pardon everyone who sets his heart on seeking God—the LORD, the God of his fathers—even if he is not clean according to the rules of the sanctuary.' And the LORD heard Hezekiah and healed the people" (2 Chronicles 30:18–20).

Amazing. The actions of the people were completely wrong. Yet their hearts were right, and God chose to forgive.

Most assuredly the Lord wants our actions to reflect our love for Him, but the heart motivation is the key. First Samuel tells us, "Man looks at the outward appearance, but the LORD looks at the heart" (1 Samuel 16:7b). The Old Testament prophets consistently denounced the Israelites' worship, not because they were doing the wrong things but because their hearts were not in it. God always looks first at the heart. He knows that this side of heaven we are not going to be perfect, and so He deals with us accordingly. Psalm 103 says, "For he knows how we are formed, he remembers that we are dust" (Psalm 103:14). In spite of our actions, He looks at our hearts and sees that we desire to do the right thing.

There are some people who do not care when they do wrong. It makes absolutely no difference to them at all. They reach a point where their hearts are cold and calloused. They have no honest sorrow for their sins. There is no repentance, no desire to change.

My experience has been that those people are rare in the Church. Most people loathe their sins. Their attitude is like Paul's in Romans 7. "I hate what I am doing!" As long as the heart is still longing for God, as long as the Holy Spirit is still bringing conviction, there will always be forgiveness.

I recently heard a Christian radio talk show. During the show, listeners were given the opportunity to call in and ask questions. A young woman called and asked a couple of seemingly mundane questions. Finally, the host directly asked her what her real question was. She began to cry. Through sobs and strained voice she confided that some Christian friends had told her that she had committed the unpardonable sin, blaspheming the Holy Spirit (see Mark 3:29) and that she could no longer be saved. She wanted to know what to do.

The talk-show host handled it perfectly. I didn't write down his exact words, but in essence he said this: "You did not commit the unpardonable sin. Please hear what I am saying to you. I am not saying, 'I don't think you did' or 'You probably did not.' I am telling you without any wavering or doubting that you did not commit the unpardonable sin. I can say that, even without knowing the details of what you've done, because I can hear your repentance. If you had committed the unforgivable sin, your heart would be completely hard. There would be no regret. You would be cold and hard and calloused. But you're not. You are very obviously sincerely sorry for whatever it is that you have done. With that kind of heart attitude, God will always take you back and offer forgiveness."

He is exactly right. The important point to the Lord is our heart attitude. If we are not repentant, if we really don't care about our sins, then we are truly lost. However, if there is a sincere desire for change, a sincere repentance in our hearts, God always offers forgiveness.

What God is most interested in is our hearts. Some people who profess to be Christians engage in practices that the Bible clearly refers to as sin. These people see nothing wrong with their actions. Some even flaunt them. However, because there is no heart repentance there can never be forgiveness.

You and I also sin every day. In all honesty, from God's perspective there is no difference in the awfulness of our sin and the sin of the people I just mentioned. The difference is that you and I, just like the apostle Paul, are devastated by our sin. We are repentant, and because we are repentant, there will always be forgiveness.

When a child does wrong, what is it that a parent hopes will result from disciplining the child? If you could, without spanking, without raising your voice, achieve a desired result in the child, what would that result be? Obviously, we need to rule out perfect sinlessness, because that will not happen this side of heaven. What then would be the desired result? I pondered that question one day and finally arrived at the obvious answer: that the remorse over the sin would be an even stronger discipline than what I could verbally or physically administer. That the agony over doing wrong would be far more painful than any spanking or harsh words. In other words, my goal is that there would be genuine, heartfelt repentance. That's exactly what God is looking for from His children.

God desires for us to have hearts that are quick to repent. You see, even if our actions look good on the surface, we may very well have sin "hidden" in our hearts. More than just an outward appearance of goodness, the Lord is looking for hearts that turn to Him asking for forgiveness and desiring what He desires.

Adapted from the book *Living Beyond the Ordinary* by Tom Kraeuter (Lynnwood, Wash.: Emerald Books, 2000).

Zadok or Abiathar?

BY GERRIT GUSTAFSON

> 🌿 *Zadok and Abiathar were priests.*
> 2 SAMUEL 20:25

Once there were two priests by the name of Zadok and Abiathar. Though they had much in common, their lives took very different turns. In the end, Zadok's lineage was favored; Abiathar's was judged.

For most of their lives, they ministered together. Zadok and Abiathar were at the top of King David's list when he wanted consecrated priests to bring the ark of the covenant to his tabernacle. Again, it was Zadok and Abiathar that David put in charge of the ark when he temporarily left Jerusalem because of Absalom.

However, in the last days of David's rule, these two priests were sharply divided over who should follow David as king. Abiathar stood with Adonijah, who, according to 1 Kings 1:5, "put himself forward and said 'I will be king.'" Zadok had no respect for Adonijah's blatant self-promotion and, at David's command, anointed Solomon as God's choice.

In 1 Kings 2:27 we learn that "Solomon removed Abiathar from the priesthood of the Lord, fulfilling the word the Lord had spoken at Shiloh about the house of Eli." In contrast, four hundred years later, Ezekiel records in chapter 44 that Zadok's descendants are still enjoying a favored position of faithful ministry to the Lord.

191

What was it that made such a difference? How can we secure Zadok's reward for our own descendants? Zadok's and Abiathar's lives are a fascinating and instructive contrast of deep-seated motivations...motivations that preceded them, and motivations that are still with us today. Let's look more closely.

Zadok was a descendant of Phinehas, who, five hundred years earlier, was promised a lasting priesthood because he hated what God hated. In Numbers 25:11, Phinehas received this trophy from God: "He was as zealous as I am for my honor" among the Israelites.

Abiathar, in contrast, inherited a motivation from his great-great-grandfather Eli's self-serving ministry: "You honor your sons more than me." His own sons were guilty of immorality, gluttony, and abuse of office, and Eli had honored, above God, what was not honorable.

Here we get to the heart of the matter. Zadok's lineage honored God above all; Abiathar's honored something worthless above God. The contrast is a zeal for pleasing God versus a zeal for serving self. One is the spirit of Christ Himself who, according to John 5:30, lived to please the One who sent Him. The other is the spirit of this age as described in 2 Timothy 3: "People will be lovers of themselves...[and] lovers of pleasure rather than lovers of God." The irony is that this passionate worship of self will be wrapped in religion—"having a form of godliness."

Eli and his sons were in the ministry. Like worship leaders today, they were in charge of the sacrifices. Eli's issue—his defining moment—was his failure to confront his sons' allegiance to the god of Self.

Similarly, Abiathar, Eli's descendant, was a well-respected priest, just like Zadok. His defining moment—the issue when his true motivation was revealed—was Adonijah's self-promotion.

For us, our defining moment may or may not be how we discipline our children or our political choices. It might be in how we handle ourselves in a church split. Or, if you're a performing musician, it may come when you're offered a contract that will really get your music out but the price tag is compromise. Or maybe, if you keep silent about something on the job, your job is secure. What's in you then?

Actions follow decisions, which follow values, which follow deep-seated motivations in our hearts, which are tied to what we really worship. As the Old Testament poet says in Proverbs 4:23, "Above all else, guard your heart, for it is the wellspring of life." Outcomes are determined in our hearts.

Worship is not just about the songs we sing or the styles we choose. It's about honoring God in every decision. Just because you're into contemporary worship doesn't exempt you from the danger of acting more like an Abiathar than a Zadok.

True worship is about being living sacrifices in the midst of an indulgent world. It is daily taking up our crosses and choosing obedience to Him even when it puts us at odds with the majority. It is being careful not to honor anything above God—not a person, an ambition, or a possession. In John 7:18, we find these words of Jesus: "He who speaks on his own does so to gain honor for himself, but he who works for the honor of the one who sent him is a man of truth; there is nothing false about him." Such worshipers are true sons of Zadok.

The essence of Zadok is ministry to the Lord. It's surprising to me that we hear so little about worship being ministry unto the Lord. Ezekiel, in chapter 44, makes the distinction crystal clear. There were many priests who could minister to God's people, but only the sons of Zadok could minister to the Lord.

In 1 Samuel 2:35, an unnamed prophet spoke of the demise of the house of Eli and then, speaking of Zadok, added, "I will raise up for myself a faithful priest, who will do according to what is in my heart and mind. I will firmly establish his house, and he will minister before my anointed one always."

These words were probably Zadok's daily meditation: faithful to what is in God's heart and mind...and constancy in ministry unto the Lord.

May all of us—every worship team and each worshiper—have this same passion of Zadok!

Setting a Good Example

BY TOM KRAEUTER

> In everything set them an example by doing what is good...so that those who oppose you may be ashamed because they have nothing bad to say about us.
> TITUS 2:7–8

The minister of music was fairly new at the church. He had left his former church in another city to accept this position as worship leader. Although he had been at the church only a few months, he was extremely enthusiastic about the people with whom he now interacted. As we visited together he expressed these thoughts: "I have the opportunity here to work with some of the most talented musicians I have ever worked with in my ten years of worship ministry. However, the really exciting part of my job is the fact that the people involved in the worship ministry here consistently demonstrate a level of maturity I only dreamed about at my previous church. There is not the constant petty bickering or the juvenile I-want-to-be-pampered attitude. These folks actually endeavor to live the way Jesus said we should."

The worship leader paused for a moment and then continued. "Oh, don't get me wrong. They're not perfect. But when someone's quick temper gets the best of them or a prideful attitude surfaces, there is always repentance and forgiveness. It's just so very different from the people in the worship ministry where I was before. I had always thought that talent and godly character were contradictory ideas. Not any longer."

194

Although I was happy to see him in such a positive situation, I was saddened to think that a veteran worship leader would have the idea that talent and godly character were opposing concepts. I know that they are not because over the years I have known many extremely gifted musicians who also exhibited a large measure of godly character.

Unfortunately, I had to admit that his previous experience is probably more the norm than his new one. I too have frequently seen the very talented, artistic people who seem to exhibit very little godly character in their lives. Many church's worship ministries are hotbeds of unrest. There are people vying for position, climbing the mountain of success. The infighting and even hostility can be nasty. This type of behavior is clearly not the path that God wants us to follow.

Our text for this section says that we should set an example "in everything." More than just setting the example, however, there is clearly an intended goal in these verses. Paul is expecting some sort of outcome because we are setting an example "so that those who oppose you may be ashamed because they have nothing bad to say about us." The example that we set should cause people to see a positive difference in our lives. As a result, they will have nothing bad to say about our behavior.

There is a very good chance that you might be criticized for doing too many fast songs (or too many slow songs or too many hymns or too many choruses). You might receive flak for the sound being too loud (or too quiet or overly weighted toward the vocals or overly weighted toward the instruments). Negative feedback may suggest that you repeat songs too many times (or not enough times). Someone might even accuse you and others involved in the worship ministry of not looking happy enough (or looking too happy). Any or all of these may be stated honestly. However, all of these are subjective concepts. What should not be able to be stated about those involved in the worship ministry is that their lives are a poor example. As our text says, "In everything set them an example by doing what is good...so that those who oppose you may be ashamed because they have nothing bad to say about us" (Titus 2:7–8).

Let's get personal. Do you occasionally have, in the words of my friend (mentioned previously), a "juvenile I-want-to-be-pampered attitude"? Are you involved in the occasional "petty bickering"? Is your life truly the example it should be?

If not, God has an answer: "If we confess our sins, he is faithful and just and will forgive our sins and purify us from all unrighteousness" (1 John 1:9). Be honest with the Lord about your shortcomings. Tell Him you're sorry for your sin. Then ask Him to give you the strength to do better in the future. He will.

Dem Bones, Dem Bones, Dem Dry Bones

BY ARLEN SALTE

> *Moses took the bones of Joseph with him because Joseph had made the sons of Israel swear an oath. He had said, "God will surely come to your aid, and then you must carry my bones up with you from this place."*
> EXODUS 13:19

I own a very old Martin D-28 acoustic guitar. It's beat up. It has cracks from airport baggage mishandlers. It has the imprint of a crashing Shure SM58 microphone on the top. The neck is somewhat twisted, and the action would challenge even Arnold Schwarzenegger. But it's mine, and every dent, scratch, split, and twist carries a ministry story behind it. Yet it's more than the ministry stories. It's a reminder of the Christian heritage I'm blessed with. I will never sell it. Someday it will pass to one of my children.

At this point, the keyboard players may be thinking, "It's just a guitar. What's the big deal about something that's always going out of tune?"

Well, there's quite a story behind this out-of-tune piece of wood.

My father was a pastor. When I was seven, our family was in a terrible car accident as we returned from Bible camp. My father was thrown from the car and brutally killed. My mother was left with three young children, a fourth on the way, and very little money to meet our needs. But what she was left with was tremendous faith in a powerful God.

My father had a small insurance policy that provided a few hundred dollars for each child. When the money was released to me as a young adult, I had an important decision to make. What would I buy with this money from my father? I wanted to buy something that would remind me of my father as I continued the ministry that was cut off at his prime. By now, you've guessed the rest of the story. That's how I was able to purchase this beautiful old Martin.

For twenty-five years, wherever I ministered with this guitar, I would be reminded of God's faithfulness. I would remember how He provided for my mother in miraculous ways. I would be reminded about my father's passion for God and my challenge to continue to share his words of hope.

In the scramble to be "contemporary," we must not forget the lessons of the past. Our lessons from the past remind us that God has been with us before and will certainly be with us again.

Our reading today refers to that. Over four hundred years before the Exodus, Joseph had his family pledge that they would carry his bones back to his homeland when they left Egypt. Did you read that? Four hundred years! That's over three and a half million hours of caring for a pile of old bones.

Did Joseph really need his bones carried out of Egypt? I don't think so. So what was the purpose?

These bones were a reminder for generations living in Egypt that they had made a pledge to God and that He had made a pledge to them as well. Once they left Egypt carrying these bones, they were reminded that God had fulfilled His promise to them, even four hundred years later. As they trampled through the desert, those old dry bones helped to remind them that God would be with them as they faced the challenges to come.

How has God shown His faithfulness to you in your worship ministry? Have you remembered His faithfulness lately? How has God shown His faithfulness in your past?

- Did you once need a bass player and God brought one to you?
- Was a member of your praise team struggling in a relationship and God brought healing?
- Have you won the fight to have drums in church?
- Did God come through for you with an upgraded sound system?

As I travel North America, I hear worship teams tell countless stories of God's faithfulness. I also meet many teams who have forgotten God's blessings. There is a danger of forgetting God's faithfulness in our scramble to find the "hot new thing." We can also forget in the midst of our struggles.

God knew that His people could easily forget His promises and decrees. He formed us and He knows that we're made of dust. That's why He stated,

> Hear, O Israel: The Lord our God, the LORD is one. Love the LORD your God with all your heart and with all your soul and with all your strength. These commandments that I give you today are to be upon your hearts. Impress them on your children. Talk about them when you sit at home and when you walk along the road, when you lie down and when you get up. Tie them as symbols on your hands and bind them on your foreheads. Write them on the doorframes of your houses and on your gates. (Deuteronomy 6:4–9)

Do you have physical reminders of your spiritual heritage? Whether it's four-hundred-year-old bones, candles, stained glass, or chalices, the church has used physical reminders of God's faithfulness for thousands of years. These symbols weren't just to beautify sanctuaries. They were to help us remember and to build our faith.

Can you look around your church and see physical reminders? Perhaps you see it in the eyes of your team members. Why don't you take a few minutes now to recount some of the ways God has proven His faithfulness in the past? From now on, every time you start to lead worship, perhaps you'll be reminded of the trustworthiness of God as you see a physical representation of His faithfulness.

What are the old Martin guitars in your worship ministry? Never forget your past as you move toward your future.

"Send Me, Sire, I'll Go"

BY TOM KRAEUTER

Obey your leaders and submit to their authority.
HEBREWS 13:17a

Quite some time ago I was reading C. S. Lewis's classic fantasy *The Chronicles of Narnia* to my oldest son. In the second book, good Prince Caspian, the rightful heir to the Narnian throne, and his band of renegade talking animals are about to engage in battle with the evil king. Caspian has in his possession a magical horn that according to legend will summon help in the time of greatest need. Because he perceives that they have reached that time, he is ready to blow the horn. Unfortunately, he has no idea what form the help will take or to where in the land of Narnia the help will be summoned. After careful discussion the leaders agree that the help, whatever it may be, will arrive in one of three places. Because they are presently situated at one of those places, Caspian needs two messengers to go stand watch at the other two locations. He asks for volunteers, and two dwarfs speak up. One, Nikabrik, adamantly and gruffly refuses any thought of going. At this, Trumpkin, the other dwarf, who has repeatedly stated that he did not believe the horn would actually cause any help to come, speaks up.

"Thimbles and thunderstorms!" cried Trumpkin in a rage. "Is that how you speak to the King? Send me, Sire, I'll go."

"But I thought you didn't believe in the Horn, Trumpkin," said Caspian.

"No more I do, your Majesty. But what's that got to do with it? I might as well die on a wild goose chase as die here. You are my King. I know the difference between giving advice and taking orders. You've had my advice, and now it's time for the orders."[16]

In the twenty-third chapter of Matthew, Jesus launches into a tirade against "the teachers of the law and the Pharisees." Throughout the rest of the chapter Jesus calls them such names as "hypocrites," "blind guides," "snakes," and "vipers." Obviously, Jesus did not think very highly of these men. However, at the beginning of the chapter, He makes a statement to the people that is mind-boggling. "The teachers of the law and the Pharisees sit in Moses' seat. *So you must obey them and do everything they tell you*" (Matthew 23:2–3). He then begins to tell these leaders what horrendous people they really are. Still, He prefaces His diatribe by telling the common people that they must obey the Pharisees and teachers of the law. Even though they are not perfect, they are still to be obeyed. Even though they are terribly misguided (not the same as rebellious), they are still to be followed. This is not quite the way we think today.

Too often today the scriptural ideal for following leadership does not coincide with our way of doing things. Because we are so tainted by our oft-repeated cultural slogan "question authority," we are usually amazed that even when King Saul pursued David and threatened his life, David still absolutely refused to harm the king because the Lord had placed Saul in that position. Today we might look at Saul and say that he should be killed. At the very least we would suggest that he should be removed from office, forcibly if necessary. David knew better.

Scripture does not just allude to this idea but spells it out plainly, "Obey your leaders and submit to their authority" (Hebrews 13:17). This does not sound like a suggestion to me. We too often simply do not understand the biblical view of submitting to leadership.

Let me explain that the local church I am a part of is not a perfect church. We cannot be. We are human beings. I frequently offer my advice before a decision is made. However, I am fully committed to the people and the leadership. Once the decision is made, once the play is called, I am going with it. It is the only way we will move ahead in a united manner.

Am I comfortable with everything that happens at our church? Of course not. There are mistakes, even major mistakes. There are decisions made that I am certain I could improve upon. However, I am committed to the leadership, and I understand, just like Trumpkin the dwarf, that "I know the difference between giving advice and taking orders. You've had my advice, and now it's time for the orders."

Those of us involved in the ministry of praise and worship need to understand this principle as much as anyone. Someday perhaps the Lord may put you into a position of leadership. Would you want those you lead to be constantly bucking your authority? Or perhaps mumbling about your leadership style or discussing your "flaws" behind your back? If not, don't you do it now.

Following leadership is not just a good idea. It is a direct command from God's Word.

Adapted from the book *If Standing Together Is So Great, Why Do We Keep Falling Apart?* by Tom Kraeuter (Lynnwood, Wash.: Emerald Books, 1994, 1998).

The Wind and the Rock

BY GERRIT GUSTAFSON

> 🍂 *God is Spirit, and his worshipers must worship in spirit and in truth.*
> JOHN 4:24

P eople are wired differently. As a songwriter who has never been mistaken for a manager, I am fascinated by accountants. It's a marvel to me that anyone could actually enjoy doing what they do. I'm sure they wish they could be normal like me...(you know I'm kidding!).

God delights in irony and contrasts. He made both the rhinoceros and the butterfly. Making everything the same is not His idea of a good time. Speaking of contrasts, His masterpiece is the creation of man and woman. What was He thinking?!

Here's another irony. God wants His worshipers to worship in spirit and in truth. Some of us think that spirit is fundamental and truth is incidental. For others it's just the opposite.

Bear with me for a moment as I draw some caricatures. Any resemblance to anyone in your church fellowship is purely coincidental. Let's imagine a Tuesday night home group meeting. You're the worship leader. Your name is Jack.

You really like to "flow in the spirit in worship—oh, glory to God!" And Sam, over there—bless his heart—"just can't get free." "Oh, God," you pray, "please don't let Sam interrupt this great worship time with all those trivial obscurities that he gets out of 'the original languages.' "

Meanwhile, Sam, over there is trying to figure you out. "Is he for real? Why does he always close his eyes when he sings? How long is this 'free worship' time going to last anyway? I'm ready to hear some good teaching."

Back to you, Jack. "I just wish Sam knew that God is Spirit. I wonder if he understands that the greatest commandment requires that we love God with all our heart?"

Sam: "I just wish Jack knew that God is Truth. I wonder if he understands that the greatest commandment requires that we love God with all our mind?"

Jack: "I'll bet he's not even filled with the Holy Spirit. He probably doesn't even have any worship CDs...too busy reading all those books!"

Sam: "I'll bet he's never read a book longer than two hundred pages. He probably thinks John Calvin is a jeans designer."

End of caricature. Jack and Sam have just proven what one translation of Proverbs 21:2 says: "Every way of a man is right in his own eyes" (NKJV).

Assuming that what the neuropsychologists tell us is true, the right and left hemispheres of our brains have fundamentally different functions. In his book *Worship Is a Verb*, Robert Webber tells us, "The left hemisphere of the brain specializes in verbal skills, while the right side of the brain centers on nonverbal and inductive skills such as the spatial and poetic impulses of the person. The left side of the brain is more word oriented and orderly, while the right side of the brain is more symbolic and creative."

Everyone will operate out of both sides of the brain, but the fact is, some will function more from one side than the other. Sam, for instance, has a little more circuitry in his left side. The tragedy is that relationships are broken and churches split because of not understanding and appreciating these different predispositions.

Jesus said that His Father is looking for worshipers who worship in spirit and truth—not one or the other. Here's the principle: *An acceptable sacrifice is an offering that is pleasing to God, in harmony with His Spirit, and in accordance with His Truth.*

If we genuinely want to please God in our worship, we must understand that truth without spirit is unacceptable, as is spirit without truth.

In John 5, we see the Pharisees searching the Scriptures but unwilling to come to Christ. This is an example of truth without spirit—knowledge of God without fellowship with God. How serious is this problem? It can be idolatrous!

The flip side of the problem is spirit without truth. In 1 Chronicles 13, King David led Israel in vigorous, demonstrative worship as they were returning the ark to Jerusalem. But according to 1 Chronicles 15:13–15, they had not followed God's truth. The Levites had not followed God's instructions to purify themselves and carry the ark themselves. How serious was this problem? Even as the joyful sounds of the tambourines were going strong, God's anger was growing. Uzzah touched the ark and died before the worship service was over! Pretty serious!

Several years ago, a revelation came to me at a wedding rehearsal dinner for two special friends, Rob and Braden. He was a solid, serious-minded student who has since become a pastor; she had an art degree, was more spontaneous, and has a high creativity quotient. As I was looking for words that would bless their marriage, I came to this: "God's truth is like a rock. It is eternally the same; it never changes. God's Spirit is like the wind. You don't know where it's coming from or where it's going. Truth is fixed; Spirit is dynamic. Rob is like the rock; Braden is like the wind. Here's to the marriage of the rock and the wind."

Shouldn't that be our prayer for our worship ministries, our congregations, and the Church as a whole? If you agree, lift your glasses: "Here's to worshipers who worship in spirit and truth! Here's to the marriage of the Wind and the Rock!"

Drinking Poison

BY TOM KRAEUTER

[Love] keeps no record of wrongs.
1 CORINTHIANS 13:5b

It was another cold, dreary day. John hated days like this. At least when the sun shone he had some small reason to smile. Today there was none. His boss, Walter Milligan, was in another one of his moods. For some reason Walter always singled out John for the worst treatment. John's coworkers—Ron, Susan, Brenda, Mack, and Sherry—got the good tasks. Walter apparently didn't like John as much as he liked the others—especially Sherry. Sherry was Walter's daughter, and she always received preferential treatment. Although Sherry was younger than everyone else, no one else was ever asked to carry the deposits to the bank. That was part of her job. Unless, of course, it was raining. Then John had to go. In general, Sherry's job consisted of doing all the things John really wanted to do but never got to. He hated Sherry, but even more, he hated Walter.

John Kovach hadn't always had such a bitter existence. Brought up in a Christian home, he was a happy-go-lucky kid. He was talented in many ways. Consistent straight A's in school showed his academic abilities. He had above-average artistic abilities, and his athletic prowess was clearly evident on the baseball diamond, basketball court, and football field. John's quick wit and caring, outgoing personality had made him lots of friends. He was clearly a very gifted guy.

Over time, however, all that changed. No one is quite certain what all the events were that changed John, but there were some significant ones. Like the time in seventh grade when the teacher refused to call on John, even though he knew the answer. She was sure John had the correct response to the question—he almost always did—but she wanted to give others a chance to shine. John didn't realize why Mrs. Linton hadn't called on him for the past week. He just knew that she hadn't. He was so angry that he stopped raising his hand after that. Oh, he still did the academic work and continued his straight A's, but something on the inside had died because of his bitterness.

A few years later, John's football coach singled him out in practice because of a mistake. The coach was trying to explain to the team how to avoid the same situation in the future. John didn't hear a word the coach said. He just knew that everyone was staring at him. He wanted to disappear, but he couldn't. He really wished the coach would just disappear. From that moment on, every time John saw the coach he tensed up. After that situation, John still worked hard at athletics, but not with the same drive. Something on the inside had died because of his bitterness.

Several years later John had graduated from college. He was employed by an up-and-coming computer-technology firm. His willingness to work hard coupled with his creative ideas had already been a major asset to the company. In his mind, John was in line for a promotion and a hefty raise. But it didn't happen. Someone else—coincidentally, the manager's nephew—was promoted over John. Although John got a raise in pay, it was *much* smaller than he had anticipated. John never talked with his boss about these things. He just stewed inside and became more bitter than ever.

Now he was thirty-six years old and in a dead-end job with Walter as his boss.

I hope I'm not telling your story here. However, if I am (or if you can relate even a little), please pay close attention to what I am about to say. The second half of 1 Corinthians 13:5 says that love "keeps no record of wrongs." When we hang on to that unforgiveness, when we harbor bitterness in our hearts, we are mostly hurting ourselves.

Someone once said that holding unforgiveness in your heart is like drinking poison and expecting the other person to die.

Please recognize that I am not just talking about the work-a-day world or school situations. In fact, my experience has been that some of the most difficult situations you may ever encounter will be in the midst of the worship ministry of your church. We creative, artsy types are good at getting bent out of shape over the slightest infraction. We then hang on to those hurts until the next time someone does something similar, at which point we relive the first incident all over again, embedding it more deeply into our psyche.

God's Word clearly tells us that love keeps *no* record of wrongs. It also says that we should "forgive whatever grievances you may have against one another. Forgive as the Lord forgave you" (Colossians 3:13–14). How did the Lord forgive you? Partially or completely? Don't hang on to those things. Forgive.

If you continue to harbor unforgiveness, you may well end up like John Kovach. Don't do it. Don't keep record of wrongs. Forgive one another.

The Enemy of Worship

BY PATRICK KAVANAUGH

> *If I had cherished sin in my heart,*
> *the Lord would not have listened.*
> PSALM 66:18

Last week, my wife and I were shopping together in a large department store. As I had nothing to buy and she had several things to try on, I found myself aimlessly pushing a shopping cart and waiting. I thought, "I should spend some time worshiping God," which I did. Yet I soon realized that I was not worshiping but was becoming more and more impatient with my wife.

Again I tried to worship, but soon my annoyance at the long wait grew, and ultimately, worship ceased altogether. My initial (and typical) reaction was to blame my wife. "It's all *her* fault that I can't seem to worship God tonight!" However, the Lord convicted me that the real problem was *within me*. My sin of impatience had become a barrier between me and God.

If we are harboring unconfessed, unrepentant sin, all of our attempts at worship will be in vain. We may go through the motions of worship, but we will fail to obtain the connection with a two-way relationship with the Lord.

An important requirement for true worship is purity. A beautiful image of worship is given in Psalm 24:3, that of "ascending the hill of the LORD." The very next verse gives the necessary requirements: "Who may ascend the hill of the LORD? Who may stand in his holy place? He who has *clean hands and a pure heart*, who does not lift up his soul to an idol or swear by what is false" (Psalm 24:3–4).

"Clean hands" refers to our actions. A "pure heart" refers to our motives, the unseen reasons behind our actions. "Lifting our soul to an idol" refers to *anything* that can come between us and God. And "swearing by what is false" refers to the all-important realm of our speech.

Without purity in these four critical areas of our life, our worship will be powerless. When Brother Lawrence wrote a pamphlet entitled "Means of Attaining the Presence of God," the very first section was on "a great purity of life." Based on our text for today, this makes sense.

Yet for most of us, the battles that are waged in our various areas of temptation become a lifetime struggle. As we seek to become more Christlike, we will always be engaged in the two following directives:

1. We should consciously seek to live a more sin-free life. Taking an honest assessment of our inconsistent disposition, we should note those areas of sin in which we are naturally prone. These must be attentively avoided, and we should make ourselves accountable in these specific spheres of temptation with the help of wise and trusted friends.

Paul consistently admonishes us about avoiding sin, even using the dynamic one-word command: flee! "Flee from sexual immorality" (1 Corinthians 6:18a); "flee from idolatry" (1 Corinthians 10:14b); "flee the evil desires of youth" (2 Timothy 2:22a); "flee from *all* this" (1 Timothy 6:11a).

Sin must be ruthlessly rooted out, not covered over. This principle can be illuminated by the very word processor I am using as I type this sentence. For instance, if I mistakenly type my first name as "Parick," all I have to do to fix the misspelling is to insert a "t" between the "a" and the "r" to spell Patrick. However, suppose that instead of omitting a letter, I mistakenly type my first name as "Pazrick." No amount of inserting letters will ever fix the problem. The name cannot be corrected without first eliminating (rooting out) the false letter "z" with the backspace key. (In the days of pencil writing, an eraser would have been required.)

2. We should make time for regular confession to God. As much as we are commended to avoid sin, we are also forewarned that it will happen.

Fortunately, the Lord has designed a remedy for this inevitable cycle. It is called confession, which entails asking the Lord for forgiveness.

Ongoing sinful activities in our lives will form an impenetrable barrier in your worship of God. As John Bunyan points out in *Pilgrim's Progress*, "One leak will sink a ship; and one sin will destroy a sinner." We all, of course, sin every day. Because of this we need to be in a continual state of self-examination and confession, to keep "short accounts" with the Lord. Any known sin areas in our lives must be guarded against and repented, praying for God's forgiveness and help. David prayed in Psalm 19, "Forgive my hidden faults. Keep your servant also from willful sins; may they not rule over me."

King David said, " 'I will confess my transgressions to the LORD'— and you forgave the guilt of my sin" (Psalm 32:5b). When the people repented at the preaching of John the Baptist, they were baptized after "confessing their sins" (Matthew 3:6). And 1 John 1:9 assures us, "If we confess our sins, he is faithful and just and will forgive us our sins and purify us from all unrighteousness." Through this incredible and utterly available process, we can be "washed white as snow" and again approach God in true worship.

Adapted from the book *Worship—A Way of Life* by Patrick Kavanaugh (Grand Rapids, Mich.: Chosen Books—a division of Baker Book House Company, 2001).

Pipe Organs, Steel Drums, and Aspirin

BY TOM KRAEUTER

Sing to the LORD a new song.
PSALM 96:1a

Discussion of musical styles in the Church can be a very volatile issue. All of us have our own ideas about what are acceptable styles of music. This has been true in the Church for centuries. Did you know that J. S. Bach was once almost dismissed from his position in the church because people thought his harmonies and rhythms were too sensual? Bach!

It is amazing to me to realize that missionaries in years gone by would take pipe organs into deepest, darkest Africa and compel the natives to worship in a style that was completely foreign to them. Is our Western style of music somehow more superior? Does our way of doing things somehow have more credibility with God because we have more Christians per capita? Obviously not. The music David and others composed for the psalms would sound extremely foreign to our ears.

The truth is that music is a cultural vehicle and must be seen as such. Martin Luther understood this when he adopted current tunes of his day and wrote good, theologically sound words for them. William Booth understood this when he wrote and performed songs (with his Salvation Army brass band) in the popular style of his day.

Some time ago I heard Bill Gaither speaking. He made a statement that really had an impact on me. Unfortunately, I did not copy it verbatim, but the gist of what he said is this. "The gospel has always been the same since the beginning, but how it is packaged, the way that it is presented is always changing depending on the culture and society." He went on to say that he sometimes has difficulty relating to the type of music his son plays in church. However, he admitted that he could not deny the fact that his son is reaching people that he, Bill, will never be able to reach. We must begin to admit that even though we may prefer some styles of music over others, the others are not necessarily wrong. Music is simply a cultural vehicle.

Several years ago I encountered Dr. Judson Cornwall teaching at a worship conference. During one of his messages he addressed this concept of music and culture. Dr. Cornwall explained that he had on more than one occasion been to tribal regions in Africa to minister. For the music portions of their worship services, they have what he refers to as "steel bands," any large metal object they can find to beat on to produce sound. Dr. Cornwall admitted that he preferred to have two aspirin before worshiping like that, but he could not deny the fact that the people were wholeheartedly giving themselves to God in worship. It was not his preferred style of music, but it was perfectly within the experience and understanding of that culture and society.

This concept does not give us license to use poor quality music. God is deserving of the very best quality we can offer. We must never compromise the highest standards of quality. However, even the high quality music of J. S. Bach would probably not be readily accepted and wholeheartedly embraced by the people of rural Mongolia.

Quite some time ago I met a pastor from Trinidad. During our conversation he began talking about the steel drum, an instrument invented in his native land. The steel drum has long been a popular instrument in their musical style. This man went on to tell me how, many years prior, missionaries had come to their country and insisted that the steel drum was demonic. Many people stayed away from the church simply because of this pronouncement. Fortunately, today many churches throughout Trinidad (and many other countries as well) use the steel drum in their worship of God.

Today in our society there are many churches that use a style of music very removed from that to which most people are accustomed. Often what happens in these churches is that visitors cannot even slightly relate to the style of music and therefore go elsewhere. The truth of the Word of God may be there, but the music is too far removed from the experience and understanding of the people.

I am not suggesting that we throw out traditional hymns. Never! They are a vital part of our Christian heritage. I have seen many churches refuse to use hymns, and it has been very much to their detriment. However, have you ever noticed how many times the Bible tells us to sing a new song to the Lord?

Again, we must realize that music is a cultural issue. Why do the people in our society generally wear Western styles of clothing? Why do teachers in the church use modern English instead of the vernacular popular in the 1600s? Music, just like language and dress, is a cultural issue.

We must break out of being locked into a certain style of music and be willing to try new ideas and new ways of doing things. Remember, no particular musical style or certain instrumentation is more appropriate with which to worship God. Even if you are already heavily involved in contemporary style music for your church, try something a little different. "Sing to the Lord a new song" (Psalm 96:1a).

Exalting God

BY BOB KAUFLIN

> *I will exalt you, my God the King; I will praise your name for ever and ever. Every day I will praise you and extol your name for ever and ever. Great is the LORD and most worthy of praise; his greatness no one can fathom.*
> PSALM 145:1–3

As you prepare to participate in a corporate worship gathering, what are your expectations? More important, what are God's expectations for our meetings? I think many of us hope to be refreshed or inspired at our weekly worship. Others want to experience an intimacy with God that makes them more aware of His presence and care. Some simply want to be pumped up by the music and the band. However, as we gather to worship God, the primary purpose of our coming together is to exalt God.

It may seem obvious, but in our attempts to be effective, relevant, and efficient, we can miss the most obvious purpose of our time together. David writes in Psalm 34:3, "Glorify the LORD with me; let us exalt his name together."

Why do we need to exalt or magnify God when He is so big already? Although God's span is immeasurable, He often doesn't appear very big to us. We rush into meetings hassled by life, burdened by bills to be paid, cars to be fixed, tests to be passed, relationships to be worked through, and projects to be completed. What size does God appear to be when daily worries fill our minds? Very small.

215

Gathering to worship God is similar to using a powerful telescope to gaze at the stars. To the naked eye the constellations appear like small pinpoints of light barely visible against the backdrop of night. We can step out our back door and never notice them. However, when we look at them through the right instrument, we realize they are raging spheres of fire, incomprehensibly large, and brighter than human eyes can bear.

The "right instrument" with which to see God in congregational worship is the Word of God, apprehended by faith and expressed in song. God's Word tells us who God is, despite how He appears to be through the clouded lens of our circumstances, successes, and problems. He is the omnipotent Creator who spoke the universe into existence with a word (2 Peter 3:5). He is the transcendent, majestic God who views the nations as a drop in the bucket (Isaiah 40:15). He is the Holy One, completely set apart in His moral purity and limitless perfections (Isaiah 6:1–8). He is the wise, Sovereign Ruler, whose infinite wisdom oversees and guides every detail of our existence (Psalm 139:1–18). He is the merciful Father who put forth His own Son on the cross as the substitutionary atoning sacrifice for our wickedness and rebellion. This last emphasis should pervade our congregational worship, because it is only through Jesus' finished work on the cross that we are able to draw near to God at all (Hebrews 10:19–22). Also, in the cross we see a perfect bringing together of God's spotless holiness, inflexible justice, incomprehensible wisdom, omnipotent power, and unfathomable love. What a God we worship!

Exalting God begins with the declaration of objective, biblical truth about God, but it is brought to fruition by affecting our feelings toward God. Scripture repeatedly teaches and models the fact that truth about God invites a response. In fact, it commands a response: "Delight yourself in the LORD" (Psalm 37:4). Jesus proclaimed that the example of the woman who poured perfume on His feet would be told wherever the gospel was preached (Mark 14:6–9). To find pleasure in God, and to express it, is an integral part of exalting Him.

We are not simply to recite facts about God like a student reviewing the multiplication tables. We are to delight in Him! God is exalted when all our energies are directed to one end—being satisfied in Him. In the eighteenth century, Jonathan Edwards addressed what he felt was his obligation as a pastor in regard to the place of emotions. "I should think myself in the way of my duty, to raise the affections of my hearers as high as I possibly can, provided they are affected with nothing but truth, and with affections that are not disagreeable to the nature of what they are affected with." Strong words for a Puritan, or anyone else for that matter!

Does this mean that there is always a perfect one-to-one correspondence between true worship (internal) and certain emotions or behaviors (external)? Does the external always prove the internal? Does the internal always produce the external? Not exactly.

During corporate worship, it may be difficult to tell from external evidence whether someone is delighting in God at any given moment. However, a person who remains internally unmoved while singing biblically grounded, God-honoring lyrics brings no glory to God, and an argument can be made that he or she is not truly worshiping God at all. God is exalted by the joy we take in reviewing His kind, gracious, and merciful acts toward us, not merely by the process of that review. If my professions of love for my wife never carried any hint of emotion, wouldn't she begin to doubt my sincerity? (I hope so!)

The sincerity of our exaltation is measured, first, by our commitment to truth. We are seeking to exalt the God who is presented in Scripture, not our subjective impressions of Him. Second, it is measured by the strength of our affections. God expects us to express emotion in keeping with the truths He is revealing to us about Himself. Everything from quiet reflection to unbridled exuberance can have a place. Other emotions might include wonder, amazement, deep sorrow, ecstatic joy, or sober circumspection. All are a natural result of being affected by who God is and what He has done, as we seek to worship Him in spirit and truth.

Any Five-Talent Musicians?

BY TOM KRAEUTER

 *"You have been faithful with a few things;
I will put you in charge of many things."*
MATTHEW 25:21, 23

Some time ago a man made a statement that really struck me. He said, "I have seen too many five-talent musicians in church doing one- and two-talent work." He was obviously referring to the parable of the talents that Jesus taught.

In that parable (Matthew 25:14–30), the master entrusts money to each of his servants based on the abilities of that servant. "To one he gave five talents of money, to another two talents, and to another one talent, each according to his ability" (Matthew 25:15). Part of the intent of the parable is to cause us to realize that God gives us gifts and abilities and then expects us to use those gifts and abilities for His glory.

The man who made the statement about musicians was making that very point. Although Jesus was talking about a measure of money from that culture, the principle is the same. Too often we take the gifts and the abilities that God gives us and use them to do just enough work to get by. We don't want to stretch ourselves. Our attitude is, "It's good enough for church."

Jesus taught another parable, similar to the one about the talents, the parable of the minas (Luke 19:12–27). It is often referred to as a parallel parable, but the details are a bit different. In the parable of the minas, each servant is entrusted with exactly the same amount of money. Each servant takes his mina (according to the margin notes in my Bible, that's about three months' wages) and endeavors to be a good steward of that which has been entrusted to him. One earns ten more minas, another five more, and so on. Upon his return home, the master rewards each servant based on what that servant has done. The one who earned ten additional minas is placed in charge of ten *cities*. This is not a simple incremental increase, but more of a parabolic curve. He did well with a little and consequently received a lot. The same thing happened to the servant who earned five additional minas—he was put in charge of five cities.

I find it interesting to note that the servants were rewarded based not on the gifts they were given but on how diligent they were with their gifts. In the parable of the talents, Jesus phrased it like this: "You have been faithful with a few things; I will put you in charge of many things" (Matthew 25:21, 23).

Clearly, the Lord does not compare us one to another. He does not look at us and say, "I like John better because he can play the flute so much better than Dan." Or, "I really don't like Susie because she can't sing as well as Leslie." God does not compare us one to another. The real measure in our lives is whether or not we are being faithful with the gifts and abilities the Lord has given to us. Are we being good stewards with those things with which God has entrusted us?

Allow me a moment to be extremely candid. I have very little innate musical abilities. I am a constant source of amusement for many bass players and drummers. I've been described as rhythmically challenged. Syncopated and offbeat rhythms are elusive to me. Consequently, everything I do (and have ever done) musically, I have had to put much effort into. I must work hard because it is not a natural, innate ability or gift.

There are people who, simply because of the musical gifts God has given them, can do musical circles around me with one hand tied behind their back. They are the five-talent musicians, and I'm the one-talent musician. However, if they are not working to their fullest potential, are they fully glorifying the Lord in what they do?

You see, God does not compare us one to another. He is *not* impressed by the fact that your musical abilities exceed mine by as much as Bill Gates's bank account exceeds mine. The Lord *is* interested in what we do with those abilities. In His parables, Jesus taught the people that God's real interest is not in our gifts and abilities but in our faithfulness with those gifts and abilities.

Are *you* really measuring up to your musical potential? Do you sometimes just get by because it is less work to take the easy road? Let's make a new commitment that by God's wondrous mercy and grace, we will do the best we can with the musical gifts and abilities the Lord has entrusted to us.

Giant–Eyeball Worship Bands

BY ARLEN SALTE

The body is a unit, though it is made up of many parts; and though all its parts are many, they form one body. So it is with Christ.... If the whole body were an eye, where would the sense of hearing be? If the whole body were an ear, where would the sense of smell be? But in fact God has arranged the parts in the body, every one of them, just as he wanted them to be. If they were all one part, where would the body be? As it is, there are many parts, but one body.
1 CORINTHIANS 12:12, 17–20

QUESTION: How do you get a guitar player to play more quietly?
ANSWER: Put sheet music in front of him.

QUESTION: How do you know when a drummer is at your door?
ANSWER: The knock always slows down.

QUESTION: What's the difference between a grand piano and a coffin?
ANSWER: The coffin has the dead person on the *inside*.

QUESTION: How many vocalists does it take to change a light bulb?
ANSWER: One. They hold the bulb and the world turns around them.

QUESTION: How many country bass players does it take to change a light bulb?
ANSWER: 1...5...1...5...1...5.

221

Now that I've offended most everyone in the worship team, let's all just take a deep breath.

Sometimes the sting of humor reveals a degree of truth. We can easily joke about someone else's instrument. But it kind of hurts when it hits close to home.

Each one of us tends to think that our particular instrument is the most significant one in the team. That's a very human reaction. Yet, it's the wonderful sonic mix and tonal variety that each instrument or voice lends to the overall sound that makes us an effective worship band. However, to achieve that, we need to let go of something pretty close to home. We need to see our instrument or voice as a part of the overall sound and not something more significant than others.

I teach on contemporary worship in my seminars all over North America. One of the many areas I deal with is musical arranging. One of the greatest challenges for bands is for them to see that each instrument or voice has a place in the overall sound. To play effectively in a band, it's helpful to apply Paul's concepts of the body of Christ from 1 Corinthians 12 to the worship team. Here are just a few points to ponder:

1. While we are different, we are all a part of one body. If I go for a walk around the block, my entire body goes with me. Each body part fulfills its role, but we're all going in the same direction. So it is with the worship team. We are all brought into a relationship with Jesus Christ by His grace. Each one of us desperately needs God's forgiveness no matter how "together" some may seem. What's more, we are all called to the same purpose in the worship team, that is, to lead our congregation into a deeper walk with God. You are not in the worship band to show that you are the best musician or vocalist in your region. In everything you sing and play, ask yourself the question, "How is what I'm doing enhancing the worship life of the congregation?" If you are detracting from the ultimate goal, then you're like my left leg trying to travel one way around the block while the rest of my body goes the other way. It's not a pretty picture.

2. But there is also a paradox. While the body is a single unit, there are also many parts. So it is with the praise team. You play an important role in the overall sound and attitude of the team. When we all want to fill the same role, Paul likens it to the

whole body being one big eyeball. Do you play the triangle but you wish you played the kazoo? Whatever your instrument or vocal part, stop comparing yourself to others. You're important. Play your part with the greatest execution possible. We each fill a role, and we should let the other parts do their job.

3. Just as the body isn't one big eyeball, so we're not all bass players. This means that for the bass parts to do their job and cut through in a mix, we need to stay out of their way and give them their place. For keyboard players, this means simplifying your left hand. If you have a bass player, you don't want to fill their role in the "body." If you're a single-note instrument, you don't want to play so busily above the vocalists that the melody is lost. If you have three acoustic guitar players, try playing different things, even if they're not as flashy. Don't be a giant six-stringed eyeball.

4. Every one of us needs to take our turn at being quiet. One of the chronic challenges as a vocalist or instrumentalist is that we want to play all the time. We can't stand the thought of idle fingers or silenced vocal chords. Yet, our sound turns into one giant pot of porridge when we do this. If you're a drummer, when was the last time you said, "I think this song would sound great with just keyboard and guitar. I'll just sit back here and worship the Lord with my hands in the air." If you're a keyboard player, when was the last time you said, "I think this song begs for a single acoustic guitar." This requires discipline and the heart of a servant.

So, if you're trying to be an ear or a liver or a spleen but you've been called to be an esophagus, it's time to swallow your pride and play your part as a part of the team called to one purpose. There's no place for eyeball bands in the church.

Check Out the New Clothes!

BY TOM KRAEUTER

> *[T]ake some of the blood on the altar and some of the anointing oil and sprinkle it on Aaron and his garments and on his sons and their garments.*
> EXODUS 29:21

The garments that God designed for Aaron, Israel's first high priest, and his sons must have been mind-bogglingly beautiful. In Exodus 28, each piece of the outfit—a breastpiece, an ephod, a robe, a woven tunic, a turban, and a sash—is elaborately described to Moses in surprising detail. Throughout the discourse, the Lord repeatedly tells Moses that those who are skillful in their trades were to do the work. These outfits were not to be something off an assembly line purchased at the local WalMart. Nor even were these garments to be sewn by the men's wives. Israel's best, most skillful workers were to do the work. Weavers, designers, embroiderers, goldsmiths, and tailors were all to be involved. This was clearly not to be a simple leisurely afternoon project. These garments, when they were completed, were surely among the finest anyone in Israel had ever seen. Keep in mind that these were the official apparel that Aaron and his sons would wear for fulfilling their priestly functions.

With all this mind, what would have been the attitude of Aaron and his sons when they wore them? Oh, certainly there would have been a measure of pride. After all, most people in Israel had no clothes anywhere near this quality. Certainly no one else had an outfit that was designed by God Himself. However, when they began slaughtering animals for the Israelite sacrifices, it would seem obvious that they could easily have had a thought of, "Uh oh. What if I get these clothes messy?!" They would surely have been very afraid of somehow desecrating these marvelous garments.

My next statement should seem obvious, but I'll say it anyway. God knew this beforehand. He certainly would not have been surprised while they were in the midst of sacrificing animals that blood and other such elements were making their way onto these fine raiments. The Lord would clearly have recognized the danger long before it happened.

God told Moses that once the garments were completed the very first thing he must do was to consecrate—set apart—Aaron and his sons for their priestly duties. They were instructed to wear their new clothes for the consecration. Just like the detailed descriptions of the garments, the Lord gave very detailed instructions—most of Exodus 29—about how the consecration was to take place. There were to be animal sacrifices as well as grain and drink offerings. However, as I reread this section of Scripture recently, one part of the description struck me: "[T]ake some of the blood on the altar and some of the anointing oil and sprinkle it on Aaron and his garments and on his sons and their garments. Then he and his sons and their garments will be consecrated" (Exodus 29:21).

How do you think you would have reacted? "What?! You want us to put blood and oil on these beautiful new clothes?!" Remember that this was before new and improved laundry detergents, chlorine bleach, and dry cleaners. Those blood stains would be there permanently. Why?

Obviously the spiritual implications are that this was the beginning of what became known as the ceremonial law of Israel. The blood made the garments and the wearers holy. However, beyond this, can you imagine the immensity of pressure this act removed from Aaron and his sons? They no longer had to worry about getting blood on their spiffy new outfits. Because God had them sprinkle blood on the clothes right away this was never a concern.

I would suggest that the Lord wanted them to be able to focus on fulfilling the ministry to which He had called them. This would have been difficult—nearly impossible—if they had to spend much of their time endeavoring to keep their outfits spotless. How could they really minister to the people if they were constantly worried about their clothes becoming soiled? "Dad, quick, check behind my left shoulder...I think I might have just gotten some blood on this thing. Oh, why won't Yahweh let us wear old clothes for this job, and then we could just wear these when we're making hospital visits?" With one simple act the Lord removed all those concerns.

In many ways, the role of those involved today in the ministry of worship parallels the role of the Old Testament priests. By way of application, God does not want us so concerned about image as with fulfilling His plan. A missed note here, a wrong chord there, a less-than-perfect "performance" are of little concern to the Lord. The far bigger purpose—the ministry to which He has called us—is the higher interest. Allowing His Word and His Holy Spirit to work through us will accomplish far more than even our finest musical efforts ever could.

This *does not* give us an excuse to be musically sloppy. It *does* cause the focus to be in the proper place. We, as those involved in the ministry of praise and worship, should be studying and growing in God's Word regularly. We should be praying for those to whom we are ministering. Our focus should be less on the mechanics and more on the spiritual implications. Again, this does not give us license to slack off on our musical preparation. Instead, we should do all that we can to be musically prepared. Still, we must recognize that the spiritual ramifications—our ministry to God and to His people—are of far greater importance.

Let's Make a Whistle

BY BILL RAYBORN

> *He took a little child and had him stand among them. Taking him in his arms, he said to them, "Whoever welcomes one of these little children in my name welcomes me; and whoever welcomes me does not welcome me but the one who sent me."*
> MARK 9:36–37

Do you know how to make a whistle?"

This was the odd question my dad posed to me that summer morning in 1943. I loved for him to ask me fun questions like that because it was usually before something exciting was going to happen. What I didn't know was just how exciting and life-changing the results of this question would be.

Dad and I got into the family car (there was only one car per family in 1943, and gasoline was rationed) and drove to Tulsa's Mohawk Park. Then he began to search for just the right kind of tree. Dad reminisced about how as a boy in Missouri in the early 1900s he had to make many of his own toys, and making a whistle was great fun.

We finally found the right tree. Although I can't recall the name of the tree, it was one where you could make a cut and slip the bark off the wood underneath. He cut the bark, firmly twisting it off. Then he cut down a portion of the wood where the bark had been. Slipping the bark back on the wood, he made a notch for the air to come out and the sound to resonate and…guess what? He had a whistle.

But whistles and trees and parks are not what this story is about.

227

When we finally returned to the car, Daddy said he wanted to talk with me about something. He wanted to talk with me about becoming a Christian, about accepting Christ as my Savior. Gently, he told me the old story of how Jesus had died for me and was now living with His Father in heaven. Dad said if I would just ask Him, Jesus would come into my heart, and I could live forever too!

Now, I had been in church since before I was born, and I had heard the gospel message hundreds of times. However, *when it came from my own father*, it took on a whole new meaning and seriousness.

My family had left our regular church to help with a "mission" on the eastern edge of Tulsa. At that time our Sunday worship was in a storefront building planted by First Baptist Church. Dad was in charge of the Sunday school, and Mom played the piano.

I remember that night as if it were yesterday. I didn't want to go to church. I was too busy playing. So I bargained with my mom. If I could keep on my jeans and bring the baseball with me, I would go with no argument. So there I was—jeans, baseball, and all—when God spoke to me. I walked over to my dad and said I felt like I should respond to the invitation given by our pastor, the Rev. Oscar Pigg. (Really!) Dad said, "Go ahead."

Mom was playing the piano and had her back to me. (Bad piano placement by some music director.) When she saw I had responded to the altar call, she jumped off the piano bench, ran over, and kissed me...right in front of God and everyone! It was definitely a memorable evening.

Fifty-eight times the calendar has turned over since that night in that little storefront church on East Admiral Street. Calvary Baptist Church is now a large congregation, and Tulsa has long since grown miles and miles to the east and south.

What a rare treat for me and my dad. To be a father who cared enough to bring his son to Christ, and for me to have a father who cared enough to teach me how to make a whistle and a life eternal.

What about you? You may be able to sing or play your instrument well. However, are you sharing the real reason you do those things with those who are dear to you? Does your family understand God's plan of salvation? Have you told those who are closest to you about what the Savior has done in your life? Don't neglect your effect on your family. They are your most important ministry.

All the People Praising the Lord

BY TOM KRAEUTER

> 🍃 *May the peoples praise you, O God;*
> *may all the peoples praise you.*
> PSALM 67:3

I have attended numerous conferences where various instructors have spoken to those involved in the ministry of praise and worship. On occasion these teachers explain that what is really important is that the *people* are engaged in worship. "You can worship later at home," they have taught. "Your job is to make sure the people are focused on God."

At other worship conferences I have heard the idea—taught just as forcefully—that it makes no difference what the people do, as long as you, the person involved in the ministry of praise and worship, are engaged in true worship. "Don't worry about the congregation. You worship the Lord and give them an example. Eventually they will follow."

Both of these statements have a measure of truth. Neither of them has the full truth, however. Let me explain.

Rory Noland, music director of Willow Creek Church near Chicago, said this:

> [S]tay focused on ministering to people, as opposed to gratifying yourself artistically. Ministry is not about us and our wonderful talents. It's about people. It's about serving others.

First Peter 4:10 says, "Each one should use whatever gift he has received to serve others." Use your gifts to serve others. If you're trying to gratify yourself artistically and forget all about ministering to people, it will be an empty experience.[17]

If we are not endeavoring to cause the people to enter in to worship, they will end up frustrated. Our job is not just to do our musical gig, but to be a catalyst to cause the congregation to be involved in worshiping the Lord.

Prior to the reformation, the worship of the Church was slowly but surely transferred from the people to the clergy. The congregation ultimately became an audience. They watched and listened to the "worship" but had very little real involvement in it. Worship became something that was done *for* the people rather than something the people *did*. The entire focus ended up completely reversed from what God intended.

One of the main thrusts of the reformers was to return worship to the people. It was during the reformation that the phrase "priesthood of all believers" (based on 1 Peter 2:5, 9; Revelation 1:6; 5:10; 20:6) was coined. The reformers recognized that worship was not to be a spectator sport. By very definition of the word, worship requires involvement.

However, even when we recognize that involvement by the people is essential, it is all too easy to think that is all that is necessary. After all, as long we are doing our best musically and the hearts of the people are engaged in worship, what is else is necessary?

In his book *I Exalt You, O God*, Jerry Bridges quotes Stephen Charnock, a Puritan: "Without the heart, it is not worship; it is a stage play, an acting part.... We may be truly said to worship God, though we [lack] perfection; but we cannot be said to worship Him if we [lack] sincerity."[18]

I don't ever want to be involved in just a "stage play, an acting part" when I should be leading people in worship. I don't want to be pretending to worship in order to get someone else truly to worship. God doesn't want just our actions; He wants our hearts.

We cannot truly be said to be leading in worship if we are not engaged in worship ourselves. The oft-quoted statement is still true: You can't take someone to a place where you are not going.

As Psalm 67 says, "May the peoples praise you, O God; may *all* the peoples praise you" (Psalm 67:3). Not just "those folks out there" or just "us folks up here" but *all* the people.

If we are truly to lead people in *worship*, then we must be engaged in worship. However, if we are to be truly leading *people*, then it is essential that we not be so far ahead of them that they end up simply watching a "show," with no real heart focus toward the Lord. Both are necessary for those of us involved in the ministry of praise and worship: *worshiping* God and *leading* the people.

"May the peoples praise you, O God; may all the peoples praise you" (Psalm 67:3).

The Eighteen-Inch Drop

BY ARLEN SALTE

My soul yearns, even faints, for the courts of the LORD; my heart and my flesh cry out for the living God.
PSALM 84:2

Tuba! Of all the cool instruments that there were to play in the school band, I was stuck with the tuba! It looked like an oil refinery with a spit valve. It wasn't an issue of my having the perfect tuba embouchure. It's just that I was one of the only ones big enough to carry it around when we marched. All the other adolescent boys played cool instruments like saxophones. Saxes looked cool. Girls liked them. Tubas? They were great targets for people to lob their old lunches into in the middle of practice. Tubas only looked cool to girls in Bavaria if you wore lederhosen.

Nevertheless, my big day finally arrived. It was time for a parade. In my small rural town, this usually meant a few wagons pulled by tractors, covered with hay bales and a pretty country girl who was Miss Corn Roast or Miss Dairy Land or Miss John Deere Combines. At the end of the parade was the marching band. At the end of the whole marching band was the tuba. One tuba. Just me laying down the "oom pa pa."

This was my big moment. My family lined the street with the other proud parents. I had practiced until I had a ring around my lips. I dutifully placed my charts on the little clip-on music stand attached to the tuba. We walked. We marched. People waved. Some of the twirlers actually caught their batons.

Then, I had a strange sensation. It wasn't a good sensation. All of a sudden, I was playing a tuba solo. I wasn't supposed to be playing a tuba solo. With my left hand I snatched the music from in front of my face and looked out at an empty street. The band had followed the parade and had taken a right turn. I'd been so busy watching the music chart and making sure I was playing the perfect notes that I had forgotten to watch the conductor and had continued down the street in total oblivion.

Sometimes in our worship bands we forget about the conductor. I'm not talking about the church's worship leader; I'm talking about God. In our struggle for the perfect execution of musical notes, we too frequently forget that worship is founded in a relationship.

Music that's played without heart is merely mathematics. Music that's married with heart is transcendent. It's the difference between my giving my wife a cheap greeting card filled with trite, pretty poetry and taking her for a walk along the lake and expressing the deepest emotions of my heart. Both impart information, but only one truly communicates effectively.

If you saw the movie *Mr. Holland's Opus,* you may remember the scene of the clarinetist who closes her eyes and transforms a mathematical musical formula into the expressions of her heart. When she was obsessed with the chart in front of her, the notes were lifeless. When she closed her eyes, however, and played from the heart, wonderful music was created. She made what many have called the eighteen-inch drop from the head to the heart.

This scene reminds me of church. I have been in many churches with stellar players whose musical execution was nearly flawless. Yet, the worship music felt as lifeless as a plate of cold macaroni and cheese. Other times, I've been in churches where one out-of-tune guitar player was drenched in such passion for the Lord that the music took wing and soared like an eagle, bringing the hearts of the congregation along for the heavenly ascent.

We still need to stretch for excellence in our musical execution, but not at the price of passionate expression. Not at the expense of losing sight of our glorious conductor.

Our relationship with God is to be one of beauty that absolutely infuses us with so much fervor that we are unable to contain our joy. Our songs resonate with love. In our desire to express our fire for God, our music becomes another blessed way of expressing the beauty of this relationship.

We have all heard secular performers sing love songs with such great swells of human emotion that audiences are enraptured. If we can become so expressive in our songs of faulty human love, how much more should our hearts burn when we sing of God, the greatest lover?

The psalmist in our scripture today states that his heart's yearning is so great that he faints for the courts of the Lord. His heart and flesh cry out for God. Talk about a song of passion! His relationship with God is not simply a sharing of cold, lifeless, mathematical information. He is so captivated with God that he faints because of his longing to be with his Lord.

In Psalm 103:1, David writes, "Praise the LORD, O my soul; all my inmost being, praise his holy name." Here, he commands his very inner being to worship with passion.

When was the last time you were so profoundly moved in worship that tears rolled down your face? When was the last time that despite your current situation you commanded your very inmost being to express without hindrance?

Perhaps it's time to shake things up a bit. It's time that we outdo the world in our worship. It's time that we express our love for our Savior to such a great extent that the love songs of the world pale in comparison.

Next time you lead worship, make a commitment that no senti-mental top-40 song will top your worship of the most high God. Worship with all your heart, soul, mind, and strength.

It's time to follow our glorious conductor with passion. It's time for the eighteen-inch drop from the head to the heart!

Want the Blessing of God?

BY TOM KRAEUTER

> *How good and pleasant it is when brothers live together in unity!... For there the LORD bestows his blessing, even life forevermore.*
> PSALM 133:1, 3b

Some time ago I was teaching a worship seminar at a church. To stress a particular point, I told a story about a husband who had left his wife. At the conclusion of the story, I noticed the worship leader from the church was crying noticeably. I considered stopping to pray for her, but I did not believe that was the right thing to do at the time. Later, during a break, I asked her about the tears. She explained that a while back her husband had left her. Not only had he left her, but he had left her for a woman who was her cousin and who was also the youth leader at the church. He and the worship leader had married early in life, and he had become practically everything to her. When he left she was devastated. She was so badly wounded that there were times when she did not show up for worship ministry rehearsals. There were even times she was absent on Sunday mornings—even when she was scheduled to lead worship.

This same church has an administrator for their worship ministry. This frees the worship leader to do what she does best and not be bothered with the details of organization. When the above scenario was going on, the administrator approached the other members of the worship ministry with a choice: "We can either ask her to leave the team and totally devastate her life, or we can help her through. Which one do you want to do?" Please understand that most of these people were not just passing acquaintances. They were close friends. They chose to help her through.

So when she did not show up for rehearsals, they went on without her. On Sunday mornings when she was supposed to lead and failed to appear, the administrator posed the challenge to the music team: "Okay, folks, who's going to lead this morning?" In the midst of all this, they covered so well for her that although the congregation was aware of her situation, they were completely oblivious to the depth of her struggle.

When the worship leader began to pull her life back together, she went to the music team and thanked them. "You'll never know what you did for me," she said. "You loved me when I was so unlovable. You helped me through the toughest time of my entire life. Thank you!"

At our church we have a Christian school, grades K-12. Over the years the varsity basketball program has produced some very fine players, and our family frequently attends the school's basketball games. Being a very black-or-white person, I sometimes disagree with the referee's calls. Usually my opposition is voiced only to myself or those around me, but occasionally, if I perceive the call to be really bad, I may be more vocal.

Interestingly, a friend of mine from our church is a basketball referee. He does not usually officiate our school's games, but when he does I have found that I seldom disagree with his calls. As I began to ponder why this was so, I realized it was not necessarily that he did a much better job as a referee. The reason is that he and I have a relationship. It is more difficult for me to find fault because I know him and like him. We are friends.

A while back, after ministering at a church, I went to lunch with the pastor. During the course of the conversation, he mentioned that they had previously had a bit of friction between two members of the church's worship ministry. The reason stemmed from the fact that one was very outspoken and often expressed his feelings freely. The other person was much more reserved and did not necessarily want to hear the feelings of the other, especially as those feelings related to her musical abilities.

After explaining the situation, the pastor told me that the problem had been solved. "Do you know how we did it?" he asked.

"No, but I'd like to know," I responded.

He explained that one day the entire music ministry spent the day together at an amusement park. The two who were occasionally at odds with each other spent a great deal of time together during that day. They got to know each other. They became friends. The problem was solved because of their deepened relationship.

Strong relationships are essential to long-term ministry. If relationships are superficial, conflict will seldom be totally resolved. Relationships that are only at the surface level have no real commitment or loyalty. Without strong, healthy relationships, the music ministry of the church will almost always be in turmoil.

However, the converse of these statements is also true. When strong relationships with true loyalty and commitment are present, no amount of conflict or difficulty will rend them.

Psalm 133 says that God bestows His blessing when brothers dwell together in unity. This promise from God's Word is as true in the worship ministry as it is in any part of life.

Adapted from the book *Things They Didn't Teach Me in Worship Leading School* by Tom Kraeuter (Lynnwood, Wash.: Emerald Books, 1995).

Why Do We Do It?

BY BOB KAUFLIN

> *So whether you eat or drink or whatever you do, do it all for the glory of God.*
>
> 1 CORINTHIANS 10:31

The tension in the air is palpable. Beads of sweat roll ever so slowly down your brow. Yes, worship team auditions have arrived once again. While the worship leader does everything he can to put each musician at ease, trembling hands and wobbly voices reveal an underlying nervousness. "Can I cut it? What if I don't make it? Well, at least I'm better than *her*."

If you can't relate to this scene, thank God right now. If you can, you might be helped by a quick review of the foundations for worship team membership. The Bible doesn't carry specific details regarding who should be on the worship team and who shouldn't. However, there are general principles concerning gifting and serving that apply to musicians as well as any other form of ministry in the church. The key phrases to remember are God's grace, God's calling, and God's glory.

God's grace is the foundation for our worship. First Corinthians 4:7 asks this penetrating question: "For who makes you different from anyone else? What do you have that you did not receive? And if you did receive it, why do you boast as though you did not?"

We wouldn't even be Christians, let alone musicians, apart from the grace of God. The second chapter of Ephesians tells us that "it is by grace you have been saved, through faith—and this not from yourselves, it is the gift of God—not by works, so that no one can boast." It is God's grace that has turned us from worshiper of ourselves to worshiper of the true and living God. It's also God's grace that is responsible for any gifting we have. Peter reminds us that "each one should use whatever gift he has received to serve others, faithfully administering God's grace in its various forms" (1 Peter 4:10). Furthermore, if that weren't enough, we learn in 2 Corinthians 9:8 that God's grace is responsible for any fruit we bear. "And God is able to make all grace abound to you, so that in all things at all times, having all that you need, you will abound in every good work." God doesn't leave much room for taking pride in our position.

Secondly, we need to realize that God's call is the reason we are on the worship team. While I may believe with all my heart that I'm supposed to be one of the musicians up front on Sundays, it's not an issue of how strongly I feel. God is the One who gives gifts, and God is the One who calls us to ministry. Occasionally, this is for life, but more often, it's only for a season.

I'll never forget serving in a church with a particular drummer named Neal. Neal was an average drummer but a true servant. He told me early on that he would do the best job he could and even bought a set of new drums to use on Sundays. But he insisted that if I ever found someone else more gifted, he would gladly step aside to serve in another ministry. The new drummer could even use his drums! I was shocked. I was elated. Sure enough a better drummer came along, and Neal moved on to another area of ministry. Imagine for a moment what effect it would have if every musician on a worship team followed Neal's example. I can guarantee you that worship leaders across the country would find a new zeal for their job. Few things make a worship leader's task more enjoyable than knowing that he's free to move people in and out of the group in a way that will best honor the Lord. That's the result of musicians trusting that their leaders can tell when God has called them to a position.

Finally, God's glory is our primary goal in serving on the worship team. Our purpose as worship musicians is to draw attention to God, not ourselves. There is an obvious tension that exists every time we stand (or sit) in front of people to lead them in praising God. It's necessary that we be heard and seen, or there's no reason to be leading. However, if people focus on what we're doing, worship has become entertainment. The only reason for being noticed is so we can direct someone's attention and focus to the One who deserves all our worship, affections, and praise. We must be committed to confronting and overcoming our inner craving to be applauded, noticed, admired, and approved. That desire is in direct opposition to our stated purpose for being on the worship team: to bring God glory.

God's grace, God's calling, God's glory. If we get these three foundations right, serving in the music ministry will be a true joy, not only for us but also for God Himself.

The Deadly Disease of...Perfectionism

BY TOM KRAEUTER

> [H]e knows how we are formed,
> he remembers that we are dust.
> PSALM 103:14

"What's the matter with you?" my wife asked.

"Nothing."

"Excuse me, but I know you better than that. Now, what's wrong?"

"Okay, okay," I responded. "Everything went wrong in the service this morning."

"*Everything* went wrong?" she asked incredulously. "I can't remember *anything* being wrong."

"Where were you? The transition between 'Holy, Holy, Holy' and 'Blessed Be the Lord God Almighty' sounded like a train wreck. The drummer totally missed the endings of two songs. And when we went back up after the sermon, our monitors were not working at all. The whole service was a catastrophe!"

My wife smiled. "Let me get this straight," she replied. "All but one transition went well, the drummer did great except for the ending of two songs, and the monitors worked well except for the closing song. Is that correct?"

"Well...yeah, I guess."

"So really almost everything went *right*." Her smile broadened. "Right?"

"Oh, you just don't understand."

In retrospect, I have realized that it was I who didn't understand. It took me a long time to admit it, but I suffer from a potentially deadly affliction that plagues many musicians: perfectionism. Statistics indicate that nearly five out of every five musicians have it. If you have this horrendous disease, you know exactly what I'm talking about. It can sap your strength and steal your joy. If ninety-nine things go right and one goes wrong, the only one you remember is the one that went wrong.

Services like the one described in the scenario above have been commonplace throughout my twenty-five years of leading worship. Of the hundreds of meetings for which I have led worship, there have been perhaps only a few where everything went exactly right. The truth is that many worship leaders have told me they have never had even *one* service where everything went just right (and I thought *my* case of perfectionism was severe!).

Rory Noland's book *The Heart of the Artist* has had a big impact on me. At one point in the book Rory, music director at Willow Creek Community Church, talks about the perfectionist mentality. Part of his dealing with this issue in his life has been through accentuating the positive. He consciously recognizes the things that have gone right as well as the ways that God has worked through him in spite of his imperfections. He said this:

> My wife once told me something interesting about Amish crafts. The Amish, whenever they produce any of their crafts, purposely put a flaw somewhere in their work. It could be one piece of thread that's out of line or a part of a quilt that's slightly off center, but it's there to remind them that only God is perfect. When I gave this teaching about perfectionism to our vocal team years ago, I wanted to give them a visual reminder to savor the good things God does in and through us—to stop minimizing the positive. My hardworking long-time assistant, Lisa Mertens, graciously volunteered to cross-stitch the phrase "Savor it" for everyone on the team and put each one in a nice frame. But in keeping with the Amish tradition that reminds us of our human frailty, she put a slight

mistake in each cross-stitch. She purposely didn't dot the *i* in *it*, to remind us that only God is perfect.[19]

I am certainly not advocating that we stop doing our best. God is worthy of the very best we can give. However, "he knows how we are formed, he remembers that we are dust" (Psalm 103:14). God knows that we will make mistakes and those around us will make mistakes. Fortunately, that's where His grace comes in. When the level of perfection that we expect doesn't happen, His grace is still sufficient.

Over the years I have been amazed at what God has done through services that were seemingly riddled with errors. When we did most things wrong, the Lord still, as the people said of Jesus in Mark 7:37, "has done everything well."

In spite of us, God is always faithful. Recognizing the fullness of His faithfulness and grace has helped me to start to live beyond the perfectionism syndrome. I still always endeavor to put forth the best possible effort, but the results will always be His responsibility. When I am tempted by the perfectionist mentality to think that "everything went wrong," I simply trust His grace and concentrate on what He did right.

Adapted from the book *More Things They Didn't Teach Me in Worship Leading School* by Tom Kraeuter (Lynnwood, Wash.: Emerald Books, 1998).

On Becoming a Good Butler

BY GERRIT GUSTAFSON

> 🌿 *So then, men ought to regard us as servants of Christ.... It is required that those who have been given a trust must prove faithful.*
> 1 CORINTHIANS 4:1–2

Scenario 1: You have received an invitation to dine with a distinguished community leader. On the appointed day, you anxiously arrive at the massive entrance to his palatial estate, ring the bell, and wait. Immediately you are greeted by a gracious butler who takes your coat, puts you at ease with just the right words of how glad the host is that you have come, and escorts you down the hallway to the presence of the revered and generous host. After greetings and introductions, a great feast begins...

Scenario 2: Same invitation...same palatial estate...same massive entrance. This time, however, the butler, after taking your coat, strikes up a conversation with you in the foyer about the weather, his health, what his children want to study when they go to college, and so forth. You're drawn into the conversation, and after a lengthy and engaging chat, you take your coat and go home. On the way home, you come to an alarming realization. You never saw the host!

You say, "It would never happen!" But sadly, it happens all too often. Worship leaders and musicians (...and really all ministers) are like butlers whose job it is to bring the congregation before the King. Many people on their way home from the service, however, find themselves with a nagging dissatisfaction...they didn't get to see the King.

244

How can we who serve in God's house make sure we are good butlers? Let's consider three words: purification, consecration, and service.

First, purification. Many church musicians were, as I was, musicians trained by the world. I played jazz and learned to love that feeling that came when you aced your solo and the crowd clapped and cheered.

Guess what? You can get addicted to that. Guess what else? That addiction's got to go before you're ready for God's service. In God's rehab—i.e., discipleship—you'll learn that there's another audience you'll be performing for—God Himself. His "well done, good and faithful servant" is what you live for now.

Deep-sea divers have decompression chambers. Our music ministries need something similar. In Christian music, whenever our shepherds notice that we're drinking too deeply of the people's accolades, they should invite us to the decompression chamber: "Take a couple of months off until the joy of singing in your living room before God alone is greater than singing before the congregation."

Music, apart from God, has a contaminating mark that goes all the way back to the origin of human culture in Genesis 11 and the story of the tower of Babel. Their governing passion was to make a name for themselves.

In contrast, God told Abraham in Genesis 12 that if he would walk in obedience, he would bless nations, and God Himself would make Abraham's name great.

Purification is about moving from Genesis 11 to Genesis 12...from a self-promoting passion to a God-honoring passion...from wanting to make your name great to wanting to glorify God and be a blessing.

Consecration means to be set apart or devoted to a specific sacred task or purpose. Before the ark of God's presence returned to the city of David in 1 Chronicles 15, the priests consecrated themselves. Before the glory of God filled Solomon's temple in 2 Chronicles 5, the priests consecrated themselves.

Modern-day worship ministries need to be consecrated too. In 2 Chronicles 5, we see the dynamics of consecration:

> All the priests who were there had consecrated themselves.... All the Levites who were musicians...stood on the east side of the altar, dressed in fine linen and playing cymbals,

harps and lyres. They were accompanied by 120 priests sounding trumpets. The trumpeters and singers joined in unison, as with one voice, to give praise and thanks to the LORD. (2 Chronicles 5:11–13).

Of interest to me is that they "joined in unison, as with one voice to give praise and thanks to the LORD." They weren't uncertain about their purpose. Oh, the awesome force of being united in purpose! When they put those linen garments on, it was like a football team dressing out for the state championship, except their task at hand was to bring sacrifices of praise to God! It wasn't to entertain the congregation. It wasn't to make a name for themselves as the best music group in the Middle East. It was to minister to the Lord.

May I suggest that on every occasion of public ministry, before you walk through the doors, you and your team mentally put on the linen garments of praise…that you unite yourselves in the holy purpose of leading God's people to the One who is really worthy of praise…that you remind yourselves that it's about Him and not you.

Did you know that in Hebrew and Greek, the words for service, worship, and ministry are almost synonymous? Worship is service. Service is ministry.

Service is the kingdom ambition that our King so perfectly exemplifies. Jesus said He came not to be served but to serve. What an amazing contrast to the way of the world! Here is the Creator of the universe—that's pretty important—not trying to convince anyone how important He is but serving His Father's honor and the needs of those around Him. As a result, His Father highly exalted His name!

I love to think of the Church as heaven's colony on earth, where its citizens reflect the ways of their King…a kingdom where everyone, including the musicians, is a servant.

Worship servants…cleansed of the Babylonian taint…consecrated and united for a holy purpose…devoted to a lifestyle of service.

"May I take your coat. My Master is eager to see you. Here…right down this hall."

Difficulties, Anyone?

BY TOM KRAEUTER

> *Not only so, but we also rejoice in our*
> *sufferings, because we know that suffering*
> *produces perseverance; perseverance,*
> *character....*
> ROMANS 5:3–4

Years ago I heard a man talking about the process used to refine gold. I'm not certain it is still done the same way today, but this was an older man who had been a smith (silver and gold) for years. He told of heating the gold until it became liquid. As the gold heated, the impurities (the dross) rose to the top. These impurities were skimmed off, and soon more dross rose to the top. It was a rather lengthy process and required a great measure of patience. The final indication to the goldsmith that the gold was pure was that he could see his face reflected in the surface of the gold. That's what God does in our lives. He keeps turning up the heat and patiently skimming off the impurities. His goal is to see His character, Christlikeness, formed in us.

Frances Jane Crosby was born in 1820. When she was barely a month old, her parents noticed a serious problem with her eyes. Unfortunately the community doctor was away. In desperation her family sought out a man who claimed to be a physician. The "doctor" insisted that extreme heat would draw out the infection, so he put a hot poultice on her eyes. Years later other doctors diagnosed Crosby's blindness as having been caused by the incompetent treatment.

In spite of her blindness, Frances Jane—more commonly known as Fanny—Crosby went on to write more than 9,000 Christian hymns. Her poetry and her speaking influenced hundreds of thousands of people.

Far from feeling self-pity, Fanny felt that on the whole, blindness was a special gift of God. She often said, "It was the best thing that could have happened to me," and, "How in the world could I have lived such a helpful life as I have lived had I not been blind?" She felt she would never have had the opportunity for an education had she not been blind. Had she not gone to the Institution [for the blind] in New York, she would not have had the contacts to enable her to write hymns for a nationally known publishing firm.

Moreover, she believed that sight must be a distraction. She attributed her great powers of concentration to blindness. She also felt that her lack of sight enabled her to develop a wonderful memory and enhanced her appeal as a speaker, creating a bond of sympathy between her and her audiences that made them more receptive to the gospel message.[20]

Fanny had a very interesting perspective on the entire situation. "She knew there was always a good reason for affliction. She would often quote Hebrews 12:6, saying, 'Whom the Lord loveth, He chasteneth,' and commenting, 'If I had no troubles, I'd think the Lord didn't love me!' "[21]

Difficult times can push us either away from God or closer to Him. The apostle Paul said, "We do not want you to be uninformed, brothers, about the hardships we suffered in the province of Asia. We were under great pressure, far beyond our ability to endure, so that we despaired even of life. Indeed, in our hearts we felt the sentence of death. *But this happened that we might not rely on ourselves but on God*, who raises the dead" (2 Corinthians 1:8–9). Hardships drove them to Jesus.

My wife recently attended a women's retreat where the main speaker invited the women to chart their spiritual lives. She asked them to recall high and low points during their lives and see if they could draw any conclusions. My wife noticed that it was at the very times when she was going through turmoil that she had the greatest spiritual growth. God used those difficult situations to cause her to come to a higher level of maturity in Him.

For several years my family and I have enjoyed a theme park called Silver Dollar City in Branson, Missouri. Besides the fun rides and family atmosphere, there are numerous old-time craft demonstrations, such as basket weaving, candy making, and glassblowing. One of the exhibits I find fascinating is the blacksmith shop. You probably recall seeing a blacksmith working in an old Western movie. A piece of iron is heated to the point where it glows white-hot. Then the smith puts the metal on an anvil and pounds it with a hammer. Sparks fly as he attacks the glowing piece of iron. The smith uses intense heat and lots of pressure to shape that piece of iron into something useful. Similarly, God frequently uses intense heat and lots of pressure to shape and transform us into the image of Jesus.

Scripture says this about Jesus in the Garden of Gethsemane: "And being in anguish, he prayed more earnestly" (Luke 22:44a). Jesus allowed His anguish to push Him *toward* the Father, not away. Every trial we walk through is a place of decision for us. Those difficult times can repel us away from the Lord. Or we can choose to draw closer to Him and, in doing so, allow Him to form His character in us.

What about your life? Do you allow God to work through the trials and tribulations of life to cause you to become more like Jesus? If not, ask Him to work in your heart so you will allow those difficult times to draw you closer to Him and have His character formed in you.

Adapted from the book *Oh, Grow Up!* by Tom Kraeuter (Lynnwood, Wash.: Emerald Books, 2001).

Called to Be Friends of God

BY KENT HENRY

> 🍃 *The* LORD *would speak to Moses face*
> *to face, as a man speaks with his friend.*
> EXODUS 33:11

The ultimate reason for our existence is to fellowship with God, to become His friend. Of course, we have a calling to be priests who offer acceptable sacrifices and heartfelt worship to Him. However, our first priority is simply to be friends who live near to the heart of God. It's through friendship that I begin to know and understand His purposes in my life for His kingdom.

When I sum up all my daily activities, I find myself yearning and longing for a deeper relationship with God. I want to draw ever nearer to the divine presence, but I still need to understand friendship with God on a higher level.

My son, Matthew, is very special to my heart. We thoroughly enjoy spending time together any chance we get. We may play with our dog, throw the football around, or mow the grass together. It doesn't make any difference what we do—we're friends. We just like to hang out together. All the while, Matthew's natural need to be with his father is being fulfilled. This is the time where our relationship is built and friendship is deepened.

This is the message our heavenly Father is sending to each one of us today. It's like the song Larnell Harris sings that used the friendship theme as its centerpiece: "Lord, I would spend time with You, but...." The song keeps coming back to these words in the chorus while the verse states all the reasons why he doesn't take the time to fellowship with God. This song really spoke to my heart when I first heard it. It accurately lists many of my personal excuses as to why I don't take time with God.

I enjoy reflecting on the lives of those in the Scriptures who had an honest friendship with the Lord. In 2 Chronicles 20:7, Abraham is referred to as God's friend. In Isaiah 41:8, God says, "Abraham, my friend." James 2:23 tells us, " 'Abraham believed God, and it was credited to him as righteousness,' and he was called *God's friend.*" Abraham truly was a friend of the Most High.

One of my favorite Scripture passages is where our verse for today comes from. Exodus 33:9–11 records the life-changing event where God speaks to Moses as a man speaks to his friend. "As Moses went into the tent, the pillar of cloud would come down and stay at the entrance, while the LORD spoke with Moses.... The LORD would speak to Moses face to face, as a man speaks with his friend." Wow! What would you or I give for a relationship with God like that?

It's really not that difficult to be friends with God. He didn't make it a mysterious relationship full of mazes and tests. One great example of the beginning of friendship is told in Luke 10:38–42. This is where Mary sat at the feet of Jesus to learn from Him.

Jesus had come to Martha's house at her invitation. The Bible records that Martha became busy about many things. She became overwhelmed with the task of serving the guests in her house. Mary, Martha's sister, chose a spot close to Jesus' feet and settled in there to listen to the Master. Martha was seriously upset because she was left alone to do all the work.

Here's the point. We have to deal consistently with the "too busy" attitude. This is one of the greatest hindrances to friendship with God. In our schedules, most of us know what the daily priorities are going to be. Does spending time with God often end up at the bottom of your list?

When I was in my early twenties, the church I attended had a conference that dealt with getting our priorities in order. A few days after the conference, some of us were sitting around talking about how we were going to change our schedules and really get our devotional life together. My friend Dave said, "I don't believe it for one minute. Your real priorities are what you're doing every day. When I see you doing it, then I'll know it's a real priority."

I'm certain the desire of our heavenly Father's heart is to be our friend. In turn, He wants us to be His friends, friends who have come to know His thoughts and ways intimately, friends who live by the same code—love, honor, and singleness of heart.

Judging Others

BY TOM KRAEUTER

> 🌿 *When Eliab, David's oldest brother, heard him speaking*
> *with the men, he burned with anger at him and asked,*
> *"Why have you come down here? And with whom did*
> *you leave those few sheep in the desert? I know how*
> *conceited you are and how wicked your heart is; you*
> *came down only to watch the battle."*
>
> 1 SAMUEL 17:28

How could David's oldest brother have so misjudged him? David had been sent by their father, Jesse, on an errand of help. He was to bring food to his brothers and take back news of the battle for Dad. He was carrying out his father's wishes. However, Eliab accuses him of coming "only to watch the battle." He tells David that he is conceited and says that his heart is wicked.

Just one chapter earlier, Samuel the prophet was visiting Jesse. His task was to search for the one that God had called to be the next king over Israel. God had clearly shown Samuel that it was to be one of the sons of Jesse. The first son that Samuel saw was Eliab, who was apparently tall and handsome. Samuel was certain this must be the one. Such a fine specimen of a man was surely God's choice for king. However, the Lord told Samuel, "Do not consider his appearance or his height, for I have rejected him. The LORD does not look at the things man looks at. Man looks at the outward appearance, but the LORD looks at the heart" (1 Samuel 16:7).

After viewing all of Jesse's sons except David, Samuel began to think he had made a mistake. God had said no about each of them. Samuel must have wondered whether he had completely missed hearing the voice of the Lord. "Are these all the sons you have?" Samuel inquired. "There is still the youngest," Jesse answered, "but he is tending the sheep." Samuel must have been grateful for this one last possibility. So they waited while someone went to get David from his sheep tending. When David was finally brought before him, God, who "looks at the heart," told Samuel that this was the one who would be king.

God knew David's heart even better than David knew it. Why, then, would Eliab have called David's heart "wicked"? Obviously the Lord didn't think so. It must be understood right from the start that Eliab's perception of David's heart was wrong.

However, the question remains: Why would Eliab suggest that his kid brother's heart was wicked? Perhaps Eliab was jealous. After all, Samuel had anointed David in front of the entire family. The runt kid—the baby—was going to be king of Israel. "Hold on a minute! I'm the oldest! I'm bigger, better looking, and certainly smarter! Why on earth would the Lord choose that little kid instead of me?!" Eliab could easily have been miffed and still have been hanging on to that grudge. It's certainly conceivable.

Or perhaps David was the classic little brother. "Dad, Eliab kicked me today for no reason."

"Eliab," Jesse's voice sounding stern, "how many times have I told you not to pick on your little brother? You'll watch the sheep tonight while the rest of us are eating supper."

Is it possible that typical family interaction had left Eliab with a mental image of David that was very different from reality? He did not see David the same way their across-town friends saw him or the same way Gramma saw him. Eliab's perception may well have been skewed when He saw David as simply the brat kid brother.

Very often, when we interact with one another in the worship ministry setting, someone may say or do something that causes us to question his or her sincerity or motivation. We may think, as Eliab thought, that this person is being impudent or perhaps even antagonistic. Perhaps there is something in the tone of voice, or a look, or a mannerism that causes us to wonder about the person's motives. We may honestly believe that this person is out to get us, or doesn't like us, or any number of other possible conclusions. However, this may not be the case at all. We cannot, as God can, know the person's heart.

Perhaps what we should do is take some advice from the apostle Paul: "In humility consider others better than yourselves" (Philippians 2:3b). Don't try to judge someone's heart or motivations. Most of the time we end up finding out how wrong we were. More often than not we are 180 degrees from reality.

Instead, let's begin to see one another as better than ourselves. We must, in humility, consider those other people more important than ourselves. When we do that, it automatically dispels the judgmental attitude.

Faith: Don't Worship Without It

BY BOB KAUFLIN

> 🍂 *And without faith it is impossible to please God, because anyone who comes to him must believe that he exists and that he rewards those who earnestly seek him.*
> HEBREWS 11:6

Much of the debate about worship centers on worship styles. Should our worship be contemporary or traditional? High church or low church? Reverent or celebratory?

Whatever the practice of your church might be (or even your personal feelings on the subject), there is a more important issue to be aware of in the matter of worship. I'm speaking of faith. Whatever our worship looks like on the outside, it is meaningless apart from faith. Singing music that I like, using biblical words, or even being part of a church that teaches on worship does not ensure that worship is actually taking place! The scripture for today states in no uncertain terms that we come to God by faith, or we do not come at all. It is only "in him and through faith in him we may approach God with freedom and confidence" (Ephesians 3:12).

So what does faith involve? At least three things are crucial to biblical faith. The first is a knowledge of God's Word. Romans tells us that "faith comes from hearing the message, and the message is heard through the word of Christ" (Romans 10:17). We must *know* what God says. That includes what He has told us about Himself, His works, and

His promises. Faith is based on eternal truth, not passing feelings or opinions.

The second element of faith is *belief*. We must consciously believe that what the Bible says is true. James, however, tells us that devils believe and tremble. Certainly, that's not faith.

That leads to the third aspect of faith that pleases God—*trust*. Biblical faith trusts God's perspective, His power, His wisdom, and His sufficiency. We not only believe the truth but also receive and rely on it. Playing music, singing, and lifting hands doesn't mean faith is present. We must actively believe what we're singing and saying. We must believe to the point that it alters our mindset, our perspective, and our lives.

As we sing songs of praise to God in our corporate gatherings, what engages our minds? I'm sure I'm not the only one who struggles with thoughts of what I'll be having for lunch, what I'm doing later that night, or some "to do" item I haven't gotten to yet. Those are the kinds of thoughts that crowd out faith and make our songs meaningless. Faith takes hold of the glorious truths we are singing about and affects our hearts. When we sing, "A mighty fortress is our God, a bulwark never failing; our helper He amidst the flood of mortal ills prevailing," we receive strength to face difficult circumstances. Proclaiming, "I sing for joy at the work of Your hands; forever I'll love You, forever I stand. Nothing compares to the promise I have in You," reminds us of the ineffectiveness of temporal earthly joys to truly satisfy. Every time we participate in corporate praise we have another opportunity to gain a fresh perspective on the worth and works of our great God.

Aside from exercising faith through the words we sing, we need to place our faith in the finished work of Jesus Christ as we come to worship Him. Our worship would not rise past the ceiling if God had not provided a way for us to draw near to Him. We must believe that it is Jesus' atoning death that is solely responsible for gaining us access to God. We have nothing in ourselves to offer Him or to make us worthy of being in His presence.

This is easier to understand if we know Old Testament history. For centuries, the Israelites were forbidden to approach God apart from the blood of a sacrificed animal. However, those sacrifices were insufficient because they were unable to secure eternal forgiveness for sins.

That sacrificial system makes clear to us that it is impossible on our own initiative, without invitation, to enter God's holy presence. God, however, has provided a solution to our problem. The author of Hebrews writes, "Therefore, brothers, since we have confidence to enter the Most Holy Place by the blood of Jesus, by a new and living way opened for us through the curtain, that is, his body, and since we have a great priest over the house of God, let us draw near to God with a sincere heart in full assurance of faith, having our hearts sprinkled to cleanse us from a guilty conscience and having our bodies washed with pure water" (Hebrews 10:19–22).

How do we draw near? Through our music? Through our skill? Through our talents, or earnest desire? No. We draw near through the work of Jesus Christ on our behalf. What encouragement this should give us to wholeheartedly declare God's praises as we gather together! God doesn't accept us based on whether or not we had a quiet time this morning or how many people we've shared the gospel with or how great the band sounds. He accepts us on the basis of what His Son accomplished in becoming sin for us, taking our punishment on Himself, and clothing us in His own righteousness. We need to remember, by faith, that His work is just as complete at the beginning of the service as at the end.

There will come a day when faith will no longer be necessary as we gaze with unrestrained joy on the face of our Creator and Redeemer. Until that time, faith will always be an indispensable part of our worship. Let's not take it for granted.

Seek the Giver Not the Gifts

BY TOM KRAEUTER

> As long as he sought the LORD,
> God gave him success.
> 2 CHRONICLES 26:5b

This scripture passage is referring to a man named Uzziah, king of Judah. King Uzziah began his reign when he was just sixteen years old. Actually, compared with the beginning of his grandfather's reign as king, Uzziah was mature. His grandfather was Joash, and he became king at just seven years of age.

Uzziah is often remembered from a very different passage of Scripture. In the sixth chapter of the book of Isaiah, the prophet sees a vision of the Lord "seated on a throne, high and exalted, and the train of his robe filled the temple" (Isaiah 6:1b). The passage starts off by saying, "In the year that King Uzziah died...." This is the same King Uzziah mentioned in 2 Chronicles 26.

Uzziah started out as a very godly king. God caused him to be victorious over his enemies in numerous battles. His well-trained army of more than 300,000 men was a powerful machine that no foe could withstand. At least four nations are mentioned as those he conquered. His weapons for warfare (catapults and large bows) brought him great notoriety.

The Lord also gave Uzziah wisdom in handling the various domestic affairs of his kingdom. Apparently Judah enjoyed great financial prosperity. Uzziah and his people prospered, and his fame spread throughout the surrounding nations. Through God's blessing, Uzziah had everything going for him.

Then comes 2 Chronicles 26:16: "But after Uzziah became powerful, his pride led to his downfall." Uh oh. How many times have you and I seen this same scenario? God blesses individuals in a mighty way. Perhaps they prosper financially. Maybe their ministry or artistic gifts are recognized and showcased. Possibly their consistent servant attitude has caused them to be noticed by someone with the ability to promote them. Whatever the case, once the recognition comes, all too often they forget what caused them to get to that point in the first place.

Perhaps you've seen this scenario in your own life. When things begin to go well for us—when our proverbial ship comes in—it seems as though the usual reaction is to begin to think we're really special. Our mindset is, "Well, of course I'm being recognized. Look what I've done. See the things I've accomplished." Paul reminds us in his letter to the Roman Christians, "Do not think of yourself more highly than you ought" (Romans 12:3).

When we and others begin to recognize some fine gift the Lord has given us, we can easily become consumed by the need to get more of the gift. We like the power, the pleasure, and the recognition "our" accomplishments bring. We begin to dwell on seeking more of the gift instead of seeking the Giver of the gift. We are more self-focused than God-focused.

"As long as he sought the LORD, God gave him success" (2 Chronicles 26:5b). Scripture plainly depicts Uzziah's tremendous success. However, it lasted only as long as he sought the Lord. When he stopped seeking the Lord, the success came to a screeching halt.

It seems to me that Uzziah was fortunate. The Lord sent him a reminder message. His wake-up call came in the form of declining success. We are not always so fortunate. God does not always remove the success when we stop pursuing Him. Sometimes it just keeps going, and for us, there is no warning like Uzziah had. And yet there is. Uzziah's life stands as a clear warning to all of God's people: Seek the Lord!

Jesus did not mince any words when He taught the same thing. In the sixth chapter of Matthew, Jesus had just finished telling the people not to worry about food and clothing. He spoke of lilies of the field and birds of the air. They are clothed splendidly and are well fed. They don't worry, He reminded us. Why should we? Then Jesus went on to say, "But seek first his kingdom and his righteousness, and all these things will be given to you as well" (Matthew 6:33). He promised them that if they would seek Him and His kingdom first, then they would get these other temporal things.

We are not to pursue the things. We are to pursue God. However, the interesting thing is that if we pursue God we get the things. If we pursue the things, we may well miss both.

Don't become proud and haughty about the gifts and talents the Lord has given you. Continue to seek Him. Seek the Giver not the gifts.

Preach the Songs!

BY BILL RAYBORN

 How, then, can they call on the one they have not believed in? And how can they believe in the one of whom they have not heard? And how can they hear without someone preaching to them? And how can they preach unless they are sent? As it is written, "How beautiful are the feet of those who bring good news!"
ROMANS 10:14–15

As we strive to obey the Great Commission, sometimes we tend to leave the "preaching" to those who have been called into full-time Christian work. We sometimes assume preaching is left to the ordained minister of the church. However, if we leave "preaching" up to the "professionals," we will lose the challenge and joy of telling the world about Jesus.

Do we assume any new responsibilities when we commit to serve God through the ministry of music? Are there different demands presented to us as leaders of music ministry? And, after all, who is a preacher anyway?

My friend Bob Burroughs had an experience one Sunday that has stuck with me for several years. It happened innocently enough when his young child approached him and asked the question, "Daddy, when are you going to preach the songs?"

Preach the songs?

Why not? The dictionary says that to "preach" is "to proclaim or to urge acceptance of an idea or course of action." Our songs—

congregational, choir, and solo—do just that. We *proclaim* the gospel of our Lord every Sunday. We preach the songs!

So that brings up this thought. If we, as choir members, *preach the songs,* doesn't that make us preachers? Many of the songs we sing in our congregation and as choir presentations are directly from Scripture or are based on Scripture. One who proclaims the Word of God is surely a "preacher." One does not need to be ordained by a denomination or a church to consider himself or herself a *proclaimer* of the gospel. Since we *are* ministers, does not this place additional responsibilities on us as church musicians?

When our choirs stand before our congregations each Sunday, we "preach" the good news as surely as any ordained preacher. That means each of us who is "preaching the songs" is a minister of the gospel. And what should we expect from a minister? We should expect conduct and dedication just a bit above those who sit in the pews.

We are all familiar with the words of Jesus when He said, "All authority in heaven and on earth has been given to me. Therefore go and make disciples of all nations, baptizing them in the name of the Father and of the Son and of the Holy Spirit, and teaching them to obey everything I have commanded you. And surely I am with you always, to the very end of the age" (Matthew 28:18–20).

Do we pass this off as words spoken to someone else? Could He have been speaking to us as choir members? Surely our service in the local church is designed to help spread the gospel and lead the saints in worship. If not, what is the need of our singing?

When I was minister of music at First Baptist Church in Aiken, South Carolina, our pastor, Dr. Austin Roberts, spoke about the need for us to live the dedicated Christian life. He said that while every Christian should lead the most dedicated life possible—we all have responsibilities to Christ and to one another—even so, we should expect the person carrying the flag at the front of the parade to stand a little straighter.

We who preach the songs before our church each Sunday carry the standard of Christ for all to see. We must all stand a little straighter as we carry the "cross of Jesus going on before." After over thirty years of serving as a minister of music, I, along with my wife, sing in the choir at First Baptist Church in Euless, Texas. Even though the choir has over two hundred members, it is not unusual for members of the church to say to us, "Oh, you sing in the choir, don't you." We think people don't notice us. Think again. People are watching.

Next time you stand before your church leading congregational singing—whether you are singing in an ensemble, on a praise team, or as a member of the choir presenting special music—*carry your banner high*! Remember, you are there to "preach the songs."

God: Our Home Sweet Home

BY TOM KRAEUTER

> *Lord, you have been our dwelling place throughout all generations.*
> PSALM 90:1

My family and I like to go on vacations together. We have wandered in the mountains of Tennessee and frolicked in a lake in Maine. Swimming is generally a family favorite whether in the ocean off the coast of Florida, in Lake Michigan, or even in the pool at a hotel where we might be staying. We have visited fascinating museums in Washington, D.C., Chicago, and Philadelphia. From the Louisville Slugger baseball bat factory in Louisville, Kentucky, to Niagara Falls, we enjoy those fun-filled times experiencing new things with one another. Setting aside the daily routine of life and getting away can be a very enjoyable experience. It can even help rejuvenate us physically and mentally.

However, after a trip of a few days or even a couple of weeks, it is always a great feeling to be back home. Staying in other people's homes or in hotels is nice, but there is nothing like being back in our own beds. There is a comfortableness in the routine of home. The old saying is true: "Be it ever so humble, there's no place like home."

Many people view their relationship with God like going on vacation. It is a great place to go and relax, but it's not their home.

Scripture says, "Lord, you have been our dwelling place" (Psalm 90:1). Not just a place to visit, but our home. God is not an escape from reality. He *is* reality.

It is clear from Scripture that God is always with us. Psalm 139 says, "Where can I go from your Spirit? Where can I flee from your presence? If I go up to the heavens, you are there; if I make my bed in the depths, you are there. If I rise on the wings of the dawn, if I settle on the far side of the sea, even there your hand will guide me, your right hand will hold me fast" (Psalm 139:7–10). We can't leave His presence. Yet we can do more to recognize His presence and thereby, from our perspective, to live in His presence.

Cultivating an awareness of God in our daily lives is vital. As we recognize His presence in us and with us, then relationship with Him throughout the day is a natural occurrence. A medieval monk, Brother Lawrence, talked of practicing the presence of God. He recognized that God was with Him in all he did. Consequently, he used all he did to nurture his relationship with the Lord. His prayer was:

> My God, since You are with me, and since it is Your will that I should apply my mind to these outward things, I pray that You will give me the grace to remain with You and keep company with You. But so that my work may be better, Lord, work with me; receive my work and possess all my affections.[22]

If our relationship with an omnipresent God is to be honest, then that relationship must, as Brother Lawrence suggested, include recognizing the Lord's presence in all that we do. It is not just now and then—a nice place to visit—but our dwelling place.

When I was a boy our family had a dog. Although we moved frequently when I was growing up, we never seemed to live in an urban area. We preferred a bit more of the rural setting. You know, fields and woods. Consequently, it was not terribly unusual for us to find ticks on our dog. If you've never encountered a tick, you are very fortunate. They are disgusting. Tiny little creatures, some are so small you can barely see them. Others are the size of a small fly. Technically they belong to the arachnid family along with spiders, scorpions, and mites.

(I'm not sure I would want to be listed in such a "family"!) Anyway, here's how the encyclopedia describes their life: "Their grasping forelegs allow them to climb on a host. They quickly find a protected spot on the host's body, sink their mouthparts into the flesh, and begin to feed. When full, they drop off the host."

Quite a life! They suck out enough life to keep themselves alive for a while and live off that until they have used it all up. Then they start over.

That's the way many people act in their relationship with God. They go to church to get just enough life from Him to survive until next week and then ignore Him the other six days.

What about you? Do you just occasionally visit, or is God really your dwelling place? Do you just play your instrument or sing your part for the worship ministry, or is the Lord actually your home, the place where you live?

Worship and Compound Interest

BY ARLEN SALTE

 "Do not store up for yourselves treasures on earth, where moth and rust destroy, and where thieves break in and steal. But store up for yourselves treasures in heaven, where moth and rust do not destroy, and where thieves do not break in and steal. For where your treasure is, there your heart will be also."
MATTHEW 6:19–21

- Do you have a computer at home? Make $60 an hour. Call 555–1111.
- I lost 30 pounds in 30 days! New Herbal formula. Call 555–2222.
- Gain washboard abs while you sleep. Takes 4 size-C batteries. Call now for three easy payments.
- New Mac & Cheese Deluxe. No need to add water or milk. Just microwave 60 seconds.

Do these phrases sound familiar to you? I've made it a rule never to trust a sign on a light pole, never to buy anything on cable after midnight, and never to eat a complete meal from a can. Yet it's tempting, and the most tempting of all is the get-rich-quick scheme.

The e-mail blasts across my computer screen. "Secret investments of the wealthy. Respond to this e-mail and triple your money in 30 days." Read any respectable investment book, and it will let you know that "get rich quick" usually leads to "get broke quick." These deceptions come in all forms, from pyramid schemes to shady tax shelters.

One of the first things you learn when you begin investing is that regular investments, started early, with reasonable rates of return will bring about good results. Through the wonder of compound interest, you can have a very respectable balance sheet if you give it enough time.

You know, it's not just in finances, exercise, and weight loss that people try to get overnight results. It exists in the spiritual world as well. Walk into any bookstore and you'll see get-spiritual-quick books all around you. Some of them are even written by Christian authors.

Maybe you've wanted to apply some of those easy steps in your life. You want a spiritual breakthrough as quickly as you can make ravioli from a can. You want to be so constantly spiritually alive that you are a worshiper every second of your life. You want it yesterday. Just add holy water and stir.

Unfortunately, that's not the normal Christian life. In the Bible, when God formed character, He used the wonder of compound *spiritual* interest. He sent Moses to the wilderness. He left David with the sheep. He kept Joseph in a prison. Even Jesus did not begin His public ministry for three decades. What's the secret ingredient in all these formulas? Time.

It's time to start the wonder of compound *spiritual* interest in your life. What deposits are you making today? As you study the lives of the great women and men of the faith, you will see that they were fervently dedicated to a daily time in the Word of God and in prayer.

Many people are into microwave Christianity. They figure that if their heart isn't hot in a week, then the investment isn't working. You'll seldom see life-transforming results in a week. Over time, however, you will. You will come to see your time with God as the most important investment of all. The return on your investment will be a deep, abiding trust in God, no matter what your earthly circumstances may be. This is better than buying Microsoft stock when it first went public. According to the verse from today, our heavenly wealth can never be taken away.

The closing verse in our scripture from today really sums it up. It says, "For where your treasure is, there your heart will be also." It's also a simple formula, as simple as compound interest. Today, the most precious commodity is time. That's why we want to drive-thru for fast food with cell phones in our ears. Where you invest your time is where your heart will be. If you invest your time mostly in sports, you'll leap when the home team runs for the end zone, but you may stay quiet when God makes a touchdown in someone's life. If you invest lots of time in television, you may be intrigued with the latest sitcom development but have little fascination with the developments of the Most High.

If the spiritual balance sheet of your heart today is showing a deficit, why not make a lasting investment? Why not discover the eternal wealth of compounding daily investments in your heavenly treasure? In time, you will experience worship that is rich beyond comparison because the treasure of your heart is not just a bank statement, it's a Person. And that Person is Jesus.

Quite the Conglomeration

BY TOM KRAEUTER

> *All these men were under the supervision of their fathers for the music of the temple of the LORD, with cymbals, lyres and harps, for the ministry at the house of God.... Young and old alike, teacher as well as student, cast lots for their duties.*
> 1 CHRONICLES 25:6a, 8

What a picture this verse of Scripture concocts! Young and old, students and teachers, all tossed together making music. Can you see it?

Front and center is the first-chair violinist from the Jerusalem Symphony. He's the ideal picture of the finest musician around. Clearly the best in Israel. Maybe even the world. Right next to him, much to his consternation, sits a kid—certainly no more than fourteen—who still makes those horrendous squawking noises on his violin, a little too regularly. "Oh, how I wish he'd spend less time playing hide-and-seek in the olive grove and more time practicing his instrument," agonizes Mr. First-chair.

Off to the left is the horn section. The elderly French-horn player certainly deserves to be here. However, as he plays, he ponders about the two green-haired trombonists next to him. "I wonder when they will get their slides caught in each other's nose ring?"

Near the back, in his dignified black tuxedo, stands the young, serious, orchestral percussionist. He just received his master's degree in percussion, and he has very definite opinions on what good music comprises. Immediately to his right sits a forty-something big, burly

271

guy with tattoos covering his arms. This guy seems to be always banging out heavy rhythm on the trap set, with just a bit too much variation in tempo to suit the tux-clad percussionist.

No doubt about it, this is definitely a scene to behold. It is most certainly a study in contrasts: The London Symphony Orchestra merges with the neighborhood garage band.

Actually this picture reminds me of the worship ministry in the average church. There is generally quite the conglomeration of different people. Some are younger, and others are older. Some are quite proficient on their instrument(s), while others—let's be kind—haven't been at it quite as long. There is clearly a difference, not only in musical tastes but in abilities as well.

The dilemma in all of this, of course, is how to get all of these various folks to work together. Preferably, to get them to work together and like one another. At the very least, to work together and not kill one another.

My experience has shown me that the single most significant factor in making this happen is for the better, more mature musicians to help and encourage those whose abilities are not quite as good. In practical terms, this requires a few different attitudes to be realized in our lives.

First, setting aside pride is imperative. Anyone can look down his nose at someone who is not quite as talented. That's easy. It takes real maturity to recognize, "This person is a part of the team, and I need to do my best to help and encourage him."

Setting aside pride has an underlying theme: dying to self. As part of the worship ministry team, our attitude should *not* be, "How can I show how really talented I am?" Rather, it *should* be something along these lines: "How can I help this team to be the very best we can be, together?" This means that if I have the ability, I show the less-proficient musician how to play something that will work better on a particular song. Perhaps I help him with a specific musical concept with which he has been struggling. My attitude is not a condescending one either. Instead, I help him because I care and want him to be the best he can be for God's glory.

For our mature musicians to mentor others, they must display an attitude of encouragement. Too frequently I have seen gifted musicians who cannot tolerate anything less than perfection. Their attitude in dealing with those whose musical abilities are not on their same level is often the same as the attitude of teenagers who form their thumb and index finger into an "L" and place it against their foreheads (connotation: loser). We would probably not say or do anything quite so harsh in the context of the worship ministry, but the attitude is still frequently there. Instead, we should have an attitude of helping and encouraging one another. An honest attitude of caring and compassion will go a long way in helping musicians of varying abilities working together over the long term.

Although he wasn't talking specifically to musicians, the apostle Paul summed it up well: "Do nothing out of selfish ambition or vain conceit, but in humility consider others better than yourselves. Each of you should look not only to your own interests, but also to the interests of others" (Philippians 2:3–4).

The Great American Worship Contest

BY GERRIT GUSTAFSON

> *Then you call on the name of your god,*
> *and I will call on the name of the LORD.*
> *The god who answers by fire—he is God.*
> 1 KINGS 18:24

Imagine this: The whole nation is gathered around millions of television sets throughout every state, city, and county to watch the Event of Events. Assured of an unprecedented viewing audience, advertisers have put up astronomical amounts of money to sponsor this epic showdown, which had only months before been the harebrained proposal of some unknown coalition of Christians.

Quite unexpectedly, all four major networks agreed to simultaneously broadcast this controversial program when a second coalition of well-known entertainers, writers, educators, media personalities, and other New Age gurus accepted the challenge of the Christians to what is now being called the Great American Worship Contest.

The day of the event, which is being held in the largest stadium in America, has finally come. The preliminaries, complete with clever commentaries, endless interviews, and erudite speculations, have explained for weeks the story behind the contest.

The coalition of Christians is very intense in its belief that the increase of violence and murder in America and our economic and political demise are directly related to a departure from the God of the

Bible and to the widespread worship of God substitutes. The New Age practitioners accepted the challenge, hoping to put to rest once and for all what they call "the archaic notion of an intervening God who judges."

The ground rules, as agreed by both sides, are simple:

1. Both sides are given time to meditate, pray, chant, and worship in any way they see fit.
2. The god who answers by fire will be recognized as the true God.
3. The audience concludes the contest by calling a "900 " number to register their response.

Everyone seems to know that the stakes are high. Congress has agreed to accept the outcome as a mandate in regard to several public policy and budgetary decisions. The Senate is actually withholding confirmation of two hotly contested nominees for the Supreme Court until after the contest.

The hour has come. The Christians are definitely outnumbered in the stadium as the New Agers begin their incantations. Everyone is wondering, "How will the day end? Who will be America's God?"

This imaginary story is, of course, a contemporary version of the Old Testament account found in 1 Kings 18 of Elijah and the prophets of Baal and Asherah. At Mt. Carmel, God did in fact answer Elijah's worship with fire, and all the people "called their 900 number" and cried out "The LORD—he is God! The LORD—he is God!" A whole nation was turned back to God, and the land was purged of the voices of delusion. The power of an acceptable sacrifice!

As to the outcome in our generation, the verdict is still pending. The story is "to be continued." The following thoughts are offered with the hope that we, as God's people, might become "a spiritual house offering acceptable sacrifices," and that we too would see His intervening presence attend our worship.

Since Cain and Abel offered their first sacrifices in Genesis 4, there has been a continuous contest of worship: acceptable versus unacceptable sacrifices. Cain was jealous of the favor that accompanied his brother's worship. If we look carefully, this jealousy is behind every international and ethnic conflict. Even in the final chapters of history, as recorded by John in Revelation 14, we find this contest is again center stage: the worship of the beast versus the worship of the Lamb.

Everyone throughout time will worship something, for man was made to worship. The real issue is not "will we worship?" but "whom will we worship?" We will yield our hearts and minds to either God or Satan. To suppose that man is ultimately autonomous and can create his own reality is simply to bow one's mind in obeisance to Satan's deceit.

We must settle the issue that Christians cannot worship multiple gods. We may think that idolatry is only a problem they have in far-away places or forgotten times. However, the biblical definition of idolatry includes greed in Ephesians 5:5, inordinate love of pleasure or being entertained in 2 Timothy 3:4, and obsessive appetites in Philippians 3:19. That hits pretty close to home!

In 2 Kings 17, verse 33, we see where the people in Samaria "worshiped the LORD, but they also served their own gods." We must seriously examine our hearts in regard to the sin of contemporary idolatry and rediscover the first two commandments that forbid false worship.

The fact that we are worshipers is not controversial. It is that we are worshipers of God alone. To say that Christ is *a* way to God will not be contested, but to say that Christ is *the only* way to God is to cause us to become an object of vicious cultural scorn.

Though there's a great challenge to all who participate in this worship contest, there's an even greater promise. God will distinguish true worship from false with the fire of His presence.

In the 1970s, a simple truth inaugurated a worship revolution. This truth was that genuine praise brings us through invisible gates into an experience of God's revealed presence. That hallmark truth is going to grow in its implications as the revolution is now attracting a new generation. When single-minded, wholehearted devotion replaces casual, "ho-hum" worship in our churches, the fire of His presence will grow brighter and brighter. The great anticipation is that God will yet answer by fire!

So what about the outcome of the Great American Worship Contest? To be honest, we don't know when the final scores are going to be posted. But if we're there at its epic conclusion, we'll know then that the outcome was determined in days just like today, in churches and homes just like our own, by folks just like you and me.

Let's fearlessly fill this generation with glorious praise of our glorious King!

Lost Luggage?

BY TOM KRAEUTER

> *...because I know whom I have believed, and am convinced that he is able to guard what I have entrusted to him for that day.*
> 2 TIMOTHY 1:12b

I fly a lot. I consider myself very fortunate in that I have never completely lost any baggage. Although I have encountered people who have lost luggage, mine has always eventually turned up.

There are at least two ways to lose luggage when traveling by air. The first is to leave your bag unattended in the airport and have someone walk off with it. If that were to happen, the scene might look something like this:

Returning from the rest room, I find my bag gone. I approach the gate agent and explain that my bag is missing. He might request a description of the bag and its general contents. He will most certainly ask where I saw it last.

"I left it right over there on that seat when I went to use the rest room, and now it's gone."

"Oh, I see," he responds. "Well, I could make an announcement about it and see if anyone turns it in. However, it is much more likely that your bag really is gone." He is not going to expend much energy to help when he realizes that my carelessness is the reason my bag is missing.

The other way to lose luggage is when the airline misplaces it. I've had this happen. When I explain where I've come from and show my baggage claim receipts, the airline employees willingly bend over backward to help. They request an address where I will be staying and promise to have the bag(s) delivered either later that day or the next morning—at the airline's expense. This scenario is very different from the first one. Why? Because I have entrusted my luggage into their care, and they are now responsible for it.

When we entrust ourselves to God, we become His responsibility—"because I know whom I have believed, and am convinced that he is able to guard what I have *entrusted* to him for that day" (2 Timothy 1:12b). We must yield ourselves into His hands, trusting His faithfulness to keep us.

However, it is clear from Scripture that this is not simply a once-and-for-all action. It must be repeated consistently. Entrusting yourself to the Lord in general is good. You recognize that "you are not your own; you were bought at a price" (1 Corinthians 6:19b–20a). This overall yielding to Him is important, but there must also come a consistent yielding to Him to walk fully in submission.

Paul the apostle said, "Therefore, I urge you, brothers, in view of God's mercy, to *offer your bodies as living sacrifices*, holy and pleasing to God" (Romans 12:1). I like to think of doing this on a daily basis. What would happen if each day when you awaken you were to pray something along these lines: "Lord, today I'm Yours. Wherever I go, whatever I do, I want You to be glorified in my life. I willingly yield myself to You and ask that You would work in and through me"? Would honestly praying something like that in a true, heartfelt way each morning make a difference in your life? Of course it would.

Clearly we are to offer our "bodies as living sacrifices," but this in and of itself is not enough. Someone once commented that the problem with a living sacrifice is that it keeps crawling off the altar. Have you found this to be true in your own life? Besides a general yielding and even a daily yielding, there needs to be a consistent, ongoing giving ourselves to God.

In the Garden of Gethsemane, three times Jesus committed Himself to His Father, praying, "Not as I will, but as you will" (Matthew 26:39), and, "May your will be done" (Matthew 26:42). Jesus was clearly committed to His Father, but He further entrusted this specific time in His life to God.

Throughout that day and into the next, Jesus' situation grew even more intense. The questionings, the insults, the humiliation, the beatings, and finally the cross. This must have been a highly emotional and difficult time for Jesus. Peter sums up Jesus' reaction in his first letter: "When they hurled their insults at him, he did not retaliate; when he suffered, he made no threats. Instead, *he entrusted himself to him who judges justly*" (1 Peter 2:23).

We need to do that. Regularly, on an ongoing basis, we should entrust ourselves to the Lord. He has promised to lead us as we commit our ways to Him. "Commit to the LORD whatever you do, and your plans will succeed" (Proverbs 16:3). "In all your ways acknowledge him [the LORD], and he will make your paths straight" (Proverbs 3:6).

When we entrust ourselves to the Lord, He is free to work in us. Like the airline employee who diligently searches for the luggage that was entrusted to his care, so 2 Timothy 1:12 promises us that God will take care of the things we entrust to Him.

Those of us involved in the ministry of praise and worship must regularly commit ourselves as well as our talents, gifts, and abilities to the Lord for His use. Consistently yielding to God gives Him more opportunity to work in and through us. Instead of being the living sacrifices with that tendency to crawl off the altar, we become committed to Him. His plans become our plans. His thoughts become our thoughts. His will—just as Jesus prayed in Gethsemane—becomes our will. Regularly entrusting ourselves into God's hands will give Him greater access to us—an important issue for those leading people in worship.

Adapted from the book *Oh, Grow Up!* by Tom Kraeuter (Lynnwood, Wash.: Emerald Books, 2001).

Fleas and Furnaces

BY TOM KRAEUTER

> 🌿 *And we know that in all things God works for the good of those who love Him, who have been called according to His purpose.*
> ROMANS 8:28

Is your life absolutely ideal all the time? Is your church perfect? Is the worship ministry of your church always flawless in every way? Okay, stop laughing. I really didn't think it was, but I wanted to be certain.

Have you noticed that God sometimes allows us to be involved in less-than-positive circumstances? The good news is that He has promised to work in and through all of these situations. "And we know that in *all things* God works for the good of those who love him, who have been called according to his purpose" (Romans 8:28).

In her book *The Hiding Place*, Corrie ten Boom tells about the time she and her sister Betsie were moved from one prison camp to another. The new residence was a filthy, smelly, overcrowded barracks. Not long after they arrived, Corrie noticed something pinch her leg. Then she felt it again.

"Fleas!" Corrie cried. "Betsie, the place is swarming with them!"

Immediately Corrie was in a foul mood over their living conditions. The smell and the overcrowding were one thing, but fleas?! After praying about their situation, Betsie shared with Corrie 1 Thessalonians 5:16–18: "Be joyful always; pray continually; give thanks in all circumstances, for this is God's will for you in Christ Jesus."

"That's it, Corrie! That's His answer. 'Give thanks in all circumstances!' That's what we can do. We can start right now to thank God for every single thing about this new barracks!"

Corrie reluctantly agreed and thanked God that she and Betsie were still together, that they had a Bible, and even that there were so many people together in the barracks because that would give them plenty of opportunities to share their faith. But when Betsie suggested that she thank God for the fleas, Corrie was adamant. "Betsie, there's no way even God can make me grateful for a flea."

" 'Give thanks in *all* circumstances,' " she quoted. "It doesn't say, 'in pleasant circumstances.' Fleas are a part of this place where God has put us."

Although Corrie was sure Betsie was wrong, they stood between piers of bunks and gave thanks for fleas.

Despite the unsanitary conditions, they enjoyed tremendous freedom in their new home. They held Bible studies and church services, unhindered by outside interference of the prison guards. It was some time later that they found out the reason for such freedom in the barracks. The guards refused to enter their quarters because of the fleas![23]

We do not always like all the things that happen to us. However, just as Romans 8:28 promises, somehow God causes all of those things to work together for good.

Okay, we know that, but let's be really candid. There have been times when I honestly wanted the Lord to return some semblance of normalcy to my life. I was tired of all the trials and testings. Unfortunately, God didn't seem swayed by my whining.

Proverbs 17:3 tells us, "The crucible for silver and the furnace for gold, but the LORD tests the heart." If you understand the Hebrew writing style, the writer here is comparing the crucible and the furnace—the intense heat, the skimming off of impurities—and how God tests us. I really don't like that comparison. However, it's not my decision to make.

Johann Sebastian Bach is considered by many to be the finest composer of all time. Bach composed some of the most beautiful music in history. However, he had a life that was anything but beautiful. Both his parents died before he was ten. He was resentfully raised by an older brother who did not need—or even want—another person to feed. Bach's first wife died after thirteen years of marriage. He later remarried, and of the children he fathered between his two marriages, ten died in infancy, one died in his twenties, and one was mentally retarded. Eventually Bach himself went blind and was paralyzed from a stroke.

Yet in the midst of all this, Bach wrote wonderful music. His music is filled with obvious praise and thanksgiving to God. It seems apparent that it was not because God had given him the ideal life that Bach wrote such music. Rather, it was because Bach knew such intense trials and tribulations that he also knew the heights of faith and praise.

Whether in everyday life or in the midst of the worship ministry, we need to be able to say with Paul the apostle, "I have learned to be content whatever the circumstances" (Philippians 4:11b). Don't let the outward trying situations of life cause you to become unsettled on the inside. Realize that it really is true: "In *all things* God works for the good of those who love Him."

Lessons from the Praise of Prisoners

BY BOB KAUFLIN

> 🌿 *The crowd joined in the attack against Paul and Silas, and the magistrates ordered them to be stripped and beaten. After they had been severely flogged, they were thrown into prison, and the jailer was commanded to guard them carefully. Upon receiving such orders, he put them in the inner cell and fastened their feet in the stocks. About midnight Paul and Silas were praying and singing hymns to God, and the other prisoners were listening to them.*
> ACTS 16:22–25

Although Paul and Silas are never described as "worship leaders," there are some significant truths about worship we can learn from this amazing narrative in the book of Acts.

Imagine this: You and your co-laborer have traveled hundreds of miles preaching the good news of Jesus Christ. You've arrived at the city of Philippi, where you're starting to see a response to the gospel. As you travel to the place of prayer one day, you cast out an evil spirit from a slave girl. Her owners, furious that you've taken away their means of making money, drag you into the marketplace to face the authorities. After presenting fabricated lies in a spurious trial, the crowd turns against you, and the city rulers have you stripped and beaten. Exhausted, bruised, and alone, you're thrown into prison to mingle with the thieves, murderers, and rebels. Your feet are placed in stocks, and appointed guards watch your every move.

The hours come and go with agonizing predictability. Midnight arrives. What would you be doing? In my very best scenario, I'd be hoping to shut out the persistent physical pain by grabbing a few minutes of sleep. The thought of worship would be totally out of the question and out of my mind. Not Paul and Silas. There they are, at midnight, in prison, "praying and singing hymns to God." What can we learn from their example?

1. WORSHIP IS FOR ANY TIME.

How often we confine worship to Sunday mornings and Wednesday nights, as if God were uninterested in our praises any other time of the week! The psalmist says, "At midnight I rise to give you thanks for your righteous laws" (Psalm 119:62). Apparently, Paul and Silas took that scripture literally. Midnight or midday, dawn or dusk, any time is appropriate to declare the glories of our awesome God.

2. WORSHIP IS FOR ANY PLACE.

Isn't it interesting how certain elements can make a building seem more "worshipful" to us than others? It might be stained-glass windows, steeples, altars, or even pews that lead our minds and hearts toward God. Certainly, the way a building is designed and furnished can accent different attributes of God that are important as we come together to declare His praise. However, we need to remember that architecture, while important, is never determinative. A worshiper finds reason to worship God no matter what surrounds him. In the midst of the filth, scum, and darkness of a prison, Paul and Silas were captivated by the glorious light of the gospel. Their voices rang out in praise, not because they were *in* a church, but because they *were* the church. Viewing our relationship with God this way will turn any location into a house of worship.

3. WORSHIP IS FOR ANY CIRCUMSTANCE.

All things considered, leading worship is one of the easiest things we do. Who wouldn't want to stand in front of people week after week, encouraging them to join fellow worshipers in proclaiming God's greatness and goodness? The problem comes when I'm dealing with an unexpected bill, a persistent illness, or an irritating coworker. God uses these trials to reveal the true focus and direction of our hearts. If I'm confident in God's sovereign hand ruling over my life, if I'm sure of His almighty power to guide my circumstances, if I have unwavering faith in His desire to do good to me all the days of my life—then I can sincerely worship Him in every situation I encounter.

4. WORSHIP IS TO GOD.

Paul and Silas weren't putting on an evangelistic concert. They were having a worship service. They counted it pure joy to suffer for the gospel and couldn't contain their gratefulness. The object of their singing was God Himself. We need to beware of worship that is done merely for the sake of others. God alone is the recipient of our praises and the reason we worship.

5. WORSHIP BENEFITS OTHERS.

While worship is an end in itself and not a means to something else, God will often use our worship to draw others to Him. At the very least, when outsiders see us encountering God in a way that is sincere, biblical, and profound, their curiosity is provoked. This is "seeker-sensitive" worship, biblically defined—God, the almighty Seeker, relentlessly pursuing those who don't know Him—even at midnight in a prison cell.

Luke goes on to tell us that this impromptu "hymn sing" resulted in an earthquake. While that won't always be the effect of our worship, we can be sure that God is ready to do amazing things whenever we apply these lessons learned from the praise of prisoners.

An Alaskan Tale

BY TOM KRAEUTER

> He [Jesus] said to them, "You are the ones who justify yourselves in the eyes of men, but God knows your hearts. What is highly valued among men is detestable in God's sight."
>
> LUKE 16:15

Yes, I know that Jesus was talking to the Pharisees in this verse. However, from time to time all of us tend to display some pharisaical attitudes. In his book *Understanding Music and Worship in the Local Church*, Vernon M. Whaley tells the following story from his childhood:

> I was raised in the home of a missionary. For the better part of my growing-up years, we lived in Alaska. Among their other ministries, my mother and father had the unique vision and desire to reach out to people with various types of disabilities. After several years, we had a good number of disabled people attending our church. If they could not get to church on their own, my father would pick them up in his aging station wagon.
>
> The entire congregation was a picture of God's grace: an alcoholic turned deacon; a prostitute transformed into a Sunday School teacher; a blind man who taught an adult Sunday School class and played the piano for worship services; a young man, a former fugitive from the law who helped to keep the church grounds; a young lady crippled from birth who greeted people

at the door on Sunday mornings; a young man with Down's syndrome who helped take up the offering. All of these people were members of the kingdom of God and were serving God together to the best of their abilities. You can imagine the impact of such a congregation on a ten-year-old boy.

A tragic situation in this church, or so it seemed to me at the time, was a man and wife who had a daughter born with serious physical disabilities. She could not walk. She could not talk. Someone had to assist her in meeting all of her physical needs. She could not feed herself. She communicated by pointing to an alphabet printed on the slate she carried with her everywhere. She was home schooled because the school system had no provision for meeting the needs of someone in her condition. In spite of her limitations, my mother and dad shouldered the responsibility of transporting her to church every time the doors were open for services. Even then, she had to be strapped to her wheelchair so she would not fall over while in the car. Although her mom and dad bitterly blamed God for inflicting this plight on their family, this young girl was full of life and overflowed with joy. She had a genuine love for the Lord.

My father was a great one for having extended times of singing during the Sunday night services at our little church. My father entered the ministry during the 1940s when giant Youth for Christ rallies were held all over the country. He never lost the excitement of those rallies and their impact on his life. So on almost every Sunday night our congregation resounded with an extended time of singing: usually simple choruses interchanged with spontaneous testimonies of praise.

On one such Sunday evening, I remember Dad asking the congregation if anyone wanted to stand up and praise the Lord for His goodness. Suddenly, there was a rather significant stir from the middle of the congregation. I turned around to see this young girl slowly steering her wheelchair to the front of the church. About that time the converted alcoholic stepped over and helped her up to the area right in front of the pulpit. She motioned to my dad to come over to the wheelchair. By this time he was beginning to seriously question what was going on with his usually uneventful Sunday night service. The girl was undaunted. She spelled out on her alphabet slate her desire to sing a solo. My father looked dumbfounded. How could this girl, except for a few groans and guttural sounds, expect to make any kind of music with her lips to the Lord? My dad asked her what she wanted to sing. She pointed to the hymn "Amazing Grace" in her open hymnal. My father turned to the blind pianist and said, "Jimmy, can you play 'Amazing Grace'? We have someone special to sing for us tonight." Jimmy played a brief introduction, and she began to make groans and moans in time with the music. I was not able to clearly understand a word she sang. But somehow the musicianship and articulation of words did not matter. All of us understood intuitively what she was doing and more importantly—why she was doing it. There was no doubt. We all knew she was singing from her heart to the living God. There was not a dry eye in the audience. Even the children were captured and stilled by the moment. And I am certain God was honored to be praised. That young girl, I believe, was worshiping God in spirit and in truth.[24]

Do you ever have the attitude that your music is what makes the worship special—that your voice or your particular instrument is the thing that causes people's heart to be drawn toward the Lord? God has given you gifts and abilities. There is nothing wrong with having and using these things. However, God is always far more interested in our hearts. "God knows your hearts. What is highly valued among men is detestable in God's sight" (Luke 16:15b).

Don't ever let a pharisaical attitude turn your heart from truly worshiping God. Our music, our gifts, our abilities are not about us. All of these things are for *God's* glory. Don't get caught up in them. Get caught up in Him.

True Stewardship

BY PATRICK KAVANAUGH

> 🌿 *Blessed are those who dwell in your house; they are ever praising you.*
> PSALM 84:4

In Christian teaching today, we hear a great deal about stewardship. Unfortunately, this excellent teaching on stewardship is often limited to the areas of finance and giving. While this is certainly important, it is perhaps the easiest area of our life in which to practice good stewardship. Indeed, it is possible to tithe or double-tithe our income and yet have very little *of ourselves* to give toward a relationship with God.

Some believers will take this teaching to a higher level and discuss the very significant aspect of the stewardship of our time. How we spend our time is undeniably a key to our Christian walk. Obviously, how much time we give to the Lord will say a great deal about our relationship to Christ.

However, there is another level that should be considered: our thought life. This is the ultimate stewardship, because our thoughts are known only by ourselves and God. How we spend our finances and our time are external; our thoughts are completely internal. They are the truest reflection of who we really are.

The expression "we become what we think about" is true. It comes directly from the King James Version of Proverbs 23:7, which states,

"As [a man] thinketh in his heart, so is he." It is further founded upon the words of our Lord, who explained that "out of the overflow of the heart the mouth speaks" (Matthew 12:34b). It is our habitual thoughts that fill up the overflow of our heart, and these will always control our words and actions. No wonder Paul insists that "we take captive every thought to make it obedient to Christ" (2 Corinthians 10:5b).

This means that as we worship God and become more Christlike, our actual thoughts are relinquished to His leading. This is the ultimate and glorious surrender to God's Lordship of us, and its results can have amazing consequences in our lives. This Christ-led thought life reminds me of the words of the illustrious astronomer Johannes Kepler. During the mental tasks of studying astronomy, he proclaimed to the Lord, "O God, I am thinking Thy thoughts after Thee."

At this point, there may be some readers who are saying, "I just can't do it! I can't think about God constantly. I can't worship the Lord every second of the day, or in every little opportunity that comes my way. I'm not in heaven yet!"

Neither am I. None of us can do all these things every day, anymore than we could eat every dish offered at a huge smorgasbord. However, it *is* tremendous to have so many dishes from which to choose.

Even the devout medieval monk Brother Lawrence realized that some of us worship the Lord with greater ease than others. He wrote, "Everyone is able to have these familiar conversations with God, some more, some less—He knows our capabilities." Brother Lawrence also admitted that "some perseverance was needed at first to form the habit of conversing at all times with God and referring all actions to Him." Like any new habit or discipline, there is a need for persistence, but not guilt.

The Lord does not want us to feel guilty anytime we are not worshiping Him. He has put us in this world, which is filled with many responsibilities and necessities. In Mark's Gospel, Jesus Himself condemned His contemporaries who ignored family duties to supposedly be more devoted to God (Mark 7:10–12).

It is not a question of worshiping God and ignoring everyone else, including those in your care. It is a question of priorities. We are called to put God first, that is, to put our relationship with Him before all others. To use the term *first* presupposes that there might be a second, third, fourth, or fifth. The supremacy of our bond with Christ does not mean that we neglect the others in our life.

For most of us, to worship God more does not necessitate spending less time with our family or our responsibilities. It may mean spending less time in activities of lesser importance. Our motivation for this should not be guilt but be a desire to know the Lord more deeply.

Each person must prayerfully examine his own life to find the critical balance of how to best spend his time and thoughts for God's glory. Even the smallest efforts have value. It is not the amount of time that pleases the Lord. It is a heart that desires to worship Him whenever possible. The French novelist Anatole France gave us a wonderful image: "The time God allots to each of us is like a precious tissue on which we embroider as we best know how." What better embroidery can there be than our worship of the Lord?

Adapted from the book *Worship—A Way of Life* by Patrick Kavanaugh (Grand Rapids, Mich.: Chosen Books—a division of Baker Book House Company, 2001).

O Canada!

BY ARLEN SALTE

🍁 *The LORD called Samuel a third time, and Samuel got up and went to Eli and said, "Here I am; you called me." Then Eli realized that the LORD was calling the boy. So Eli told Samuel, "Go and lie down, and if he calls you, say, 'Speak, LORD, for your servant is listening.'" So Samuel went and lay down in his place. The LORD came and stood there, calling as at the other times, "Samuel! Samuel!" Then Samuel said, "Speak, for your servant is listening."*
1 SAMUEL 3:8–10

We were in Canada. The sanctuary was packed to capacity. Extra chairs even extended into the foyer. Our worship team was prayed up, set up, tuned up, and ready to roll. The set list was thematically designed, copied, and passed to the whole band.

The service was launched. Hands lifted into the air. Voices of praise raised the roof. Hearts were focused on God. Everything was neat and tidy. Then God wanted to mess it up!

We were partway through the set list when God spoke quietly to my heart, "Arlen, sing 'O Canada.'"

"What?!" I asked with more than a hint of panic. "God, that would be really goofy. We put time into the set list. Besides, the apostle Paul said we should be orderly in worship. Furthermore, my reputation is at stake. There's a huge crowd here tonight. They're all going to think I'm nuts!"

In desperation, I went on with the next song. Unfortunately, God wasn't about to listen to my protests. "Sing 'O Canada,'" He whispered.

It took a few more promptings, but I finally surrendered to the still small voice. I steeled my nerves, closed my eyes, threw away my thoughts of maintaining any decent reputation, and started to blurt out, "O Canada, our home and native land."

Our worship band did a double take. I'm sure they were thinking that I had finally flipped out. To be honest, I think I asked myself the same question. Our poor musicians were thrown into a flurry of chords that don't exist in most contemporary worship choruses. They searched their minds for memories of hockey games as they tried to remember the music for the national anthem.

However, the Lord clearly knew what He was asking. We had been touring in the U.S., and I wasn't in tune to what was happening in Canada. But God knew! That night, the province of Quebec was voting to separate from Canada.

As we came to the line, "God, keep our land," it hit us why God had wanted us to sing our national anthem. People dropped to their knees in prayer for our country that we would not be ripped apart with discord. Many tears flowed that night. Many requests were placed before the throne of God. Fifty-one percent of Quebec voted to remain in Canada.

We may have had a written map for the evening, but God knew the destination. I could not have planned for a national anthem in the midst of that night of worship. God knew that as well.

Yes, the apostle Paul did state in 1 Corinthians 14:40, "But everything should be done in a fitting and orderly way." However, there are times when He is calling us to step out of the box. Sometimes these promptings are so out of the ordinary that we would never design them in our worship orders. So God waits for the moment in the service when He will speak to our hearts about a spontaneous change. It may be as simple as an extra chorus that drives the PowerPoint operator crazy. Or it may be something far more unusual.

I have encountered many people who show concern about this type of spontaneity because they've seen abuse. So how do we get to know the voice of God as we lead in worship? Here are three points to help us:

1. We need to maintain a soft heart toward God. This means walking in obedience and communing with Him throughout the day. When we fall—and we will—we need to quickly come to

Him in repentance and seek restoration. Samuel had been dedicated to the Lord as a child. We too need to walk in dedication.

2. We need to crawl before we can walk. Before you are ready to sound like you're launching a hockey game, you need to take smaller steps. Perhaps that's to change your introduction to a song as God prompts you. Maybe it's as simple as raising your hands as an example to the congregation. Samuel began his ministry doing simple tasks in God's house before he became a mighty prophet.

3. Don't be afraid to talk this over with your pastor and your worship team. Review the steps of faith you take in listening and responding to the voice of God. Make sure that there is theological integrity and sensitivity to what you are doing. Samuel went to his mentor Eli to make sure that what he was hearing was the voice of God. We need to respect those in authority as they help us to hear the voice of God. God will only call us in accordance with His Word.

I believe that God is calling each of us to listen more carefully and to respond more quickly. Why don't you let God know that you are willing to listen to His still, small voice? He is very willing to speak to us. I encourage you to say just like Samuel, "Speak, for your servant is listening."

However, I want to give one small disclaimer. If you think that God is calling you to sing the song folio from *The Sound of Music* in the middle of the worship service, I'd like to suggest that this just might be the anchovies from the pizza you ate last night and not the voice of the Lord.

Fortunately, God has never asked me to sing "O Canada" again!

"You Ain't Even Close!"

BY TOM KRAEUTER

> *For by the grace given me I say to every one of you: Do not think of yourself more highly than you ought.*
> ROMANS 12:3a

All the bridesmaids have just walked slowly down the aisle. The organ bursts forth with the first strains of "The Wedding March." The back door of the church opens wide. The bride appears, and there is a collective gasp at her breathtaking beauty. All over the building there are murmurings of "Isn't she beautiful?" and "My, how lovely!" Most of these comments are too soft and too far away for her to hear, but several are within her earshot. Suddenly she begins to realize how absolutely gorgeous she really is. Immediately one hand goes on her hip, and she strikes a pose for the photographer. She then drops her bouquet and puts her other hand behind her head giving the camera buffs another great shot of her beauty. As this continues, the crowd turns toward the groom. The comments of "Isn't she beautiful?" have now changed to "Oh, the poor man. She loves herself more than she loves him."

What an unthinkable scenario this is. However, I would suggest that this scene is a fairly accurate portrayal of the worship ministry of too many churches. When people comment on how great the music sounds or how talented the people are, those involved in the music ministry can become proud, even haughty. We can begin to think more highly of ourselves than we ought.

Because of our talents and abilities, we can begin to think that we are really something special. The more gifted we are, the easier this becomes. Over the years it has been my observation that the people who are the most gifted, the most talented, have the most difficulty maintaining their humility. Why? Because they think that compared to others around them they are really something special.

In his classic book *Mere Christianity*, C. S. Lewis discusses the issue of pride. He says this:

> Pride gets no pleasure out of having something, only out of having more of it than the next man. We say that people are proud of being rich, or clever, or good-looking, but they are not. They are proud of being richer, or cleverer, or better-looking than others. If every one else became equally rich, or clever, or good-looking there would be nothing to be proud about. It is the comparison that makes you proud: the pleasure of being above the rest.[25]

I have never been prideful when I find that I can do something well. I have too often become prideful (literally "full of pride") when I find that I can do that thing better than you. There is a competitiveness—Lewis calls it a comparison—in our sinful nature. We do not just want to be good at something, we want to be better than others. More important, we want people to know that we are better than others.

The apostle Paul told the Christians in Rome, "Do not think of yourself more highly than you ought" (Romans 12:3a). This verse goes on to say, "but rather think of yourself with sober judgment." The Greek word for "sober judgment" literally means "of sound mind." Paul is saying, "Don't fantasize about being the best. Look at yourself honestly." Let's be really candid. You might be pretty good at what you do compared to some other human being. However, compared to God...well, let's just say, "You ain't even close!"

Rory Noland, music director of Willow Creek Community Church near Chicago, said it this way:

Whatever you do, don't do what Hezekiah did (2 Kings 20). When King Hezekiah became deathly ill, God not only promised that He would heal him but even made the sun regress six hours, from noon to dawn, as a sign that Hezekiah would be healed. Emissaries from neighboring Babylon came to call on Hezekiah because they saw the sun move backward and had heard that God had done it on behalf of Hezekiah. The Babylonians were sun worshipers, so this was a great opportunity to give witness to the one true God. But instead Hezekiah took his guests up to the treasure room and proudly showed them all the kingdom's gold, silver, spices, oils, and armor. God had done this miraculous thing, and Hezekiah was showing off his personal trophy room. God's doing great things around us all the time. Let's not get stuck on how great we are, because it doesn't compare at all with God's greatness.[26]

If you and I took all of our talents and pooled them together and then added in the talents of thousands of other gifted people, we still could not impress God with our abilities. Compared to Him, we're not in the same ballpark. We're not in the same league. We're not even in the same universe. God's abilities are so far beyond us that we cannot begin to compare. So what do we have to be proud of? Nothing!

Remember, Romans 12:3 says, "Do not think of yourself more highly than you ought."

Preferences and Essentials in Worship

BY GERRIT GUSTAFSON

> 🍂 *"Why do you break the command of God for the sake of your tradition?"*
> MATTHEW 15:3

When someone decides to become a Christian, the next thing he has to decide is "which kind?" I first heard this in Russia, but the problem is universal. Which "brand" of Christianity should the new convert choose?

When a congregation decides to become a worshiping church, it has a similar dilemma: "Which style of worship will we adopt? Should we learn a contemporary worship style? Traditional? Seeker-sensitive?"

Then there are different kinds of contemporary worship...different flavors of traditional...and different degrees of "visitor consciousness." Further, if you finally decide on a "blended style," then you have to decide on what proportions. Will you be 80:20 in the contemporary-traditional mix or 30:70 the other direction?

Hmmm? It's getting complicated. Then, if you really want to see some fireworks, just let the congregation decide!

Unfortunately, most discussions on how to do worship never get past the issue of personal preferences. "If we get too contemporary, we'll lose the older folks." "Yes, but if we're too traditional our young people will go somewhere else." "Hey, I know...let's have a contemporary service *and* a traditional service; then everybody will be happy."

Personal tastes are not unimportant, but neither are they all-important. How about asking something like this: "God, do you have anything to say on the subject? After all, you are the Head of the Church!" Now that would be a good move!

Consider these three statements as a starting place in discovering biblical essentials for worship:

1. It is essential that we worship in spirit and in truth (John 4:24).
2. It is essential that worship involve the totality of the human personality (Matthew 12:30).
3. It is essential that we employ songs, hymns, and spiritual songs (Ephesians 5:19; Colossians 3:16).

Jesus didn't actually say much about worship, but what He did say is an inescapable imperative: "True worshipers...must worship in spirit and in truth." He didn't say, "I would strongly suggest that you worship in spirit and in truth, but it's really up to you and how you feel about it." Nor did He say, "If it's compatible with your target audience, you might consider worshiping in spirit and in truth."

"Okay," you say, "but what does it mean to worship in 'spirit and truth'?"

Worship "in spirit" has these three characteristics. First, Christ is central. Second, the energizing is from God, not self. Finally, it has a spontaneous element.

In John 16, Jesus said the Holy Spirit will bring glory to Him. Paul described those who worship by the Spirit in Philippians 3:3 as those who "glory in Christ Jesus." It's all about Jesus.

The flesh refers to man's capabilities apart from God or, as *The Message* translates it, "the old do-it-yourself life." If we can worship without God's energizing, that is not the worship Jesus was talking about.

We know this about the Spirit: He's like the wind. You can't control wind or predict it. Even though careful planning is important, there should always be room for God's Spirit to do the unexpected.

Worship "in truth" has two qualities. First, it's in accordance with God's Word. Second, it's genuine. The New Testament word for truth, *aletheia*, has both meanings. This covers not only the content of our worship but also the reality of it. It's so easy to go through the motions, to draw near with our words but not our hearts. External expression without internal reality is unacceptable worship.

The second essential is derived from the Great Commandment: "Love the Lord your God with all your heart and with all your soul and with all your mind and with all your strength." The key word is *all*! Since worship is simply our love for God expressed, we should worship Him as we're commanded to love Him: vigorously, with all we have intellectually, emotionally, spiritually, and physically. This is not optional; it's required!

The third essential comes from Paul's instruction to both the Colossian and Ephesian churches: sing psalms, hymns, and spiritual songs.

To sing a psalm is not necessarily the equivalent of singing from the book of Psalms. The term *psalm,* like song, can be used in a general or specific sense. In the general usage it could include hymns, just as there are hymns in the book of Psalms. In the specific sense, however, a song contrasts with a hymn. A song, like our praise choruses, is generally simpler, shorter, more testimonial, and less theological than a hymn.

A great hymn has a timeless quality about it. A song employs current vernacular. The life spans of songs and hymns contrast like flowers and trees—both God's creation—neither more important than the other.

A "spiritual song" is even more a song-of-the-moment than a "song." When Paul referred to singing with his spirit in 1 Corinthians 14, he contrasted it with singing with his mind and said he would do both. This "less rational" song form, which consists of spontaneous melodies and words inspired by the Holy Spirit and sung around a chord or slowly moving chord progression, may seem strange to our Western way of thinking, but apparently it was an integral part of the early Church's worship. Maybe part of our music rehearsals should include time learning to do spiritual songs.

If nothing else, these three song forms show us God's love for diversity. He doesn't want us to have just one groove. Churches that practice this divine diversity will attract the feelers, the thinkers, and the intuitive folks. At the same time, this biblical worship challenges each of us to a greater totality of worship expression.

Are you ready for the worshiper's pledge? If so, repeat with me: "I will worship in spirit and truth...I will worship with all my being...and I will sing songs, hymns, and spiritual songs."

The Holographic Worship Team

BY TOM KRAEUTER

> *Above all, love each other deeply.*
> 1 PETER 4:8

Not long ago someone suggested to me an intriguing idea: a holographic worship team. Instead of real people, the "people" would simply be holograms programmed to play their instruments extremely well. We would never need to worry about someone being sick and missing a service. Our lead guitarist who occasionally hits those sour notes would be a thing of the past. The thing I really thought was so exciting about this concept was that as a worship leader, I would never need to deal with relationship issues within the worship ministry. No more, "She's singing my part" or "Why is he always so uncaring about anyone but himself?"

However, in reality, a holographic worship team would miss the essence of true Christianity. After salvation, the thing that Jesus spoke of the most when He was visibly here on earth was walking in unity. We need to understand that our relationships with one another, even with those we do not fully understand or relate to, are vital.

Suppose for a moment that you had the opportunity to meet the apostle Peter. If you were to ask him what he thought was the most important thing for us to learn about the kingdom of God, how do

301

think he would respond? What would Peter—the man whose shadow touched people and they were healed, the man who walked closely with our Lord Jesus for three years—say our top priority should be?

In his first epistle, mainly a letter of encouragement and admonition, Peter tells us very clearly what he believes is most significant for us. He says, "*Above all*, love each other deeply" (1 Peter 4:8). These are strong words. Nearly every translation I checked used the phrase "above all." This is not just a side issue. Additionally, instead of "deeply," some translations used "fervently" or "intensely." This obviously is not meant to be a halfhearted action.

Of course, in making this statement Peter is assuming that our relationship with the Lord is strong. However, his words echo the words of Jesus.

One day the Pharisees asked Jesus, "What is the greatest commandment?" He responded, " 'Love the Lord your God with all your heart and with all your soul and with all your mind.' This is the first and greatest commandment. And the second is like it: 'Love your neighbor as yourself' " (Matthew 22:37–39).

Most of us understand the first one. Loving God with all our heart is a given. To us this is a foundation in our walk with the Lord. However, that second part is often a bit more difficult for us. Loving imperfect people is always more challenging than loving a perfect God. People have flaws. People have opinions that differ from ours. People fail us. Loving them can be difficult.

Not long ago I heard singer/songwriter Barry McGuire being interviewed on the radio. He recited a little poem that I thought was quite accurate:

> To dwell up above with the saints that we love,
> Oh, that will be glory;
> But to live here below with the saints that we know,
> Well, that's another story.

For us as Christians, loving a perfect, holy God is easy. It's the unholy, imperfect people that we hang around with who are often much more challenging to love.

"If it weren't for people, life in the kingdom of God would be wonderful." I have frequently heard people make this remark in jest. Unfortunately, I fear that many actually believe this statement. We too often choose to ignore people or, at best, simply to tolerate them. We must move beyond this and choose to honestly, as Peter implores us to, love one another deeply.

I am not referring to simply an outward show of affection. We in the Church are often very good at outward demonstrations of "unity."

On my home computer I have a game called "Battle Chess." It is unique in that the chess pieces come to life and actually fight with one another. Of course, the correct piece always wins, but each piece interacts differently with each different opponent. A normal chess game ends when checkmate is reached. This version, however, actually finishes out the game and takes the king at the end. If the queen is the one taking the king, she walks over to him, hugs him, and stabs him in the back. That scenario reminds me of some relationships I have seen in the Church! We are often much too ready to put on an outward show of affection while, inside, there is no real love in the heart.

The fact of the matter is that unless you have a holographic worship ministry, you will always have to deal with people. Unfortunately, people will often hurt you, mistreat you, and sometimes point out things in your life that really do need to change. How will you respond? Will you endeavor to love them anyway?

Adapted from the book *If Standing Together Is So Great, Why Do We Keep Falling Apart?* by Tom Kraeuter (Lynnwood, Wash.: Emerald Books, 1994, 1998).

Big–Eared Ambassadors

BY ARLEN SALTE

> We are therefore Christ's ambassadors,
> as though God were making his appeal
> through us.
> 2 CORINTHIANS 5:20a

It was humiliating! I was just an innocent little kid. I was visiting my grandfather in a little village on the prairies, and he decided to take me downtown. He held my hand and proudly paraded me down Main Street from store to store.

I'm not complaining about the walk. Believe me, it wasn't a long walk in Torquay, Saskatchewan. It was the humiliation that came with it in every conversation.

From store to store, my grandfather would proudly show off my ears and compare them to his gigantic muffs. "See, he has the Salte ears," he'd proudly proclaim. I wanted to dive underneath the store displays. Was it my fault that I looked like a '56 Chevy driving down the street with the front doors open?

The worst part was looking at my grandfather and seeing my future. Not only were his ears big, but also it seemed as though his hair had receded from his head and was poking through his ears in big clumps. Not only did I have even bigger ears to look forward to; they were also going to be hairy.

I can't help it. One of the genetic traits in my family is huge ears. We're not talking about slightly larger than normal audio receivers.

304

We're talking about flaps that intimidate Dumbo the elephant. On a windy prairie day, if we weren't careful, our ears could get caught up and spin our heads like roosters on the barn roof.

If I ever questioned my heritage, all I had to do was look at my own shadow. Remember Dopey in *Snow White*? He must have been a relative. As much as I tried to hide my ears with hair or hats, they'd pop out at the most inconvenient of times and reveal my true genetic code.

You've been coded as well. You're a part of the worship team. Everywhere you go people are watching. That's a lot of responsibility to hold. That's true for all Christians, but especially true of those who stand on the platform on Sunday morning.

We can call it role modeling. We can call it being an example. The apostle Paul simply called us ambassadors.

That's a tall order to fill. To be an ambassador, you have to give up your rights. You never have a day off. You represent your country in all you say and do. Every action reflects on your country. You forfeit certain freedoms and take on extra responsibilities. An ambassador is never to be absorbed by the country where the embassy is located. He is watched at every turn. People watch the ambassador from Norway to see what Norwegians are like. When you think of it, it's not an easy job.

Your job isn't easy either. Your job doesn't end once you step off the platform. Your public position comes with a price. You're an ambassador for your church. More important, you're an ambassador for your God.

People are watching you to see what a true Christian is like. "But that's not fair," I hear you say. "That wasn't a part of the formal job description," you protest. "My job description revolved around strings and picks and capos and E flat chords written by malicious keyboard players."

Nevertheless the truth is out. You're coded. The sword has been drawn. You've been dubbed an ambassador.

Now the challenge is to know your citizenship very well. It's time to dig into the visitors guide, the Bible. It's time to let the culture of God infuse your very being until you think, act, and breathe the very nature of your citizenship.

Here's your new job description as an ambassador. The apostle Paul already wrote it for you:

Therefore, as God's chosen people, holy and dearly loved, clothe yourselves with compassion, kindness, humility, gentleness and patience. Bear with each other and forgive whatever grievances you may have against one another. Forgive as the Lord forgave you. And over all these virtues put on love, which binds them all together in perfect unity.

Let the peace of Christ rule in your hearts, since as members of one body you were called to peace. And be thankful. Let the word of Christ dwell in you richly as you teach and admonish one another with all wisdom, and as you sing psalms, hymns and spiritual songs with gratitude in your hearts to God. And whatever you do, whether in word or deed, do it all in the name of the Lord Jesus, giving thanks to God the Father through him. (Colossians 3:12–17)

Remember, though, that when you're feeling weak as an ambassador, there's another truth you need to remember. You have diplomatic immunity. There's always a fresh start in Jesus Christ.

If you haven't lived your citizenship for a while, why don't you start today? God is calling you as His ambassador.

Your heavenly Father wants to take your hand and show you off to the world. He cares nothing about your ears. It's your kindred heart He's looking for.

Frozen Bubbles

BY TOM KRAEUTER

> *[Love] always protects, always trusts,*
> *always hopes, always perseveres.*
> 1 CORINTHIANS 13:7

Several years ago I was ministering in Chicago. It was during the winter, and the weather was cold. Unusually cold. The nighttime temperatures were -50°F. Did I mention that it was really, really cold?

One evening as I was watching a local news broadcast, the meteorologist did something I've never seen before. Broadcasting live from outdoors, he took some bubble-blowing liquid and blew bubbles. No, he wasn't crazy. There was a reason for his seemingly silly antics. When the bubbles hit that icy cold air (did I mention how cold it was?), they froze instantly. Then he popped each bubble, and it shattered into tiny crystals. It was fascinating.

Of course, when I got home to where I live near St. Louis, Missouri, I had to try it. Although not quite as cold as it was in Chicago (our evening temperature was a balmy -10°F), it was still cold enough to freeze the bubbles. I took our kids outside in their pajamas and winter coats (my wife thought I had really gone off the deep end) and showed them the frozen-bubble-blowing trick. They loved it. When we broke the bubbles they burst into thousands of beautiful crystals. We took great delight in watching those crystals float gently to the ground, never to be seen again.

We in the Body of Christ have an enemy who clearly takes great delight in breaking us apart. His goal is for us to be divided so that we are weakened. There are few things he would rather see than for us to float aimlessly away from the Body of Christ, never to be seen again.

This morning I was reading the book of Titus. It's a short letter written by Paul to Titus, his "true son in our common faith." As I read, a particular passage jumped out at me. "Warn a divisive person once, and then warn him a second time. After that, have nothing to do with him. You can be sure that such a man is warped and sinful; he is self-condemned" (Titus 3:10–11). Wow! After I read these verses, I thought, "Paul, why don't you tell us how you really feel about this topic. Don't hide your emotions. What's your true opinion?" Of course I'm being facetious. Paul clearly articulated his honest thoughts in these verses. Words like *warped* and *sinful* don't need much interpretation, do they?

The context of these verses is talking about how we as believers should interact with one another. Paul tells us that a person causing division gets two warnings and then is shunned. He goes on to say that such a person is self-condemned. Those are strong assertions. He does not, however, suggest any possible exceptions to these rules. He does not offer thoughts on times when being divisive might be acceptable. There are no footnotes about occasions for proper divisiveness. He is clearly telling us that being divisive is sinful.

As human beings, we have a tendency to rate sins the way Olympic events are rated. We rate things like adultery or embezzling church funds as 9.0 or higher. Divisiveness, however, we would probably only rate as 2 or 3. We don't see it as sinful as many other things. God clearly does not use the same rating scale that we do.

Galatians 5:19–21 lists out "the acts of the sinful nature." Of course, there are the things that we would all expect in such a list: sexual immorality, debauchery, idolatry, witchcraft, and hatred. However, right along with those things are listed discord, dissensions, and factions. These things are just as objectionable to the Lord as the others.

Our Bible verse for today tells us that love does a number of things. "It always protects, always trusts, always hopes, always perseveres." It seems obvious to me that we in the Church rarely operate in the realm of "always" mandated by this verse. What would happen if we indeed had that kind of attitude toward one another? What would the people of God be like if we truly *always* protected one another, *always* trusted one another, *always* offered hope to one another, and *always* helped each other persevere through difficult times? Would we be different than we are now? Of course we would.

Let's get personal. Let's talk about the worship ministry of your church. I know as well as you do that creative, artsy people can sometimes be difficult to interact with. However, as I mentioned earlier, there are no loopholes in Scripture that allow us to be divisive. Dealing with difficult people does not give us an excuse. Sorry.

We have an enemy who wants to shatter us just like those frozen bubbles. Right now, in your own heart, with the help of God Almighty, make a new declaration to refuse to be divisive. Instead, reach for the level of "always" in expressing love for one another.

Notes

1. J. Robert Clinton, "Four Observations on Giftedness," in *Worship Leader* magazine May/June 1999.
2. John Fischer, *Twelve Steps for the Recovering Pharisee (Like Me)*, (Minneapolis, Minn.: Bethany House Publishers, 2000), p. 107.
3. Rory Noland, *The Heart of the Artist* (Grand Rapids, Mich.: Zondervan Publishing, 1999). p. 89.
4. Jim Cymbala, *Fresh Wind, Fresh Fire* (Grand Rapids, Mich.: Zondervan Publishing House, 1997), p. 70.
5. Lewis Smedes, *The Art of Forgiving* (New York, N.Y.: Ballantine, 1996), p. 178.
6. John R.W. Stott, *The Contemporary Christian* (Downers Grove, Ill.: InterVaristy Press, 1992). pp. 227–228.
7. Os Guinness, *The Call* (Nashville, Tenn.: Word Publishing, 1998).
8. Ibid.
9. *Sky* magazine, April 1999, "Travelin' Man."
10. Paul and Gretyl Haglin, *Letters of Faith* newsletter (Hawk Point, Mo., September 2000).
11. C. S. Lewis, *Mere Christianity* (New York, N.Y.: Macmillan Publishing Co., Inc., 1943, 1945, 1952).
12. Jim Cymbala, *Fresh Wind, Fresh Fire* (Grand Rapids, Mich.: Zondervan Publishing House, 1997), p. 50.
13. Dr. Donald W. McCullogh, *The Trivialization of God* (Colorado Springs, Colo.: NavPress, 1995).
14. C. S. Lewis, *Perelandra* (New York, N.Y.: The Macmillan Company, 1944).
15. Tim Hansel, *You Gotta Keep Dancin'* (Elgin, Ill.: LifeJourney Books, 1985.)
16. C. S. Lewis, *Prince Caspian* (New York, N.Y: Macmillan Publishing Company, 1951.)
17. Rory Noland, *The Heart of the Artist* (Grand Rapids, Mich.: Zondervan Publishing, 1999). p. 63.
18. Puritan Stephen Charnock, quoted by Jerry Bridges in *I Exalt You, O God* (Colorado Springs, Colo., Waterbrook Press, 2001).
19. Rory Noland, *The Heart of the Artist* (Grand Rapids, Mich.: Zondervan Publishing, 1999). p. 124.
20. Bernard Ruffin, *Fanny Crosby—The Hymn Writer* (Uhrichsville, Ohio: Barbour Publishing, 1995).
21. Ibid.
22. Brother Lawrence, *The Practice of God's Presence*, trans. Robert J. Edmonson (Orleans, Mass.: Paraclete Press, 1985), p. 120.
23. Adapted from Corrie ten Boom with John and Elizabeth Sherrill, *The Hiding Place* (Old Tappan, N.J.: Spire Books, 1971).
24. Vernon M. Whaley, Ph.D., *Understanding Music & Worship in the Local Church* (Wheaton, Ill: Evangelical Training Association, 1995.) pp.10–12.
25. C. S. Lewis, *Mere Christianity* (New York, N.Y.: Macmillan Publishing Co., Inc., 1943, 1945, 1952).
26. Rory Noland, *The Heart of the Artist* (Grand Rapids, Mich.: Zondervan Publishing, 1999). p. 64.

Index by Topic

311

Index by Title

Index by Author

Index by Scripture Reference